Pro Windows Phone 7
Development

Rob Cameron

Apress®

Pro Windows Phone 7 Development

ISBN-13 (pbk): 978-1-4302-3219-3

ISBN-13 (electronic): 978-1-4302-3220-9

President and Publisher: Paul Manning
Lead Editor: Jonathan Hassell
Technical Reviewer: Robert Garrett
Editorial Board: Steve Anglin, Mark Beckner, Ewan Buckingham, Gary Cornell, Jonathan Gennick, Jonathan Hassell, Michelle Lowman, James Markham, Matthew Moodie, Jeff Olson, Jeffrey Pepper, Frank Pohlman, Douglas Pundick, Ben Renow-Clarke, Dominic Shakeshaft, Matt Wade, Tom Welsh
Coordinating Editor: Debra Kelly
Copy Editor: Tracy Brown
Compositor: MacPS, LLC
Indexer: BIM Indexing & Proofreading Services
Artist: April Milne
Cover Designer: Anna Ishchenko

Distributed to the book trade worldwide by Springer Science+Business Media, LLC., 233 Spring Street, 6th Floor, New York, NY 10013. Phone 1-800-SPRINGER, fax (201) 348-4505, e-mail orders-ny@springer-sbm.com, or visit www.springeronline.com.

For information on translations, please e-mail rights@apress.com, or visit www.apress.com.

Apress and friends of ED books may be purchased in bulk for academic, corporate, or promotional use. eBook versions and licenses are also available for most titles. For more information, reference our Special Bulk Sales–eBook Licensing web page at www.apress.com/bulk-sales.

The source code for this book is available to readers at www.apress.com. You will need to answer questions pertaining to this book in order to successfully download the code.

To my beautiful wife, Ally, whose love and patience is unending,
and to my daughters Amanda and Anna, who make me so proud every day.

Rob

Contents at a Glance

Contents

About the Author

■ **Rob Cameron** Employed by Microsoft since 2001, Rob Cameron is an Industry Architect Evangelist with Microsoft Corporation based out of Atlanta, Georgia. As part of Microsoft's Communication Sector Developer & Platform Evangelism team, Rob focuses on development tools and technologies targeting mobile devices, gaming, and embedded devices for telecommunications, cable, and media & entertainment companies. Rob has also worked on six books for Apress including authoring the latest Pro Windows Phone 7 Development. He has a master's degree in information technology management and a bachelor's degree in computer science. Visit Rob's blog at http://blogs.msdn.com/RobCamer.

About the Technical Reviewer

 **Rob Garrett** has worked with SharePoint since the early beta version of MOSS 2007 and has leveraged his talents for SharePoint architecture and design with Portal Solutions—a SharePoint consultant company in Rockville, MD. Rob has extensive background in .NET technologies and has developed software for Microsoft Frameworks since the early days of C++ and MFC. In pursuit of his career dreams, Rob left his birthplace in England for a journey to the United States on Thanksgiving Day 1999. Upon arrival, he enjoyed his first American meal from a gas station.

Acknowledgments

I would like to acknowledge the incredible support provided by the Apress team who patiently waited as I struggled to balance all the demands in my life the past year. Jonathan Hassell has been there with me through all of my books with Apress, and I sincerely appreciate his support. Debra Kelly has been a trooper prodding me along to keep this book on track through the final push.

Introduction

Authoring a book on mobile development with a title that starts with "Pro" is a daunting task. Put in too much introductory material and you lose the knowledgeable developer looking to take his application to the next level. Breeze through key concepts and the cross-platform professional mobile developer may struggle learning how to work with targeting a relatively new platform in Windows Phone 7.

Another challenge is culling down what to cover between Silverlight and the XNA Framework. Both are fabulous and interesting technologies so I strived to cover both in a single text, though this book is more geared toward Silverlight developers who are interesting in learning about the XNA Framework as well.

This book provides a comprehensive overview of XAML and Silverlight since it is a critical aspect of WP7 development. It also focuses on many of the more challenging topics such as correctly architecting Silverlight for Windows Phone 7 applications using the Model-View-ViewModel architecture as well as working with services, encryption, and gestures.

There are many tidbits throughout this book extracted from many long hours of working with top media brands to bring their content and applications to Windows Phone 7. I hope that sharing this knowledge on memory and CPU optimization gleaned from these experiences helps to bring your applications to the top of the rankings in the Windows Phone 7 marketplace.

Who This Book Is For

If you are an existing Silverlight developer, this book will provide details on how to leverage your Silverlight skills for Windows Phone 7. If you are a mobile developer looking to port an existing application to Windows Phone 7, then this book will give you the information you need, covering the core concepts and techniques fundamental for Silverlight for Windows Phone 7 development.

Having an understanding of the .NET Framework will help, but if you are an experienced developer new to the .NET Framework, you will still be able to learn Windows Phone 7 development using this book because much of the development is in the XAML markup language as well as in code.

Note You still may want to grab a programming in C# text such as Adam Freeman's *Introducing Visual C# 2010* (Apress, 2010) if you are not confident with C#.

The example code in this book is written in C#. However, much of the development is in the XAML, not in C#, so if you are a VB.NET developer, the markup is almost exactly the same. For the examples that do include C# code in the code-behind, the code translates pretty easily, as the .NET Framework for Silverlight for Windows Phone is language agnostic.

How This Book Is Structured

This book consists of chapters that focus on individual topic areas of Windows Phone 7 and is intended to be read in the order in which it is written; however, I strive to point to related sections in other chapters so if you need to skip ahead to a specific topic feel free to do so.

I spend a bit more time on Silverlight than the XNA Framework, but both are covered throughout the book. Chapter 1 starts with an introduction to the Windows Phone Platform, the AppHub marketplace, Silverlight, and concludes with a detailed introductory sample on the XNA Framework. Chapter 2 focuses exclusively on Silverlight UX development. Chapter 3 covers input, leveraging examples both for Silverlight and the XNA Framework. With the fundamentals for professional development on Windows Phone 7 out of the way, Chapter 4 dives into the programming model with Silverlight as well as how to integrate into the Windows Phone 7 platform via tasks and choosers. Chapter 4 also covers the Bing Maps control and the WebBrowser control, including how to communicate between Silverlight and JavaScript.

Chapter 5 covers Advanced Silverlight UI development starting with a detailed investigation of the Model-View-ViewModel pattern. While this may seem odd in a chapter focused on UI, good architecture focuses on separation of concerns, which leads to better user experience and cleaner XAML. Chapter 6 covers advanced programming model concepts, including Advanced Data Binding, the Silverlight toolkit for WP7, working with the Media Library, creating a Photos Extra and Music plus Video hub application, as well as other integration scenarios.

Chapter 7 dives in deep on XNA Framework development for 2D applications, building on the introductory sample from Chapter 1. It includes coverage on how to leverage the Game Management sample from AppHub to create a professional looking application. Chapter 8 starts off with adding polish to the Chapter 7 2D game development sample, covering saving and load as well supporting tombstoning in XNA. A simple particle system is added to the 2D game to add explosions. Chapter 8 then delves into the world of 3D game development, covering working with primitives and models in 3D.

Prerequisites

You will need a version of Visual Studio 2010, with Service Pack 1 of Visual Studio 2010 applied. You will also need to install Windows Phone Developer Tools available here:

http://create.msdn.com/en-us/home/getting_started

You will want to download the Silverlight Toolkit for WP7 available here:

http://silverlight.codplex.com

I also highly recommend that you review the Design Resources for Windows Phone 7 available here:

http://msdn.microsoft.com/en-us/library/ff637515(VS.92).aspx

Downloading the Code

The code is available in zip file format in the Source Code/Download section of the Apress web site. Please review the readme.txt for setup instructions.

Contacting the Author

To reach the author, please go to his blog and click the Email link to send him an email.

Rob Cameron: http://blogs.msdn.com/RobCamer.

■ ■ ■

CHAPTER 1

Introduction to Windows Phone 7 and Marketplace

Windows Phone 7 presents an exciting new opportunity for developers to build and monetize mobile applications. It represents a major new investment into mobile computing by Microsoft, and in many ways is a break from the past.

Up until roughly 2007, Windows Mobile was a growing, well-received platform targeting primarily enterprise users. Windows Mobile was taking share from competitors such as Palm and going head-to-head with RIM Blackberry, but overall it was considered fairly successful. The release of the iPhone and its consumer focus and applications store it turned the mobile device market on its head, and was a major wake-up call for Microsoft. Tack on the surge by Google's Android operating system, and the smartphone market became hyper-competitive.

■ **Note** Microsoft originally dubbed this new platform Windows Phone 7 Series. After some initial "feedback" from the market, Microsoft dropped the "Series" from the name. It is still a faux pas to call it Windows Mobile 7.

Windows Phone 7 represents a sea change in approach by Microsoft toward mobile computing. Although Windows Mobile 6.x and earlier resembles a miniaturized version of desktop Windows, with its iconic Start screen, Windows Phone 7 is very different with a user interface that is more similar to the ZuneHD interface – on steroids.

When the ZuneHD was introduced, it received positive feedback from critics, but it wasn't highly marketed toward consumers. It also did not have a third-party application Marketplace. Still, it was an opportunity for Microsoft to try out new mobile computing concepts on a mass audience of a few million users.

Learning from its own stumbles, taking what works from Zune, and then looking at the existing mobile landscape, Microsoft came up with Windows Phone 7 with a dramatically different user experience from Windows Mobile, a new mobile development paradigm, and a completely different approach in the market.

With Windows Phone 7, Microsoft makes the end-user consumer the top priority, whereas in the past, with Windows Mobile, the original equipment manufacturer (OEM) was Microsoft's primary customer. This does not mean that Microsoft is OEMing the device directly. Instead, Microsoft spec'd out the hardware and software for the platform such that OEMs can take that specification as a basis for further innovation. OEMs can build devices with or without a keyboard, or with slightly different physical sizes, different screen types, and additional features like a camera and more storage, to name a few options.

This may make you nervous as a developer, but it is important to remember that every Windows Phone 7 device at launch will have an 800 × 480 screen resolution, the exact same user interface and APIs, and the same range of sensors no matter what the OEM or Mobile Operator. This means that developers can build an application and be confident that it will run on all available devices. I cover hardware in more detail later in the chapter.

Note Microsoft has stated that it may add a new screen resolution in the future, and will provide guidance and tooling to ease development and ensure applications can run on all screens.

From a software standpoint, the programming model for Windows Phone 7 is very different from Windows Mobile. With Windows Mobile, developers created applications with either C++ or .NET Windows Forms via the .NET Compact Framework. For Windows Phone 7, the available programming models are Silverlight and the XNA Framework. This represents a clean break from the past, which will be painful for existing Windows Mobile ISVs, but in the end it provides a much more powerful programming model for developers. I cover the software and capabilities in more detail in the following sections.

Why Should I Care?

As a developer, you may wonder whether you should invest in building applications for Windows Phone 7. Is there room in the marketplace? Is Microsoft committed to mobile platforms? These are all reasonable questions.

Smartphone Growth

The mobile phone has become a major computing platform, experiencing incredible growth. As I write this, Smartphone shipments make up approximately 10% of the market worldwide. It is expected to grow to 70% of the market over the next three or four years. Much of the growth potential is still ahead. A new or remade player in the market, such as Android and Windows Phone 7, can come on to the scene and capture the imagination of both developers and consumers with the right level of marketing and engineering commitment.

Is Microsoft Committed?

This is a tricky one, because I work for Microsoft and am biased, but what I see in terms of activity and energy around Windows Phone 7 reminds me of what I observed as an IT pro and developer working outside of Microsoft when Windows 95 launched. I was earning my Master's degree and spending a lot of time with other platforms like Unix and IBM OS/2 Warp, generally looking down on Windows for Workgroups 3.11. Microsoft's client OS, WfW 3.11 was looking long in the tooth, very dated, and limited. Out of nowhere Windows 95 exploded on to the scene and changed everything.

Can Windows Phone 7 change the market? Time will only tell, as it is just getting started. However, I see a tremendous level of commitment at Microsoft focused on Windows Phone 7. It is a great platform in version one. Can it improve? Absolutely, but I can honestly say that I imagine this is what it was like at Microsoft when Windows 95 launched, and I am thrilled to be a part of it and to be working with customers and partners on building applications for Windows Phone 7!

Current Microsoft Developers

If you are an existing .NET Framework, Silverlight, or XNA Game Studio developer, you are well on your way to having the skills needed to create great Windows Phone applications. However, there are many unique aspects to mobile device development, as well as features that are specific to Windows Phone 7, that require new skills. This book will present to you the information you need to bring your existing skills to bear on this new and exciting platform and to build great mobile application experiences.

■ **Note** Windows Phone 7 development initially supported C# only at launch. Since launch, Microsoft has added support for Visual Basic .NET development with Silverlight. XNA Framework game development still requires C#.

If you are new to Silverlight and XNA Game Studio, I spend time in this chapter introducing you to the basic concepts in these technologies to get you started. Combine this chapter with the online references available, and you will have the necessary foundation to proceed with the rest of this text.

If you are an existing Windows Mobile developer, you have a great depth of understanding of .NET and deep knowledge of mobile development considerations as well. This book will help you bring your existing knowledge to Silverlight and XNA Game Studio so that you can port your existing applications to Windows Phone 7.

Non-Microsoft Developers

If you are an existing mobile developer on another platform, this book will help you bring your mobile development skills to bear on Windows Phone 7. Windows Phone 7 applications are written in C#, which is similar to the Java language and has roots in C, so many of the language constructs will be straightforward. For additional information on C# in general, check out the Apress title *Beginning C# 2010: From Novice to Professional*, Second Edition, by Adam Freeman.

The Mobile Market

The smartphone segment of the mobile device market is expected to continue significant double-digit growth in the foreseeable future. This growth stems from new users purchasing devices, as well as existing function phone and feature phone users moving to smartphones. Despite the hype, it is way too early to suggest that one platform or another has "won" the smartphone war. There is plenty of new growth to be had in the market before competing platforms will need to focus on taking share from one another.

Take Android as an example, which has stormed onto the market and has out-sold iOS devices so far in 2011. Regarding Windows Phone 7, Microsoft CEO Steve Ballmer claims that his company is "all-in" with respect to commitment to the mobile market and Windows Phone 7. The partnership with Nokia announced in early 2011 demonstrates the high-level of commitment and desire needed to bring a third ecosystem to market.

In describing my perspective on what Windows Phone 7 means to Microsoft, I like to use an analogy. When Microsoft first introduced the Xbox game console, the general consensus in the market was that the Sony PlayStation had "won" the market and there was no way the Xbox could catch up. Today, I don't think anyone would question Microsoft's investment or commitment with respect to the Xbox 360. Likewise, who would have guessed that Nintendo would have made a comeback like it did with the Wii. Competition is a wonderful thing for consumers. Expect even more competition and dynamism in the mobile device market!

Windows Phone 7 Platform Overview

In this section, I provide an overview of the design philosophy behind Windows Phone 7. I also cover the available development model to familiarize you with underlying platform architecture and developer capabilities.

Phone Design Philosophy

When Microsoft introduced Windows Phone 7, its executives spoke about "integrated experiences" and "smart design." Without a doubt, Windows Phone 7 presents a unique user interface as compared to other current smartphone operating systems, as shown in Figure 1-1.

Figure 1-1. Windows Phone 7 Start screen

The Windows Phone 7 Start screen presents a lot of information in a clear fashion. Information and content is presented in a straightforward, easy to navigate manner without distraction. Controls have a minimalistic feel, allowing the user to focus on the content. This is a high-level overview of what Microsoft calls smart design. I focus more on design in Chapter 3.

Also shown in Figure 1-1 are several top-level tile icons pointing to the built-in "hubs," such as the People, Office, Pictures, Zune, Marketplace, and Xbox LIVE hubs. The hubs are the built-in, top-level panoramic experiences, meaning they scroll left and right to present content in a rich fashion. Figure 1-2 shows an early concept of the People hub. Notice that the focus is on the content, not "chrome."

Figure 1–2. Windows Phone 7 People hub Panorama experience

Figure 1–2 shows a wide view of the full user interface width of the Panorama experience. A user swipes left and right to view content in addition to scrolling up and down on each viewable section. Hubs provide an integrated view on data. For example, if you register an Exchange, Facebook, and Windows Live account, the contact data is pulled together into a single integrated view called the People hub. This allows the user to explore contacts as well as see a scrolling view of status updates.

In addition to Panorama, the other major navigation paradigm is called Pivot, with very similar navigation behavior to what you see in the ZuneHD. Figure 1–3 shows an example Pivot interface running in the Emulator.

Figure 1–3. Windows Phone 7 Pivot experience

In the application shown in Figure 1–3, the users touches the categories at the top, such as DVDs, instant, and so on, to switch between lists of data. Selecting an item displays the details. The Pivot experience provides a great navigation experience for displaying large amounts of categorized or filtered data.

The Panorama and Pivot experiences are all part of the Metro UI design language, which is the underlying design approach for all of the Windows Phone 7 built-in experiences. The controls available when developing for Windows Phone 7 are skinned for Metro by default. You will see more of this in the "Silverlight Framework" section of this chapter.

Of course, you are not limited to Panorama or Pivot for application design and navigation. Windows Phone 7 supports a page navigation metaphor as well. In addition, many applications may simply consist of a single-page application that takes advantage of animations to render out the user experience.

I cover application user interface design in more detail in Chapter 3, but it is important to have an understanding of the platform philosophy up front in order to help you start to think about your application in terms of what it means to be a Windows Phone 7 application. For more information on Windows Phone 7 design, please check out the design resources available at `http://msdn.microsoft.com/en-us/library/ff637515%28VS.92%29.aspx,` or simply search for "design resources for Windows Phone" in your favorite Web search engine.

Hardware Capabilities

Unlike the iPhone or Blackberry, Microsoft does not produce the phone directly. Instead, Microsoft has chosen to continue to partner with mobile device OEMs in order to scale production and to promote differentiation. However, unlike with Windows Mobile 6.x and its predecessors, Microsoft has taken a more hands-on approach in specifying the underlying hardware such as chipset, CPU, GPU, Camera, Sensors, minimum memory, and so on, in addition to authoring many of the drivers.

OEMs are still free to innovate in terms of providing additional capabilities such as a physical keyboard, additional memory, and storage, but the underlying consistency ensures that applications work well across device manufactures, which greatly simplifies the efforts required of developers.

Every Windows Phone 7 device has the following capabilities:

- Capacitive 4-point multi-touch screen
- DirectX 9 hardware acceleration
- Digital camera
- Accelerometer
- Assisted GPS
- Compass sensor
- Light sensor
- Proximity Sensor

Windows Phone 7 hardware includes a powerful ARM v7 "Cortex/Scorpion" CPU, a powerful NVidia Tegra GPU, a minimum of 256 MB of RAM, and 8 GB or more of flash storage. Windows Phone 7 includes a large WVGA (800 × 480) display at launch.

At some point in the future Windows Phone 7 will also be available with an HVGA (480 × 320) display to provide for additional hardware differentiation. Microsoft will provide tools and guidance to assist developers with creating applications that support both resolutions. However, as you learn more about Silverlight, you will be well on your way to correctly writing applications that work well on both resolutions.

For XNA Framework-based games, the Windows Phone 7's powerful hardware scaler can assist with scaling assets as needed, whether to allow sharing of assets with Xbox and PC versions of a game or to assist with scaling assets for the HVGA version of Windows Phone 7 when it becomes available at some point after initial launch.

Software Capabilities

Windows Phone 7 includes two programming models: the Silverlight and XNA Frameworks. Both Silverlight and XNA Game Studio are in version four of their desktop focused versions, bringing a high level of maturity to mobile development. Figure 1–4 illustrates the iconic breakdown shown by Microsoft when discussing the Windows Phone 7 Application Platform at Mix, TechReady, and pretty much any other setting.

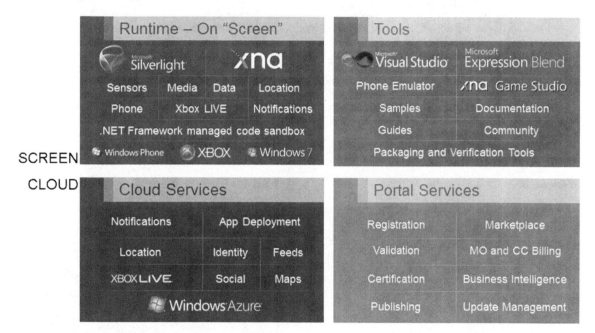

Figure 1–4. Windows Phone 7 application platform

The upper left-hand corner of Figure 1–4 lists the two major programming models, Silverlight and XNA Framework, with the various integration points developers can take advantage of. Note that all of the underlying capabilities are accessible from either Silverlight or XNA Framework. All of these capabilities run inside the .NET Framework common language runtime in a sandboxed environment.

The upper right-hand corner of Figure 1–4 lists the two primary tools you use to create Windows Phone 7 applications, Visual Studio 2010 and Expression Blend 4. Visual Studio 2010 is the development tool most developers are familiar with already. XNA Game Studio sits inside of Visual Studio 2010 via a plug-in for game development.

A critically important tool listed in the upper right-hand corner is the Windows Phone Emulator. The Windows Phone Emulator is a virtual machine that allows developers to create applications and games without having a physical device. If you have a touch-enabled monitor, the emulator will pick up touch interactions as if running on a device. You can also simulate location and accelerometer.

▦ **Tip** Microsoft limits the Phone Emulator to a single processor and injects sleep events to better simulate actual device performance, but generally performance will be better in the emulator than on a device, because there are far more resources available on a desktop PC. It is therefore important to periodically test your application on a real device.

In Figure 1–4, the lower left-hand corner of the diagram represents code that you access in the cloud, such as notification services and location services that Microsoft provides, as well as custom-code you write to support your application such as web services, REST data, and so on.

The lower right-hand corner of in Figure 1–4 contains a reference to the tools that help you ship and promote your applications, primarily the Windows Marketplace for Mobile, or Marketplace for short.

Now that I covered a high-level overview of the application platform, let's dive into the programming models, Silverlight and XNA Framework. You build user experiences in Silverlight via Xml Application Markup Language (XAML) with a C# code-behind model. XAML is the serialization format of the UI elements added to the form. Since XAML is well-formed XML, it provides excellent tooling and validation support. It is also a namespace-based human-editable serialization format, allowing developers to easily modify XAML by hand.

The UI for Silverlight can be created in both Visual Studio and Expression Blend 4 for Windows Phone, though Expression Blend 4 can make some design operations such as animations and data binding much easier to code visually.

XNA Framework applications, on the other hand, are developed purely in C# code in Visual Studio, though there are third-party frameworks that can assist with game development through visually designing levels and the like Figure 1–5 provides a high-level breakdown of Silverlight vs. XNA Framework.

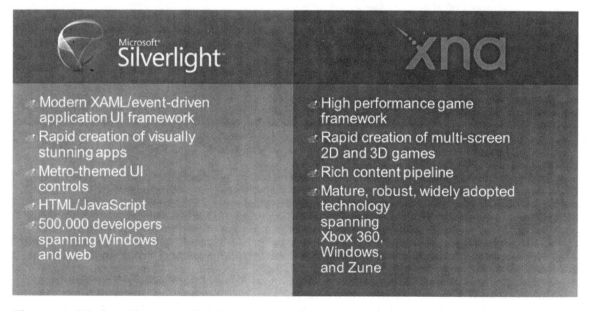

Figure 1–5. Windows Phone 7 application programming frameworks

Both Silverlight and XNA Framework share the same application model built on top of the .NET Common Language Runtime (CLR), allowing access to libraries across frameworks. So, a Silverlight application can access the audio APIs available in XNA Framework. Likewise, an XNA Framework application can access remote server access APIs available in Silverlight.

■ **Note** 3.7 is the version of the .NET Compact Framework under the covers, but it is more relevant to think in terms of Silverlight 3+ and XNA Game Studio 4.0.

Windows Phone Developer Tools

The Windows Phone Developer Tools are a free download available from AppHub at http://create.msdn.com. The tools include Visual Studio 2010 Express for Windows Phone, XNA Game Studio 4, and Expression Blend 4 for Windows Phone – all you need in a single free download.

If you are currently a Visual Studio 2010 Professional or later developer, fear not – you will not lose access to all of your favorite features available in the Professional or later products. When you install the Windows Phone Developer Tools over Visual Studio 2010 Professional or later, the tool simply folds into the existing installation with no loss of functionality.

Download and install the tools to prepare for the next two sections. The first section provides an overview of the Silverlight Tools and Framework. The section after covers XNA Game Studio in detail, because this book does not dive in deeply with XNA Game Studio until Chapter 7. Finally the chapter closes with an overview of AppHub and Marketplace.

Silverlight Tools and Framework Overview

In general, Silverlight is Microsoft's cross-web browser, cross-platform, and cross-device plug-in for delivering the next generation of .NET Framework-based rich interactive applications for the Web and the Windows desktop. On the Web, Silverlight runs on Windows in Internet Explorer 6 or later, Mozilla Firefox, and Chrome build 1251 and later. Silverlight also runs on the Apple Mac in both Safari and Firefox, as well as on Linux in Firefox as part of the Moonlight project (www.mono-project.com/Moonlight), a collaboration project between Novell and Microsoft to bring Silverlight to Linux.

Silverlight for Windows Phone

Windows Phone 7 brings Silverlight to Windows Phone. Silverlight on Windows Phone 7 is based on Silverlight 3, with some Silverlight 4 features that were brought forward to the platform. There are some notable differences between Silverlight for the desktop and Silverlight for Windows Phone 7:

- Silverlight for Windows Phone 7 applications are deployed via Marketplace on the device and via the Zune client. Silverlight applications are not deployed from the Web or side-loaded from a PC to Windows Phone 7.

- Silverlight for Windows Phone 7 applications do not run in IE Mobile. Silverlight applications run directly on the phone via a host process in isolation from one another. If you are a Silverlight developer, you can think of it as a Silverlight out-of-browser application only – applications do not run in a browser.

- Some Silverlight Framework APIs are not applicable to Windows Phone 7. One example is the APIs that enable Silverlight in the web browser to communicate with the host browser. Because Silverlight does not run in the browser on Windows Phone 7, these APIs are not applicable.

- Silverlight for Windows Phone 7 includes additional functionality to make underlying device capabilities available to developers such as the built-in sensors, tasks, and choosers to enable selecting a contact, send an SMS or email, and so on.

Despite these differences, the vast majority of the Silverlight Framework is compatible between Silverlight for the Web/desktop and Silverlight for Windows Phone so learning Silverlight is a great way to also learn how to build cross-platform applications between the Web, desktop, and Windows Phone 7.

■ **Note** For more information on Silverlight go to `http://Silverlight.net` and `www.microsoft.com/expression/products/Blend_Overview.aspx`.

Hello Silverlight for Windows Phone

Now that you have a high-level overview of the application platform and programming model, let's dive a little bit deeper into Silverlight development with the Windows Phone Developer Tools. We start first with an overview of Visual Studio 2010.

Silverlight development was available in Visual Studio 2005 and 2008; however, support for Silverlight really shines in Visual Studio 2010, making it a first-class citizen development technology with great tooling support. I also provide a very high-level overview of Expression Blend, now in its fourth version and included as a free download for Windows Phone development as part of the Windows Phone Developer Tools.

Visual Studio 2010 Tour

Once you have the Windows Phone Developer Tools installed, fire up Visual Studio 2010 and select File ➤ New ➤ Project… to bring up the New Project dialog. Select Silverlight for Windows Phone on the left of the dialog and then select Windows Phone Application. Enter a name and location and then click OK to create it.

After the project is created, double-click on MainPage.xaml in the Solution Explorer tool window on the right to bring up the main application form or page. Figure 1–6 shows the UI with key items highlighted.

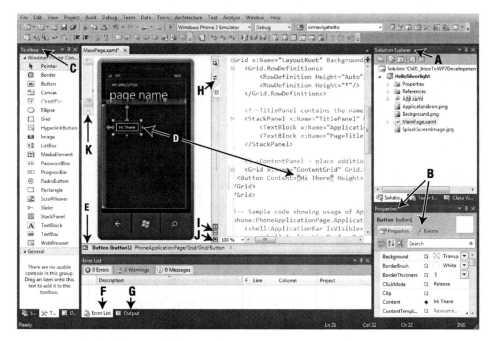

Figure 1–6. Windows Phone 7 Silverlight for Windows Phone design-time

Table 1–1 explains the identified items in the figure. If you are an experienced .NET developer, some of these may be obvious to you, but other items may not be so familiar.

Table 1–1. Visual Studio Silverlight Developer Tools

Letter	Description
A	Solution Explorer tool window: Lists the projects and project files for the entire solution. Right-clicked enabled for those new Visual Studio, so you will want to explore. The toggle buttons at the top show/hide hidden files, refresh file lists, and provide short cuts so show the code or designer for a particular file.
B	Properties tool window: Lists the properties for the selected item in the designer or the item where the cursor is in the XAML markup file. Click the lightning bolt to switch to view the events for the selected object.
C	Toolbox tool window: Lists the controls available for drag-and-drop on to the designer.
D	The main area where designer and code files are viewed and edited. On the left is the Windows Phone designer view of the XAML code on the right. Notice the button that was dropped onto the designer. The areas point to both the design-time visualization of the button, as well as the XAML markup that actually defines the button. You can edit in either view and the changes are reflected in both views.

Letter	Description
E	Document Outline tool window: Actually the button that displays the Document Outline as shown in Figure 1–7. It may not look like much but it presents the XAML markup, an XML tree, in a hierarchical view. As you design and develop your application, the nesting can be deep. When you select an item in the Document Outline, the focus shifts to that item for the Properties tool window. The Document Outline is an important part of your workflow to quickly find controls, modify properties, and so on.
F	When you build your project, errors show up in this tool window. Many times you can double-click on an error and it takes you to the correct line of code.
G	The Output tool window will show you what's going on during a build. It is also the window where Debug.WriteLine messages appear if you have them in your code.
H	Click this button to swap the sides where the Windows Phone designer view and the XAML view appear.
I	This arrow points to two buttons that position the Windows Phone design view and XAML view either side-by-side-or vertically.
J	Click this button to expand the Windows Phone designer to full screen.
K	Use this slider to Zoom the designer in size to fit your screen best or to drill in for more exact positioning of controls.

Figure 1–7 shows the Document Outline tool window. Once you start using it as part of your development workflow, you will find it invaluable for anything but the most trivial projects.

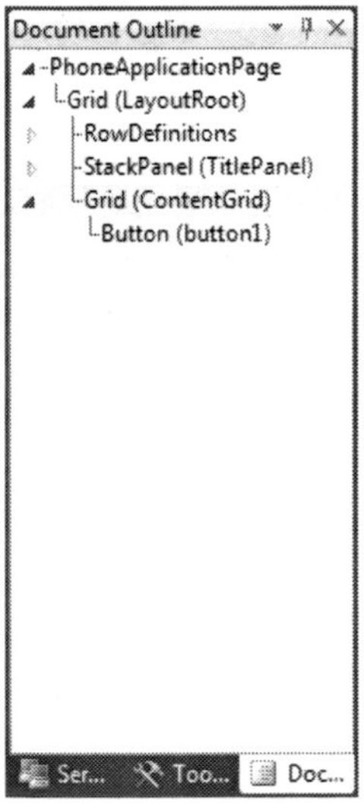

Figure 1–7. Document Outline tool window

Now that I have provided a quick tour of Visual Studio 2010 for Windows Phone development, let's dive in with some code. Add a button toward the top middle portion of the form. Double-click on the button to create the default event handler for the control, which is the Click event for a Button control. Doing so creates the following event handler that is edited to adjust the content for the button:

```
private void button1_Click(object sender, RoutedEventArgs e)
{
  (sender as Button).Content = "Hi There Reader";
}
```

We can reference the button by name, button1, created by default. In the above code, since the button1 is also the sender, we simply cast sender to button and set the Content property. A question you may be asking is how is the event handler associated with the Button object? The answer is via the XAML markup for button1, shown here:

```
<Button Content="Hi There" Height="72" HorizontalAlignment="Left" Margin="47,101,0,0"
Name="button1" VerticalAlignment="Top" Width="160" Click="button1_Click" />
```

All of the XAML was automatically generated when the control was dropped onto the designer surface except for the value configured in Content property and this line of code that associates the event handler in the MainPage.xaml.cs code-behind with the Click event for the control:

```
Click="button1_Click"
```

You can also generate event handlers by editing XAML directly. Drag another button on to the design-surface below the first. Change the Width property to Auto for this button, more on that later. Next go to the markup and type Click= inside of the <Button …> markup for the second Button control. Figure 1–8 shows the IntelliSense pop-up.

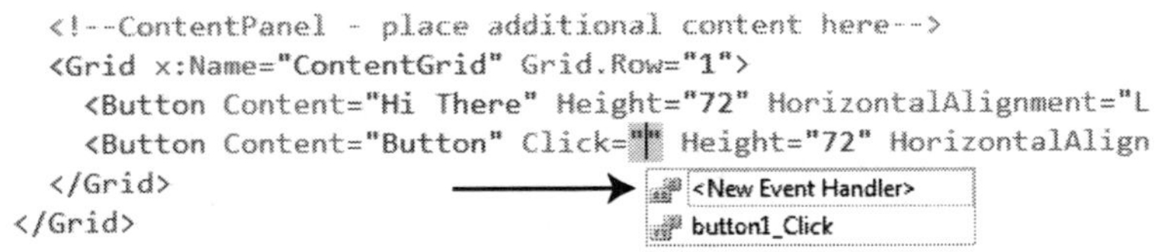

```
<!--ContentPanel - place additional content here-->
<Grid x:Name="ContentGrid" Grid.Row="1">
   <Button Content="Hi There" Height="72" HorizontalAlignment="L
   <Button Content="Button" Click=█ Height="72" HorizontalAlign
</Grid>                          ─────►  ▣ <New Event Handler>
</Grid>                                  ▣ button1_Click
```

Figure 1–8. XAML IntelliSense

You can arrow up or down in the pop-up window shown in Figure 1–8 to select an existing event handler, or simply type **Tab** to generate a new event handler into the code-behind file named button2_Click by default. We copy the same code from the first event handler into the second event handler and click F5 or the green arrow in the toolbar in Visual Studio to run the application the emulator as shown in Figure 1–9.

Figure 1–9. *HelloSilverlight application in the emulator*

In Figure 1–9, the image on the left shows the initial state, and the image on the right shows the state after clicking both buttons. Notice that the text is clipped on the top button while the bottom button automatically expanded. Remember that when I added the second button the Width was set to Auto. By setting the Width to Auto, we rely on the Silverlight layout system to determine the appropriate width for the control. I cover the layout system in more detail in Chapter 2.

Expression Blend 4 for Windows Phone Tour

Expression Blend is a relatively new tool available from Microsoft. It was first introduced with Windows Presentation Foundation as the user experience design tool. I discussed XAML as part of the overview in this section and a little bit during the walkthrough in the previous section, but to reiterate, the UI Markup language for WPF and Silverlight is Xml Application Markup Language XAML, It has great tooling support provided in both Visual Studio and Expression Blend, which I cover here.

Expression Blend is positioned as a designer tool, more for a technical designer who takes mock-ups from Adobe Photoshop or another drawing tool and turns it into XAML. Expression Blend 4 can import from Adobe Photoshop as well as Adobe Illustrator files to help jumpstart from mock-up to XAML. Figure 1–10 shows the Expression Blend 4 UI with the Ch01_IntroToWP7Development solution open.

■ **Tip** If you are a designer, please check out the Windows Phone Design Resources available at
http://msdn.microsoft.com/en-us/library/ff637515(VS.92).aspx. It includes design guidance as well as
templates for Adobe Photoshop to help jumpstart Windows Phone design efforts.

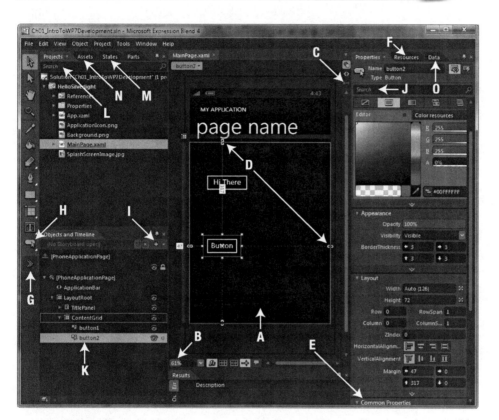

Figure 1–10. *HelloSilverlight application in Expression Blend*

Figure 1–10 shows Expression Blend 4 with a simple project opened in order to provide an overview
of the tool's major features. Table 1–2 provides a quick description of the lettered arrows.

Table 1–2. Expression Blend 4 Features

Annotation	Description
A	This is the designer surface, also known as the Artboard, which supports drag-and-drop editing.
B	Use this to zoom in or out of the designer surface as needed. Zoom out to see the entire application, or zoom in close to perform precise visual editing.
C	Tabs allow you to switch between the design surface, the XAML markup, or split view to see both the design surface and XAML.
D	These represent grid lines for laying out controls in the UI. When you move the mouse over the edge of the Grid control, the UI provides a visual cue that you can add a grid line.
E	This is the Properties window; here, several sections are collapsed so that they fit in the view.
F	The Resources window lists available resources such as styles and templates. I cover these resources throughout this book, particularly in Chapters 2, 4, and 5.
G	Clicking this chevron brings up the Asset Library, where you can search for a control if you are not sure what the icon is or whether it is visible. The Asset Library is similar to the Visual Studio toolbar area where controls are listed.
H	The little arrow in the lower right-hand corner under some of the controls shown in the Asset Library is a visual cue that related controls are available for quick access. Clicking and holding the arrow brings up a small window listing the related controls. Click a control and it becomes the visual control for that section of the Asset Library.
I	Clicking this button creates a new Storyboard object. You use storyboards to design animations. We talk more about storyboards later in this chapter.
J	This is the extremely useful Search text box. Type a property name, and Expression Blend 4 will search the list of properties available for the control and bring the property into view for easy access. Be sure to clear the Search text box when you've finished. Otherwise, it can be confusing when you switch objects and the filter entered in the Search text box does not apply, resulting in a blank properties window.
K	The XAML visual tree is listed in this area of Expression Blend 4. The yellow frame around the LayoutRoot control indicates that the LayoutRoot control is the active element. This means that double-clicking a control in the Asset Library will insert that control as a child to the LayoutRoot control. Double-clicking another control, such as the StackPanel, would make that one the active element and the insertion point for child controls dragged on the visual design surface.
L	New in Expression Blend 4, this extremely useful Search text box allows you to find project files quickly.

Annotation	Description
M	The Visual State Manager has an improved user interface in Expression Blend 4. More states for controls are displayed with a warning indicator when a property has been changed in more than one state group.
N	New in Expression Blend 4, the Assets tab provides fast access to project, controls, styles, behaviors, and effects assets in a nicely organized list.
O	The Data tab provides designers with the ability to create either a sample or live data source that makes it easier to design a data binding UI.

Expression Blend has many features that developers and designers will want to take advantage of, such as design-time data, animations, visual states, UI templates, and control templates.

This completes the quick overview of the Silverlight tools and programming model. I will cover user interface development in both Visual Studio and Expression Blend in more detail in Chapters 2 and 5.

In the next section I spend a bit more time on XNA Game Studio development as part of this chapter to cover the fundamentals. I also cover the XNA Framework in Chapter 3 related to input and in Chapter 4 related to the programming model. Chapter 7 covers 2D game development and Chapter 8 covers 3D game development in much greater detail.

XNA Game Studio and Framework Overview

XNA Game Studio and game development with the Xbox LIVE Hub are major features of Windows Phone 7. The XNA Framework for Windows Phone is part of XNA Game Studio 4.0, which is a plug-in for Visual Studio 2010 that enables developers to create games for Windows, Xbox and now Windows Phone 7.

The XNA Framework enables developers to write applications, primarily games, using managed .NET Framework code. The XNA Framework is consistent across the target platforms mentioned previously. Applications targeting a specific platform will have unique user input capabilities, such as the mouse and keyboard for the desktop, Xbox controller for Xbox and on the desktop if a USB controller is connected. For Windows Phone 7, the primary input is the touch screen and sensors. Otherwise, much of the code for a cross-platform game would be exactly the same.

Although Chapter 3 focuses on user input that applies to both Silverlight and the XNA Framework, this book has more chapters focused on Silverlight overall. Therefore, I would be remiss to not cover XNA Game Studio in this chapter, such that you can go start to create games for Windows Phone 7. To that end, this section will provide an XNA Game Studio overview to help provide background on the tools and a little bit on the platform. Chapters 7 and 8 are dedicated to XNA Game Studio, covering both 2D and 3D game development.

▓ **Note** This book does not go into game development theory in detail, because it is an incredibly broad topic that would consist of several courses at a university. You could easily purchase multiple books that cover an individual aspect of game development theory such as books completely focused on 3D math, game physics, artificial intelligence, game engine design, and so on.

What this book does provide you with is an understanding of the mechanics of game development so that you could port an existing game that you developed for another platform to Windows Phone 7, incorporate existing XNA Game Studio samples located at http://create.msdn.com, as well as apply game development theory obtained through additional reading into your own Windows Phone 7 games.

Hello XNA for Windows Phone

When you install the Windows Phone Developer Tools it includes XNA Game Studio, with a dedicated template folder XNA Game Studio 4.0 in the Visual Studio 2010 New Project dialog to create either a Windows Phone game or a Windows Phone game library assembly.

All game development is done non-visually through code. You do not use Expression Blend to create games unless building the game experience in Silverlight. This makes the Emulator that much more important for XNA Framework game development. The good news is that the Windows Phone Emulator is hardware accelerated on the Windows Vista or Windows 7 development machine, enabling a great game development experience with the emulator to visually see the game in action without having to always deploy to a device.

■ **Tip** Traditional third-party game engines have ported their visual tools and frameworks to XNA Game Studio with support for Windows Phone 7. The AppHub partner link has more information here:

http://create.msdn.com/en-us/resources/partners

In Visual Studio, let's create a new project and call it HelloXNA in our existing Chapter 1 code solution. Right-click on the solution explorer and select Add… ➤ New Project, select Windows Phone Game (4.0), and then type **HelloXNA** as the project name. Be sure to right-click on the new HelloXNA project and set it to the startup project for the solution if is not already.

After the project is created, you can see that the project layout is very different from a Silverlight project, as shown in Figure 1–11.

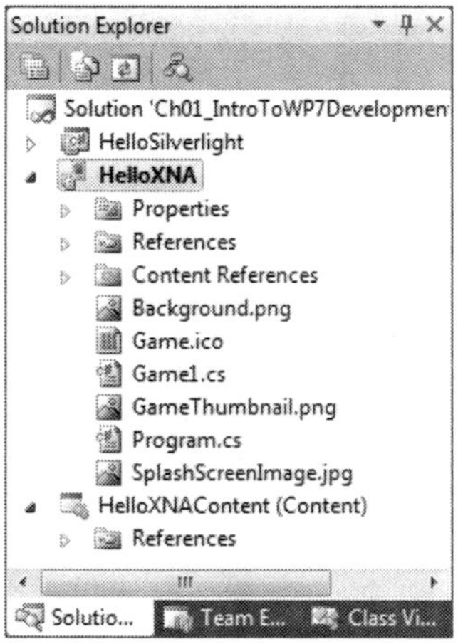

Figure 1–11. XNA Game Studio default project layout

Notice in Figure 1–11 there are actually two projects listed, HelloXNA and HellXNAContent. The primary project with the output remains the HelloXNA project. The HelloXNAContent project is the content project for the HelloXNA project, which I cover in the next section.

Game Content

As noted in the previous paragraph, the content project is where the content is located – the sprites, textures, 3D models, and so on for the game. Sprites and textures generally refer to 2d images you move around the screen (sprites) and the background or surface image (textures). In our sample we create three simple .tga files to represent a background texture for the simple game, a spaceship sprite, and a hero ship sprite that the user controls and a missile sprite that is fired from the hero ship. Figure 1–12 shows the content project layout, as well as the properties for the hero ship sprite.

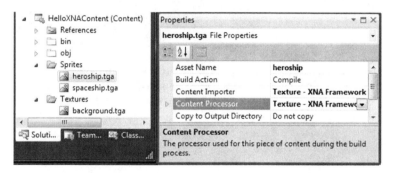

Figure 1–12. HelloXNAContent project files

Notice in Figure 1–12 that the heroship.tga image file has an AssetName, a Content Importer and Content Processor properties. The Content Importer and Content Processor property automatically selected when the content is added. Internally, the XNA Framework stores content assets in a custom compressed format so it uses content importers and processors to import external content into the internal format. XNA Game Studio ships with several built-in converters for common content listed here, with explanations for the less than obvious converters:

- Effect: DirectX High Level Shader Language (HLSL) .fx file (not supported on WP7)

- AutoDesk FBX: .AutoDesk file format for three dimensional models

- Sprite Font Description

- MP3 Audio File

- Texture: Essentially a bitmap

- WAV Audio File

- WMA Audio File

- WMV Video File

- XACT Project: XACT is a DirectX audio tool for building rich game audio

- X File: DirectX 3D model file

- XML Content

You can create custom content importers as well as purchase third-party converters for file formats not available out of the box. However, in most cases the previous list supports the vast majority of content and content creation tools available.

The other property for content is the AssetName, which is based on the filename without the extension. When you load content into your game you load it via the AssetName property, as you will see shortly.

■ **Tip** Make friends with a graphic artist if you are not very artistic. Content is just as important, if not more so then the coding in a game. There are third-party content providers that sell content you can tweak as well as higher graphic artist talent on a contractual basis. Programmer art won't cut it.

The Game Loop

Let's continue to explore the code and functionality in the HelloXNA project by exploring the default game loop code. When learning to build games, development centers on the game loop summarized here:

1. Load the game content and related objects.

2. Update the object's state.

3. Draw the object to the screen.

The XNA Framework provides a typical game loop development model consisting of initial content load, followed by repeated calls to the update, and draw methods. By default the XNA Framework game loop is fixed-step game loop at 30 frames per second with each frame represented by calls to draw and update. It is set to 30 frames per second (fps) to be aligned with the refresh rate of the hardware. You can change the frame rate to 60 fps using the following code:

```
GraphicsDeviceManager.SynchronizeWithVerticalRetrace = false;
game.TargetElapsedTime = FromSeconds (1/60f);
```

However, if you increase the frame rate, it will impact battery performance with possibly minimal tangible benefit. One way around this is to call update twice per each draw call by creating a custom game loop. This would be the recommended course of action over adjusting the frame rate above 30 frames per second.

Now let's dive in to the code. When we created the HelloXNA game project, it generates a code file Game1.cs, which is the main code file and includes the game loop logic. Listing 1–1 has the full code listing for reference.

Listing 1–1. Generated Game1.cs

```
using System;
using System.Collections.Generic;
using System.Linq;
using Microsoft.Xna.Framework;
using Microsoft.Xna.Framework.Audio;
using Microsoft.Xna.Framework.Content;
using Microsoft.Xna.Framework.GamerServices;
using Microsoft.Xna.Framework.Graphics;
```

```csharp
using Microsoft.Xna.Framework.Input;
using Microsoft.Xna.Framework.Input.Touch;
using Microsoft.Xna.Framework.Media;

namespace HelloXNA
{
    /// <summary>
    /// This is the main type for your game
    /// </summary>
    public class Game1 : Microsoft.Xna.Framework.Game
    {
        GraphicsDeviceManager graphics;
        SpriteBatch spriteBatch;

        public Game1()
        {
            graphics = new GraphicsDeviceManager(this);
            Content.RootDirectory = "Content";

            // Frame rate is 30 fps by default for Windows Phone.
            TargetElapsedTime = TimeSpan.FromTicks(333333);
        }

        /// <summary>
        /// Allows the game to perform any initialization it needs to before starting to run.
        /// This is where it can query for any required services and load any non-graphic
        /// related content.  Calling base.Initialize will enumerate through any components
        /// and initialize them as well.
        /// </summary>
        protected override void Initialize()
        {
            // TODO: Add your initialization logic here

            base.Initialize();
        }

        /// <summary>
        /// LoadContent will be called once per game and is the place to load
        /// all of your content.
        /// </summary>
        protected override void LoadContent()
        {
            // Create a new SpriteBatch, which can be used to draw textures.
            spriteBatch = new SpriteBatch(GraphicsDevice);

            // TODO: use this.Content to load your game content here
        }

        /// <summary>
        /// UnloadContent will be called once per game and is the place to unload
        /// all content.
        /// </summary>
        protected override void UnloadContent()
        {
```

```
      // TODO: Unload any non ContentManager content here
    }

    /// <summary>
    /// Allows the game to run logic such as updating the world,
    /// checking for collisions, gathering input, and playing audio.
    /// </summary>
    /// <param name="gameTime">Provides a snapshot of timing values.</param>
    protected override void Update(GameTime gameTime)
    {
      // Allows the game to exit
      if (GamePad.GetState(PlayerIndex.One).Buttons.Back == ButtonState.Pressed)
        this.Exit();

      // TODO: Add your update logic here

      base.Update(gameTime);
    }

    /// <summary>
    /// This is called when the game should draw itself.
    /// </summary>
    /// <param name="gameTime">Provides a snapshot of timing values.</param>
    protected override void Draw(GameTime gameTime)
    {
      GraphicsDevice.Clear(Color.CornflowerBlue);

      // TODO: Add your drawing code here

      base.Draw(gameTime);
    }
  }
}
```

Listing 1–1 is insightful reading to help you understand the game loop implementation in XNA Game Studio. The comments help you understand what to do where in the game loop code but we briefly cover the methods here starting with the constructor for Game1 in Listing 1–1. The constructor initializes a reference to the GraphicsDeviceManager, which represents the graphics device. It also sets the content root directory to the Content folder, which is where all of our content will reside. Finally it sets the frame rate to 30 fps.

The Initialize() method is where developers query for required game services. Game services are objects defined by a custom Interface you create that you want to access for the entire life of the game. It is a way to expose an object, such as a 3D camera object, to many other objects. I demonstrate game services in Chapters 7 and 8.

I'm sure you can guess what the LoadContent() method does. It is called once per game with the idea that you load all of your content upfront so as to not impact the game loop timing by loading content on the fly in the middle of a frame.

For a game with a lot of content, this may not make the best use of resources. In this case, the game can be broken up into levels and a developer can dynamically load content at the start of each level. Users won't mind waiting a few seconds up front as the level loads, as long as the return is better game play during the level by pre-loading the content.

After loading the content in the LoadContent method, the next method in Listing 1–1 is the UnLoad method. While you have to explicitly load content in LoadContent, the opposite is not required. Any content that you load in the LoadContent method is automatically managed by XNA Framework.

However, for any content that you load dynamically and that is not explicitly managed by a ContentManager object. An example object is a DynamicVertexBuffer that requires the Dispose() method to be called. Otherwise, content that is loaded by ContentManager will automatically be unloaded either when the game exits or if a developer manually removes a GameComponent object. A GameComponent is an XNA Framework feature that allows a developer to encapsulate a complex game object into the game loop in an object oriented way. I cover GameComponents in Chapter 7.

As mentioned, the Update() and Draw() methods are the heart of the game loop. The default Update method checks to see if the user pushes the hard key Back button on the Windows Phone 7 device. If so, the game exits. The other code calls base.Update(gameTime) to allow the minimum game loop logic to occur. The Update method takes one parameter of type GameTime. The GameTime type contains a snapshot of game timing state that can be used by variable step (real time) or fixed-step (game time) games. The GameTime object has three properties all of type TimeSpan:

- **ElapsedGameTime:** The amount of time since the last call to the Update method.

- **IsRunningSlowly:** A Boolean value. If it has a value of true, this indicates that the ElapsedGameTime is running longer than the TargetElapsedTime for the game loop. The game should do something to speed up processing in the Update method such as reducing calculations; otherwise the game frame rate will potentially decrease by skipping calls to the Draw method.

- **TotalGameTime:** The amount of time since the start of the game.

Developers can use these values to perform game-related calculations ,such as when a grenade object should explode after it was initially tossed, as an example.

When developing a game, always keep in mind that games, videos, movies, and so on all depend on tricking the human eye into believing that it is watching continue motion. In general, 30 fps is the minimum before the human eye starts to perceive that it is not watching continuous motion. I mentioned the two types of game loops, fixed-step and variable step. The type of game loop affects how a developer manages the user perception of motion, which we dig into in the next two sections.

Fixed-Step Game Loop

A fixed-step game loop tries to call its Update method at a regular interval, providing a fixed chunk of time for the developer to perform calculations in Update before drawing the scene. The fixed-step game loop is the default for XNA Framework. For the Xbox and Windows, the default frame rate is 60 fps in a fixed-step game loop, which means that Update is called every 1/60 of a second.

For Windows Phone 7, the default frame rate for a fixed-step game is 1/30 of a second, which aligns with the hardware screen refresh rate. Visually, a higher frame rate does not provide any benefit, but it would impact battery life more.

Based on this information, the value TargetElapsedTime from the gameTime parameter for Update (and Draw) will have a value of 1/30 of a second for the value of its TimeSpan. The Update and Draw methods are called every 1/30 of a second, unless IsRunningSlowly returns true. In that case, the call to Draw is skipped so that Update catches up, resulting in a reduced frame rate.

■ **Note** When the game pauses in the debugger, the Update method is not called until the debugger resumes the game.

Variable-Step Game Loop

In this type of game, `Update` and `Draw` are called continuously without regard for the value set to the `TargetEllapsedTime` property resulting in a variable frame rate. With the fixed refresh rate for the screen of 30 fps, there may not be much gained by a viable-step loop without potentially negatively impacting battery performance.

Now that you have background on XNA Game Studio development, how content is loaded, and the game loop, let's dive in and create a simple game.

Implement the Game

In this section we start with the default game loop code generated when we created the `HelloXNA` project to create a simple space ship shooter game. Our game will be a simple top-down shooter where alien space ships attempt to strike the hero ship. The hero ship can shoot missiles at the alien ships to cause them to explode. Score is based on the number of alien ships blown up.

Now that we have an understanding of the game play, let's get started. We alternate between coding and background detail as we develop the game to explain key concepts. In the Game1.cs code file we declare four variables of type `Texture2D` named `HeroShip`, `SpaceShip`, `Missile`, and `BackgroundImage` that are initialized in the `LoadContent` method:

```
HeroShip = this.Content.Load<Texture2D>("Sprites/heroship");
SpaceShip = this.Content.Load<Texture2D>("Sprites/spaceship");
Missile = this.Content.Load<Texture2D>("Sprites/missile");
BackgroundImage = this.Content.Load<Texture2D>("Textures/background");
```

Since these assets are loaded by a `ContentManager` object, we do not need to worry about releasing the objects in the `UnloadContent` method. The `ContentManager` will take care of that for us when it goes out of scope.

Now that we loaded the content, we next cover modifications to the `Update()` and `Draw()` methods. We cover `Draw` first because we want to draw the background on the screen. To actually do the drawing to the graphics device you use a `SpriteBatch` object.

By default, the XNA Game Studio project template creates a member named `spritePatch` of type `SpriteBatch`. Within the `Draw` method, you first call `spriteBatch.Begin`, then `spriteBatch.Draw` any number of times, and then `spriteBatch.End`. It is more efficient for the graphics hardware to draw to the back buffer as a batch and then draw to the back buffer to the device as opposed to drawing items one at a time directly to the graphics device. `SpriteBatch.Begin` method sets up the back buffer and the call to `SpriteBatch.End` indicates that the batch is ready to be drawn to the device.

```
spriteBatch.Begin();
spriteBatch.Draw(BackgroundImage,graphics.GraphicsDevice.Viewport.Bounds, Color.White);
spriteBatch.End();
```

Figure 1–13 shows the background image in the Emulator.

Figure 1–13. Drawing the background in the Emulator

The background is static for our simple game so we are finished with it. We covered Begin and End for the SpriteBatch class but not the Draw method, which has several overloads that look intimidating at first, taking rectangle objects, rotation, scale, etc.

All overloads of the Draw method have a couple of parameters in common in that all of the overloads take a Texture2D (the image to draw) and a position to draw it either in the form of a Vector2 or a Rectangle object. I cover SpriteBatch.Draw in detail in Chapter 7, but we will cover the specific overloads we use to build the game as we go along. For the background image shown in Figure 1–13, we draw with this overload:

```
spriteBatch.Draw(BackgroundImage,graphics.GraphicsDevice.Viewport.Bounds, Color.White);
```

BackgroundImage is the Texture2D to be drawn. For the place to draw the texture, we pass in the Rectangle size of the entire screen, which is defined by graphics.GraphicsDevice.Viewport.Bounds. We could hard-code the values to be the shipping screen resolution of 800 × 480. However, we do not want to hardcode this value, because at some point in the future an additional screen resolution will be introduced that is 480 × 320. The last parameter in this Draw method overload allows you to tint Texture2D in a particular color. Color.White represents no tint at all.

Now let's shift over to the Update method. It is in the Update method where calculations are performed to determine where the alien ship, space ship, and missile should be drawn. In addition to the variable representing the sprite image, we also need variables to track the position and speed of the objects as well. First let's have a quick discussion on vectors.

When Windows Phone 7 initially hits the market, the screen resolution is 800 pixels in height and 480 pixels in width. In XNA Framework, the 2D coordinate system puts 0,0 in the upper left hand corner of the screen with the positive X direction flowing to the right and positive Y direction flowing down the screen, as shown in Figure 1–14.

Figure 1–14. The Windows Phone 7 Portrait 2D Cartisian Plane

■ **Note** The XNA Framework expects your game to appear in wide-screen or landscape mode by default. It is possible to build a game that runs vertically as well — I cover how in Chapter 7.

A Vector2 consists of an X and Y component that represents a direction and magnitude from the origin. As an example, since the screen is 480 pixels wide, the X axis represented as a Vector2 would have zero for the Y component, and 480 for the X component like this (480,0). Likewise, a Vector2 that represents the Y axis would have zero for the X component and 800 for the Y component like this (0,800).

A Vector2 can represent either a position or a speed. As a position, you set the X and Y component to be the values you want to place an object on the Cartesian plane. As an example, to place the upper left-hand corner of a sprite or image in the middle of the screen, you would set the sprites position to this value (240,400), which is half the screen width and height respectively.

■ **Tip** When you position a sprite, it is always relative to the upper left-hand corner of the sprite, which is considered (0,0) in terms of height and width for the sprite. If you don't take this into account and think you are positioning the center of a sprite, it will be off by half the height of the sprite toward the bottom and half the width of the sprite to the right.

Position is pretty straightforward in a 2D plane. Representing Speed as a Vector2 is similar except that the Vector2 is interpreted by its magnitude or length and direction. Imagine an arrow with its tail at position (0,0) and its head at (X,Y) such as (10,10) on a 2D plane, as illustrated in Figure 1–15.

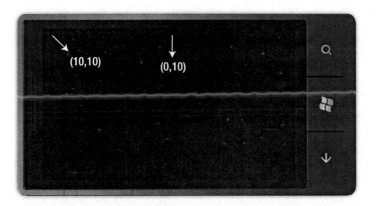

Figure 1–15. Vectors in a 2D plane

If the imaginary Vector2 (0,10) represents a speed, it means that the object is moving straight down at 10 pixels per frame. If the Vector2 (10,10) represents a speed, it means that for each frame, the object is moving 10 pixels to the right and 10 pixels down. Figure 1–16 depicts a ball that has a position of (300, 160). A speed Vectors2 (50,50) is applied to the ball in a given frame.

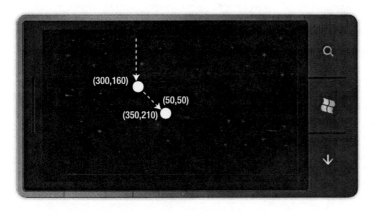

Figure 1–16. Applying speed to an object via vector addition

Applying a speed of (50,50) redirects the ball to a southeastern direction in the plane, giving a new position of (350, 210) for the ball. We know this intuitively because X is positive to the right and Y is positive in the down position, so the Vector2 (50,50) moves the ball 50 pixels to the right and 50 pixels down. Note that we could just as easily have a speed of (-50, 50), which would intuitively move the ball to the southwest direction.

Now that you have a basic understanding of position and speed as Vector2 objects, let's go back to the XNA Game Studio project. We will perform speed and position calculations in the Update method. We also need to check to see if an object has either collided with another object/sprite, or if the object collided with an edge of the screen.

If it an object collides with an object we can do several things. If the object is a golf club and the other object represents a golf ball, a developer would want to simulate the club connecting with the ball and send it flying in the opposite direction based on the ball and club Vector2 position, the angle of impact. Another example action upon a collision is that if the collision is between an alien space ship and a missile fired from the player's space ship, the game could simulate an explosion and the alien space ship disappears from the screen.

Speaking of the player space ship, the other key component handed in the Update method is user input, which is also calculated using Vector2 objects. For Windows Phone 7 user input can be in the form of a screen tap, a gesture, or the accelerometer as the major game input methods.

With the background on the screen coordinate system and Vector2D objects out of the way, you should have a pretty good idea of what the code will look like in the Update method in pseudo code:

- Handle User Input

- Apply User Input to objects

- Update Position of objects

- Detect Object and Edge Collisions

- Determine the final state and position of all objects

A key point to consider is that if the Update method takes too long the Game loop will decide to skip a call to the Draw method, resulting in dropped frames. Keep this in mind when writing code in the Update method.

■ **Note** Performance considerations in game development are covered in more detail in Chapters 7 and 8.

Armed with an understanding of what we need to do in the Update method in general, let's dive into coding the game logic. We need to add a couple of member variables to represent the position and speed for our game objects, which include the hero ship, the enemy space ship, and the missile. We need to track each object's position, and speed so we declare six additional variables:

```
//Define Speed and Position vectors for objects that move
Vector2 HeroShipPosition;
Vector2 HeroShipSpeed;
Vector2 SpaceShipPosition;
Vector2 SpaceShipSpeed;
Vector2 MissilePosition;
Vector2 MissileSpeed;
```

We initialize these values in a separate method named InitializeObjects executed in LoadContent just after we load the related sprite images.

```
private void InitializeObjects()
{
  //Initialize Positon and Speed
  SpaceShipPosition = new Vector2(
    graphics.GraphicsDevice.Viewport.Width / 2 - SpaceShip.Width / 2, -SpaceShip.Height);
  SpaceShipSpeed = new Vector2(0, 2); // 2 pixels / frame "down"

  //Center hero ship width wise along the X axis
  //Place hero ship with 20 pixels underneath it in the Y axis
  HeroShipPosition = new Vector2(
```

```
    graphics.GraphicsDevice.Viewport.Width / 2 - HeroShip.Width / 2,
    graphics.GraphicsDevice.Viewport.Height - HeroShip.Height - 20f);
HeroShipSpeed = Vector2.Zero;

//Center Missile on Space Ship and put it 50 pixels further down
//off screen "below" hereoship
MissilePosition = HeroShipPosition +
    new Vector2(HeroShip.Width / 2 - Missile.Width / 2, HeroShip.Height + 20f);
MissileSpeed = new Vector2(0, -6); // 6 pixels / frame "up"

}
```

I mentioned this earlier but it is worth restating: when you draw a sprite, the position provided to the Draw method is the origin of the sprite when drawn meaning that the provided position becomes the upper left-hand corner of the sprite. In order to draw the alien spaceship and hero spaceship centered width-wise on the screen, we subtract half of the sprite's width from the position so that the middle of the sprite is centered on the screen.

I already covered how to draw in the Draw method, and we are already drawing the background, which was easy to position since it fills the entire screen. We haven't written the code to draw the hero ship, the alien spaceship, or the missile. Since we now have position information for these objects to reference in the form of the initialized variables, let's update the Draw method. We add these three lines of code to the Draw method right after we draw the background image:

```
spriteBatch.Draw(SpaceShip, SpaceShipPosition, Color.White);
spriteBatch.Draw(Missile, MissilePosition, Color.White);
spriteBatch.Draw(HeroShip, HeroShipPosition, Color.White);
```

Figure 1–17 shows the results.

Figure 1–17. Sprite Initial Position

We are pretty much down with the Draw method for our simple game and will focus on the Update method to make the game interactive. The first thing we do is add the basic update formula for all three objects to the Update method:

```
HeroShipPosition += HeroShipSpeed;
SpaceShipPosition += SpaceShipSpeed;
MissilePosition += MissileSpeed;
```

If you run the game right now, you will see the enemy spaceship move down the screen and the missile move up the screen at a slightly faster rate. Figure 1–18 shows a snapshot of the movement.

Figure 1–18. *Moving Sprites*

While pretty cool, it doesn't do much. The sprites pass through each other and then fly off to infinity in the up direction for the missile and the down direction for the alien spaceship. We can make a couple of modifications to make it somewhat more interesting as well as explain a couple of concepts.

The first modification that we make is edge detection. In the Update Method we type CheckScreenBoundaryCollision(gameTime); and then right-click on it and select Generate ➤ Method Stub.

In the newly generated method, we check to see if the missile, which has a default speed of -4 pixels / frame in the Y direction, has flown off the top of the screen, which would be a negative Y value. Since the alien space ship drops straight down at 2 pixels per frame, we check to see if it has a Y value greater than the screen height. Here is the method:

```
private void CheckScreenBoundaryCollision(GameTime gameTime)
{
  //Reset Missile if off the screen
  if (MissilePosition.Y < 0)
  {
    MissilePosition.Y = graphics.GraphicsDevice.Viewport.Height -
                        HeroShip.Height;
  }

  //Reset enemy spaceship if off the screen
  //to random drop point
  if (SpaceShipPosition.Y >
        graphics.GraphicsDevice.Viewport.Height)
  {
    SpaceShipPosition.Y = -2*SpaceShip.Height;
  }
}
```

Notice that we avoid using actual number values. As an example, we could use 480 instead of graphics.GraphicsDevice.Viewport.Height, but when the second screen resolution becomes available the game will break, because screen height in landscape mode will be 320.

The second modification to the game is to detect collisions between the alien spaceship and the missile. We create a new method, CheckForCollisions(gameTime); as before and edit the generated stub. There are many different algorithms available to detect for collisions with different levels of accuracy. The most accurate method is to compare for equality each point of the first image with every possible point in the other image. While most accurate, it is also the most CPU intensive and time consuming.

A simple method to check for collisions is to use bounding boxes. The idea is to wrap an object in a rectangle and check for collisions. The rectangle is based on the maximum length and width of the object. This can be inaccurate for irregular shapes, but costs much less in terms of CPU and time. In our simple game we generate two Rectangle objects that wrap the alien spaceship and the missile and then call the Intersects method to detect a collision. Here is the code:

```
private void CheckForCollisions(GameTime gameTime)
{
  //Alien and Missile
  Rectangle AlienRec = new Rectangle((int)SpaceShipPosition.X,
            (int)SpaceShipPosition.Y,SpaceShip.Width, SpaceShip.Height);
  Rectangle MissileRec = new Rectangle((int)MissilePosition.X,
            (int)MissilePosition.Y,Missile.Width, Missile.Height);

  if (AlienRec.Intersects(MissileRec))
  {
    SpaceShipPosition.Y = -2*SpaceShip.Height;
    MissilePosition.Y = graphics.GraphicsDevice.Viewport.Height - HeroShip.Height;
  }
}
```

We create the two Rectangle objects and then check for collision by calling if (AlienRec.Intersects(MissileRec)) and then update position similar to when there is a screen edge collision.

We now have an application that shows a dropping alien spaceship intersected by a missile over and over again. While not the most functional game, specifically because it doesn't incorporate user input or interactivity at all, it allows us to demonstrate key concepts for XNA Game Studio without inundating you with new concepts. Listing 1–2 shows the full code for our incomplete game.

Listing 1–2. Modified Game1.cs

```
using System;
using System.Collections.Generic;
using System.Linq;
using Microsoft.Xna.Framework;
using Microsoft.Xna.Framework.Audio;
using Microsoft.Xna.Framework.Content;
using Microsoft.Xna.Framework.GamerServices;
using Microsoft.Xna.Framework.Graphics;
using Microsoft.Xna.Framework.Input;
using Microsoft.Xna.Framework.Input.Touch;
using Microsoft.Xna.Framework.Media;

namespace HelloXNA
{
  /// <summary>
  /// This is the main type for your game
  /// </summary>
  public class Game1 : Microsoft.Xna.Framework.Game
```

```
    {
        GraphicsDeviceManager graphics;
        SpriteBatch spriteBatch;

        //Define Texture2D objects to hold game content
        Texture2D HeroShip;
        Texture2D SpaceShip;
        Texture2D BackgroundImage;
        Texture2D Missile;

        //Define Speed and Position vectors for objects that move
        Vector2 HeroShipPosition;
        Vector2 HeroShipSpeed;
        Vector2 SpaceShipPosition;
        Vector2 SpaceShipSpeed;
        Vector2 MissilePosition;
        Vector2 MissileSpeed;

        public Game1()
        {
            graphics = new GraphicsDeviceManager(this);
            Content.RootDirectory = "Content";

            // Frame rate is 30 fps by default for Windows Phone.
            TargetElapsedTime = TimeSpan.FromTicks(333333);

        }

        /// <summary>
        /// Allows the game to perform any initialization it needs to before starting to run.
        /// This is where it can query for any required services and load any non-graphic
        /// related content.  Calling base.Initialize will enumerate through any components
        /// and initialize them as well.
        /// </summary>
        protected override void Initialize()
        {
            // TODO: Add your initialization logic here

            base.Initialize();
        }

        /// <summary>
        /// LoadContent will be called once per game and is the place to load
        /// all of your content.
        /// </summary>
        protected override void LoadContent()
        {
            // Create a new SpriteBatch, which can be used to draw textures.
            spriteBatch = new SpriteBatch(GraphicsDevice);

            HeroShip = this.Content.Load<Texture2D>("Sprites/heroship");
            SpaceShip = this.Content.Load<Texture2D>("Sprites/spaceship");
            Missile = this.Content.Load<Texture2D>("Sprites/missile");
            BackgroundImage = this.Content.Load<Texture2D>("Textures/background");
```

```
    InitializeObjects();
}

private void InitializeObjects()
{
    //Initialize Positon and Speed
    SpaceShipPosition = new Vector2(
        graphics.GraphicsDevice.Viewport.Width / 2 - SpaceShip.Width / 2, -SpaceShip.Height);
    SpaceShipSpeed = new Vector2(0, 2); // 2 pixels / frame "down"

    //Center hero ship width wise along the X axis
    //Place hero ship with 20 pixels underneath it in the Y axis
    HeroShipPosition = new Vector2(
        graphics.GraphicsDevice.Viewport.Width / 2 - HeroShip.Width / 2,
        graphics.GraphicsDevice.Viewport.Height - HeroShip.Height - 20f);
    HeroShipSpeed = Vector2.Zero;

    //Center Missile on Space Ship and put it 50 pixels further down
    //off screen "below" hereoship
    MissilePosition = HeroShipPosition +
        new Vector2(HeroShip.Width / 2 - Missile.Width / 2, HeroShip.Height + 20f);
    MissileSpeed = new Vector2(0, -6); // 6 pixels / frame "up"

}

/// <summary>
/// UnloadContent will be called once per game and is the place to unload
/// all content.
/// </summary>
protected override void UnloadContent()
{
    // TODO: Unload any non ContentManager content here
}

/// <summary>
/// Allows the game to run logic such as updating the world,
/// checking for collisions, gathering input, and playing audio.
/// </summary>
/// <param name="gameTime">Provides a snapshot of timing values.</param>
protected override void Update(GameTime gameTime)
{
    // Allows the game to exit
    if (GamePad.GetState(PlayerIndex.One).Buttons.Back == ButtonState.Pressed)
        this.Exit();

    // TODO: Add your update logic here
    CheckScreenBoundaryCollision(gameTime);
    CheckForCollisions(gameTime);

    HeroShipPosition += HeroShipSpeed;
    SpaceShipPosition += SpaceShipSpeed;
    MissilePosition += MissileSpeed;
```

```
      base.Update(gameTime);
    }

    private void CheckForCollisions(GameTime gameTime)
    {
      //Alien and Missile
      Rectangle AlienRec = new Rectangle((int)SpaceShipPosition.X,
                  (int)SpaceShipPosition.Y, SpaceShip.Width, SpaceShip.Height);
      Rectangle MissileRec = new Rectangle((int)MissilePosition.X,
                  (int)MissilePosition.Y, Missile.Width, Missile.Height);

      if (AlienRec.Intersects(MissileRec))
      {
        SpaceShipPosition.Y = -2 * SpaceShip.Height;
        MissilePosition.Y = graphics.GraphicsDevice.Viewport.Height - HeroShip.Height;
      }
    }

    private void CheckScreenBoundaryCollision(GameTime gameTime)
    {
      //Reset Missile if off the screen
      if (MissilePosition.Y < 0)
      {
        MissilePosition.Y = graphics.GraphicsDevice.Viewport.Height -
                            HeroShip.Height;
      }

      //Reset enemy spaceship if off the screen
      //to random drop point
      if (SpaceShipPosition.Y >
            graphics.GraphicsDevice.Viewport.Height)
      {
        SpaceShipPosition.Y = -2 * SpaceShip.Height;
      }
    }


    /// <summary>
    /// This is called when the game should draw itself.
    /// </summary>
    /// <param name="gameTime">Provides a snapshot of timing values.</param>
    protected override void Draw(GameTime gameTime)
    {
      GraphicsDevice.Clear(Color.CornflowerBlue);

      // TODO: Add your drawing code here
      spriteBatch.Begin();
      spriteBatch.Draw(BackgroundImage, graphics.GraphicsDevice.Viewport.Bounds, Color.White);
      spriteBatch.Draw(SpaceShip, SpaceShipPosition, Color.White);
      spriteBatch.Draw(Missile, MissilePosition, Color.White);
      spriteBatch.Draw(HeroShip, HeroShipPosition, Color.White);
      spriteBatch.End();
```

```
        base.Draw(gameTime);
    }
  }
}
```

In this section I provided an introduction to the XNA Framework. I cover programming in XNA Game Studio in detail in Chapters 7 and 8, including adding much more interactivity to what we started here in Chapter 1. The next section provides a high-level overview of the Windows Marketplace for Mobile.

AppHub and the Windows Marketplace for Mobile

There are many reasons a developer like you wants to build an application for Windows Phone 7. To make your creation available to customers, you submit it for certification to the Windows Marketplace for Mobile, which is the official name. Henceforth, we will refer to it as the Windows Phone Marketplace.

Windows Phone Marketplace Registration

Registering for the Windows Phone Marketplace is a straightforward process, which you can do at AppHub here: http://create.msdn.com. Registration takes some time to fully complete because Microsoft vets every publisher identity via GeoTrust. The timeline is partially dependent on actions by you, such as clicking the email link to validate your email address and providing the necessary documentation to GeoTrust in a timely manner

Publisher Verification ensures that consumers can feel confident that the publisher is who they say they are. This protects the consumer from a nefarious publisher impersonating their bank as a way to obtain a user's account information.

Registration costs $99. This allows you as the publisher to submit an unlimited number of for pay applications and five free app certifications. As of this writing, each additional certification event is $20 per application. Updates to free applications are no-charge certification events unless the application fails certification during the update.

▨ **Tip** If you are a member of one of Microsoft's "Spark" programs such as BizSpark for startup business or DreamSpark for the academic community, you may be eligible for a reduced or possibly free Marketplace registration.

Microsoft is continuously updating policies to better serve its developer community. The AppHub FAQ is a great place to start for the most recent updates: http://create.msdn.com/en-US/home/faq.

Submitting Applications to Marketplace

When you submit an application to Marketplace, the estimated average time for an application to be approved is five days. Microsoft validates the application against the criteria set forth in the document "Windows Phone 7 Application Certification Requirements" available for review at http://create.msdn.com. This document covers application policy guidelines, content policy guidelines, and application certification requirements.

Making Money

The application publisher sets the price of the application. As the publisher you collect 70% of the revenue and Microsoft keeps 30% for paid applications, which is in line with other application store revenue models. The 30% primarily covers the costs of marketplace, certification costs, and so on.

Microsoft also provides an advertising-based revenue model offering for Windows Phone 7. You are not required to use Microsoft's advertising offering but it does provide a very easy way to take advantage of advertising revenue. The Microsoft Advertising SDK is discussed in detail as part of Chapter 5.

An important component to getting paid is potential application reach. At initial availability, Windows Phone 7 currently support 5 languages; English, French, Italian, German and Spanish, otherwise known as EFIGS. The Windows Phone Marketplace supports applications purchases in 30 countries as of this writing with more countries to be added in 2011.

• Australia	• Hong Kong	• Poland
• Austria	• India	• Portugal
• Belgium	• Ireland	• Russia
• Brazil	• Italy	• Singapore
• Canada	• Japan	• Spain
• Denmark	• Luxembourg	• Sweden
• Finland	• Mexico	• Switzerland
• France	• Netherlands	• Taiwan
• Germany	• New Zealand	• United Kingdom
• Greece	• Norway	• United States

In order to participate and sell your applications and get paid, you must be registered in Marketplace and have a bank account for one of these countries. Microsoft announced early in 2011 that more countries and languages will be added later this year. Go to http://create.msdn.com/en-US/home/faq/windows_phone_7#wp7faq53 to check on supported countries for the latest status.

Marketing Matters

Making money is more than setting a price. As part of the submission process, the developer supplies the detailed description, screen shots, and marketing art for items like the background panorama for the Marketplace hub. Your tile icon is determined by the background.png file that is part of your Visual Studio Windows Phone 7 project so be sure to update it so that it looks good on the Windows Phone 7 Start screen. The applicationicon.png file is the smaller icon displayed in the App List. Figure 1–19 shows the App List in the emulator.

Figure 1–19. App list

The marketing art for Marketplace is incredibly important because that is what the end-user sees when viewing your application in Marketplace on the device. Also, if you study successful applications on other platforms, the mobile ISV generally includes four people or roles, a business person, a marketing person, and a couple of developers. Someone has to wear the marketing hat to promote the application beyond Windows Phone Marketplace, such as via Social Networking channels, outreach to application review web sites, and so on. The most successful applications are those with a great business plan and great marketing behind them.

Bing Visual Search for Windows Phone 7

Not really an official web marketplace, however, the Bing Maps Visual Search provides a visual filterable search for the top 3000 applications. To review the search go to http://bing.com and enter **Windows Phone 7 Top Apps**. A new menu appears under the search box titled "visual search." Click it to bring up the results as shown in Figure 1–20.

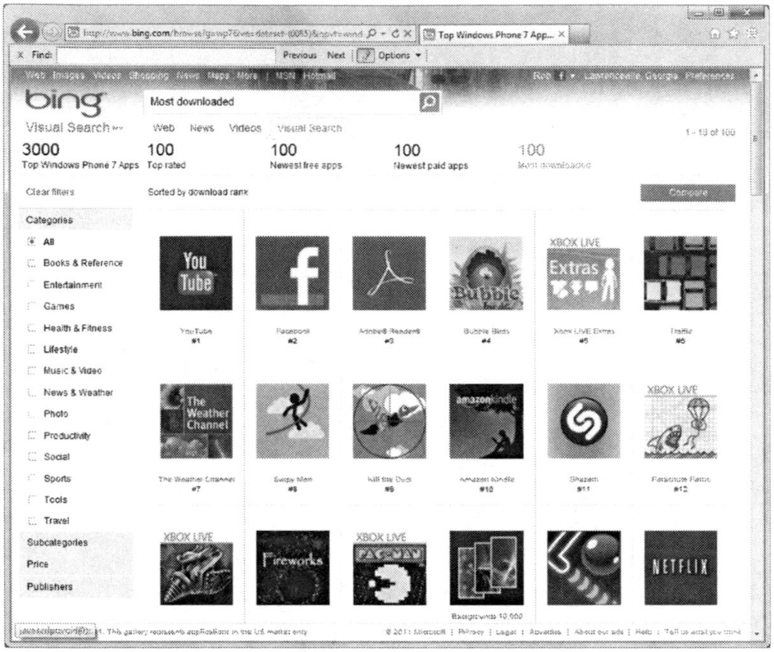

Figure 1–20. Windows Phone 7 Bing Maps visual search

You can filter the search by category on the left as well as filter using the headers across the top such as 100 Newest paid apps, and so on. Clicking on an application or game provides additional details on the application as well as a deep link for the Windows Phone 7 desktop marketplace, which is covered in the next section.

Windows Phone Marketplace on the PC

Windows Phone 7 does not connect to your PC via Microsoft's ActiveSync or Windows Mobile Device Center. If you happen to own a Microsoft Zune media player, then you are already familiar with the Windows Phone Marketplace on the PC, which is the Zune client software available at http://Zune.net. Figure 1–21 shows a game found using the built-in Search functionality.

Figure 1–21. *Windows Phone 7 Application in the Zune client*

The Zune client provides the full Microsoft Zune experience for Windows Phone 7, including ZunePass if you are a subscriber. In addition to the media content such as music, videos, TV, and movies, end-users can browse and select applications for download using the Zune client for their Windows Phone 7 device. If the device is tethered either via USB or connected over a wireless network, the application will download via PC. Otherwise, if the device is not connected to the PC the application will download the next time the user launches Marketplace on his or her device.

The Windows Phone Marketplace is the only mechanism available to install an application on Windows Phone 7. It is not possible to "side load" an application on to a Windows Phone 7 device outside of the Windows Phone Marketplace mechanisms unless registered in AppHub and using the Windows Phone Developer Registration tool.

▓ **Note** Applications greater than 20 MB must be installed via Zune client or over Wi-Fi.

An important function provided by the Zune client is that it allows a developer to deploy code to a connected device from Visual Studio 2010 or Expression Blend 4 for Windows Phone. I cover how to do that in the section titled "Limited Distribution of Applications" later in this chapter.

Marketplace on the Device

Marketplace on the device is a top-level hub experience that provides a one-stop shop location to find applications and games that are not managed XboxLIVE titles.

▓ **Note** Premium Xbox LIVE games can be found in Xbox LIVE Hub. We cover Windows Phone 7 game development in Chapter 7.

Figure 1–22 shows a mockup of the Marketplace panorama where you can see the featured app, which in this example is the eBay application. You also see categories, popular apps, what's new, and all of the featured applications. Selecting a featured app places its panoramic image as the background for the marketplace hub. In this example the eBay application is selected and its corresponding image is what is shown in the background. As a developer you can provide the panoramic art when you submit your application to Marketplace.

Figure 1–22. *Windows Phone 7 Marketplace hub*

When you select an application, the application details page is displayed. An example is shown in Figure 1–23.

Figure 1–23. Example Marketplace application details page

The application details view provides the following information to the consumer:

- Publisher and detailed product information
- Price and Try Before You Buy
- Application screenshots
- Access to user ratings and application reviews
- Size and available options for downloading (PC or Wi-Fi only for apps greater than 20 MB vs. Over-The-Air)
- List of related applications if any
- Optionally, game content ratings for games
- More apps by the developer publisher

This information allows consumers to make an informed decision on whether to download and purchase an application. Purchasing is enabled two-ways that are self-explanatory:

- Associate a credit card with their Windows Live ID
- Mobile Operator Billing for applications

Users can make a purchase with just two taps, Buy and then a Confirm Download dialog. Mobile Operator billing provides a great user experience to end-users as the application purchase simply shows up on their monthly bill. Microsoft has found that mobile operator billing increases the likelihood of a purchase transaction by 300%.

Once purchased and downloaded, the application is available in the application list or App List to the right of the Start screen. End-users can choose to pin your application to the bottom of the Start screen by clicking and holding the application icon in the app listing selecting "Add to Quick Launch." When you download a game, it will appear in the Xbox LIVE Hub.

▓ **Note** Applications cannot pin themselves automatically to the Start screen quick launch area. Only users can pin an application to the Start screen.

Supported Business Models

This is a very important and common question asked of Microsoft: what are the supported business models? Microsoft supports four business models in the Windows Phone Marketplace:

- Paid

- Try Before Buy

- Ad-Funded

- Free

A Paid business model is very straightforward. You set a price and get paid. Try Before Buy is the concept of end users trying a free version and then purchasing the full version of the application. To take advantage of Trial mode, it is a very simple API call add a using statement:

```
using Microsoft.Phone.Marketplace;
```

Instantiate a LicenseInformation object to gain access to the IsTrial() method call:

```
if (licenseInfo.IsTrial())
{
    ….//Only show level one
}
```

As the developer, you determine how the trial application functions relative to the fully paid application.

Ad-funded is where you plug your application into your own or a third-party advertising network. As users download and use your application, they view the advertisements as they go and you get paid for views, clicks-throughs, and the like, similar to on the Web. "Free" isn't really a business model per se, but it can be if the free application enables access to an existing subscription available via the web. As an example, if a newspaper or music services offers a paid Web-based subscription, they can extend that subscription to Windows Phone 7 for free to their existing subscribers enabling anytime access via the phone.

Search, Browse, and Discover Applications

The Windows Phone Marketplace provides several types of content that users can select from such as Applications, Games, Premium Xbox LIVE Games, music, and special applications from either the Mobile Operator or the OEM who manufactured the device that a user can download.

When a user selects a category such as Featured, the panorama jumps to a Pivot experience to let a user navigate through the different categories available to make it easy for the user to filter, search, and discover applications.

When in the Marketplace app on the phone, click the Search hardware button to search within Marketplace. You can also search within the Zune marketplace windows client.

Application and Game Updates

Within the on-device marketplace in the content area of the hub users can find a list available application updates. If consumer purchases and downloads your application and you as the publisher provide an updated version in marketplace, you can make the update available automatically to your end-user installed-base and it will be listed on the Marketplace hub as an application update.

As the developer you can provide details on the update to the end-user such as bug fixes, improved performance, additional game levels, and so on, so that your installed base understands what the update provides them.

Connecting with Your End Users

When a user purchases and installs your application, it appears in the App List or Xbox LIVE Hub. The end-user can choose to make your app a favorite and pin it to the Start screen. It initially appears at the bottom of the list but end users can move it up towards the top by tap and holding the tile, then dragging it to the desired location.

Stay Connected to Users via Live Tiles

Developers can enable Live Tiles in your application so that when your end-users pin the application to the Start screen, they can receive notifications and updates dynamically directly on the application for a richer, more connected, experience. These updates include changing the background image, a count value, and a title. The update is delivered via the Windows Phone 7 Push Notification Services, covered in Chapter 6.

Temp Users to Purchase with Try Before You Buy

The Windows Phone Developer tools and the Windows Phone application framework provides a trial API that allows developers to call IsTrial within the application to find out if the user has actually purchased the application or whether the application is still in trial mode. This API connects to marketplace under the covers to make this determination. This means that the trial version is the same application as the full version.

You as the publisher/developer get to determine what type of trial as well as how long the trial period lasts. For type of trial, you can determine if it is time based, based on levels, and so on. Trial applications are a powerful way to let users try the app and then convert them to paying customers.

Limiting Distribution of Applications

Once an application is published on Marketplace, it can be downloaded by any Windows Phone user. A common question is how to make an application available to a limited number of users. The next sections answers that.

Deploy an Application to Your Phone for Testing

Probably the most limited distribution for an application is deploying an application to your phone, whether a pre-production developer device or a retail phone purchased after launch. The process to developer unlock a device requires three steps:

1. Register at `http://create.msdn.com`.

2. Install the Zune Client and connect your device.

Launch the Windows Phone Developer Registration tool in the Windows Start screen.

I covered registration at create.msdn.com and the Zune client already. The last step is achieved by installing the Windows Phone Developer Tools download. Once installed, a Windows Start Menu folder titled Windows Phone Developer Tools is created. Navigate there to launch the Windows Phone Developer Registration tool shown in Figure 1–24 for a device that has already been registered.

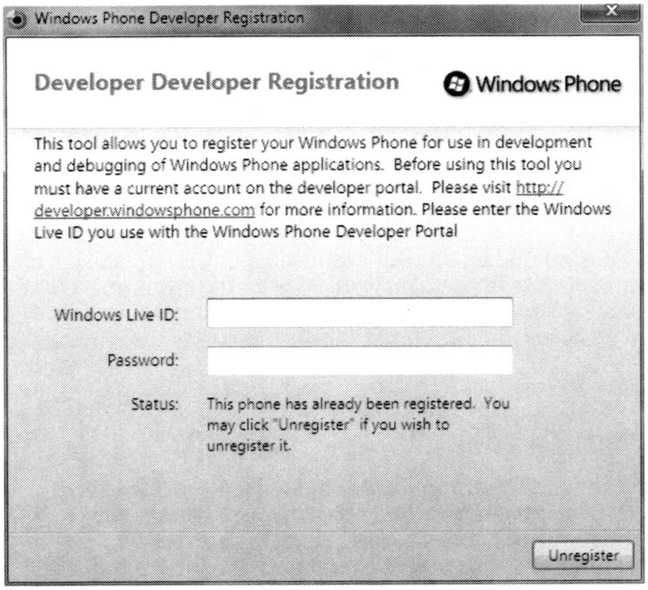

Figure 1–24. The Windows Phone Developer Registration tool

Ensure that the Zune client is open and your Windows Phone 7 device is connected before proceeding. Next enter your Windows Live ID and Password you used when you registered in marketplace at `http://create.msdn.com` and click Register. Upon success, you can now deploy code to your device.

Table 1–3 shows a list of possible error codes and related cause when deploying applications to a device either via Visual Studio or the Developer Registration tool.

Table 1–3. *Device Connectivity Error Codes*

Error Code	Explanation
0x8973180E	Zune software is not installed. Please install the latest version of Zune software.
0x8973180F	Incorrect version of the Zune software installed. Please download the latest version.
0x89731810	Corrupted device configuration. To correct this problem, reinstall Visual Studio 2010 Express for Windows Phone.
0x89731811	Zune software is not started. Please try again from the Zune to ensure that the software is running.
0x89731812	Connection to device failed. Please ensure the phone is connected and the not on the lock screen.
0x89731813	Application failed to start. Please ensure that the device has been registered and unlocked. Explanation on how to register can be found here: http://go.microsoft.com/fwlink/?LinkId=195284.
0x81030110	Failed to install the application. Runtime error has occurred. Capabilities WMAppManifest.xml file located in the attribute content is incorrect. (This link might help)
0x81030118	Installation of the application failed. Device is developer locked. Register for the developer unlock program before deploying the application.
0x81030119	You cannot install the application. You have reached the maximum number of applications being developed for the device can be installed on this development. Please uninstall a previous developer application.

Limit Availability to Beta Testers

Microsoft will offer the ability to conduct limited beta testing of applications prior to making their application available to all users in the Marketplace. As of this writing, the functionality is not yet available; however, Microsoft has stated that beta testing functionality is a priority for Marketplace functionality future updates.

Enterprise Applications in Marketplace

Initially at launch, the Windows Phone Marketplace does not provide a way for an enterprise to create and distribute a custom Line of Business (LOB) type application to only its employees. Microsoft has publically stated that they will enable this capability at some point in the future after Windows Phone launch.

With that said, an enterprise can choose to publish an application to Marketplace, but have the application require a password to enable functionality. Perhaps a retail store enterprise wants to create an application for its in-store employees. The retail store enterprise could create and submit the application to the Marketplace, making it available to download for anyone.

If a non-employee downloads the application, they would not have a username and password to log in. The application could be written in such a way to allow a non-employee to browse the retailer's catalog or even make in-store pickup purchases. While this scenario may not be an option for enterprise, it may be workable for many enterprises as an interim step.

Conclusion

In this chapter I provided an overview of Windows Phone 7, the platform. I introduced the application platform and the two major programming models: Silverlight and XNA Framework. I then dove deeper into XNA Framework programming model to balance out technology coverage as we dive into Silverlight development over the next several chapters. Finally, I covered the Marketplace so that you have a solid understanding of how to publish and monetize applications that you create. In the next chapter I will cover user interface development for Windows Phone 7 using Silverlight.

CHAPTER 2

■ ■ ■

Silverlight User Interface Development

Since all client applications require some sort of end-user experience, user interface development is the first topic I will dive into after the introduction provided in Chapter 1. Also, for client-application development, it is usually the first aspect of the application that developers start to experiment with in learning a new technology.

The user interface is usually the hallmark of a great application proposal or application prototype. It helps communicate what an application will look like, as well as what it will actually do. How an application looks and feels is just as important as what the application actually does. It is understandable, as users expect more from client-applications, especially non-Web-based client applications such as mobile applications.

First up is an overview of the Windows Phone 7 application design and design resources. The Windows Phone 7 product team is incredibly passionate about the user interface they created for Windows Phone 7. In an effort to help jumpstart great user experience (UX) design and development for Windows Phone 7 developers, the Windows Phone 7 design team created some great resources and guidance, which I cover in this chapter.

After covering design, the chapter dives into developing UX in Visual Studio 2010, with a quick background on the underlying architecture of the Silverlight programming model and the.NET Framework for Silverlight. This book is not an introductory one, but this section provides hopefully enough background to fill in the major blanks as well as help understand the important namespaces and classes if you are new to Silverlight development.

The markup language for Windows Phone UX is Xml Application Markup Language (XAML). XAML development started out in Visual Studio 2005 with a basic design surface for Windows Presentation Foundation. Expression Blend was created to provide a design tool to make it easier for designers to work in XAML, but in a visual way. Both Visual Studio 2010 and Expression Blend XAML tooling has improved greatly, with unique support for phone development with Silverlight. I cover the built-in controls and capabilities using Visual Studio 2010 as the backdrop.

After covering Visual Studio 2010, UX development with Expression Blend 4 is next. As a developer, you need to learn Expression Blend 4 – it is definitely not just a tool for designers, and you will find some tasks are much easier to do in Expression Blend, such as data binding and sample data. The section covers laying out controls in Blend, sample data, data binding, the Silverlight Toolkit for Windows Phone 7, and animations in Expression Blend as well.

Designing for Windows Phone 7

This section covers design-oriented content that a developer will find very useful. I phrase it that way because this book in general is not geared toward designers; however, just as end-users were no longer satisfied with character-based UI when graphical UI came into vogue, today's end-users expect even more from client-based mobile applications when compared to the rich UX available via the desktop. Developers are an integral part to the design/development cycle, which is why it is strongly encouraged that developers embrace design concepts as much as possible to help create better UX beyond designer mock-ups.

Design Approach

The design team at Microsoft refers to the "design language" of Windows Phone 7, codenamed "Metro," when describing the approach they took when designing the Windows Phone 7 UI. The Metro codename is inspired by the graphics found in transportation systems worldwide, which rely on big, bold, beautiful graphics and text to communicate to the "end-user" or traveler where they need to go. It is inspired by other sources as well, such as Zune, video games, product packaging, and the like, which focus on these key principles:

- **Light and simple:** Focus on primary tasks, achieving a lot with very little (little user effort and few phone resources, steps, and so on). Use whitespace to its full advantage.

- **Typography:** Focus on beautiful, not just legible, with sensitivity to font weight, balance, and scale to communicate a sense of hierarchy for the content.

- **Motion:** Responsive and alive UI. Transition between UI is just as important as the design of the UI. Create an animation system, not just transitions.

- **Content, not chrome:** Reduce visuals that are not content. Navigate via content itself.

- **Honest:** Design for the form factor, keeping things simple and direct. Be authentic. Content makes the UI beautiful.

Probably the most important design approach *not to take* is to simply port an iPhone or Android application to Windows Phone 7 without modifying the user interface to match the platform. The application will look odd and out of place if it does not at least use the default templates for the built-in controls and font styles for text. In the next section I cover the great design resources available to help you build an authentic Windows Phone 7 user interface, whether you are creating a new application or porting an existing one.

Design Resources

The Windows Phone 7 documentation includes several designer-oriented resources to help generate a beautiful user experience. If you are new to Windows Phone 7 design or development, you will want to review these resources.

Windows Phone Design System – Codename Metro

The Windows Phone Design System – Codename Metro is available here:

`http://go.microsoft.com/fwlink/?LinkID=189338`

This document describes what the product team calls its design language: seven areas of differentiation, and "red threads," or guiding principles. The user experience of Windows Phone 7 is partly inspired by the image of the simple and effective communication style provided by metropolitan public transportation system signage as shown in Figure 2–1.

Figure 2–1. Metropolitan signage as inspiration

The product team describes Metro as

"…our code name for our design language. We call it metro because it it's modern and clean. It's fast and in motion. It's about content and typography. And it's entirely authentic."

There are key points to take notice of in this description. "Modern and clean" means an application should provide just what is needed to get the task done, whether that task is to provide a movie, the news, or a weather forecast.

"Fast and in motion" means anything other than snappy performance is unsatisfactory. While this may seem obvious, the key here is that a user's perception is what's important. No doubt some tasks take time, so the key is to provide animation and indicators that help shape the user's perception that the application is responsive.

"Content and typography" means that the focus of the application is on the content, not application chrome. Navigate via the content with touch instead of a scroll bar is one example. Typography is incredibly important, so much so that the design team created a special font type for Windows Phone 7 called Segoe WP that looks great onscreen and is pleasing to the eye. Finally, "authentic" means that the application does not try to do more than what it is.

UI Design and Interaction Guide for Windows Phone 7

Here is a link to the UI Design and Interaction Guide for Windows Phone 7:

`http://go.microsoft.com/fwlink/?LinkID=183218`

It cannot be overstated: this document is a must-read for both designers and developers. It covers all of the user experience customizations, input methods, and controls to help developers and designers understand how to build a great looking Windows Phone 7 user interface.

Reviewing this document will help you combine Metro with your company's brand in the best way, resulting in an authentic user experience that is true to your brand and Windows Phone 7. Figure 2–2 is a page from the document with annotations.

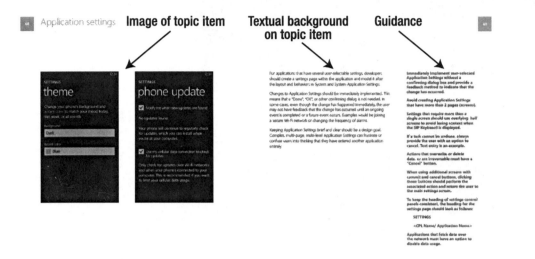

Figure 2–2. UI Design and Interaction Guide format

The UI Design and Interaction Guide for Windows Phone 7 v2.0.pdf document prints out in a large format and is best viewed on a large monitor. Each section provides a topic item, such as "Application settings" (as shown in Figure 2–2). It displays an image and textual context for the topic item, along with guidance for designers and developers with do's and don'ts. As far as I am concerned, this document is required reading for anyone who designs or develops a Silverlight-based Windows Phone 7 application.

Application Icons

Windows Phone 7 design resources includes a zip of icons to use directly in your application or as a model for custom application icons you build. The application icons come in .png and XAML vector format. The .png format comes in both a light and dark variant to support the light and dark themes in Windows Phone 7. Figure 2–3 shows the included icons, as well as other sample icons. The image is taken from the Windows Phone Design System – Codename Metro.pdf document.

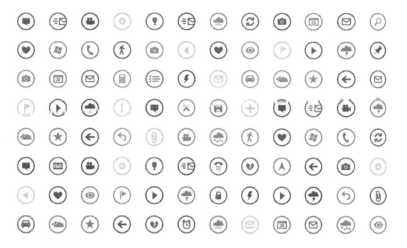

Figure 2–3. Collage of application icons for Windows Phone 7

The icons are included with the Windows Phone 7 design resources, as well as installed by the Windows Phone Developer Tools, at C:\Program Files (x86)\Microsoft SDKs\Windows Phone\v7.0\Icons on an x64 Windows machine. The icons come in black and white to match the built-in application themes available in Windows Phone 7.

The most common place to use the icons is for the Application bar if included in your application; however, they be incorporated into the main UI as well.

Design Templates for Windows Phone 7

The design templates for Windows Phone 7.zip file includes 28 Adobe Photoshop files that designers can use to create pixel-perfect UX. Share this download with your Windows Phone 7 designer friends and they will be forever grateful. It takes the guesswork out of how to size the design. It will also save rework for developers, as the templates will be ready to go when imported – more on this in the next section.

One little gem you will not want to ignore is the Design Templates for Windows Phone 7.pdf document that is included in the template download zip located here:

http://go.microsoft.com/fwlink/?LinkId=196225

This document details how to use the templates, which is especially important for controls that are not shipped as part of the Windows Phone Developer Tools. A great time to use this document is when you need to build UI, like a notification, where there isn't an existing control. The guidance is provided to help designers and developers match both visually and in interaction the built-in version of the control that appears in Windows Phone OS 7.0.

■ **Tip** Many additional controls are shipped in the Silverlight Toolkit for Windows Phone, which is available for download at CodePlex: http://silverilght.codeplex.com.

This section concludes the overview of the design resources for Windows Phone 7. Please do checkout these resources as it will save you rework later. The next section covers the mechanics of how designers and developers can work together to build a Silverlight for Windows Phone 7 user interface.

Designer and Developer Mechanics

As with most client application development, Windows Phone 7 applications begin as comprehensive artwork, or "comps" for short, that can start out as a rough sketch wireframe that is refined into a full user interface mock-up handed over to developers for development. Quite often the actual development results in a far less stunning UI when compared to original comps. This is a result of a mismatch of the output from the design process, usually a vector drawing flattened into an image format and the input of the development process, which is a development language.

Starting with Windows Presentation Foundation, XAML was introduced as a language to describe UX that is both user- and tool-consumable, meaning a developer can author XAML directly or tools vendors can build applications that allow a designer and developer to visually create UX that generates the appropriate XAML. Silverlight was introduced after XAML as a lightweight version of WPF that fits into a small (approximately 5 MB) cross-platform, cross-browser desktop plug-in. Initially Silverlight included a subset of the most commonly used features of WPF. Since its introduction, Silverlight has steadily added additional capabilities to match more closely the full capabilities available in WPF. Examples include more support for triggers, Commanding, and COM interop, making offline desktop Silverlight a capable alternative to WPF for many desktop application scenarios.

Silverlight for Windows Phone 7 is based on Silverlight 3 with some Silverlight 4 features pulled forward, putting XAML-based development front and center in mobile application development. Also, since Silverlight for Windows Phone 7 does not run in a browser, some features, like browser-interoperability available in Silverlight for the desktop, are removed from Silverlight for Windows Phone. Fundamentally, however, they share core capabilities.

The reason XAML is so important and useful is that the output of visual design tools can be directly consumed by developers, since the output of the visual design is human-readable XAML. Designers can use Expression Design to create rich visual designs for application control templates as well as general application UX. Expression Design supports exporting XAML.

While Expression Design is a great tool, the world of designers is dominated by the Adobe toolset. What may not be well-known by many designers is that Expression Blend 4 has excellent import capabilities to pull in the vector output from the Adobe toolset directly into Expression Blend as XAML. The Expression Blend 4 import capabilities are shown in Figure 2–4.

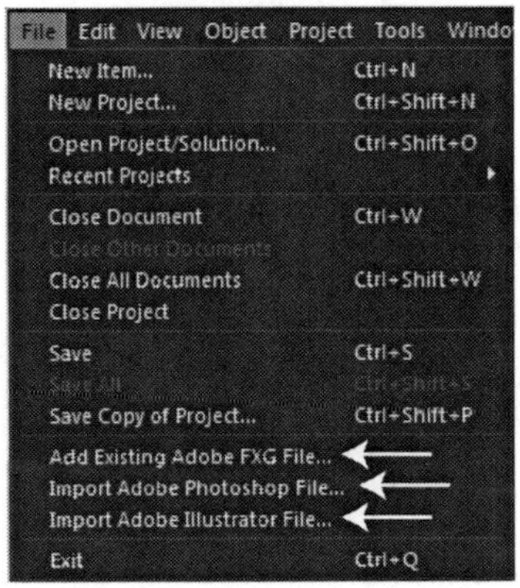

Figure 2–4. Expression Blend 4 file menu import capabilities

The menu offers import capabilities for three Adobe file formats: .fxg, .psd (Photoshop), and .ai (Illustrator). The .fxg file is the new file interchange format introduced in Adobe Creative Suite 5 that provides a common interchange format for the Adobe toolset. The format is very similar to .svg format. The other two file formats are the native format of Adobe's well known Photoshop and Illustrator tools. Figure 2–5 shows one of the Windows Phone 7 design templates opened in Photoshop.

Figure 2–5. *Windows Phone 7 design template in Photoshop*

Let's say the example in Figure 2–5 is part of a real application that you are building. In Expression Blend, you can import the background using the File ➤ Import Photoshop File … menu item and then selecting the desired layer as shown in Figure 2–6.

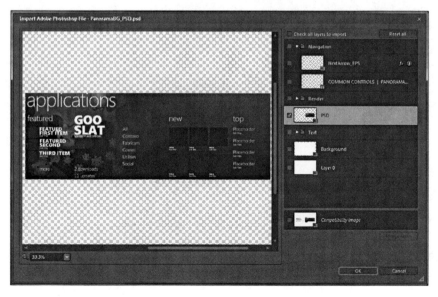

Figure 2–6. *Import a layer from a sample Photoshop file*

When you click OK in the dialog shown in Figure 2–6, a Canvas object is added to the currently opened XAML file and the image assets are brought into the project in a new folder named with the same name as the imported asset but with the suffix _images appended. At the bottom on the right of Figure 2–6 there's an option to generate a "Compatibility image" instead of attempting to import the vector components of the image as XAML. What this option does is take the selected layers and "flatten" it to a .png image. This is a handy option when you just need a flattened image instead of the layers, which in many cases has better performance than having to calculate vector-based layout.

This section provided an overview of how designers and developers can work in their preferred tools while allowing for the smoothest work stream possible with Expression Blend 4 as the bridge between a pure designer and developer.

The technical designer or developer who works in Expression Blend will also build out the interaction model for the user experience using the built-in animation capabilities, which I cover later in this chapter. Before I jump into Expression Blend 4, I next cover Visual Studio 2010 with an introduction to the .NET Framework for Silverlight and an overview of the available controls.

User Interface Development in Visual Studio 2010

I highlighted in the introduction to this chapter the much improved design surface available in Visual Studio 2010 as compared to Silverlight support in previous editions of Visual Studio. I also gave you a whirl-wind tour of the improved tooling, so I will not cover it in this section. Be sure to refer to Chapter 1 for a refresher if needed.

Visual Studio 2010 Windows Phone Developer Tools include several additional controls and project templates to help developers get started building their mobile application. Figure 2–7 shows the available templates.

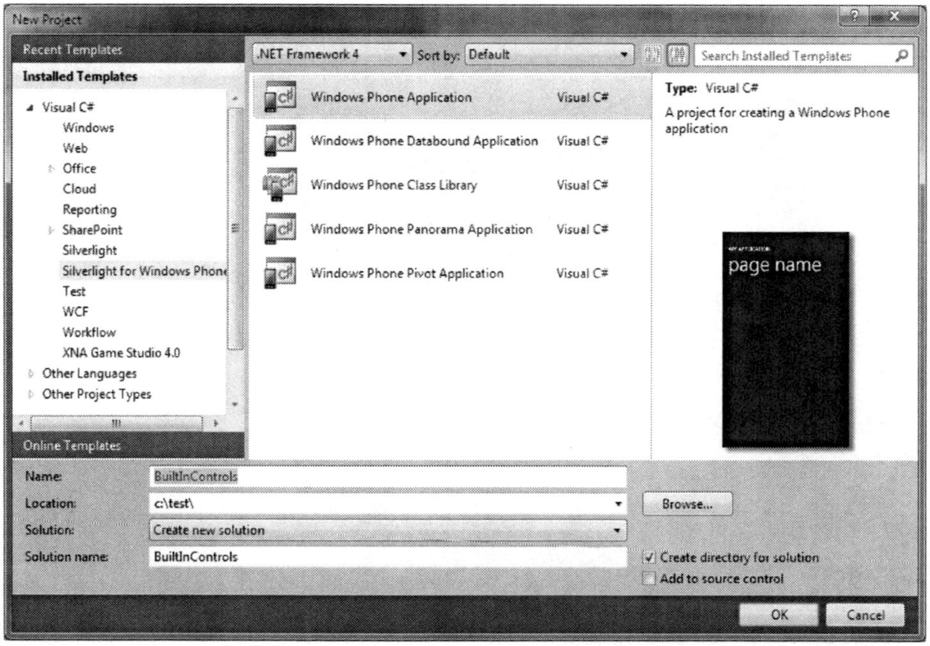

Figure 2–7. Visual Studio 2010 File ➤ New Project – Silverlight for Windows Phone dialog

The first three application templates existed in the beta tools. The last two templates, Windows Phone Panorama Application and Windows Phone Pivot Application, were added to the final release and hint to the fact that the shipped tools include Panorama and Pivot controls that match the built-in Windows Phone 7 application experience. I cover the Panorama and Pivot controls later on in this chapter, since they define unique application UI navigation architectures.

The first thing you will notice when reviewing a Silverlight for Windows Phone application is that the control templates follow the Windows Phone 7 theme style, defaulting to the dark theme. The other available theme is the light theme

---

■ **Note** The built-in controls will automatically adjust to application theme changes by the user; however, the developer may need to adjust the rest of the UI such as images, backgrounds, and so on, if the end-user changes the phone theme to light or vice versa.

We create the BuiltInControls project by selecting File ➤ New ➤ Project… and select the Windows Phone Application template. Figure 2–8 shows the Solution Explorer tool window for the BuiltInControls project.

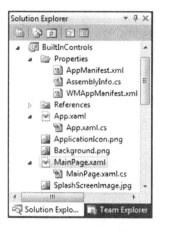

Figure 2–8. Initial project file layout in the Solution Explorer tool window

A typical Windows Phone 7 project consists of an App.xaml and App.xaml.cs file that represents the non-visual Application object that is the root of the project and application structure. MainPage.xaml with the MainPage.xaml.cs code-behind file is the default initial UI for the application. There are three graphic files associated with the project structure:

- **Background.png**: This is a 173 × 173-pixel image that represents the application's "tile" when pinned to the Start screen. The user has to pin your tile. Applications cannot pin themselves.

- **ApplicationIcon.png:** This is a 62 × 62–pixel image that is the icon in the application list when installed on a device.

- **SplashScreenImage.jpg:** This is a 480 × 800-pixel image displayed when an application first launches. Developers do not have to do anything to show the image or hide the image. The framework handles it.

■ **Tip** From the certification requirements applications must show UI within 5 seconds and be functional within 20 seconds after launch. The splash screen image is displayed until the UI is shown.

The next section covers the Windows Phone manifest file in more detail.

WMAppManifest.xml File

A file unique to the Windows phone 7 Visual Studio project templates is the WMAppManifest.xml file under the properties folder. Listing 2–1 shows the default WMAppManifest.xml file for the BuiltInControls project.

Listing 2–1. WMAppManifest.xml Configuration File

```xml
<?xml version="1.0" encoding="utf-8"?>
<Deployment xmlns="http://schemas.microsoft.com/windowsphone/2009/deployment"
 AppPlatformVersion="7.0">
  <App xmlns="" ProductID="{1ea898d1-33a3-4064-a3e2-ad6cc6a5a38a}" Title="BuiltInControls"
RuntimeType="Silverlight" Version="1.0.0.0" Genre="apps.normal"  Author="BuiltInControls
author" Description="Sample description" Publisher="BuiltInControls">
    <IconPath IsRelative="true" IsResource="false">ApplicationIcon.png</IconPath>
    <Capabilities>
      <Capability Name="ID_CAP_GAMERSERVICES"/>
      <Capability Name="ID_CAP_IDENTITY_DEVICE"/>
      <Capability Name="ID_CAP_IDENTITY_USER"/>
      <Capability Name="ID_CAP_LOCATION"/>
      <Capability Name="ID_CAP_MEDIALIB"/>
      <Capability Name="ID_CAP_MICROPHONE"/>
      <Capability Name="ID_CAP_NETWORKING"/>
      <Capability Name="ID_CAP_PHONEDIALER"/>
      <Capability Name="ID_CAP_PUSH_NOTIFICATION"/>
      <Capability Name="ID_CAP_SENSORS"/>
      <Capability Name="ID_CAP_WEBBROWSERCOMPONENT"/>
    </Capabilities>
    <Tasks>
      <DefaultTask  Name ="_default" NavigationPage="MainPage.xaml"/>
    </Tasks>
    <Tokens>
      <PrimaryToken TokenID="BuiltInControlsToken" TaskName="_default">
        <TemplateType5>
          <BackgroundImageURI IsRelative="true" IsResource="false">Background.png
</BackgroundImageURI>
          <Count>0</Count>
          <Title></Title>
        </TemplateType5>
```

```
        </PrimaryToken>
      </Tokens>
    </App>
</Deployment>
```

When you configure project settings by right-clicking the BuiltInControls project node in the Solution Explorer and select Properties, the values are updated in AssemblyInfo.cs just like for every other .NET Framework project, but it also updates values in WMAppManifest.xml. The WMAppManifest.xml is rewritten when you submit your application to marketplace based on capabilities detection and based on the metadata provided to marketplace when submitting the application.

You can carefully edit the WMAppManifest.xml during development to help identify certification requirements. As an example, if you do not believe your application needs location information, you can remove ID_CAP_LOCATION from the Capabilities XML element. When you run your application, you will discover errors indicating that your application needs that capability. Using location means that certain certification requirements need to be met such as asking for permission as well as having a setting to disable location. Capabilities are an important part of certification.

■ **Note** You can use the Capabilities Detection Tool available for download as of this writing in the January 2011 Tools update located here: www.microsoft.com/downloads/en/details.aspx?FamilyID=49B9D0C5-6597-4313-912A-F0CCA9C7D277.

Continuing to explore WMAppManifest.xml , the App element contains several key pieces of information. You should not change the ProductID once the application is published in Marketplace. If you change the ProductID when submitting an update, Marketplace will infer it to be a new product and not an update to an existing product. Existing users will never see the update in this case.

The Genre is configured based on user selection in the marketplace metadata. The default for Silverlight and XNA Framework is apps.normal. You can change it to Apps.Games to force the application to appear in the Games Hub on a device.

One item to be aware of is that if you rename MainPage.xaml, you should also update the DefaultTask element under the Tasks element to match the first UI Xaml page that should be displayed. If you do not, the application will fail to launch. For more information on the WMAppManifest.xml file, go to:

http://msdn.microsoft.com/en-us/library/ff769509(VS.92).aspx

Anatomy of a WP7 Application

As mentioned, App.xaml and App.xaml.cs are the code files for the application object that hosts the individual pages. Listings 2–2 and 2–3 contain a default App.xaml file and its code behind file.

Listing 2–2. App.xaml File

```
<Application
    x:Class="BuiltInControls.App"
    xmlns="http://schemas.microsoft.com/winfx/2006/xaml/presentation"
    xmlns:x="http://schemas.microsoft.com/winfx/2006/xaml"
    xmlns:phone="clr-namespace:Microsoft.Phone.Controls;assembly=Microsoft.Phone"
    xmlns:shell="clr-namespace:Microsoft.Phone.Shell;assembly=Microsoft.Phone">
```

```xml
<!--Application Resources-->
<Application.Resources>
</Application.Resources>

<Application.ApplicationLifetimeObjects>
    <!--Required object that handles lifetime events for the application-->
    <shell:PhoneApplicationService
        Launching="Application_Launching" Closing="Application_Closing"
        Activated="Application_Activated" Deactivated="Application_Deactivated"/>
</Application.ApplicationLifetimeObjects>
</Application>
```

Listing 2–3. App.xaml.cs Code File

```csharp
using System;
using System.Collections.Generic;
using System.Linq;
using System.Net;
using System.Windows;
using System.Windows.Controls;
using System.Windows.Documents;
using System.Windows.Input;
using System.Windows.Media;
using System.Windows.Media.Animation;
using System.Windows.Navigation;
using System.Windows.Shapes;
using Microsoft.Phone.Controls;
using Microsoft.Phone.Shell;

namespace BuiltInControls
{
  public partial class App : Application
  {
    /// <summary>
    /// Provides easy access to the root frame of the Phone Application.
    /// </summary>
    /// <returns>The root frame of the Phone Application.</returns>
    public PhoneApplicationFrame RootFrame { get; private set; }

    /// <summary>
    /// Constructor for the Application object.
    /// </summary>
    public App()
    {
      // Global handler for uncaught exceptions.
      UnhandledException += Application_UnhandledException;

      // Show graphics profiling information while debugging.
      if (System.Diagnostics.Debugger.IsAttached)
      {
        // Display the current frame rate counters.
        Application.Current.Host.Settings.EnableFrameRateCounter = true;
```

```
            // Show the areas of the app that are being redrawn in each frame.
            //Application.Current.Host.Settings.EnableRedrawRegions = true;

            // Enable non-production analysis visualization mode,
            // which shows areas of a page that are being GPU accelerated with a colored overlay.
            //Application.Current.Host.Settings.EnableCacheVisualization = true;
        }

        // Standard Silverlight initialization
        InitializeComponent();

        // Phone-specific initialization
        InitializePhoneApplication();
    }

    // Code to execute when the application is launching (eg, from Start)
    // This code will not execute when the application is reactivated
    private void Application_Launching(object sender, LaunchingEventArgs e)
    {
    }

    // Code to execute when the application is activated (brought to foreground)
    // This code will not execute when the application is first launched
    private void Application_Activated(object sender, ActivatedEventArgs e)
    {
    }

    // Code to execute when the application is deactivated (sent to background)
    // This code will not execute when the application is closing
    private void Application_Deactivated(object sender, DeactivatedEventArgs e)
    {
    }

    // Code to execute when the application is closing (eg, user hit Back)
    // This code will not execute when the application is deactivated
    private void Application_Closing(object sender, ClosingEventArgs e)
    {
    }

    // Code to execute if a navigation fails
    private void RootFrame_NavigationFailed(object sender, NavigationFailedEventArgs e)
    {
      if (System.Diagnostics.Debugger.IsAttached)
      {
        // A navigation has failed; break into the debugger
        System.Diagnostics.Debugger.Break();
      }
    }

    // Code to execute on Unhandled Exceptions
    private void Application_UnhandledException(object sender, ↲
ApplicationUnhandledExceptionEventArgs e)
    {
      if (System.Diagnostics.Debugger.IsAttached)
```

```
    {
      // An unhandled exception has occurred; break into the debugger
      System.Diagnostics.Debugger.Break();
    }
  }

  #region Phone application initialization

  // Avoid double-initialization
  private bool phoneApplicationInitialized = false;

  // Do not add any additional code to this method
  private void InitializePhoneApplication()
  {
    if (phoneApplicationInitialized)
      return;

    // Create the frame but don't set it as RootVisual yet; this allows the splash
    // screen to remain active until the application is ready to render.
    RootFrame = new PhoneApplicationFrame();
    RootFrame.Navigated += CompleteInitializePhoneApplication;

    // Handle navigation failures
    RootFrame.NavigationFailed += RootFrame_NavigationFailed;

    // Ensure we don't initialize again
    phoneApplicationInitialized = true;
  }

  // Do not add any additional code to this method
  private void CompleteInitializePhoneApplication(object sender, NavigationEventArgs e)
  {
    // Set the root visual to allow the application to render
    if (RootVisual != RootFrame)
      RootVisual = RootFrame;

    // Remove this handler since it is no longer needed
    RootFrame.Navigated -= CompleteInitializePhoneApplication;
  }

  #endregion
  }
}
```

Applications can locate application-wide resources such as data sources, styles, and templates in the Application.Resources element of App.xaml. The ApplicationLifetimeObjects element in App.xaml can contain references to classes that extend application services without having to subclass the Application class. The order of the services listed dictates the order that they are initialized and the order that lifetime event notifications are received. A class must implement the IApplicationService interface and optionally the IApplicationLifetimeAware interface in order to be an ApplicationLifetimeObject service.

The default extension that is configured in the ApplicationLifetimeObjects is the Microsoft.Phone.Shell.PhoneApplicationService extension that manages lifetime events such as Launching, Closing, Activated, and Deactivated for tombstoning, which I cover in Chapter 4. In the next section we create a Configuration Settings service that you can use to manage your application's configuration.

Configuration Settings Service

As part of user interface development, customizable settings are an important component to the user experience. In the sample source code is the ConfigSettingsDemo project that demonstrates how to create an application service for managing settings beyond the UI. The project contains an application lifetime service named ConfigurationSettingsService, which implements the IApplicationService interface. The project includes a Services folder containing the ConfigurationSettingsService.cs code file as shown in Listing 2–4.

Listing 2–4. ConfigurationSettingsService.cs Code File

```
using System;
using System.Collections.Generic;
using System.IO;
using System.Linq;
using System.Net;
using System.Windows;
using System.Xml.Linq;
using ConfigSettingsDemo;

namespace ConfigSettingsDemo.Services
{
  public class ConfigurationSettingsService : IApplicationService
  {
    private string _configSettingsPath = @"\Settings\";
    private string _configSettingsFileName = " ConfigurationSettings.xml";

    //Event to allow the Application object know it is safe to
    //access the settings
    public event EventHandler ConfigurationSettingsLoaded;

    #region IApplicationService Members
    void IApplicationService.StartService(ApplicationServiceContext context)
    {
      LoadConfigSettings();
    }

    private void LoadConfigSettings()
    {
      //TODO - Load ConfigSettings from isolated storage

      //Check to see if the event has any handler's attached
      //Fire event if that is the case
      if (ConfigurationSettingsLoaded != null)
        ConfigurationSettingsLoaded(this, EventArgs.Empty);
    }

    private void SaveConfigSettings()
    {
      //TODO - Save ConfigSettings to isolated storage
```

```
    }

    void IApplicationService.StopService()
    {
      SaveConfigSettings();
    }
    #endregion

    //Stores configuraiton settings in
    public Dictionary<string, string> ConfigSettings { get; set; }
  }
}
```

The sample doesn't implement the actual loading or saving of the data until I cover Isolated Storage later in Chapter 4; however, the service is fully wired up within the application. First we have to list the `ConfigurationSettingsService` in the App.xaml `Application.ApplicationLifetimeObjects` element. To do so, we have to make the class available in Xaml by adding an xml namespace:

```
xmlns:services="clr-namespace:ConfigSettingsDemo.Services"
```

The service can now be added to the `ApplicationLifetimeObjects` using the services namespace:

```
<services:ConfigurationSettingsService />
```

Adding that line of code completes the changes in App.xaml. In App.xaml.cs the `ConfigSettingsDemo.Services` is added via a using clause. The `App()` constructor is modified to get a reference to the `ConfigurationSettingsService` and to add an anonymous event handler that allows the configuration settings to load before launching the main user interface:

```
ConfigurationSettingsService service =
  App.Current.ApplicationLifetimeObjects[1]
  as ConfigurationSettingsService;

service.ConfigurationSettingsLoaded += new EventHandler((s, args) =>
{
  // Phone-specific initialization
  InitializePhoneApplication();
});
```

The splash screen will display until this event fires. As a test, modify `ConfigurationSettingsService.LoadConfigSettings()` and add this line of code:

```
 System.Threading.Thread.Sleep(10000);
```

The splash screen will display for about 10 seconds. This demonstrates the effect of the anonymous event handler in allowing the configuration settings to fully load.

This completes our overview of how to create a lifetime service. I will now shift gears to a quick discussion of the events present in App.xaml.cs. The App.xaml.cs code-behind file contains the events and methods associated with the Application object. There are several important methods and events available to applications that we cover in the next few sections.

The Default App() Constructor

Besides wiring up the Application_UnhandledException event, the default constructor enables the `Application.Current.Host.Settings.EnableFrameRateCounter` if the debugger is attached as shown in code Listing 2–3. The frame rate counter is much more valuable on the device than in the emulator and it is something to monitor throughout development as features are added. Figure 2–9 shows the counters:

Figure 2–9. Frame rate counters

Table 2–1 explains the counters identified by letters in Figure 2–9.

Table 2–1. Frame Rate Counters

Letter	Counter	Description
A	Render Thread FPS	This is the frame rate for the render thread where animations, etc., run. Applications should try to push as much render processing as possible to the render thread from the UI thread.
B	UI Thread FPS	This is the frame rate for the UI thread where application runs. Application code execution directly affects this frame rate.
C	Texture Memory Usage	Indicates the video memory used for storing application textures.
D	Surface Counter	A count of the number of surfaces that are passed to the graphics chip.
E	Intermediate Texture Count	The number of intermediate textures created for compositing.
F	Screen Fill Rate	A metric representing the number of complete phone screens being painted each frame.

Jeff Willcox, a senior software development engineer on the Silverlight phone and devices team at Microsoft, provides some target framerates for good performance on his blog: www.jeff.wilcox.name/2010/07/counters/, but here is a summary:

- **Render Thread FPS:** 60 fps is great performance. 30 fps or below will show a poor experience. Turns red below 30 fps.

- **UI Thread:** This is the busiest thread. Applications must try to take as much work as possible off of the UI thread by leveraging the Render Thread or a background thread. Turns red below 15 fps.

- **Screen Fill Rate:** Below 2.0 is ideal. Above 2.5 indicates overdraw.

The frame rate counters can be zero when there isn't an animation playing on the thread at the moment and then spike during an animation or transition. Applications can play a simple continually playing animation to always show a frame rate.

The best way to leverage the frame rate counters and the screen fill rate counter is to continuously monitor them when testing on an actual device. The best time to address frame rate issues is after making a change and it results in a drop in performance. Check out the Creating High Performing Silverlight Applications for Windows Phone Samples for more information on UX performance:

www.microsoft.com/downloads/en/details.aspx?displaylang=en&FamilyID=3a8636bf-185f-↵
449a-a0ce-83502b9ec0ec

Application UnhandledException Event

The Application_UnhandledException event is where you can log, report, and display an error message to a user when something unexpected happens in your application that causes an unhandled exception. Applications should customize this event to present a friendly message to the user. Many users welcome the ability to enter feedback regarding a failure so displaying a simple UI to collect information on what the user was doing at the time and recording to a local error log for review can help increase application quality.

In the Chapter 2 Solution's ConfigSettingsDemo project's App.xaml.cs, the Application_UnhandledException event handler is modified to show an error message to the user when an exception is encountered.

```
private void Application_UnhandledException(object sender,↵
 ApplicationUnhandledExceptionEventArgs e)
{
  MessageBox.Show(
    "Error!  We logged the error.  Click OK to turn on logging mode.",
    "Error Diagnostics", MessageBoxButton.OKCancel);
  //TODO - Add logging service
  //Log error to logging service here
  //Turn on logging mode for logging service if OK clicked by user
  //Use the Microsoft.Phone.Tasks.EmailComposeTask
  //to collect exception information and offer to the user
  //to send in the exeception info.
  //Set e.Handled to true if recoverable  e.Handled = true ;

  if (System.Diagnostics.Debugger.IsAttached)
  {
    // An unhandled exception has occurred; break into the debugger
    System.Diagnostics.Debugger.Break();
  }
}
```

You can intentionally cause an error to display the error message by clicking the DivideByZero button at the bottom of the main page. Run the application without the debugger connected by deploying the project and running the app manually in the emulator or on a device. You will notice that the error message displays and then the application exits.

The Application_UnhandledException event handler arguments include the familiar sender object and an instance of the ApplicationUnhandledExceptionEventArgs. The ApplicationUnhandledExceptionEventArgs class contains the following properties:

- **ExceptionObject property:** A reference to the original exception that was thrown.

- **Handled property:** Set to true to if the application can recover from the error.

In the previous code, uncomment the line e.Handled = true; and the application will continue to run after the error is thrown. This property gives the application a chance to recover without kicking the user completely out of the application, providing a much better experience.

The comments hint at creating a logging service and adding logging to the application with the implication that the user can choose to upload the logs. Such a logging service could implement IApplicationService, and therefore be available anywhere in the application via the Application. ApplicationLifetimeObjects collection along with the Configuration Service discussed above.

Consider that, in a consumer oriented application, you may not have a direct relationship to your customer, so you simply cannot ask them what they saw just before the crash. One option is to prompt the user if they would like to send more info. If the user agrees, display the Microsoft.Phone.Tasks.EmailComposeTask to send the Exception object's Message and StackTrace values to the support email alias. I cover the EmailComposeTask in Chapter 4.

Part of the overall user experience is to build applications that can recover as well as give the user an opportunity to provide additional information. Most users will be happy to do so if they like your application and want to help make it better.

Anatomy of a PhoneApplicationPage

I covered the Application object and related PhoneApplicationFrame object that hosts the application. You can get access to the PhoneApplicationFrame with code like this:

```
PhoneApplicationFrame frame = App.Current.RootVisual as PhoneApplicationFrame;
```

Once the root PhoneApplicationFrame loads, the first UI displayed after the splash screen is a PhoneApplicationPage identified as the default task in WMAppManifest.xml, named MainPage.xaml with its corresponding code-behind file named MainPage.xaml.cs. The code-behind partial class inherits from PhoneApplicationPage. MainPage.xaml is linked to the code-behind via the Class attribute on the root PhoneApplicationPage root element.

The root element includes several namespace declarations to bring in common namespaces, like the phone namespace alias that pulls in the Microsoft.Phone.Controls namespace. I cover options related to PhoneApplicationPage in the next sections.

Orientation

The root element of the page declaration includes two attributes related to page layout, SupportedOrientations and Orientation. SupportedOrientations has three options:

- Landscape

- Portrait

- PortraitOrLandscape

The Orientation attribute can be set to any of the SupportedOrientations permissible values. For the ConfigSettingsDemo project, SupportedOrientations is set to PortraitOrLandscape in order to test orientation changes. When SupportedOrientations is set to PortraitOrLandscape, the page automatically changes the display depending on how you hold the phone. We set SupportedOrientations to PortraitOrLandscape for the ConfigSettingsDemo project.

The page does not automatically change the layout of controls. So, if the page has more than 480 pixels of content when held in Portrait mode, the content will run off the screen when held in Landscape mode. An application has an opportunity to react to orientation changes by adjusting the layout content in the PhoneApplicationPage.OrientationChanged event. I cover how to handle orientation changes in detail in Chapter 5, but for this demo, I will use a simple switch statement to reposition the single UI element, the divideByZeroBtn Button object:

```
private void PhoneApplicationPage_OrientationChanged(object sender,↵
 OrientationChangedEventArgs e)
{
  switch (e.Orientation)
  {
    case PageOrientation.Landscape:
      divideByZeroBtn.Margin = new Thickness(12, 200, 235, 0);
      break;
    case PageOrientation.LandscapeLeft:
      divideByZeroBtn.Margin = new Thickness(12, 200, 235, 0);
      break;
    case PageOrientation.LandscapeRight:
      divideByZeroBtn.Margin = new Thickness(12, 200, 235, 0);
      break;
    //default is Portrait
    default:
      divideByZeroBtn.Margin = new Thickness(12, 400, 235, 0);
      break;
  }
}
```

SystemTray

The system tray is the bar across the top of the screen in Portrait mode that displays the connection signal strength, Wi-Fi, and current time. According to the *UI Design and Interaction Guide for Windows Phone 7*, the system tray or status bar is 32 pixels high in Portrait mode and 72 pixels width in Landscape mode. Developers can set it to not display by editing the XAML for the page to this value:

```
shell:SystemTray.IsVisible="False"
```

It is not recommended to hide the SystemTray, as users consider it to be valuable information. Letting the SystemTray display is helpful to the user who wants to see the current time without having to exit the application. Probably the most common reason to hide the system tray is for a XNA Game Studio game.

Application Bar

The Application Bar is located at bottom of the screen to provide menu icon buttons for actions and views related to the content presented on the page. You can put up to four icon buttons at any time. If you have additional actions, you can place them into the Application Bar Menu instead. The Application Bar Menu item text will run off the screen. The recommendation is between 14 and 20 characters.

By default, XAML for the Application Bar is available in a new page but commented it out. The default XAML is un-commented for the ConfigSettingsDemo project. Two of the Application Bar IconButton images that are installed by default in the C:\Program Files (x86)\Microsoft SDKs\Windows Phone\v7.0\Icons folder are dropped into an Images folder for the project and set as the icon for two of the objects. Figure 2–10 shows the Application Bar after swiping up on the Application Bar to display the Application Bar menu items.

Figure 2–10. *Expanded Application Bar*

If you click the back button when the Application Bar is expanded, the Application Bar will close down. The application bar height is 72 pixels both in portrait and landscape mode and cannot be changed. The Application Bar can be displayed and hidden.

Developers should resist the temptation to use the Application Bar for navigation. Developers should not put a Home button into the Application Bar either, because it breaks the back stack. Users should navigate your application via the content and the hardware Back button.

Page Navigation

Most Windows Phone 7 applications will consist of more than one page. Silverlight for Windows Phone leverages the built-in navigation framework available as part of Silverlight. Pages navigation occurs within the hosting Application PhoneApplicationFrame object via the Page.NavigationService instance of the System.Windows.Navigation.NavigationService object.

In addition to the NavigationService, the page has two methods to override called OnNavigatedTo() and OnNavigatedFrom(). I cover these options in the next two sections.

NavigationService

The NavigationService has several properties and methods to aid in application navigation listed in Table 2–2.

Table 2–2. NavigationService Key Properties and Methods

Member	Description
CanGoBack	Indicates whether there is an entry in the back stack to navigate to backward in the stack.
CanGoForward	Indicates whether there is an entry in the forward navigation history to navigate to forward to in the navigation history.
GoBack	Navigate to the most recent page in the back stack. Throws an exception if there isn't an entry to navigate back to in the back stack.
GoForward	Navigate to the most recent page in the forward navigation history. Throws an exception if there isn't an entry to navigate forward to in the navigation history.
Navigate Method	Navigates to the page specified by the passed in `Uri` object. This `Uri` must be of type `UriKind.Relative`.
Navigated Event	Event fires when content that is being navigated to has been located and is available.
Navigating Event	Event fires when a new navigation is requested.
NavigationFailed Event	Event fires when a navigation request encounters an error.
NavigationStopped Event	Event fires when a navigation requested when an existing navigation event is in progress. It also occurs if the StopLoading method is called.
StopLoading Method	Stops asynchronous navigations that have not yet been processed.

The NavigationService provides full control over application flow but the most common member called is the Navigate method. In this chapter's solution `PageNavigation` project, MainPage contains a TextBlock that when clicked navigates to Page2.xaml:

```
private void NavToPage2_MouseLeftButtonDown(object sender, MouseButtonEventArgs e)
{
  this.NavigationService.Navigate(new Uri("/Page2.xaml", UriKind.Relative));
}
```

When the project is run and the `TextBlock` with the Text "Navigate to Page 2" is clicked, the event fires and `Page2.xaml` is displayed. Developers can pass parameters to the navigation target using standard Query string parameters with the question mark and paramname=paramdata notation like this:

```
this.NavigationService.Navigate(
  new Uri(String.Format("/Page2.xaml?page2data={0}",textBox1.Text), UriKind.Relative));
```

Pass multiple parameters like this: Page2.xaml?ParamName1=ParamData1&ParamName2=ParamData2 and so on with an ampersand between parameter values. Generally parameters consist of keys or object IDs such that the page can look up the full object or object collection of data for rendering.

In Table 2–3, the events like Navigating and Navigated provide opportunities to display progress to the user as navigation events fire. To test this, add the below line of code to the constructor for Page2.xaml:

```
System.Threading.Thread.Sleep(5000);
```

The effect is that when the TextBlock is clicked, the UI appears frozen for about five seconds before the navigation occurs. To provide feedback to the user, a ProgressBar is added to the UI and IsIndeterminate is set to False and Visibility to Collapsed.

▓ **Note** IsIndeterminate should be set to false anytime the ProgressBar is not needed in order to conserve CPU resources. The Silverlight for Windows Phone toolkit includes a performance optimized PerformanceProgressBar control as well.

Navigation.Navigating and Navigation.Navigated are wired up to an event handler in the PhoneApplicationPage_Loaded event in MainPage.xaml.cs in the PageNavigation project. The Navigating event handler enables and makes visible the ProgressBar. The Navigated event handler hides the ProgressBar and sets IsIndeterminate to false. Here is the code from the PageNavigation project's MainPage.xaml.cs code file:

```
private void PhoneApplicationPage_Loaded(object sender, RoutedEventArgs e)
{
  NavigationService.Navigating += new navigation.NavigatingCancelEventHandler
(NavigationService_Navigating);
  NavigationService.Navigated += new navigation.NavigatedEventHandler
(NavigationService_Navigated);
}

void NavigationService_Navigating(object sender, navigation.NavigatingCancelEventArgs e)
{
  progressBar1.Visibility = Visibility.Visible;
  progressBar1.IsIndeterminate = true;
}

void NavigationService_Navigated(object sender, navigation.NavigationEventArgs e)
{
  progressBar1.Visibility = Visibility.Collapsed;
  progressBar1.IsIndeterminate = false;
}
```

The performance of the ProgressBar is choppy because, by default, it runs on the UI thread, which is put to sleep in the Page2 constructor. I cover the PerformanceProgressBar in Chapter 5 when I go over the Silverlight for Windows Phone toolkit.

■ **Tip** In Silverlight there are two threads that draw to the screen, the UI thread and the Render thread. Storyboard animations run on the Render thread. User code runs on the UI thread. Any animations that run on the UI thread can become choppy if the UI thread is very busy doing application work. Developers should strive to offload as much work as possible from the UI thread and keep an eye on the Render thread and UI thread frame rate counters to see how code changes affect render performance.

This sample so far shows how to use the NavigationService to navigate to a page, as well as hook into navigation related events. The next section covers the PhoneApplicationPage overrides available that allow additional hooks into the navigation system.

OnNavigated Overrides

There are two PhoneApplicationPage method overrides available to further plug into the navigation system:

- **OnNavigatedFrom:** Event fires when navigating from the current page.

- **OnNavigatedTo:** Event fires when navigating to the current page.

Both methods take a NavigationEventArgs object. This object includes two properties:

- **Uri:** Uri of the target for navigation.

- **Content:** The content of the target being navigated to.

The OnNavigatedFrom override is the method where you can take any final actions when the page has become inactive. The OnNavigatedTo override is called when the page becomes active in the navigation frame. Developers can access query parameters on OnNavigatedTo with code similar to the following from MainPage.xaml.cs in the PageNavigation project:

```
protected override void OnNavigatedTo(System.Windows.Navigation.NavigationEventArgs e)
{
  if (NavigationContext.QueryString.ContainsKey("page2data"))
    dataFromMainPageTextBlock.Text = NavigationContext.QueryString["page2data"];

  base.OnNavigatedTo(e);
}
```

In this code, we first check to make sure that the parameter is present and then retrieve the value. Otherwise, if you attempt to retrieve data for a non-existing key, it results in an error. We will explore navigation further in Chapters 5 and 6, but many of the examples leverage navigation so this section provides an overview. This completes the discussion on the navigating events.

Up to now, this chapter focused on overall design and then dove into project organization covering the Application object, PhoneApplicationFrame, PhoneApplicationPage, and an overview of the navigation framework. In the next section I step back a bit and provide an overview of the .NET Framework for Silverlight and programming XAML, to help prepare for more advanced topics such as data binding, control templates, and control customization.

.NET Framework for Silverlight

As I mentioned earlier, Silverlight for Windows Phone 7 is based on Silverlight 3 with some key features pulled forward from Silverlight 4, such as the WebBrowser control and offline DRM for Silverlight Smooth Streaming Support, which means you can play DRM'd content when in airplane mode. I cover DRM and SmoothStreaming in more detail in Chapter 6.

Since this chapter is focused on building application user experience in Silverlight, it provides a deeper look at the .NET Framework for Silverlight. Here is a summary of the major .NET Framework namespaces available in Silverlight for Windows Phone 7:

- System
- System.Collections
- System.Collections.Generic
- System.Diagnostics
- System.Globalization
- System.IO
- System.Linq
- System.Media
- System.NET
- System.Reflection

- System.Runtime
- System.Security
- System.ServiceModel
- System.Text
- System.Threading
- System.Windows
- System.Windows.Controls
- System.Windows.Input
- System.Windows.Shapes
- System.XML

If you are at all familiar with Silverlight and the .NET Framework in general, you can see that much of your existing skills will translate right over. If you are new to Silverlight, this book strives to help you get up to speed. However, consider reviewing an Introduction or Silverlight reference book for additional background information.

■ **Tip** Check out *Silverlight Recipes: A Problem-Solution Approach*, Second Edition, co-authored by Jit Ghosh and me (Apress, 2010) for more on general Silverlight development.

For Windows Phone 7, Microsoft adds additional assemblies and namespaces related to phone specific functionality that I cover in this chapter and throughout this book:

- Microsoft.Devices
- Microsoft.Phone
- Microsoft.Phone.Controls
- Microsoft.Phone.Shell

These assemblies and namespaces identify a rich set of APIs available to developers in order to build powerful Silverlight for Windows Phone 7 mobile applications.

Next let's take a deeper look at Xml Application Markup Language (XAML) and how it relates to the .NET Framework for Silverlight.

XAML Overview

The .NET Framework 3.0 introduced XAML for Windows Presentation Foundation (WPF) and Windows Workflow Foundation (WF). WPF is of more interest to us since it is a desktop-based client development technology and has a lot in common with Silverlight. WPF was updated in .NET Framework 3.5, and available today in its latest incarnation in the .NET Framework 4.0.

Introduced in 2007, Silverlight is another client application technology that uses XAML to express UI. Recall from Chapter 1 that Silverlight is Microsoft's cross-browser, cross-platform browser plug-in that has rapidly evolved to have near parity with WPF in the latest version Silverlight 4.

With this rich heritage, there are a lot of great references available on Silverlight development, but it is important to provide fundamentals on the XAML language itself. As XAML is based on XML, it is hierarchical in nature, which lends itself to tooling because it is simple XML manipulation under the covers. Expression Blend 4 takes advantage of this by providing a GUI interface to XAML development that you will want to take advantage of when building animation storyboards and data binding.

Since this section is focused on XAML as a markup language, I explore the capabilities of XAML using Visual Studio 2010. We could just as easily explore XAML capabilities in Expression Blend 4. Expression Blend 4 includes syntax highlighting and IntelliSense as shown in Figure 2–11.

```
MainPage.xaml* ×
  1  <phone:PhoneApplicationPage
  2      x:Class="XAMLBasics.MainPage"
  3      xmlns="http://schemas.microsoft.com/winfx/2006/xaml/presentation"
  4      xmlns:x="http://schemas.microsoft.com/winfx/2006/xaml"
  5      xmlns:phone="clr-namespace:Microsoft.Phone.Controls;assembly=Microsoft.Phone"
  6      xmlns:shell="clr-namespace:Microsoft.Phone.Shell;assembly=Microsoft.Phone"
  7      xmlns:d="http://schemas.microsoft.com/expression/blend/2008"
  8      xmlns:mc="http://schemas.openxmlformats.org/markup-compatibility/2006"
  9      mc:Ignorable="d" d:DesignWidth="480" d:DesignHeight="768"
 10      FontFamily="{StaticResource PhoneFontFamilyNormal}"
 11      FontSize="{StaticResource PhoneFontSizeNormal}"
 12      Foreground="{StaticResource PhoneForegroundBrush}"
 13      SupportedOrientations="Portrait" Orientation="Portrait"
 14      shell:SystemTray.IsVisible="True" >
 15
 16      <!--LayoutRoot is the root grid where all page content is placed-->
 17      <Grid x:Name="LayoutRoot" Background="Transparent" >
 18          <Grid.RowDefinitions>
 19              <RowDefinition Height="Auto"/>            {} AutomationProperties          AutomationProperties
 20              <RowDefinition Height="*"/>                Background
 21          </Grid.RowDefinitions>                         CacheMode          Background
 22                                                        {} Canvas
 23          <!--TitlePanel contains the name of the applicat  Children
 24          <StackPanel x:Name="TitlePanel" Grid.Row="0" Mar  Clip
 25              <TextBlock x:Name="ApplicationTitle" Text="M
 26              <TextBlock x:Name="PageTitle" Text="page nam
 27          </StackPanel>
 28
 29          <!--ContentPanel - place additional content here-->
 30          <Grid x:Name="ContentPanel" Grid.Row="1" Margin="12,0,12,0"></Grid>
 31      </Grid>
 32
 33      <!--Sample code showing usage of ApplicationBar-->
 34      <!--<phone:PhoneApplicationPage.ApplicationBar>
 35          <shell:ApplicationBar IsVisible="True" IsMenuEnabled="True">
```

Figure 2–11. Expression Blend 4 syntax highlighting and IntelliSense

We will be looking at some C# code as well, so Visual Studio serves our purposes better in this section. But unlike with previous versions of Expression Blend, you don't have to leave Blend in order to hand-edit XAML with syntax Highlighting and IntelliSense support.

Importing a .NET Class into XAML

As you can see in Figure 2-11, the XAML markup for the XAMLBasics project includes several namespace imports using xmlns, including the xmlns:phone import that is used to declare the root element phone:PhoneApplicationPage. What may not be completely obvious at first glance is that PhoneApplicationPage is a class in the Microsoft.Phone.Controls namespace, contained in the Microsoft.Phone.dll assembly reference. Here is the xmlns import for the phone namespace:

```
xmlns:phone="clr-namespace:Microsoft.Phone.Controls;assembly=Microsoft.Phone"
```

In the xmlns import above, you see the .NET namespace, Microsoft.Phone.Controls, and the assembly name, Microsoft.Phone. This corresponds to a using clause in .NET code:

```
using Microsoft.Phone.Controls
```

The point is that markup written in XAML corresponds to objects in C# code. For example, you can create a button in C# using the code Button btn = new Button(). In XAML, you create a button with this markup: <Button />. You can essentially consider XAML as a human editable serialization format for .NET Framework for Silverlight.

With this background in hand, you can deduce that making custom C# classes available within XAML is as simple as creating a xmlns namespace import, which is correct. One consideration is that for a .NET classes to be brought in to a XAML markup page, it must have a parameter-less constructor so that you can simply declare it as <foo /> in XAML without needing parameters in the constructor, which is not supported.

Programming XAML

With the appropriate namespaces in place, creating a user experience in XAML is simple XML editing with XML Elements and Attributes. Elements generally represent a class or object such as a Button declared as <Button />. To set properties on the Button, you can add XML Attributes such as Height and Width: <Button Height="40" Width="100" />.

Some properties are of type System.Object or some other complex type, which could be difficult to set via an attribute depending on the value. The Button's Content property is of type System.Object, which means that it can point to pretty much anything. For a Button's Content property, it can be set as an attribute like so:

```
<Button Height="40" Width="100" Content="Hello Reader" />
```

For a not so simple type, The Button.Content property can be set using XML property element syntax:

```
<Button>
    <Button.Content>
        <MediaElement />
    </Button.Content>
</Button>
```

Remember that the Button.Content property is of type System.Object, so you could actually play a video as the "content" of a Button object via a MediaElement. With property element syntax, more complex objects such as a MediaElement playing a video named video1.wmv can be set as the value for the Content:

```
<Button>
    <Button.Content>
        <MediaElement Source="video1.wmv" />
    </Button.Content>
</Button>
```

Other properties can be set to an enumerated type such as a System.Windows.Media.Color value configured on a Brush type such as a SolidColorBrush object. In the example below, how does XAML know what do to with the text value "Blue" in this example?

```
<Button Background="Blue" />
```

Intuitively, the developer understands what this means, however, there is a little bit of magic to support this simplified syntax. In the XAML above, the text "Blue" is converted to a System.Windows.Media.Color value via a built in System.ComponentModel.TypeConverter for the Brush type. Without the type converter, the full property element syntax is required:

```
<Button>
  <Button.Background>
    <SolidColorBrush Color = "Blue" />
  </Button.Background>
</Button>
```

TypeConverter objects are intrinsic to straightforward XAML programming. Developers can create their own custom TypeConverter objects to simplify data binding between two XAML objects with two different types allowing the developer to avoid cluttering event handlers in the code-behind file for a XAML page.

The last XAML concept I will cover in this overview is markup extensions. Markup extensions are similar to type converters in that they allow for more straightforward XAML development. Markup extensions allow a string value to be converted into a configured object, which can greatly reduce the amount of XAML that must either be hand-written or generated by a tool.

In order to identify and parse a markup extension, since it is configured as attribute property text, a special syntax is required that uses curly braces: attribute="{ extension goes here}". The curly braces tell the XAML parser that a markup extension is inbound for parsing.

The two most common markup extensions are used for specifying a resource for an object property or attribute value and for configuring data binding for an object property or attribute value. Listing 2–5 shows the MainPage.xaml file for the XAMLBasics project where you can see Style attributes configured using the markup extension syntax:.

```
<TextBlock x:Name="ApplicationTitle" Text="MY APPLICATION"
    Style="{StaticResource PhoneTextNormalStyle}"/>
```

Listing 2–5. XamlBasics MainPage.xaml File

```
<phone:PhoneApplicationPage
    x:Class="XAMLBasics.MainPage"
    xmlns="http://schemas.microsoft.com/winfx/2006/xaml/presentation"
    xmlns:x="http://schemas.microsoft.com/winfx/2006/xaml"
    xmlns:phone="clr-namespace:Microsoft.Phone.Controls;assembly=Microsoft.Phone"
    xmlns:shell="clr-namespace:Microsoft.Phone.Shell;assembly=Microsoft.Phone"
    xmlns:d="http://schemas.microsoft.com/expression/blend/2008"
    xmlns:mc="http://schemas.openxmlformats.org/markup-compatibility/2006"
    mc:Ignorable="d" d:DesignWidth="480" d:DesignHeight="768"
```

```
     FontFamily="{StaticResource PhoneFontFamilyNormal}"
     FontSize="{StaticResource PhoneFontSizeNormal}"
     Foreground="{StaticResource PhoneForegroundBrush}"
     SupportedOrientations="Portrait" Orientation="Portrait"
     shell:SystemTray.IsVisible="True">
   <phone:PhoneApplicationPage.Resources>
     <Style x:Key="TestTextBlockStyle" TargetType="TextBlock">
       <Setter Property="Foreground" Value="#FFD49696"/>
       <Setter Property="FontSize" Value="16"/>
     </Style>
   </phone:PhoneApplicationPage.Resources>

   <!--LayoutRoot is the root grid where all page content is placed-->
   <Grid x:Name="LayoutRoot" Background="Transparent">
     <Grid.RowDefinitions>
       <RowDefinition Height="Auto"/>
       <RowDefinition Height="*"/>
     </Grid.RowDefinitions>

     <!--TitlePanel contains the name of the application and page title-->
     <StackPanel x:Name="TitlePanel" Grid.Row="0" Margin="12,17,0,28">
       <TextBlock x:Name="ApplicationTitle" Text="MY APPLICATION"
                        Style="{StaticResource PhoneTextNormalStyle}"/>
       <TextBlock x:Name="PageTitle" Text="page name" Margin="9,-7,0,0"
                        Style="{StaticResource PhoneTextTitle1Style}"/>
     </StackPanel>


     <!--ContentPanel - place additional content here-->
     <Grid x:Name="ContentPanel" Grid.Row="1" Margin="12,0,12,0" >
       <TextBox Height="72" HorizontalAlignment="Left" Margin="12,66,0,0"
        Name="textBoxOriginal" Text="Original" VerticalAlignment="Top"
        Width="374" />
       <TextBlock Height="30" Margin="35,185,0,0" Name="textBlock1"
        Text="{Binding Text, ElementName=textBoxOriginal}"
        VerticalAlignment="Top" Width="374"
        Style="{StaticResource TestTextBlockStyle}" />
       <TextBox Height="72" HorizontalAlignment="Left" Margin="12,280,0,0"
         Text="{Binding Text, ElementName=textBoxOriginal, Mode=TwoWay}"
         VerticalAlignment="Top" Width="374" Name="textBox2" />
     </Grid>
   </Grid>
</phone:PhoneApplicationPage>

<Button Style="{StaticResource CustomButtonStyle}" />
```

The next question is where is CustomButtonStyle defined? It can be defined either in App.xaml or the current XAML page in the Resources collection like this:

```
<phone:PhoneApplicationPage.Resources>
    <Style x:Key="CustomButtonResource" TargetType="Button" >
        <Setter Property="Margin" Value="20,20,0,0" />
    </Style>
</phone:PhoneApplicationPage.Resources>
```

Figure 2–12 shows the UI in the emulator for the XamlBasics project.

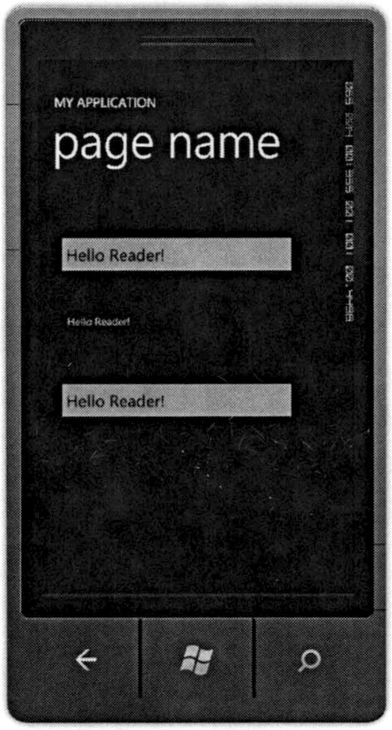

Figure 2–12. *XAML Basics UI*

The UI is pretty simple, but it helps me explain the concept of markup extensions for resources and data binding. The TextBlock has a style resource applied to it via a markup extension that makes the text very small and a reddish color. Here is the style resource wrapped in the PhoneApplicationPage.Resources element from Listing 2–1:

```
<phone:PhoneApplicationPage.Resources>
  <Style x:Key="TestTextBlockStyle" TargetType="TextBlock">
    <Setter Property="Foreground" Value="#FFD49696"/>
    <Setter Property="FontSize" Value="16"/>
  </Style>
</phone:PhoneApplicationPage.Resources>
```

The style is named TestTextBlockStyle via the x:Key attribute. The style is applied to the TextBock via the StaticResource markup extension as shown here:

```
<TextBlock Height="30" Margin="32,187,50,0" Name="textBlock1" ….
Style="{StaticResource TestTextBlockStyle}" />
```

This syntax applies to all types of resources, not just element styles. It allows for consistent UX by sharing resources across an application. Resources can be stored at the Page level or the Application level in App.xaml. Resources can also be stored in external files in Resource Dictionaries. I explore the StaticResource markup extension further when I cover Expression Blend later in this chapter, but for now this section provides solid background to help you understand how to program in XAML with resources.

Let's now move on to an overview of the data binding markup extension with Element Data binding. Element data binding allows one control's property to data bind to another control's property value. The stylized TextBlock and the TextBox below it in Figure 2–1 databind to the first TextBox via element data binding. Run the project and enter text in the first TextBox, notice the other two change values as you type.

■ **Tip** If you would like to use your keyboard when typing in the emulator, click the "pause" button on your physical keyboard. This allows the emulator OS to capture the physical keyboard and can save a lot of time typing. Exit the element and click "pause" again to switch back to the soft key keyboard within the emulator.

Element Data binding is a powerful concept, but at its simplest level it saves the developer from writing simple event handlers that do nothing but copy values from one control to another. How this works is that when you type in the first TextBox on the screen shown in Figure 2–12, the reddish text TextBlock and the TextBox below it get the same value automatically via Element Data binding. Here is the XAML for the TextBlock that uses the Binding markup extension to element databind:

```
<TextBlock Height="30" Margin="32,187,50,0" Name="textBlock1"
  Text="{Binding Text, ElementName=textBoxOriginal}"
  VerticalAlignment="Top" Width="374"
  Style="{StaticResource TestTextBlockStyle}" />
```

The Binding markup extension first identifies the target property that the property is binding to, in this case TextBlock.Text is binding to TextBox.Text. The ElementName attribute value within the Binding markup extension specifies textBoxOriginal.Text as the target control/property that textBlock1.Text is databound to by default as one-way or read-only data binding.

The third control on the page in Figure 2–12, the TextBox, also databinds to the first TextBox as shown here:

```
<TextBox Height="72" HorizontalAlignment="Left" Margin="12,280,0,0"
  Text="{Binding Text, ElementName=textBoxOriginal, Mode=TwoWay}"
  VerticalAlignment="Top" Width="374" Name="textBox2" />
```

The Binding markup extension for the textBox2 TextBox looks very similar to the TextBlock's Binding, except that it also specifies Mode=TwoWay in the Binding markup extension. This means that if you type a value in the third TextBox named textBox2, the same value propagates back to the original TextBox named textBoxOriginal, which then updates the TextBlock's value via one-way Element data binding.

Data binding in XAML is an incredibly powerful construct that extends beyond Element data binding to object data binding via collections of data retrieved from a server via web service calls. I explore data binding further in a later section in this chapter on Expression Blend.

Combining TypeConverters with Element Data binding can provide a powerful XAML construct that avoids writing what would normally be a lot of boilerplate code. As an example, you could Element Databind a TextBlock to the Position property of a MediaElement that is playing either an audio or video segment. There is a type mismatch between the TextBlock.Text property's type of String and the MediaElement.Position property's type of TimeSpan. You can get around this by writing a simple event handler that manually converts from a TimeSpan value to a String value. A more elegant way to handle this is to create a simple ValueConverter that is applied as part of the Element Data binding markup extension. TypeConverter objects are used by the XAML parser at compile time; however,

ValueConverter objects apply at runtime for converting values when data binding. I cover ValueConverters in detail in Chapter 6.

This section concludes the XAML overview. The next section dives into the class model available within Silverlight for Windows Phone and is the underlying objects behind the XAML markup.

Key Silverlight UI Base Classes

Silverlight for Windows Phone is similar to Silverlight for the desktop and traces its roots back to Windows Presentation Foundation. As such it has a similar control tree to support functionality endemic to XAML UIs such as data binding, styling, and animation to name a few.

As with all of.NET, the root base class is Object. Next in line from Object is DependencyObject, which you will find in Windows Presentation Foundation (WPF) and Silverlight. DependencyObject provides dependency property system services to derived classes. The DependencyObject includes the concept of dependency properties to enable automatic data binding, animation, and styling. Dependency Properties support three major functions over standard .NET properties: Change notification, Property value inheritance, and value providers.

The UIElement class inherits from the DependencyObject class and serves as the base class for most objects that have visual appearance and that can process basic input. Example properties and events are Visibility, Opacity, Clip, GotFocus, KeyDown, and MouseLeftButtonDown, etc. Check out the MSDN documentation for a full list of properties and methods:

http://msdn.microsoft.com/en-us/library/system.windows.uielement(v=VS.95).aspx

The FrameworkElement class is the common base class for System.Windows.Shapes namespace classes like Shape, Ellipse, and Rectangle and System.Windows.Controls namespace classes like Control, Button, and TextBox. FrameworkElement implements layout, data binding, and the visual object tree functionality. Properties and events implemented in FrameworkElement include Margin, Padding, Height, Width, SizeChanged, and LayoutUpdated. The next section covers graphic primitives followed by an overview on controls. Check out the MSDN documentation for a full list of properties and methods:

http://msdn.microsoft.com/en-us/library/system.windows.frameworkelement(v=VS.95).aspx

Graphics Primitives

Silverlight for Windows Phone supports 2D graphics primitives such as rectangles, ellipses, lines, and paths. Generally these objects have been used in Silverlight to build up images, separate UI areas, as well as incorporated within controls. One of the key reasons to use XAML primitives is to take advantage of the infinite scaling capabilities of vector-based graphics.

On Windows Phone 7, UI design is all about the content, not UI "chrome" – so you won't see a heavy use of UI control chrome in most applications. Where graphics primitives can be useful on Windows Phone 7 is in game development when you need to draw game scenes for 2D game development.

For game development, vector graphics primitives or raster images can be used to draw the scene – so which one should you use? Vector-based graphics require a level of CPU processing to convert from a vector to raster format so that the GPU can render the scene. Therefore, wherever possible, it is recommended to use a raster format like .png files to avoid the additional format conversation, saving battery. Given the fixed screen size of a mobile device, little fidelity is lost by sing raster graphics.

I cover the graphics primitives in more detail with a sample application called GraphicsPrimitives in the Chapter 2 Solution. Figure 2–13 shows the UI.

Figure 2–13. *Graphics Primitives UI*

Listing 2–6 shows the XAML markup for the GraphicsPrimitives project.

Listing 2–6. *GraphicsPrimitives MainPage.xaml File*

```
<phone:PhoneApplicationPage
    x:Class="GraphicsPrimitives.MainPage"
    xmlns="http://schemas.microsoft.com/winfx/2006/xaml/presentation"
    xmlns:x="http://schemas.microsoft.com/winfx/2006/xaml"
    xmlns:phone="clr-namespace:Microsoft.Phone.Controls;assembly=Microsoft.Phone"
    xmlns:shell="clr-namespace:Microsoft.Phone.Shell;assembly=Microsoft.Phone"
    xmlns:d="http://schemas.microsoft.com/expression/blend/2008"
    xmlns:mc="http://schemas.openxmlformats.org/markup-compatibility/2006"
    mc:Ignorable="d" d:DesignWidth="480" d:DesignHeight="768"
    FontFamily="{StaticResource PhoneFontFamilyNormal}"
    FontSize="{StaticResource PhoneFontSizeNormal}"
    Foreground="{StaticResource PhoneForegroundBrush}"
    SupportedOrientations="Portrait" Orientation="Portrait"
    shell:SystemTray.IsVisible="True">

  <!--LayoutRoot is the root grid where all page content is placed-->
  <Grid x:Name="LayoutRoot" Background="Transparent">
    <Grid.RowDefinitions>
      <RowDefinition Height="Auto"/>
      <RowDefinition Height="*"/>
```

```xml
    </Grid.RowDefinitions>

    <!--TitlePanel contains the name of the application and page title-->
    <StackPanel x:Name="TitlePanel" Grid.Row="0" Margin="12,17,0,28">
      <TextBlock x:Name="ApplicationTitle" Text="CHAPTER 2"
        Style="{StaticResource PhoneTextNormalStyle}"/>
      <TextBlock x:Name="PageTitle" Text="graphics primitives"
        Margin="9,-7,0,0" Style="{StaticResource PhoneTextTitle1Style}"/>
    </StackPanel>

    <!--ContentPanel - place additional content here-->
    <Grid x:Name="ContentPanel" Grid.Row="1" Margin="12,0,12,0">
      <Ellipse Height="146" HorizontalAlignment="Left" Margin="12,28,0,0"
        x:Name="ellipse" Stroke="White" StrokeThickness="3"
        VerticalAlignment="Top" Width="176" />
      <Rectangle x:Name="Rectangle" Fill="LightGray" HorizontalAlignment="Left"
        Margin="12,200,0,227" Stroke="White" Width="145"/>
<Image HorizontalAlignment="Left" Margin="21,213,0,0"
        x:Name="image1" VerticalAlignment="Top"
        Source="images/bookcover.png" Stretch="None" />
<Path x:Name="Line" Data="M245,28 L404,200" Fill="#FFF4F4F5"
        HorizontalAlignment="Right" Height="173" Margin="0,28,51,0"
        Stretch="Fill" UseLayoutRounding="False" VerticalAlignment="Top"
        Width="160" Stroke="White" StrokeThickness="5" />
      <Path Data="M406,307 L244,306 L239,187" Fill="White"
        HorizontalAlignment="Right" Margin="0,200,49.5,227" Width="161.5"
        Stretch="Fill" Stroke="White" UseLayoutRounding="False" Name="Pen" />
      <Path x:Name="pencil"    Height="55" Margin="24,0,19,93.143"
         Stretch="Fill" Stroke="White" UseLayoutRounding="False"
         VerticalAlignment="Bottom" Data="M31,396 C36.294918,415.62234 34.544609,412.77231↩
 57,424
 C67.599434,429.29971 74.964737,436.59296 87,439 C91.685699,439.93713 97.165527,439 102,439
 C131.96695,439 133.0285,434.60718 158,419 C181.28416,404.44739 192.78926,421.84195 221,443
 C236.51602,454.63702 255.19547,455.07272 274,430 C290.42596,408.09872 279.30313,393.7677↩
 319,407
 C334.2662,412.08875 343.0755,439.55231 359,441 C369.82889,441.98444 372.32379,433.58371↩
 379,425
 C383.57141,419.12247 397.35007,414.1167 406,417 C419.57794,421.52597 422,469.74692 422,412
 C428.6496,413.32993 435.72543,412.92343 443,413"/>
<Canvas Height="104" HorizontalAlignment="Left" Margin="6,495,0,0" Name="canvas1"
            VerticalAlignment="Top" Width="444">
        <Ellipse Canvas.Left="75" Canvas.Top="24" Height="60"
          x:Name="ellipseCanvas1" StrokeThickness="1" Width="76" Stroke="White" />
        <Ellipse Canvas.Left="290" Canvas.Top="24" Height="60"
          x:Name="ellipseCanvas2" StrokeThickness="1" Width="76" Stroke="White" />
      </Canvas>
    </Grid>
  </Grid>
</phone:PhoneApplicationPage>
```

The Ellipse and Rectangle controls are pretty straightforward except that, as a developer, you might be wondering what is setting the top and left values for the Ellipse and Rectangle objects at the top. How are they positioned?

```
<Ellipse Height="146" HorizontalAlignment="Left" Margin="12,28,0,0"
    x:Name="ellipse" Stroke="White" StrokeThickness="3"
    VerticalAlignment="Top" Width="176" />
<Rectangle x:Name="Rectangle" Fill="LightGray" HorizontalAlignment="Left"
    Margin="12,200,0,227" Stroke="White" Width="145"/>
```

Since I mentioned game development earlier, it is worth spending a little bit of time on the layout system. Silverlight includes a layout system as part of the rendering engine that places objects based on the Margin property for the Grid and StackPanel layout controls. The Margin property takes four values representing the distance from the Left, Top, Right, and Bottom sides of the containing control, in this case the ContentPanel Grid object. Notice that just the first two values are configured for the Ellipse. If the other values are not set, the Width and Height values determine sizing for the object.

For game development, it would be odd to draw game scenes using just Margin values to place game sprites or images. Silverlight includes another layout control, the Canvas object, which allows the developer to set Top and Left directly on the object. This may seem strange because graphics primitives and even controls do not include a Top or Left property. Check the Properties Tool window in Visual Studio 2010 for any object to confirm.

We added a Canvas at the bottom of the Grid and place two Ellipse objects in it. Here is the markup for the Ellipse objects.

```
<Canvas Height="104" HorizontalAlignment="Left" Margin="6,495,0,0" Name="canvas1"
        VerticalAlignment="Top" Width="444">
  <Ellipse Canvas.Left="75" Canvas.Top="24" Height="60"
      x:Name="ellipseCanvas1" StrokeThickness="1" Width="76" Stroke="White" />
  <Ellipse Canvas.Left="290" Canvas.Top="24" Height="60"
      x:Name="ellipseCanvas2" StrokeThickness="1" Width="76" Stroke="White" />
</Canvas>
```

The Ellipse objects are placed using Attached Property syntax, i.e., Canvas.Top and Canvas.Width properties. Attached properties are a special dependency property that allows the attached property to be configured on and apply to a contained object in the XAML tree. I cover attached properties in the next section, but they provide a powerful extensibility mechanism without having to create custom objects. Given that Silverlight objects tend to have many more properties then their Windows Forms counterparts already, attached properties allows controls to take advantage of additional properties without having to actually declare them in every object

The last item I'll cover here are the two <Path /> objects named Pen and Pencil. The controls have those named because that is the tool I used to draw them in Expression Blend. I cover Expression Blend later in this chapter. The Path objects include a Data property that is set to what looks like a code.

The Data property is set to a value that follows the syntax of the Path Mini-Language. The Path Mini-Language has a similar syntax as the Scalable Vector Graphics (SVG) markup Path object. Please refer to a SVG reference for more info on the syntax if interested. Otherwise, use Expression Blend to visually draw objects without worrying about the underlying Data value generated for the Path object.

The other object that is part of the GraphicsPrimitives project is the Image object. It takes an image file such as a .png as the value for its Source property. It can be configured to stretch and scale an image by setting the Stretch property to Fill or UniformttoFill. The Image object is the most common graphics primitive a developer will work with. I cover working with the Image object in detail in Chapter 6.

This wraps up the overview of the .NET Framework for Silverlight and XAML. Now let's dive into the details on controls.

Controls

Silverlight for Windows Phone 7 includes a rich set of controls that are already templated with the Metro theme" by default. Figure 2–14 shows a quick search of controls available on my laptop.

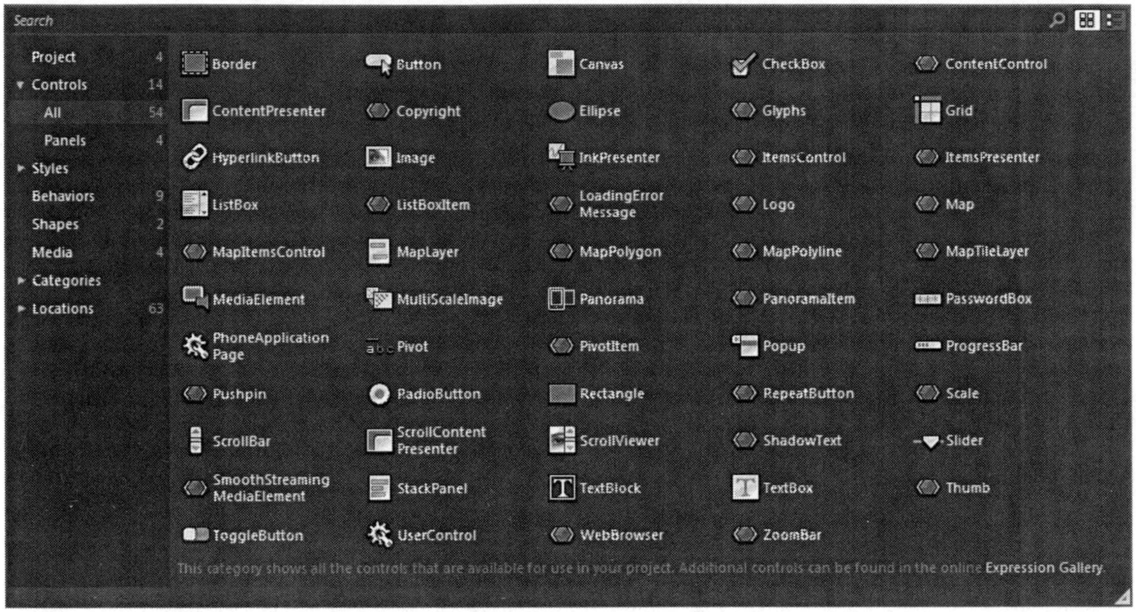

Figure 2–14. *Avaialble controls on the author's laptop*

Some of the controls are "sub" controls that are generally associated with a primary control. As an example, the ListBoxItem control always sits within a ListBox control. The ZoomBox control is part of the Bing Maps Map control, etc. Still, as you can see, there are a rich set of controls available for Windows Phone 7 developers.

▓ **Note** I cover the additional controls available in the Silverlight for Windows Phone Toolkit in Chapter 5.

The Chapter 2 solution in the code download has a project named BuiltInControls to demonstrate a few of the controls that ship with the Windows Phone Developer Tools. One control in Figure 2–4 that may not be on your system is the SmoothStreamingMediaElement control. This control plays media like the built-in MediaElement, but it also supports IIS Smooth Streaming adaptive streaming technology, which allows you to chunk up a media stream to different sizes depending on available bandwidth conditions. Smooth Streaming is especially important on mobile devices where bandwidth can vary greatly by optimizing the user experience for available conditions. You can learn more about Smooth Streaming at IIS.net. I cover media playback in Chapter 6.

There's an additional control available as part of the Microsoft Advertising SDK for Windows Phone 7. You can download it here:

www.microsoft.com/downloads/en/confirmation.aspx?FamilyID=b0f00afc-9709-4cc2-ba2c-57728db6cbd6

The download installs the control and API documentation here:

C:\Program Files (x86)\Microsoft Advertising SDK for Windows Phone 7

All that's needed is to add a reference to the control and a few lines of code to generate revenue from your free applications. I cover how to integrate advertising into your application in Chapter 6. Other controls shown in Figure 2–14 are pulled in by the Silverlight for Windows Phone 7 Toolkit, which is covered below in Chapter 5.

User Interface Development with Expression Blend 4

In this section we build on the introduction to Expression Blend 4 for Windows Phone provided in Chapter 1 by delving into key concepts such as the layout system, sample data, data binding, and control templates. I provide coverage of the Silverlight for Windows Phone 7 Toolkit and then return to an overview of the Panorama and Pivot controls.

Layout System

The Silverlight for Windows Phone 7 layout system is based on the desktop Silverlight layout system, so it behaves in a similar manner. The Silverlight layout system enables dynamic positioning of vector-based UI elements using device-independent units or pixels that default to 96 units per inch, regardless of display resolution.

For example, if you set a rectangle to be 96 units high and 96 units wide in Visual Studio 2010 or Expression Blend 4, the rectangle will be one-inch square by default, because the Windows Phone default is 96 dpi.

The Silverlight for Windows Phone layout system includes containers that manage the size and position of controls placed within the container. UI elements are placed into one of three primary containers that inherit from the Panel base class:

- **Canvas:** Defines an area within which you can explicitly position child elements by coordinates relative to the Canvas area.

- **StackPanel:** Arranges child elements into a single line that can be oriented horizontally or vertically.

- **Grid:** Defines an area containing rows and columns where elements can be placed.

I cover the container controls over the next few sections, but first let's look at the layout system in more detail. This is a critically important topic when laying out UI. The layout system is a recursive operation that first sizes, then positions, and finally draws elements onscreen.

The layout system is a two-pass system that is applied starting at the top of the visual XAML tree and then works its way through the Children collection of each control. During the Measure pass, the desired size of each child element is determined. In the Arrange pass, each child element's size and position are finalized.

Two closely related properties with respect to layout are Margin and Padding. Whereas all FrameworkElements have the Margin property, only objects that inherit from Control and the Border FrameworkElement have a Padding property. The difference is that Margin defines the extra space placed around the outside edges of the element, and Padding defines the extra spaced placed around the inside edges of the control.

You can use Margin and Padding to force mandatory separation between controls; it is applied by the layout system as the UI is resized, either programmatically or as the user resizes the browser.

Values for Margin and Padding can be specified using three notations: a unique value for each edge, such as "1,2,3,4"; two numbers, such as "3,5", which applies 3 for the left and right and 5 for the top and bottom; or a single value such as "4." If you set the property to a single value, that Margin or Padding will be applied to the left, top, right, and bottom edges of the control. If you set each edge explicitly to "1,2,3,4", the order applied is left, top, right, bottom.

Canvas

The Canvas object may feel most comfortable to developers who are not familiar with WPF or Silverlight and have built UIs in technologies similar to .NET Windows Forms. The Canvas container enables absolute positioning of UI elements – very similar to Windows Forms or other layout technologies.

StackPanel

The StackPanel arranges controls side-by-side, either vertically or horizontally, via the Orientation property, taking into account the configured Margin and Padding for each control nested within the StackPanel control.

Grid

The Grid control is similar to an HTML table in laying out controls. It supports multiple rows and columns in the RowDefinitions and ColumnDefinitions collections. By default, if a control is nested inside a Grid without any rows or columns defined, the control renders in the upper left-hand corner, which represents row zero and column zero.

When you define columns and rows on a Grid, you can specify the Width in the ColumnDefinition object for a column and the Height in the RowDefinitions object for a row in pixels. You can also leave Width and Height set at their default value of Auto or specify Auto explicitly for each.

Leaving Width and Height set to Auto causes the Grid to size rows and columns equally as much as possible; however, the ultimate size is determined by the layout system, which takes into account the size of the content. For example, if a Grid has two rows defined with the default of Auto, but the content in the first row has a minimum size that is twice that of the content in the second row, the layout system causes the first row to be twice the width of the second.

The Grid supports a much more powerful method of sizing columns and rows: star sizing. When you specify a star (*) as the Width or Height of a column or row, the column or row receives a proportional amount of space relative to the other columns or rows, respectively. This XAML has the same effect as setting Width and Height to the default of Auto:

```
<Grid.ColumnDefinitions>
  <ColumnDefinition Width="*"/>
  <ColumnDefinition Width="*"/>
</Grid.ColumnDefinitions>
<Grid.RowDefinitions>
  <RowDefinition Height="*"/>
  <RowDefinition Height="*"/>
</Grid.RowDefinitions>
```

It gets interesting when you prepend an integer to * for Width or Height. For example, to give up to twice the amount of available space to the second column and second row, specify 2* for both the Width and Height, like this:

```
<Grid.ColumnDefinitions>
  <ColumnDefinition Width="*"/>
  <ColumnDefinition Width="2*"/>
</Grid.ColumnDefinitions>
```

```
<Grid.RowDefinitions>
  <RowDefinition Height="*"/>
  <RowDefinition Height="2*"/>
</Grid.RowDefinitions>
```

Note that I said "up to twice the amount." That is because the layout system takes into account the minimum size required for content. If the second column wants twice as much space as the first column, the content in the first column may prevent the second column from getting all the requested space, depending on the minimum width values configured on the content in the first column.

Layout Controls Sample and Blend Behaviors

The project LayoutControls in the Chapter 2 solution demonstrates how the Canvas, StackPanel, and Grid layout controls work. Since this section is focused on Expression Blend, I introduce a new concept called Behaviors to provide navigation without writing any C# code.

Behaviors Overview

WPF introduced the concept of Triggers, which allowed actions to happen such as starting an animation StoryBoard object by clicking a button without writing any C# code. Behaviors were introduced in Silverlight 3 and take the concept of Triggers even further while including full Expression Blend support with drag-and-drop support to apply behaviors.

Behaviors allow developers to add logic to a control visually in Blend. You can think of them as code-less events or actions meaning no C# code is needed to utilize a Behavior. To find behaviors in Expression Blend, click on the Assets tab and select Behaviors to filter to the list of items. Figure 2–15 shows a list of available behaviors.

Figure 2–15. *Expression Blend built-in behaviors*

Additional Silverlight behaviors can be found at the Expression Blend Gallery located here:

```
http://gallery.expression.microsoft.com/en-us/site/search
```

For the LayoutControls sample project, three TextBlock controls are put into the UI of MainPage.xaml with text of Canvas, StackPanel, and Grid, respectively. Three pages are added to the project named CanvasPage.xaml, StackPanelPage.xaml, and GridPage.xaml. Switch back to MainPage.xaml to drag-and-drop a NavigateToPageAction behavior onto the TextBlock with the text Canvas. Figure 2–16 shows the Properties window for the behavior. The EventName property indicates the event to kick off the action, in this case touching the label will navigate to the page configured for the TargetPage property.

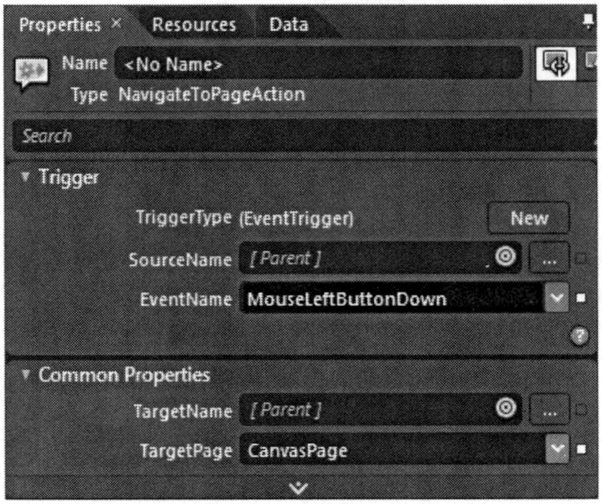

Figure 2–16. *NavigateToPageAction behavior configuration*

Without writing any code, when the Canvas TextBlock is touched, the MouseLeftButtonDown event fires and the PhoneApplicationFrame will navigate to the TargetPage of CanvastPage.xaml. We do the same for the other two labels so that they navigate to the StackPanelPage.xaml and GridPage.xaml pages respectively. Here is a snippet of the XAML added to the Canvas textbox as a result of dragging-and-dropping the behavior:

```
<TextBlock HorizontalAlignment="Left" TextWrapping="Wrap" Text="Canvas"↵
 VerticalAlignment="Top" Margin="12,43,0,0">
  <Custom:Interaction.Triggers>
    <Custom:EventTrigger EventName="MouseLeftButtonDown">
      <ic:NavigateToPageAction TargetPage="/CanvasPage.xaml"/>
    </Custom:EventTrigger>
  </Custom:Interaction.Triggers>
</TextBlock>
```

Under the hood, behaviors are just XAML markup programmed visually with Expression Blend. The navigation actions do not include animations but this quick demo touches upon just the beginning of what Silverlight Behaviors can offer in terms of simplifying code with standardized behaviors and actions. Chapter 5 covers how to add animations to page transitions.

Layout Controls

Now that the navigation has been visually programmed with Behaviors, it is time to add the layout controls starting with the Canvas control to CanvasPage.xaml. By default the Canvas control is not listed in the Asset Bar. As covered in Chapter 1, click and hold the chevron at the bottom of the Asset Bar on the left to pop-out the search UI, or click and hold on the Grid icon in the Asset Bar and the UI to switch to Canvas is presented.

Double-click on Canvas to add it to the CanvasPage.xaml UI. Type Shift-V to go back to Selection mode and then right-click on the Canvas and select Auto-Size ➤ Fill. The Canvas now occupies the content area. The interesting part is when an object is placed inside a Canvas such as an Ellipse. Click-and-Hold the Rectangle to switch to Ellipse, double-click as before to add the Ellipse to the Canvas. The Ellipse is added to the Canvas instead of the Grid named ContentPanel, because Canvas was the control selected (blue rectangle) in the Object and Timeline Tool Window.

Move the Ellipse to about the middle of the ContentPanel Grid's area. Notice that the Margin value did not change as what is normally the case when objects are placed within a Grid layout control. Because the Ellipse is within a Canvas layout control, objects are absolutely positioned using Canvas.Left and Canvas.Top attached properties instead of via Margin. Here is the XAML for the ellipse:

```
<Ellipse Fill="#FFF4F4F5" Height="100" Stroke="Black" Width="100" Canvas.Left="176"
Canvas.Top="279"/>
```

The Canvas layout control operates differently with respect to the Silverlight Layout system. Controls are absolutely positioned within a Canvas, making it the ideal layout control for Silverlight-based game development. Developers can apply Margin to controls within a Canvas but the Margin is applied relative to the Canvas.Top and Canvas.Left properties, not to the bounds of the Canvas, which is different behavior compared to a Grid.

Grid Page

For GridPage.xaml, we don't add an additional Grid, because there is already a Grid control named ContentPanel by default when adding a new page to the project. Click and hold the Rectangle to switch to Ellipse, and double-click as before to add the Ellipse to the Grid. By default it is placed in Grid.Row = 0 and Grid.Column=0. Initially the ContentPanel does not have any additional Rows or Columns so let's add a couple visually to make a tic-tac-toe type grid layout as shown in Figure 2–17.

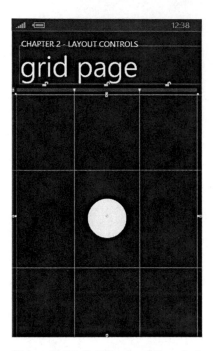

Figure 2–17. GridPage.xaml at desig time

The Ellipse is placed in the center position in the Grid control resulting in this Xaml:

```
<Ellipse Fill="#FFF4F4F5" Stroke="Black" Grid.Column="1" Grid.Row="1" Width="100"↵
 Height="100"/>
```

We see two additional attached properties used to position the Ellipse within the Grid Control:
Grid.Column and Grid.Row.

StackPanel Page

Double-click on StackPanel to add it to the StackPanelPage.xaml UI. Press Shift-V to go back to Selection mode, and then right-click on the StackPanel and select Auto-Size ➤ Fill. The StackPanel now occupies the content area. The interesting part is what happens when multiple objects are placed inside a StackPanel such as an Ellipse. Click and hold the Rectangle to switch to Ellipse, and double-click as before to add an Ellipse to the StackPanel. This time, double-click on the Ellipse icon in the Asset Bar five more times. Notice how each Ellipse is automatically added under the previous Ellipse or "stacked" on top of one another.

The StackPanel control does not support absolute positioning like the Canvas. Developers can use Margin and Padding to adjust the display within the StackPanel. Remove two of the six Ellipses so that four are stacked. Multi-select the remaining four Ellipse controls and then set the Top and Bottom Margin values to 10. This results in the Ellipses separating from each other a bit but still within the behavior of the StackPanel.

Now set a Width on all four Ellipse controls of 100 pixels to remove the stretch. By default, we now have four circles stacked and spaced. Finally, add a 100 Left Margin to the second Ellipse and 100 Right Margin to the third Ellipse resulting in Figure 2–18.

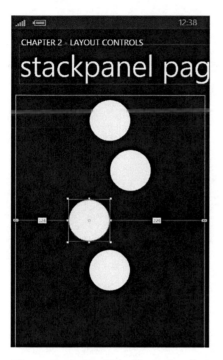

Figure 2–18. StackPanel.xaml at design time

Layout Tips

The layout controls provide an immense amount of flexibility within the layout system. Developers should use the controls to lay out UI as much as possible initially. As an example, use a Grid with Rows and Columns to separate UI first. For items that are lined up either horizontally or vertically, use a StackPanel. Adjust HorizontalAlignment and VerticalAlignment as needed.

Once the general layout is in place, Apply Margin and Padding as needed to space controls within containers. Resist the temptation to set Width and Height on every control initially. Width and Height override all other layout configurations and can result in odd layout behavior where controls appear to be cut off. Only set Width or Height when needed to ensure correct display of content.

With all that said, the Silverlight Layout System takes CPU cycles to determine positioning. In most cases following the above recommendations works fine and provides maximum flexibility with great performance. Only in cases when frame rates are dropping should a developer consider absolute positioning to reduce layout calculations and even then the gains may be marginal. In the next section, I shift gears over to another major topic in XAML development: data binding.

Data Binding

Support for data binding is engineered directly into XAML-based programming languages like WPF and Silverlight. This means most properties are of type DependencyProperty, which includes built-in support for change notifications and data binding. It would be nearly impossible to cover Silverlight user experience without also covering data binding. There are three main categories for data binding:

- Element data binding

- Object data binding

- XML data binding

Silverlight for Windows Phone 7 includes full data binding support comparable to what is related in Silverlight 3. In order to create sample code, some demo live data is needed. The next section covers the DemoLiveData project available in the Chapter 2 solution.

Demo Live Data

In addition a separate project named DemoLiveData is available to provide an object collection and an xml data file to work with for the rest of this chapter. The project contains two simple classes, a Customer class and a Customers class to serve as the live data. Listings 2–7 and 2–8 show the Customer and Customers classes.

Listing 2–7. Customer.cs Code File

```
namespace SampleData.LiveData
{
  public class Customer
  {
    public string FirstName { get; set; }
    public string LastName { get; set; }
    public string PhoneNumber { get; set; }
    public string Address { get; set; }
    public string City { get; set; }
    public string State { get; set; }
    public string Zip { get; set; }
  }
}
```

Listing 2–8. Customers.cs Code File

```
using System.Collections.Generic;

namespace SampleData.LiveData
{
  public class Customers
  {
    private List<Customer> _customerList;

    public Customers()
    {
      _customerList = new List<Customer>()
      {
        new Customer(){FirstName="Rob",LastName="Cameron",PhoneNumber="555-555-5555",
                       Address="123 Main Street", City="Atlanta",State="GA", Zip="30042"},
        new Customer(){FirstName="Amanda",LastName="Cam",PhoneNumber="555-555-5555",
                       Address="123 Main Street", City="Philadephia",State="PA",↵
Zip="19111"},
        new Customer(){FirstName="Anna",LastName="Ron",PhoneNumber="555-555-5555",
                       Address="123 Main Street", City="New York",State="NY", Zip="10001"},
```

```
        new Customer(){FirstName="John",LastName="Smith",PhoneNumber="555-555-5555",
                    Address="123 Main Street", City="Chicago",State="IL", Zip="20011"},
        new Customer(){FirstName="Jane",LastName="Doe",PhoneNumber="555-555-5555",
                    Address="123 Main Street", City="San Francisco",State="CA",↵
 Zip="30333"},
        new Customer(){FirstName="Daniel",LastName="Booth",PhoneNumber="555-555-5555",
                    Address="123 Main Street", City="Dallas",State="TX", Zip="79999"},
        new Customer(){FirstName="Arthur",LastName="Olson",PhoneNumber="555-555-5555",
                    Address="123 Main Street", City="Seattle",State="WA", Zip="50000"},
        new Customer(){FirstName="Janet",LastName="Rich",PhoneNumber="555-555-5555",
                    Address="123 Main Street", City="Portland",State="OR", Zip="43334"},
        new Customer(){FirstName="Janus",LastName="Poor",PhoneNumber="555-555-5555",
                    Address="123 Main Street", City="Sacramento",State="CA", Zip="85755"},
        new Customer(){FirstName="Alice",LastName="Mer",PhoneNumber="555-555-5555",
                    Address="123 Main Street", City="Kansas City",State="KA", Zip="48488"}
    };
  }
  public List<Customer> CustomerList { get { return _customerList; } }
  }
}
```

To instantiate the data, simply create the Customers class and data bind to the CustomerList. The XML file named ApressBooks.xml lists details on about 20 books that have been published by Apress over the years. I won't list the full XML file, but here is a summary of the schema with one of the sample book data present:

```
<ApressBook>
  <ID>4</ID>
  <ISBN>1-4302-2435-5</ISBN>
  <Author>Jit Ghosh and Rob Cameron</Author>
  <Title>Silverlight Recipes: A Problem-Solution Approach, Second Edition</Title>
    <Description>Silverlight Recipes: A Problem-Solution Approach, Second Edition is your↵
practical companion to developing rich, interactive web applications with Microsoft's↵
latest technology. This book tackles common problems and scenarios that on-the-job↵
developers face every day by revealing code and detailed solutions. You'll quickly be able↵
to integrate real-world, functioning code into your applications—and save hours of coding↵
time.</Description>
  <DatePublished>2010-07-15T00:00:00</DatePublished>
  <NumPages>1056</NumPages>
  <Price>$49.99</Price>
</ApressBook>
```

The next three sections cover the scenarios listed previously and demonstrated in the Chapter 2 solution. That includes a project named Data Binding, which includes a MainPage.xaml and a folder named pages that includes three pages to cover each topic that follows.

Element Data Binding

Element data binding is when a property on one control data binds to the value of a property on another control. To demonstrate this, we add a Rectangle and a Slider control to the page named ElementDataBindingPage.xaml with the Rectangle on the left and the Slider control oriented vertically.

The experience we want to create is that when the Slider is positioned, the Opacity on the Rectangle is modified. The Slider has a MinimumValue of zero and MaximumValue of one, with a default of one. The LargeChange property is changed to .1 and the SmallChange property is changed to .01 to keep the value consistent with what are valid values for the Opacity property.

What we want to do is data bind the Rectangle's Opacity value to the Value property of the Slider. To do this, select the Rectangle object and click the small button to the right of the field in the Properties Window to bring up the menu shown in Figure 2–19 to select the Element Property Binding... menu item.

Figure 2–19. Expanded menu options for the Opacity property

The menu shown in Figure 2–19 is mostly the same for any Property selected for a control. When Element Property Binding... is clicked, the Artboard switches to Element Property Binding mode, allowing the developer to select a control to then choose a property. Figure 2–20 shows the UI. Notice that it indicates that the Slider control will be given a name of slider. This is because the control must be named for Element Binding to work.

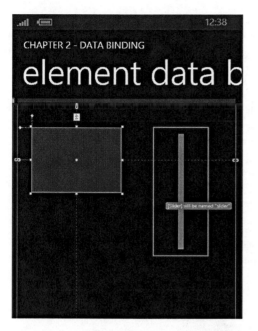

Figure 2–20. Element Binding mode with mouse over the slider

Once the Slider control is clicked, it is named slider and you can select the property to bind to as shown in Figure 2–21.

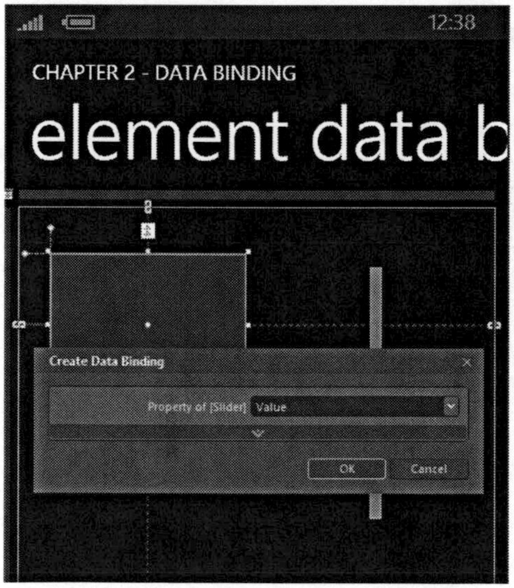

Figure 2–21. Element Binding – Create Binding dialog

The Slider.Value property is the desired property so click OK to create the element binding. The XAML or the Rectangle is updated to include element binding for the Opacity value as shown here:

```
<Rectangle Fill="#FF0000E0" Height="134" Margin="30,44,0,0" Stroke="Black"↵
 VerticalAlignment="Top"
 HorizontalAlignment="Left" Width="188" Opacity="{Binding Value, ElementName=slider}"/>
```

The Binding markup extension indicates that the Opacity property for the Rectangle should get its value from the UI element named "slider." Markup extensions are identified by the braces within the quotes as covered above in the XAML overview. Binding is a class in the .NET Framework for Silverlight that connects the property, in this case Opacity, to the data source, in this case the Value property on the Slider control.

Object Data Binding

Data binding to collection of objects is a very typical scenario. Silverlight for Windows Phone 7 has rich support for data binding to object collections, as is the case with Silverlight. We continue to customize the DataBinding project by adding a ListBox onto the ObjectDataBindingPage.xaml ContentPanel Grid. Add a reference to the DemoLiveData project to provide an object data source.

In Expression Blend, right-click on the ListBox and select the "Data bind ItemSource to Data…" menu item. Click the "+CLR Object" button in the Create Data Binding dialog shown in Figure 2–22.

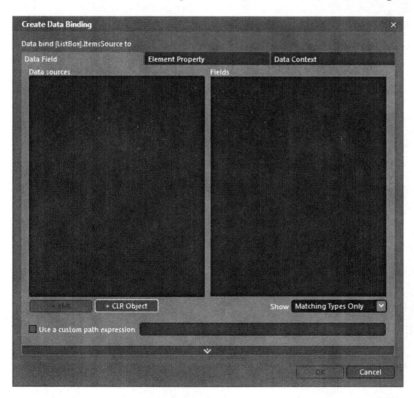

Figure 2–22. Create Data Binding dialog

This brings up the Create Object Data Source dialog shown in Figure 2–23, where we select SampleData.LiveData.Customers and click OK.

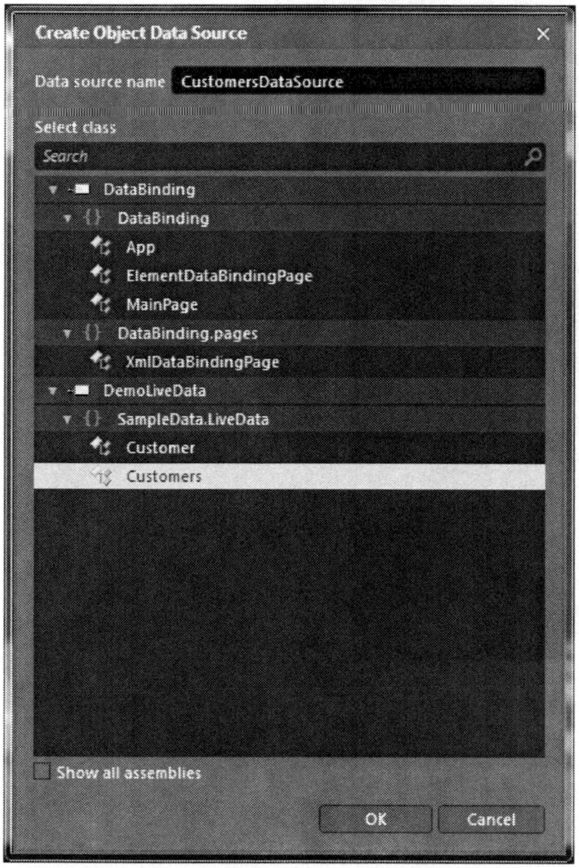

Figure 2–23. *Create Object Data Source dialog*

This returns us back to the Create Data Binding dialog with an object data source pointing to the custom object collection. Select the CustomerList Field to data bind it to the ItemSource as shown in Figure 2–24 and click OK.

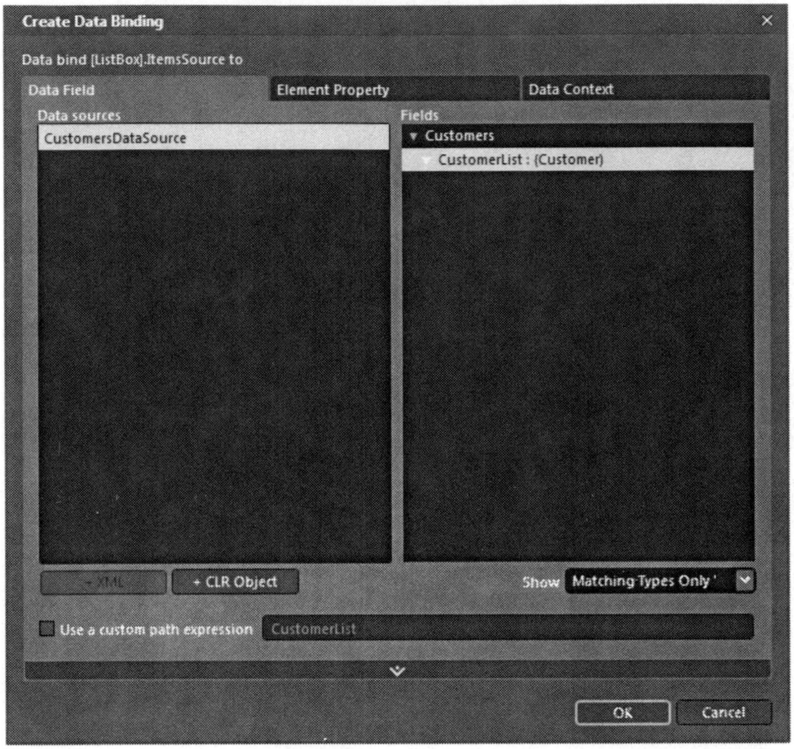

Figure 2–24. Create Data Binding with Object data source

Figure 2–25 shows the ListBox now data bound to the object data source.

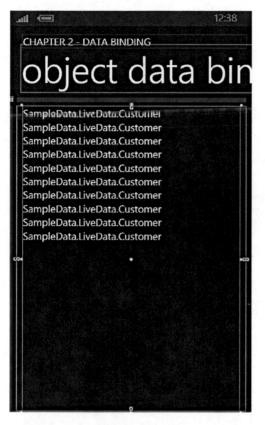

Figure 2–25. *Data-bound ListBox*

In Figure 2–25, the data source is configured but it just displays the ToString() value for the Customer object, which defaults to the full type name. This is because an ItemTemplate is not configured on the ListBox. The ItemTemplate is used to layout the individual Customer records. Listing 2–9

Listing 2–9. *ObjectDataBindingPage.xaml Code File*

```
<phone:PhoneApplicationPage
    xmlns="http://schemas.microsoft.com/winfx/2006/xaml/presentation"
    xmlns:x="http://schemas.microsoft.com/winfx/2006/xaml"
    xmlns:phone="clr-namespace:Microsoft.Phone.Controls;assembly=Microsoft.Phone"
    xmlns:shell="clr-namespace:Microsoft.Phone.Shell;assembly=Microsoft.Phone"
    xmlns:d="http://schemas.microsoft.com/expression/blend/2008"
    xmlns:mc="http://schemas.openxmlformats.org/markup-compatibility/2006"
    xmlns:SampleData_LiveData="clr-namespace:SampleData.LiveData;assembly=DemoLiveData"
    x:Class="DataBinding.ObjectDataBindingPage"
    SupportedOrientations="Portrait" Orientation="Portrait"
    mc:Ignorable="d" d:DesignHeight="768" d:DesignWidth="480"
    shell:SystemTray.IsVisible="True">
```

```
<phone:PhoneApplicationPage.Resources>
  <SampleData_LiveData:Customers x:Key="CustomersDataSource" d:IsDataSource="True"/>
</phone:PhoneApplicationPage.Resources>

<phone:PhoneApplicationPage.FontFamily>
  <StaticResource ResourceKey="PhoneFontFamilyNormal"/>
</phone:PhoneApplicationPage.FontFamily>
<phone:PhoneApplicationPage.FontSize>
  <StaticResource ResourceKey="PhoneFontSizeNormal"/>
</phone:PhoneApplicationPage.FontSize>
<phone:PhoneApplicationPage.Foreground>
  <StaticResource ResourceKey="PhoneForegroundBrush"/>
</phone:PhoneApplicationPage.Foreground>

<!--LayoutRoot is the root grid where all page content is placed-->
<Grid x:Name="LayoutRoot" Background="Transparent" DataContext="{Binding↵
Source={StaticResource CustomersDataSource}}">
  <Grid.RowDefinitions>
    <RowDefinition Height="Auto"/>
    <RowDefinition Height="*"/>
  </Grid.RowDefinitions>

  <!--TitlePanel contains the name of the application and page title-->
  <StackPanel x:Name="TitlePanel" Grid.Row="0" Margin="12,17,0,28">
    <TextBlock x:Name="ApplicationTitle" Text="CHAPTER 2 - DATA BINDING"↵
Style="{StaticResource PhoneTextNormalStyle}"/>
    <TextBlock x:Name="PageTitle" Text="object data binding" Margin="9,-7,0,0"↵
Style="{StaticResource PhoneTextTitle1Style}"/>
  </StackPanel>

  <!--ContentPanel - place additional content here-->
  <Grid x:Name="ContentPanel" Grid.Row="1" Margin="12,0,12,0">
    <ListBox Margin="12,0" ItemsSource="{Binding CustomerList}"/>
  </Grid>
</Grid>
</phone:PhoneApplicationPage>
```

The Expression Blend work results in the following XAML changes:

- Added an xmlns namespace import to the SampleData.LiveData namespace at the top of the XAML page.

- Added a CustomersDataSource resource to the PhoneApplicationPage.Resources section.

- Set the DataContext attribute for the LayoutRoot Grid to the CustomersDataSource resource via a Binding markup extension.

- Bind the ListBox ItemSource attribute to the CustomerList property of the Customers class.

It is important to note that by setting the DataContext on the LayoutRoot Grid, it makes the data source collection, individual records, and fields available to nested XAML controls automatically. As an example, an ItemTemplate can be added to the ListBox that Binds TextBlock control Text properties to the FirstName and LastName properties of the Customer class just by specifying the data field name in the Binding marketup extension. I demonstrate how to do this visually next.

Right-click on the ListBox, select Edit Additional Templates, then Edit Generated Items, and finally click Create Empty. This puts the Artboard into template editing mode with an empty Grid. Drag two TextBlock controls next to each other with some spacing to fit the FirstName and LastName fields. Next click the more actions button next to the Text property in the Properties Window for the first TextBlock to bring up Figure 2–26.

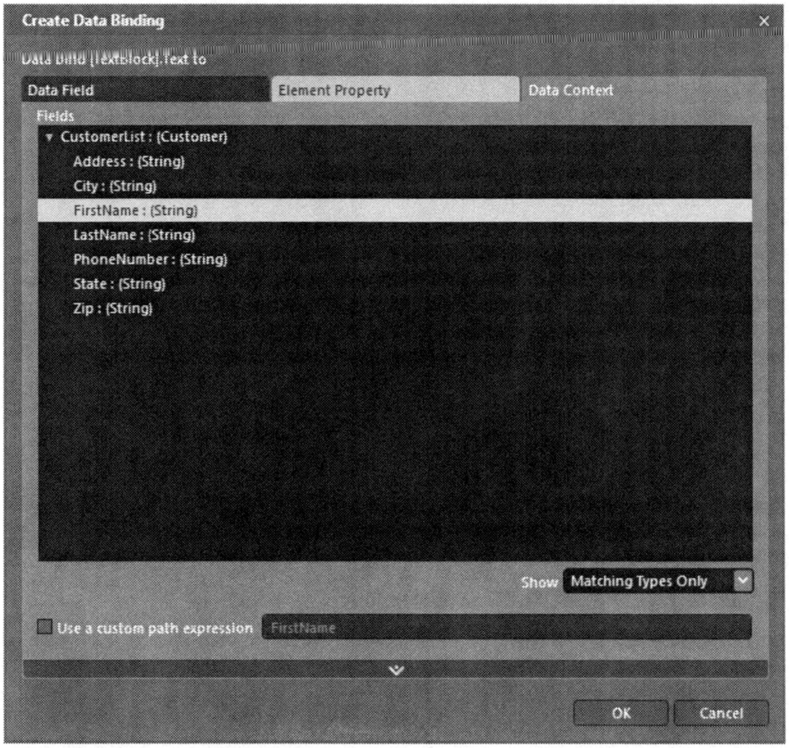

Figure 2–26. Create data binding

Expression Blend understands that we are creating an ItemTemplate to display individual Customer records in the ListBox that is data bound to the CustomersList so the fields available for controls in the ItemTemplate are Customer class fields. We select FirstName for the left TextBlock and LastName for the second TextBlock. Adding the ItemTemplate results in the much more useful display of first name and last name for each record. Here is the resulting XAML:

```
<DataTemplate x:Key="CustomersListBoxDataTemplate">
  <Grid>
    <TextBlock Margin="0" TextWrapping="Wrap"
    Text="{Binding FirstName}"
    d:LayoutOverrides="Height" Width="75"/>
    <TextBlock Margin="0,0,-148,0" TextWrapping="Wrap"
    Text="{Binding LastName}"
    d:LayoutOverrides="Height" HorizontalAlignment="Right" Width="118"/>
  </Grid>
</DataTemplate>
```

XML Data Binding

The first step to data binding to XML is to obtain the XML file, which can be retrieved from a remote server or embedded as part of the application. For this demonstration, the XML file is retrieved from the application, because I don't cover remote server access until Chapter 4.

There are two ways to parse XML data in Silverlight: the XmlReader class and LINQ to XML, which is one of the new technologies that became available in .NET Framework 3.5 and later. The XmlReader class is a fast-forward–only, non-caching XML parser. For processing large XML files, XmlReader is better suited than LINQ to XML for performance reasons. LINQ to XML provides rich object-based XML processing using the common LINQ syntax.

The work in this section is focused on the XmlDataBindingPage.xaml page, which has two ListBox controls: a ListBox named XmlDataLinqListBox that is loaded via data binding with LINQ to XML and another ListBox named XmlDataReaderListBox that is loaded via XmlReader in Code.

The ApplicationBar control is enabled with two icon buttons, one to switch between the two ListBox controls by alternatively hiding and making visible the controls. The other icon button loads data into the XmlDataReaderListBox ListBox. We configure an icon for the icon button that loads the data via XmlReader by simply browsing the list of icons available as resources and configure the Refresh icon. The other icon was created by combining the default next and back icons into one. The second icon button switches between the two ListBox controls using the Visibility property.

Now that we have the sample project set up, the next two sections cover the code to load the XML data using both methods.

LINQ to XML

The Silverlight XmlReader works in a similar manner as the XmlReader in the full version of the .NET Framework. Visit this site for details on the differences between the .NET Framework and the .NET Framework for Silverlight versions of XmlReader:

http://msdn.microsoft.com/en-us/library/cc189053(VS.95).aspx

Silverlight for Windows Phone 7 is a rich subset of the full .NET Framework 3.5 and that it includes LINQ. There are many web sites, blogs, and books that cover LINQ, so I won't dive into all the details here.

■ **Tip** A great resource on LINQ is Joseph C. Rattz Jr.'s *Pro LINQ: Language Integrated Query in C# 2008* (Apress, 2007).

Since the XML file is embedded into the application, we use an XmlResolver. In this case the XmlXapResolver, which extracts XML from the xap, and then loads the XML data into an XDocument object.

We call XDocument.Load(XmlReader) to load the contents into an XDocument so that it can be queried using LINQ. The XDocument class, located in the System.Xml.Linq namespace, is the key object in LINQ to XML functionality.

The XmlReader class can be used to read XML data from the IsolatedStorage file system as well as from streams retrieved via the network just like in the full .NET Framework. A unique Silverlight for Windows Phone 7 ability that we take advantage of in this section is to use an XmlXapResolver to retrieve XML data embedded into the application's .xap file, which is the container for Silverlight applications. An XML resolver in .NET resolves, or evaluates, external XML resources. An XmlUrlResolver is used to resolve the Url location passed into XmlReader.Create. The XmlXapResolver looks for the name passed into XmlReader.Create within the .xap file for the application:

```
XmlReaderSettings XmlRdrSettings = new XmlReaderSettings();
XmlRdrSettings.XmlResolver = new XmlXapResolver();
XmlReader reader = XmlReader.Create("ApressBooks.xml",
XmlRdrSettings);
```

The resolver is configured for the XmlReaderSettings object that is passed into the Create method. For more information on the XmlReaderSettings class, refer to the MSDN documentation here:

http://msdn.microsoft.com/en-us/library/system.xml.xmlreadersettings(VS.95).aspx

The LINQ to XML code is encapsulated in the ApressBooks class that is part of the DemoLiveData project shown in Listing 2–10.

Listing 2–10. APressBooks.cs Code File

```csharp
using System;
using System.Collections.Generic;
using System.Linq;
using System.Xml;
using System.Xml.Linq;
using System.Collections;

namespace DemoLiveData
{
  public class ApressBooks
  {
    private List<ApressBook> _apressBookList;
    public List<ApressBook> ApressBookList
    {
      get
      {
        if (null == _apressBookList)
          RetrieveData();
        return _apressBookList;
      }
    }

    private void RetrieveData()
    {
      XmlReaderSettings XmlRdrSettings = new XmlReaderSettings();
      XmlRdrSettings.XmlResolver = new XmlXapResolver();
      XmlReader reader = XmlReader.Create("ApressBooks.xml", XmlRdrSettings);

      XDocument xDoc = XDocument.Load(reader);

      _apressBookList =
        (from b in xDoc.Descendants("ApressBook")
         select new ApressBook()
         {
           Author = b.Element("Author").Value,
           Title = b.Element("Title").Value,
           ISBN = b.Element("ISBN").Value,
```

```
            Description = b.Element("Description").Value,
            PublishedDate = Convert.ToDateTime(b.Element("DatePublished").Value),
            NumberOfPages = b.Element("NumPages").Value,
            Price = b.Element("Price").Value,
            ID = b.Element("ID").Value
        }).ToList();
    }
  }
}
```

It is similar to the Customers class in the same project in that it just returns a list of objects to databind. The object type is ApressBook shown here:

```
using System;

namespace DemoLiveData
{
  public class ApressBook
  {
    public string Author { get; set; }
    public string Title { get; set; }
    public string ISBN { get; set; }
    public string Description { get; set; }
    public DateTime PublishedDate { get; set; }
    public string NumberOfPages { get; set; }
    public string Price { get; set; }
    public string ID { get; set; }
  }
}
```

The significant difference between the Customers class and the ApressBooks class is the LINQ to XML code that parses out an ApressBook object from the XML. Otherwise, the data binding process is the same within Expression Blend so we how all of the dialogs to data bind ApressBooks to the XmlDataLinqListBox ListBox control on the XmlDataBindingPage.xaml page. The next section covers reading the XML data and loading it directly into the Items collection of the ListBox control.

XmlReader

For this section, the XML records are added to the ListBox.Items collection for the XmlDataReaderListBox on the XmlDataBindingPage.xaml page without using an ItemTemplate. In Silverlight 4 XPath is supported so that you can create a Data Template that parses the bound XML object but for now we just bind the XML object as is without a template. Here is the code to load up the data:

```
private void XmlReaderIconButton_Click(object sender, EventArgs e)
{
  XmlReaderSettings XmlRdrSettings = new XmlReaderSettings();
  XmlRdrSettings.XmlResolver = new XmlXapResolver();
  XmlReader reader = XmlReader.Create("ApressBooks.xml", XmlRdrSettings);

  // Moves the reader to the root element.
  reader.MoveToContent();

  while (!reader.EOF)
```

```
{
    reader.ReadToFollowing("ApressBook");
    // Note that ReadInnerXml only returns the markup of the node's children
    // so the book's attributes are not returned.
    XmlDataReaderListBox.Items.Add(reader.ReadInnerXml());
}
reader.Close();
reader.Dispose();
}
```

Figure 2–27 shows both methods in action.

Figure 2–27. Xml Data Binding UI

In this section I covered the Silverlight for Windows Phone 7 data binding capabilities. When live data is not available, developers can take advantage of the sample data capabilities available in Expression Blend, which I cover in the next section.

Sample Data

It is difficult to build out a user experience without the content available in a usable format. Quite often, a project will have development and test services and classes to make data available within an application. Still, this means that you must have an Internet connection available, or have to VPNconfigured to access services. Being able to work with a local copy of the data is more convenient and probably quicker in terms of iterative development than connecting over and over to a data service.

Expression Blend 4 includes a Data Panel on the right in the Blend UI as shown in Figure 2–28 where developers and designers can add or import sample data.

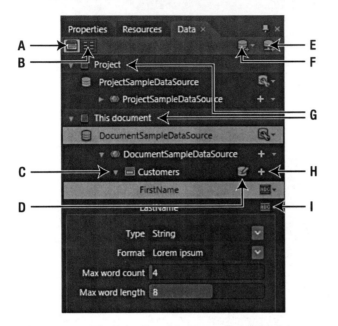

Figure 2–28. The Data Panel in Expression Blend 4

Table 2–3 identifies key aspects of the Data Panel with a couple of fake data sources configured to help explain the various capabilities.

Table 2–3. Expression Blend 4 Data Panel Features

Annotation	Description
A	Selected by default, list mode for the Data panel lets you drag the Customers collection shown in Figure 2–28 onto the Artboard and generates a ListBox data-bound to the Customers design-time datasource.
B	Details mode lets you drag a collection item like FirstName to the Artboard to create a control data-bound to that collection item. This action also configures the DataContext property of the parent container to the collection, in this example Customers.
C	This is a document-level datasource collection named Customers. In addition, a datasource named ProjectSampleDataSource is defined at the Project level.
D	Click this button to edit and further customize the collection. You can specify the type of value (String, Number, Boolean, or Image) as well as the format (for String, how many words; for Number, how many digits; and for Image, a folder location).

Annotation	Description
E	The "Create data source" button allows you to add a live or real datasource to the application to display at runtime.
F	The "Create sample data" button allows you to create a design-time datasource to help working with UI elements that display data in Expression Blend
G	You can define datasources at the document and project levels of an application.
H	Click the plus sign to add a simple property to a datasource collection, or click the down-arrow next to the plus sign to choose whether to add a simple property, a complex property, or a collection property to the design-time datasource.
I	Click the down-arrow for an individual property to edit the attributes for the property, such as its type and format, depending on the type of the property.

The Data Panel allows developers and designers to work with the design-time data in Expression Blend while also displaying the design-time data at runtime for testing and demonstration purposes. Developers can also add a live datasource to the UI that pulls data from a live datasource for display at runtime, by clicking item E in Figure 2–28.

As long as your schema is compatible between the design-time datasource and the live datasource, a developer can use both a design-time and a runtime data source in an application. The steps to use both are pretty straightforward. Start working with a design-time datasource to build an application. Next add a live datasource to the Data panel in Expression Blend. Drag items from the live datasource, and drop them onto the control displaying the corresponding sample data. This will bind the control to design-time data at design-time and runtime data at runtime.

■ **Note** Clear the check box next to Enable When Running Application in the design-time datasource properties to allow the live datasource to display data at runtime.

As long as the data schemas match, the sample data displays on the Artboard in Expression Blend and the live data displays when the application executes. This is because the sample datasource bindings are not removed or overwritten when the run-time datasource is added. Once you create a sample data source, you can work with it just like with live data as demonstrated above in the section on Data Binding.

Control Styling

By default, Windows Phone 7 controls are styled to fit the Metro design language intrinsic to Windows Phone 7. You can apply the built-in styles to your application's user interface as well as create your own styles. Silverlight styles allow you to define a set of properties related to UI that can be reused throughout an application to create a standardized look and feel.

Expression Blend 4 can apply Metro text styles as shown in Figure 2–29 by right-clicking on the control and selecting Edit Style ➤ Apply Resource ➤ and selecting a style.

Figure 2–29. Applying built-in Metro text styles

After visually applying the style, the XAML is updated with a StaticResouce markup extension applied to the Style property.

```
<TextBlock Margin="12,273,31,270" TextWrapping="Wrap" Text="Apply a Built in Style"
    Style="{StaticResource PhoneTextExtraLargeStyle}"/>
```

You can create your own styles tailored to your brand or application theme but otherwise try to use the built-in Metro styles. To create a custom Text style right-click on a TextBlock and select Edit Style as before but this time select "Create Empty…" to bring up the dialog box shown in Figure 2–30.

Figure 2–30. Create Style Resource dialog

The Name (Key) attribute is how you reference the resource when applying it as a style with this syntax Style="{StaticResource ResourceKeyNameHere}".

Resources can be defined at the application level in the <Application.Resources> element, at the page level in the <phone:PhoneApplicationPage.Resources> element, or in a separate Resource Dictionary by clicking the "New.." button. Clicking the "New…" button brings up the Resource Dictionary dialog shown in Figure 2–31.

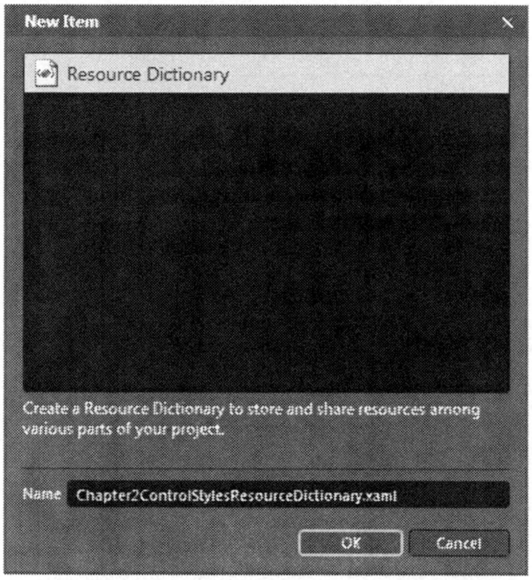

Figure 2–31. Resource Dictionary New Item dialog

Clicking OK to the dialog in Figure 2–31 enables the Resource Dictionary option and sets the name on the dropdownlist box in the dialog shown in Figure 2–30. Clicking OK to that dictionary adds an entry to the Application.Resources element in App.xaml.

```
<Application.Resources>
  <ResourceDictionary>
```

```
    <ResourceDictionary.MergedDictionaries>
        <ResourceDictionary Source="Chapter2ControlStylesResourceDictionary.xaml"/>
    </ResourceDictionary.MergedDictionaries>
  </ResourceDictionary>
</Application.Resources>
```

Resource dictionaries are a great way to segregate XAML markup to keep markup files from becoming unwieldy and achieve better project organization. Now that you understand how styles are referenced and stored, let's move on to creating a custom text style that we can apply to the TextBlock named CustomStyleTextBlock.

We continue visually editing the TextBlockStyle1 style now located in the Chapter2ControlStylesResourceDictionary.xaml resource dictionary. We set the Foreground color to Gold and the Opacity to 70%. Here is the resulting XAML markup:

```
<Style x:Key="TextBlockStyle1" TargetType="TextBlock">
        <Setter Property="Foreground" Value="Gold"/>
        <Setter Property="Opacity" Value="0.7"/>
</Style>
```

■ **Tip** Implicit styles are introduced in Silverlight 4, but they are not supported in Silverlight for Windows Phone, which is based on Silverlight 3. Implicit styles are defined without an x:key so that the style is applied to all controls that match the TargetType without an explicit Style value configured.

A style consists of a TargetType and nested series of Setter property elements. The TargetType must be a control that inherits from the FrameworkElement base class. Each Setter consists of a Property name and a Value. These identify what control properties the settings apply to as well as what the value should be. For a complex property, the <Setter.Value> </Setter.Value> syntax like this:

```
<Style x:Key="TextBlockStyle2" TargetType="TextBlock">
  <Setter Property="Foreground">
    <Setter.Value>
      <LinearGradientBrush EndPoint="0.5,1" StartPoint="0.5,0">
        <GradientStop Color="Gold" Offset="0"/>
        <GradientStop Color="White" Offset="1"/>
      </LinearGradientBrush>
    </Setter.Value>
  </Setter>
  <Setter Property="Opacity" Value="0.7"/>
</Style>
```

Another attribute available on the Style element is the BasedOn attribute, which allows a Style to inherit from another Style. The TextBlockStyle2 is modified to inherit from the built-in Metro style using this attribute setting on the Style element:

```
BasedOn="{StaticResource PhoneTextExtraLargeStyle}"
```

The last option I will cover is inline styles, where the Style is nested within the XAML markup for the control. Here is an example with a single property:

```xml
<TextBlock Height="57" HorizontalAlignment="Left" Margin="42,427,0,0"↵
 Name="InlineStyleTextBlock" Text="TextBlock" VerticalAlignment="Top" Width="162">
  <TextBlock.Style>
    <Style TargetType="TextBlock" BasedOn="{StaticResource PhoneTextLargeStyle}">
      <Setter Property="Foreground" Value="Orange" />
    </Style>
  </TextBlock.Style>
</TextBlock>
```

Any control that inherits from the FrameworkElement base class has a Style property that can be standardized across the application, though not all controls support visual editing of styles via menu items. To create a custom style for a Button, edit the XAML in the Chapter2ControlStyleResourceDictionary.xaml file to start a custom Style with a TargetType of Button and a name of ButtonStyle. Once the custom Style is manually created, you can visual edit styles using the Resources window as shown in Figure 2–32 with the ButtonStyle selected and ready to be edited visually.

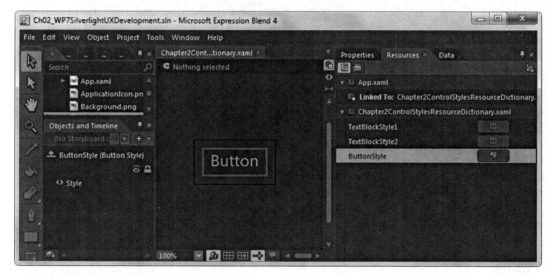

Figure 2–32. Resources window

Once the custom Button style is completed, you can apply it to an existing Button control by selecting the Button, finding the Style property in the Properties window, and clicking the button to apply a Local Resource named ButtonStyle. See Figure 2–33.

In Figure 2–33, the Properties Window is filtered by typing Style in the filter box at the top of the Properties Window.

Figure 2–33. *Applying ButtonStyle via Properties window Style property*

The Style is already applied to the Button but the arrows highlight the small green button, which is usually black until the property is customized. Green around a property indicates that a resource is applied. Additional menu items light up such as Edit Resource… and Convert to New Resource… Here is the final XAML for the ButtonStyle Style:

```
<Style x:Key="ButtonStyle" TargetType="Button" >
  <Setter Property="Foreground">
    <Setter.Value>
      <LinearGradientBrush EndPoint="0.5,1" StartPoint="0.5,0">
        <GradientStop Color="Gold" Offset="0"/>
        <GradientStop Color="White" Offset="1"/>
      </LinearGradientBrush>
    </Setter.Value>
  </Setter>
  <Setter Property="Opacity" Value="0.7"/>
  <Setter Property="BorderBrush" Value="Red"/>
</Style>
```

This completes the overview on Control Styles and customization. The next section provides background on control templates.

Control Templates

In most "real" software development projects, custom controls are needed to customize data presentation, customize how a control appears, as well as how a control functions. In Silverlight, developers generally do not create custom controls. Instead, Silverlight developers modify existing controls vial control templates.

Right-click on the ListBox control on the ListBoxTemplatePage.xaml page and you will see two menu items related to Templates: Edit Template and Edit Additional Templates. I cover both menu items in the next two sections.

Edit Template Menu Item

This menu item enables direct modification of the control for maximum customization. There are two sub-menu items "Create Empty…" and "Edit a Copy…" to create a customized control. Selecting the "Create Empty…" menu item is essentially starting from scratch. The template contains a Grid to start create a new control UI.

Most customizations start with the "Edit a Copy…" menu item, which extracts the Control's internal visual tree, including visual states and animations, and makes it available for customization. This is very similar to inheriting from an existing control in other languages but much more powerful.

Edit Additional Templates

The Edit Additional Templates menu item can have one or more options depending on the control. For example, a ListBox control has the following options:

- Edit Generated Items (ItemTemplate)

- Edit Generated Item Container (ItemContainerStyle)

- Edit Layout of Items (ItemsPanel)

The Generated Items ItemTemplate is the template applied to the data bound list of items. Without customization, the ListBox displays the .ToString() value for the data bound type. This is the most common – and necessary – customization for a ListBox control.

The ItemContaineStyle is also a customization applied to the data bound list of items. This style is applied to the container element generated for each item. For a ListBox, the generated container control is a ListBoxItem control. I don't cover ItemsContainerStyle in this section. I will discuss customizations in Chapter 5 when I cover the Visual State Manager.

The last additional template for the ListBox is the ItemsPanel template, which just has a "Create Empty…" option. This template customizes the container that all of the ListBoxItem controls exist in.

As mentioned, different types of controls can have different options for additional templates to edit. As another example, the progress bar does not have any additional templates to edit but the Button Control has a ContentTemplate that customizes content rendering for the Button control by applying a data template to the content.

I discuss editing the control template and additional templates in the next couple of sections to demonstrate these concepts with the ListBox, Button, and ProgressBar controls.

ListBox Customization

The ListBox control needs to data bind with a collection of data to be interesting. We create a sample data source at the Project level named ProductsSampleData that has 100 items. The sample data text, a url, and an image in order to make it interesting. Next up is working with the ItemTemplate in the first section.

Working with ItemTemplate

The first step we take is to drag the Products collection to the ListBox, which data binds the collection and creates an ItemTemplate automatically that can be used as a starting point as shown in Figure 2–34.

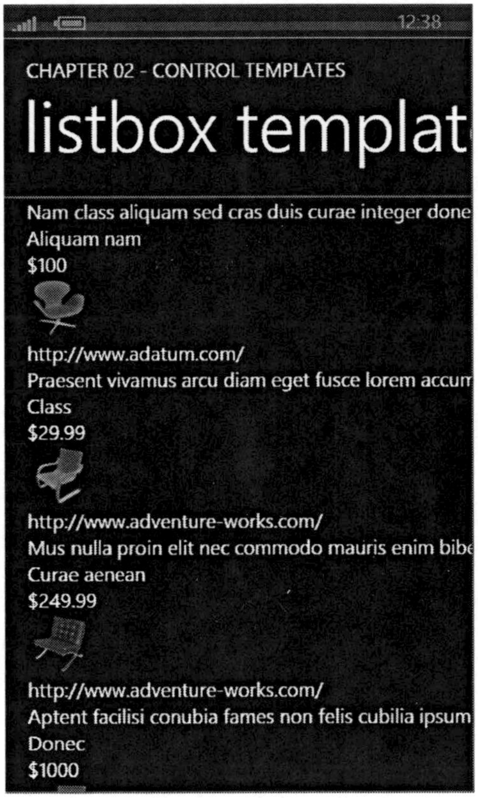

CHAPTER 02 - CONTROL TEMPLATES

listbox templat

Nam class aliquam sed cras duis curae integer done
Aliquam nam
$100

http://www.adatum.com/
Praesent vivamus arcu diam eget fusce lorem accun
Class
$29.99

http://www.adventure-works.com/
Mus nulla proin elit nec commodo mauris enim bibe
Curae aenean
$249.99

http://www.adventure-works.com/
Aptent facilisi conubia fames non felis cubilia ipsum
Donec
$1000

Figure 2–34. *Generated ItemTemplate for Products sample data*

Here is the XAML markup for the ItemTemplate that we customize in Blend shortly:

```
<DataTemplate x:Key="ProductsItemTemplate">
  <StackPanel>
    <TextBlock Text="{Binding Description}"/>
    <TextBlock Text="{Binding Name}"/>
    <TextBlock Text="{Binding Price}"/>
    <Image Source="{Binding ProductImage}" HorizontalAlignment="Left" Height="64" Width="64"/>
    <TextBlock Text="{Binding Url}"/>
  </StackPanel>
</DataTemplate>
```

To edit the template, click the drop-down arrow next to (ListBox) at the top of the ArtBoard under where the filenames are displayed and select Edit Additional Templates ➤ Edit Generated Items (ItemTemplate) ➤ Edit Current to go into template editing mode.

The first modification is to add 40px bottom margin to the root StackPanel to create space between the items. Next the items are re-arranged to present a better display with the item name, price, image, and URL at the top. Do this by re-arranging the controls in the first item visually.

■ **Note** Because it is a repeated template for each item, the ItemTemplate is dynamically applied to the items below the first item as the first item is visually edited.

To improve the display and better utilize space, multi-select the Name and Price fields, right-click, select Group Into, and pick a container control. Any one of the containers can be used to arrange the Name and Price fields, but choose the StackPanel with Orientation set to Horizontal in this case to flow the content across the screen. Grab the lower right-hand corner of the Image to increase the Image size. We next apply built-in styles to further refine the UI. Finally, set the Description TextBox TextWrapping property to Wrap. Figure 2–35 shows the final modifications to the generated template shown in Figure 2–34.

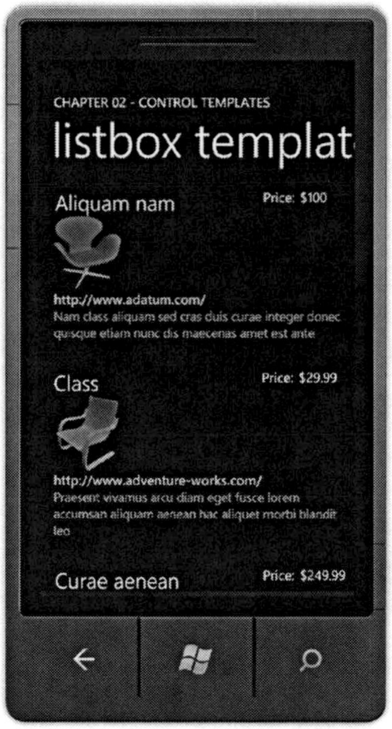

Figure 2–35. Customized ItemTemplate for Products sample data

This completes our overview on working with the ItemTemplate customization for the ListBox. Let's turn to the ItemsPanel customization next.

Custom ItemsPanel

By default, the ListBox uses a VirtualizedStackPanel as the ItemsPanel. The VirtualizedStackPanel enables much faster data refresh with very long lists, because only the visible elements are drawn. For a list that is tens of items or low hundreds of items, the VirtualizedStackPanel may not provide much benefit and can potentially impact scroll performance.

If scrolling is not smooth for your application, select the ListBox control and go to the breadcrumb menu up top of the ArtBoard near the filenames and click on ListBox, select Edit Additional Templates, Edit Layout of Items (ItemsPanel), and then "Create Empty..." to get started. The Create ItemsPanelTemplate Resource dialog box pops up. Provide a name and store the template in This Document to place the template in the Resources section. By default it creates this ItemsPanelTemplate with a StackPanel.

```
<ItemsPanelTemplate x:Key="ItemsPanelTemplate1">
        <StackPanel/>
</ItemsPanelTemplate>
```

Because there is a few hundred items, you can experience the performance differences. Without the custom ItemsPanelTemplate modification, when you click Customize ListBox, the ListBoxTemplatePage.xaml page loads immediately, because the data is virtualized in the ListBox with the default VirtualizedStackPanel items container.

When you modify the ItemsPanelTemplate to be a StackPanel, the page takes noticeably longer to load –about four or five seconds. Scrolling appears smoother, but the load time may be unacceptable. This is because all of the items, a couple of hundred, must be created before rendering, i.e., the data is no longer virtualized.

As you can see, there are always trade-offs with performance recommendations to consider and test before final implementation.

Button Customization

In this section I cover some additional control customizations available to developers. Next we transform a standard rectangle Button to an ellipse Button via a custom control template.

Custom Control Template

To get started, drag a Button on the ArtBoard, right-click on the Button, and select Edit Template, then "Edit a Copy..." to go into control template editing mode. The ButtonBackground Layer is a Border. You may be tempted replace the Border with an Ellipse control, but that would make the necessary changes much more complex due to animation dependencies and the fact that the Border is actually a container control whereas the Ellipse is not.

Instead, make a simple modification by adjusting the CornerRadius property for the Border by setting it to 50. The Button now has rounded corners and can take on various elliptical shapes depending on the Height and Width properties. Figure 2–36 shows the Button in action.

Figure 2–36. *Custom Button control template*

There are much more complex modifications possible that involve editing the Visual States defined in the template. I cover modifying states in Chapter 5, when I discuss the Visual State Manager. For this section I will expose you to control customizations by modifying the internal visual tree via a control template.

Animation Fundamentals

Silverlight has powerful animation capabilities that allow the designer or developer to animate any property value of type Double, Color, or Point. Animation lets you vary a property between two values over a specified period of time, thus providing the illusion of motion or transformation.

In Silverlight for Windows Phone, the animation engine is left to interpret how to change the value over the specified period of time between the configured values for the property that is being animated. To apply an animation to a UI element, create a Storyboard, which I describe in the next section and then move on to key frame animations.

Creating an Animation Storyboard

In the Chapter 2 project BasicAnimations, we add a navy blue Rectangle control named NavyRect to animate using a Storyboard. To apply an animation to a UI element, create a Storyboard in XAML, and set TargetName and TargetProperty to specify the element and the property of the element to animate.

Nest the animation within the Storyboard element in XAML in phone:PhoneApplicationPage.Resource like this:

```
<Storyboard x:Name="NavyRectMouseClick">
  <DoubleAnimation BeginTime="00:00:00.5" From="1" To="7"
    AutoReverse="True" Duration="00:00:00.5"
    Storyboard.TargetName="Rect1"
    Storyboard.TargetProperty="(Shape.StrokeThickness)"/>
</Storyboard>
```

The TargetName and TargetProperty attributes are attached properties for the Storyboard class. Storyboard objects are usually created as resources within either the Application.Resources or UserControl.Resources element, making it easy to interact with the Storyboard by referencing it by the x:Name value.

This XAML contains a DoubleAnimation object, which can animate a value of type Double between the values configured in the From and To properties. An additional property configured here is AutoReverse, which indicates whether the animation should automatically reverse itself and animate in the opposite direction starting at the To value and ending at the From value. BeginTime indicates how long after starting the Storyboard should the animation actually begin. Duration specifies how long the animation should take to animate between the From and To values for the property of type Double. Also, a Storyboard can contain more than one animation, allowing one Storyboard to animate multiple objects and properties.

The Storyboard class provides Begin, Pause, Stop, and Resume methods you can use to control the Storyboard programmatically. The following code starts the animation when you touch the Rectangle:

```
private void NavyRect_MouseEnter(object sender, MouseEventArgs e)
{
  NavyRectMouseClick.Begin();
}
```

The Loaded event is the only RoutedEvent supported in a Trigger for Silverlight. You can read more about RoutedEvents in the Silverlight documentation:

http://msdn.microsoft.com/en-us/library/system.windows.routedevent(VS.96).aspx

Triggers provide an elegant way of firing an animation. Silverlight for Windows Phone supports Triggers like WPF, where an animation is kicked off via XAML code only; but currently, the only supported event that can be associated with a trigger is the Loaded event. Here is an example from the BasicAnimations project:

```
<Rectangle.Triggers>
  <EventTrigger RoutedEvent="Rectangle.Loaded">
    <BeginStoryboard>
      <Storyboard>
        <DoubleAnimation Storyboard.TargetName="NavyRect"
          BeginTime="00:00:00" From="0.0" To="1.0" Duration="0:0:0.5"
          Storyboard.TargetProperty="(UIElement.Opacity)" />
      </Storyboard>
    </BeginStoryboard>
  </EventTrigger>
</Rectangle.Triggers>
```

The Loaded event is very handy to have UI fade into view as the XAML loads. Run the sample to see the effect. You may wonder why the Storyboard is embedded in the Rectangle declaration and not configured as a Resource on the Page. The reason is that Silverlight does not support loading a value for Storyboard using the StaticResource markup extension within a Trigger.

In addition to the DoubleAnimation, developers can also create ColorAnimation and PointAnimation objects within a Storyboard object. To demonstrate this, add an Ellipse named GoldEllipse to the XAML:

```
<Ellipse Name="GoldEllipse" Stroke="Navy" Height="100" Fill="Gold" Width="100"
  Margin="30,162,0,0" HorizontalAlignment="Left" StrokeThickness="1"
  VerticalAlignment="Top" MouseEnter="GoldEllipse_MouseEnter"
  MouseLeave="GoldEllipse_MouseLeave" />
```

Here are several ColorAnimation examples that are started in the MouseEnter event and stopped in the MouseLeave event. Because there isn't a mouse pointer in Windows Phone, these events fire when your finger touches and then is moved off of the Ellipse.

```
<Storyboard x:Name="EllipseMouseEnter">
  <ColorAnimation BeginTime="00:00:00" Duration="00:00:00.3"
                  From="#FFC18125" To="#FF2DBD43"
                  Storyboard.TargetName="GoldEllipse"
                  Storyboard.TargetProperty=
                  "(Shape.Fill).(SolidColorBrush.Color)"/>
</Storyboard>
<Storyboard x:Name="EllipseMouseLeave">
  <ColorAnimation BeginTime="00:00:00" Duration="00:00:00.3" To="#FFFFD700"
                  Storyboard.TargetName="GoldEllipse"
                  Storyboard.TargetProperty="(Shape.Fill).(SolidColorBrush.Color)"/>
</Storyboard>
```

To demonstrate PointAnimation, add a Path object with the shape defined by a PathGeometry:

```
<Path Name="OlivePath" Fill="Olive" Margin="46,380,75,6"
  MouseLeftButtonDown="OlivePath_MouseLeftButtonDown" >
  <Path.Data>
    <PathGeometry>
      <PathFigure>
        <ArcSegment x:Name="animatedArcSegment" Point="50,50" Size="50,150"
        RotationAngle="-20" IsLargeArc="False"
             SweepDirection="Clockwise"/>
      </PathFigure>
    </PathGeometry>
  </Path.Data>
</Path>
```

Here is the related PointAnimation that is invoked by touching the Path object via the MouseLeftButtonDown event:

```
<Storyboard x:Name="PathClick">
  <PointAnimation AutoReverse="True"
    Storyboard.TargetProperty="Point"
    Storyboard.TargetName="animatedArcSegment"
    Duration="0:0:2" To="200,200"/>
</Storyboard>
```

This section covered the basics of Storyboard animation. The next section introduces key frame animation with Expression Blend.

Creating Animations in Blend

I covered the basics of animation in the previous section using Storyboard objects. In this section we will dive deeper into creating animations using keyframe objects to explore animating multiple controls and properties in the same Storyboard, configuring the interpolation type for the animation, as well as configuring easing in, easing out, i.e., acceleration for overall animation to provide fine-tuned animation control.

To create and manage animations, you work in the Objects and Timeline Tool Window as shown in Figure 2–37.

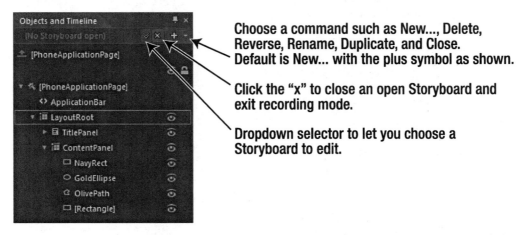

Figure 2–37. *Animation management in the Objects and Timeline tool window*

Clicking the "plus" sign to create a new Storyboard prompts for a name, name it RectStoryboard, and then click OK. With our new Storyboard, let's create an animation that re-positions and rotates the Rectangle vertically. Select just the Rectangle in the Storyboard editor as shown in Figure 2–38.

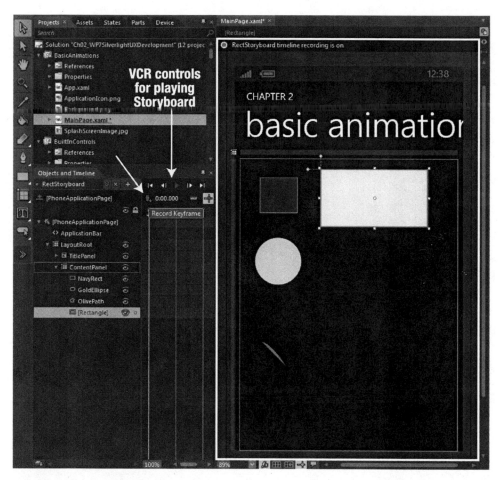

Figure 2-38. Storyboard editor

Clicking the record keyframe button (the small blue oval with the plus sign pointed to by the arrow) adds a keyframe for the selected or multiple selected objects on the Artboard. Recording a Storyboard is a matter of adding keyframes at different points of time, slide the yellow timeline marker to later on the timeline, reposition the object(s), and then click the add keyframe button again. Silverlight will interpret the animation behavior between keyframes. You simply have to position objects and record keyframes to create an animation.

Click the close animation button (the "x" button) to exit timeline recording mode. You don't want to accidentally record random editing as part of an animation.

▓ **Tip** You can always undo accidental modifications by clicking Edit ➤ Undo or Ctrl-Z.

Open the Chapter 2 BasicAnimation project to explore the Storyboard editor and play the RectStoryboard animation. Clicking on one of the keyframe objects in the timeline brings up the visual keyframe editor as shown in Figure 2–39.

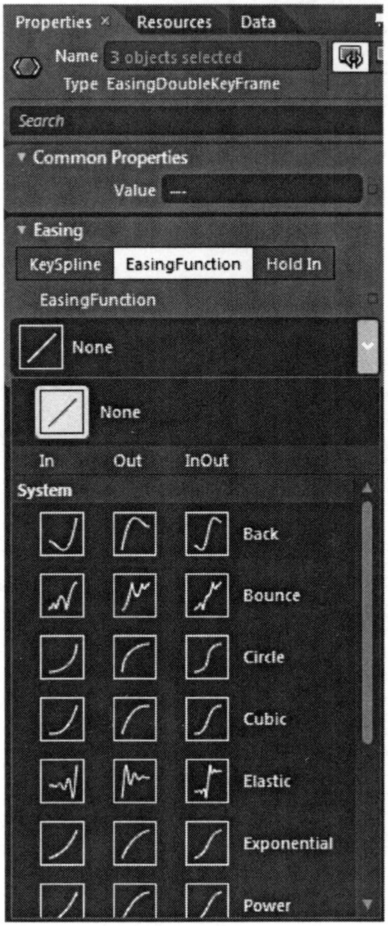

***Figure 2–39.** Individual Keyframe editor*

Select the second keyframe at one second and change the easing from the default straight line to a Cubic Out Easing Function to improve the animation's behavior towards the end of the animation. Select an "In" animation to affect the beginning of the animation. The EasingFunction options provide a quick and easy way to visually identify how the changes will affect the animation.

The other options available are KeySpline and Hold In. The Hold In easing modification holds the animation and then adjusts position very quickly at the end. The KeySpline easing modification allows for more fine grained control by adjusting the yellow control handles to modify the values as shown in Figure 2–40.

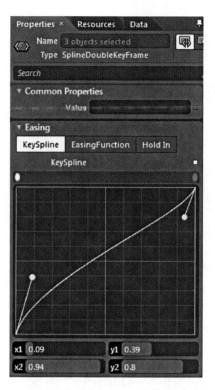

Figure 2–40. *KeySpline easing customization*

Add a TextBlock and then drop the ControlStoryboardAction behavior on to the TextBlock. Leave the EventName to MouseLeftButtonDown and the ControlStoryboardOption to Play. All that has to be changed is the name of the Storyboard. Change it to RectStoryboard, which means that when the TextBlock is clicked or touched on a device, the white Rectangle will animate. Listing 2–11 has the generated XAML from the work in Expression Blend.

Listing 2–11. *RectStoryboard Code Fragment*

```
<Storyboard x:Name="RectStoryboard">
  <DoubleAnimationUsingKeyFrames Storyboard.TargetProperty="(UIElement.RenderTransform)↵
.(CompositeTransform.TranslateY)" Storyboard.TargetName="rectangle">
    <EasingDoubleKeyFrame KeyTime="0" Value="0"/>
    <EasingDoubleKeyFrame KeyTime="0:0:1" Value="198.876">
        <EasingDoubleKeyFrame.EasingFunction>
                <CubicEase EasingMode="EaseOut"/>
        </EasingDoubleKeyFrame.EasingFunction>
    </EasingDoubleKeyFrame>
  </DoubleAnimationUsingKeyFrames>
  <DoubleAnimationUsingKeyFrames Storyboard.TargetProperty="(UIElement.RenderTransform)↵
.(CompositeTransform.TranslateX)" Storyboard.TargetName="rectangle">
    <EasingDoubleKeyFrame KeyTime="0" Value="0"/>
    <EasingDoubleKeyFrame KeyTime="0:0:1" Value="-35.955">
```

```
    <EasingDoubleKeyFrame.EasingFunction>
            <CubicEase EasingMode="EaseOut"/>
    </EasingDoubleKeyFrame.EasingFunction>
  </EasingDoubleKeyFrame>
</DoubleAnimationUsingKeyFrames>
<DoubleAnimationUsingKeyFrames Storyboard.TargetProperty="(UIElement.RenderTransform)↩
.(CompositeTransform.Rotation)" Storyboard.TargetName="rectangle">
  <EasingDoubleKeyFrame KeyTime="0" Value="0"/>
  <EasingDoubleKeyFrame KeyTime="0:0:1" Value="89.949">
    <EasingDoubleKeyFrame.EasingFunction>
            <CubicEase EasingMode="EaseOut"/>
    </EasingDoubleKeyFrame.EasingFunction>
  </EasingDoubleKeyFrame>
</DoubleAnimationUsingKeyFrames>
</Storyboard>
```

As you can see in the generated XAML, The animation class is DoubleAnimationUsingKeyFrames. Just like DoubleAnimation, ColorAnimation, and PointAnimation objects, the keyframe animations work on certain types, including Color, Double, Point, and Object with the corresponding keyframe class of ColorAnimationUsingKeyFrames, DoubleAnimationUsingKeyFrames, PointAnimationUsingKeyFrames, and ObjectAnimationUsingKeyFrames.

Each of these classes includes a KeyFrames collection containing keyframe objects that correspond to the type being animated, with an additional wrinkle of the algorithm used to interpolate between keyframes.

The available animation interpolation options are linear, discrete, and splined. Linear interpolation animates at a constant rate for the duration of the segment and is the default. Discrete or Hold interpolation animates at discrete intervals without interpolation over time.

KeySpline interpolation is more similar to linear than discrete but provides the ability to accelerate or decelerate the animation within the duration of a segment. The spline interpolation method has an additional property called KeySpline that defines a Bezier curve to create more realistic effects. The KeySpline property defines a Bezier curve with two control points that go from (0,0) to (1,1). The first control point defines the curve factor of the first half of the curve, and the second control point defines the curve factor for the second half of the curve; the curve factor defines the rate of change or acceleration for the spline keyframe as shown in Figure 2–40.

This concludes my exploration of animations in Blend. I will build on this work throughout the text as needed to demonstrate more advanced concepts such as handling orientation changes in Chapter 5. The next section covers an example of how to create animation in code.

Creating Animations in Code

On Windows Phone 7, such as when you click a tile or other objects in the phone UI, there is a Tilt animation to give visual feedback that the action was registered. This link provides an overview of the Tile Effect sample in the Windows Phone 7 documentation.

http://msdn.microsoft.com/en-us/library/ff941094(v=VS.92).aspx

This link references a code sample that contains a file named TiltEffect.cs. This link describes how to use the TiltEffect code sample but I'll also cover the steps here:

http://msdn.microsoft.com/en-us/library/ff941108%28v=VS.92%29.aspx

We add TiltEffect.cs code file to the BasicAnimations project and change the namespace to BasicAnimations. We add the xmlns:tilt="clr-namespace:BasicAnimations" namespace to MainPage.xaml. We also add this line to the PhoneApplicationPage element to enable Tilt:

tilt:TiltEffect.IsTiltEnabled="True". We also add a ListBox control with a few items to test the TiltEffect. Run the sample to see the TiltEffect in action. Note that it only applies to controls that inherit from ButtonBase or ListBoxItem by default. Developers can add additional control types programmatically via code:

```
TiltEffect.TiltableItems.Add(typeof("AdditionalControl"))
```

Application Layout

Windows Phone 7 provides a differentiated user experience with unique interaction models. In Chapter 1 and at the beginning of Chapter 2, I discussed the Metro design language with examples provided by the "Hubs" like People, music+video, and so on. Hub experiences are based on a Panorama control. The built in Outlook application is based on a Pivot control. I cover both the Panorama and Pivot controls in the next two sections.

Panorama

The Panorama control allows Windows Phone 7 developers to build "Hub-like" experiences within their own applications. Generally an application will have one Panorama as the first screen in the application. It is not recommended to have multiple Panorama controls within an application.

Think of the as the magazine cover and table of contents of an application. From a design perspective, a Panorama control should not be jammed-packed with content. Rather an application's Panorama page should highlight top items, favorites, and a menu to navigate to the details of an application hosted on Pivot pages for detailed lists of items or regular pages for individual item details.

The control provides full design-time experience to switch between PanoramaItem panes and visually edit content. The built-in Panorama control matches the look and behavior of the built-in Windows Phone 7 experience, including the gesture-and-flick support.

A Panorama control includes automatic page animations so that transitioning between panes, with different layers moving at different speeds, providing a nice parallax effect. The layers consist of a Title layer at the top left-aligned on the PanoramaItem pane furthest to the left by default. The next layer is the header for the individual PanoramaItem panes.

A Panorama control consists of multiple panes or PanoramaItem objects that span beyond the phone screen horizontally. Generally a Panorama application spans between three and five PanoramaItem objects wide, though four is the recommended maximum. The number of PanoramaItem panes that perform well depends on the content weight in each Pane. Having four PanoramaItem controls richly packed with images and content may well bog down an application with performance issues. Keep an eye on the UI performance counters when working with the Panorama control especially.

■ **Caution** Keep an eye on transitions, animations, and scrolling. If transitions and animations cut short or don't render, that's an indication of too much work on the UI thread. Poor scrolling performance is also an indicator. Reduce rendering complexity as well as offload work from the UI thread wherever possible in these situations.

In situations where performance is suffering, developers can hide individual PanoramaItems until content is visible. Dynamically loading and unloading PanoramaItems may help in some cases as well. Pay attention to the graphic performance counters covered previously to see the impact of changes as content is added.

PanoramaItem panes overlap onscreen such that 24 pixels of the pane to the right show on the current pane in view as shown in Figure 2–41. The content to the right of the line with arrows overlaid on to the screenshot is from the PanoramaItem item to the right, giving a hint to swipe right and reveal the content.

Figure 2–41. The "peek" on a PanoramaControl

Notice the straight edges and grid like nature of content on the screen. It is perfectly OK for a PanoramaItem object to extend into two panes such as the "History" section of the music+video Hub on a Windows Phone 7 device. You can set the PanoramaItem control's Orientation property to Horizontal to flow into additional panes and achieve the same effect.

■ **Note** Across Windows Phone 7 applications, whether Panorama or not, content should align on the left margin at 24px. In general, examine margin values and try to apply margin to the largest container possible in order to achieve alignment while reducing calculations.

A Panorama can have a background image. It is recommended to keep a Panorama background image less than 2,000 pixels wide and 800 pixels in height. If the image is not 800 pixels in height, the image will be stretched automatically without consideration to aspect ratio. The background image should span the entire width of the Panorama control or be a single-colored background. I demonstrate how to add a custom image as well as correct the Title layer positioning in the next section.

Correct Title Position

We start by creating a new project named PanoramaApp using the Windows Phone Panorama Application project template. This template is a fully functioning application that is based on the Panorama control leveraging sample data.

A 2272 wide x 1704 in height photo from a recent vacation is added to the project. We modify the photo to be 800 pixels in height, maintaining aspect ratio, in Paint.NET to prevent stretching the image when the project is debugged. In the emulator, the image fits nicely but the White text doesn't show very well against the image – it needs more contrast. Open the image in any editing too, such as Paint.NET and add a layer that is 30% Black over the entire of the image to provide more contrast with the White text while allowing the background image to show through when the project is run again in the emulator.

Notice though that, when you swipe over to the second pane, part of the text is clipped in the Title, as shown in Figure 2–42. The lower case 'l' and 'I' are clipped at the top.

Figure 2–42. Clipped Title text

To fix this, you can modify the control template in Expression Blend. Select the Panorama control, right-click, select Edit Template, Edit a Copy to create a Style resource. Click OK to the dialog box to go into Style editing mode. Select the TitleLayer in the Objects and Timeline Tool Window. Adjust the Top Margin to slide the title down a bit by changing the value from -76 to -68. When you run the application, this puts the top of the 'l' right against the top of the screen to fully display the text. Otherwise, the application behaves just as before.

Image as Title and Themes

Let's say you want to put your company name and logo as the title for a Panorama application. Once again, we can edit the Panorama control's template to create a custom Style to support this. First we add a new wrinkle to the sample code. The image for the Title in the Panorama will be an Apress logo. In the spirit of customizing the design to fit the logo, the Panorama background is changed to a solid color to a yellow similar to Apress' logo yellow.

In Expression Blend, the Device tab shown in Figure 2–43 can help you test out your application by changing the Orientation, Theme, and Accent color at design time. It also allows you to choose to preview the application in the emulator or device.

Figure 2–43. Device tab in Expression Blend

Switching the Theme from the default of Dark to Light changes the font from White to Black. The darker font of the Light theme looks much better; however, this is a setting that a user can change on a whim. By default Windows Phone 7 obey the theme settings automatically because of the default control styles applied to controls.

Applications can override the default theme by setting custom values for Foreground color and the like on individual controls but that can be error prone. A better way to do this is to redefine the built-in Metro styles to force the foreground color to Color.Black regardless of theme setting, making the change in effect for the entire application with just a few lines of code.

In the App Application object constructor, remove the pre-defined resource and then add back the resource with modifications. Here is example code to redefine the pre-defined styles:

```
this.Resources.Remove("PhoneForegroundColor");
this.Resources.Add("PhoneForegroundColor",  Colors.Black);

this.Resources.Remove("PhoneAccentColor");
this.Resources.Add("PhoneAccentColor",Color.FromArgb(200,200,200,200));

this.Resources.Remove("PhoneBackgroundColor");
this.Resources.Add("PhoneBackgroundColor ",  Colors.White);
```

Now that the resources are redefined to better fit the branding colors, we will now convert the title from a text title to an image. You can make this modification two different ways. The simplest method is to set Panorama.Title to an Image without editing the control template using code like this:

```
<controls:Panorama.Title>
  <Image Source="images/panorama_title.png" Height="80" Width="420" Margin="-20,80"/>
</controls:Panorama.Title>
```

The other way to modify the Title is to edit the Panorama's TitleTemplate by right-clicking on the Panorama, select Edit Additional Templates, and then Create Empty… to enter template editing mode in Expression Blend. This updates the Panorama's TitleTemplate to point to a resource:

```
<controls:Panorama  Background="#FFFFCC00"
TitleTemplate="{StaticResource PanoramaTitleDataTemplate}">
```

Here is the XAML for PanoramaTitleDataTemplate:

```
<DataTemplate x:Key="PanoramaTitleDataTemplate">
  <Grid>
    <Image HorizontalAlignment="Left" VerticalAlignment="Top"
      Source="images/panorama_title.png" Margin="-20,80,0,0"/>
  </Grid>
</DataTemplate>
```

Dynamic Background Image

A nice application customization is to make the Panorama.Background image dynamic. The Title property can be databound to a Brush type, which can be a png image or color Brush or it could simply be set when the page is Loaded or Activated via a background thread. If the Image is downloaded dynamically, you would not want to perform the download in the main UI thread. For the same reason, the background image could be configured on a Timer control as well.

Programmatically Set the Current PanoramaItem

The Panorama control lands on the most left PanoramaItem by default. Many applications implement a navigation menu on the left most pane but want the user to land on a PanoramaItem with content by default. We modify the PanoramaImageTitle project by adding a PanoramaItem to the left of the two existing PanoramaItem objects and mock up a menu.

The new PanoramaItem is named MenuPanoramaItem. The second PanoramaItem with the first set of content is named DefaultPanoramaItem, and will be displayed when the application first loads. A line of code is added to the MainPage_Loaded event to display the DefaultPanoramaItem upon load:

```
MainPanorama.DefaultItem = DefaultPanoramaItem;
```

When the user loads the application, it lands on the content page as before, but when wiping right the user will find the second set of content and then swiping again brings up the menu. The circular page scrolling in the Panorama control makes discoverability of the navigation menu via the menu very easy.

Now that I've discussed the Panorama control, let's switch over to the other major navigation control, the Pivot control.

Pivot

Upon initial examination, the Pivot control appears to be very similar to the Panorama control. It has a title and header, and swipes left and right to view additional content. However, upon closer examination, you will find significant differences. Create a new project and name it PivotApp based on the Windows Phone Pivot Application project template to get started. Figure 2–44 shows the default UI for the PivotApp project.

Figure 2–44. *Visual differences for a Pivot compared with a Panorama*

As you can see in Figure 2–44, there are visual differences compared to the Panorama. Also, note that while the Panorama has "peek" to indicate content to the right, the Pivotcontrol header items show the selected PivotItem in the normal font Foreground color and additional PivotItem controls to the right or left in a faded font Foreground color.

The other significant difference for the Pivot control is that PivotItem objects are dynamically created as they are scrolled to, which is unlike the Panorama control that loads all PanoramaItem objects upfront. This has implications in terms of start-up behavior, page weight, memory consumption, and so on.

Generally, a Pivot control can hold more containers of data than a Panorama control because of the dynamic memory allocation. Also, the Pivot is used more often to present a denser view of content as compared to the Panorama control. I cover additional differences below in the section titled Panorama vs. Pivot.

Pivot Background Image

Like the Panorama control, the Pivot control supports having a Background configured as a Brush (Color or Gradient), as well as an image in the same way that a Panorama can be configured. This includes data binding the background image as well as dynamically loading the image.

Pivot Title Customization

The Pivot Title property can be modified exactly like the Panorama as demonstrated in the section above covering either modifying the TitleTemplate or simply setting the value onto the Title property via element property syntax.

Programmatically Set the Current PivotItem

The Pivot control exposes a SelectedItem property that can be set in order to display a particular PivotItem other than the default leftmost PivotItem. Simply provide a name to the Pivot and PivotItem controls so that they can be identified in code. This code in MainPage_Loaded in MainPage.xaml sets the second PivotItem as the default:

```
MainPivot.SelectedItem = SecondPivotItem;
```

In the next section I conclude this chapter with a comparison of the Pivot Control vs. the Panorama control.

Pivot vs. Panorama

As mentioned, the Panorama and Pivot controls have a lot in common in terms of base functionality. Both controls mimic the built-in native control versions in terms of behavior and animations yet provide a simple programming interface with strong customization available. The controls include built-in touch navigation with support for flick and pan for a great navigation experience.

From a programming standpoint both controls function like tab controls with an Items collection for either Panorama or PivotItem controls allowing rich content presentation in compact amount of space. Both controls allow the developer to focus on building the content within the Item control panes, which is usually a matter of customizing a ListBox control, greatly simplifying programming tasks while providing a rich user experience.

The controls themselves can be data bound with content template properties and item container styles for the Title, Header, and Item Panel, and so on. The controls also include full Blend support such as control template modification and visual states.

In terms of usage, the vast majority of Windows Phone 7 Silverlight applications will open to an initial page containing either a Panorama or Pivot control. For rich initial content presentation, the Panorama control is usually the better choice. For denser content presentation, or larger amounts of content, the Pivot control is ideal.

Many applications will consist of a root Panorama control with a PanoramaItem dedicated to a menu. The menu items then use the navigation framework to navigate the UI to sub-pages consisting of Pivot controls or plain old page depending on content needs. The hardware Back button provides navigation back to the root Panorama control and is in incredibly important part of the navigation framework.

Conclusion

In this chapter I provide a sweeping overview of the Silverlight user experience controls starting with layout controls, data binding, and a demonstration of how to take advantage of sample data. I then move on to a discussion of control templates and an overview of animation in Expression Blend. In the last section I cover an overview of the Panorama and Pivot controls, which are the major navigation controls in Windows Phone 7. In the next chapter I will cover input on Windows Phone 7.

CHAPTER 3

■ ■ ■

Handling Input on Windows Phone 7

Handling input is a critical aspect of any application, but it is an especially unique challenge on a mobile device. The first consideration is that the user is most likely not sitting in a comfortable chair sipping coffee, casually browsing the Internet. A mobile application user is most likely on the go, looking to just get a task done or find the needed information and be on their way.

The second consideration is that user input on a mobile device is quite different than handling input on the PC or even on the XBOX 360 for XNA Framework game development. A Windows Phone 7 mobile device may or may not have a physical keyboard, so you cannot author your application to depend on it. Even at 800px x480px screen resolution, screen real estate is still at a premium.

Mobile devices have unique hardware input capabilities for innovative user experiences, such as capacitive touch, accelerometer, and location. In this chapter, I cover handling user input in both Silverlight and XNA Windows Phone 7 applications.

■ **Note** The gesture samples use the Silverlight for Windows Phone Toolkit, available at
`http://silverlght.codeplex.com`. Please download the toolkit to compile the sample code.

■ **Note** This code in this chapter is broken up into two separate Solutions in the sample source code: Ch03_HandlingInput and Ch03_HandlingInput_Part2. Sample code starting in the location sample on forward is in the Part 2 solution.

The Keyboard

The last thing a mobile user wants to do is type on a mobile keyboard, but it is inevitable for many applications to require some form of text input. In this section I discuss keyboard capabilities and API enhancements to ease typing on the keyboard on Windows Phone 7 devices.

Physical Keyboard

Windows Phone 7 devices may also have a hardware slide-out keyboard, but your application will not pass certification in AppHub if it is dependent upon the hardware keyboard. Otherwise, from a software development perspective, programming for hardware keyboard input "just works." Of the six devices available at Windows Phone 7 launch, only one had a full slide-out keyboard, and another had a vertical QWERTY keyboard. The other four devices were pure touch devices without a physical keyboard.

Soft Input Panel (SIP) Keyboard

All Windows Phone 7 devices have a SIP keyboard used for entering text. Typing on the SIP keyboard built into Windows Phone 7 is a pretty comfortable means of entering text; however, it is still a small keyboard, so anything that a developer can do to ease typing can really help improve the overall user experience.

Programming with the Keyboard

Typing text on a mobile phone should be minimized as much as possible, but if text input is required, a developer should take advantage of capabilities to make typing as simple as possible. In the next section I cover InputScope, which is a must-have feature to take advantage of when typing is required in your Windows Phone 7 applications.

When testing keyboard input, you will be tempted to type on your PC keyboard; however, it does not work. You must use the mouse with the SIP keyboard in the Emulator for input.

■ **Tip** Click the Pause/Break button on your PC keyboard to enable typing in the emulator with your PC keyboard instead of having to use the mouse to "touch" the SIP.

InputScope

The InputScope property is available on the TextBox control, which is the primary control for text input. InputScope lets the developer customize the keyboard for the expected type of input. For example, the default behavior is that when you click into a TextBox, the SIP keyboard pops up, as shown in Figure 3–1.

Figure 3–1. Default SIP keyboard

The second TextBox has an InputScope of Text, which enables word selection just above the keyboard, as shown in Figure 3–2.

Figure 3–2. InputScope of Text SIP keyboard with word suggestion

With just one simple attribute, text input becomes much easier for the end user. Figure 3–3 shows three additional text input options, which I explain just after the figure.

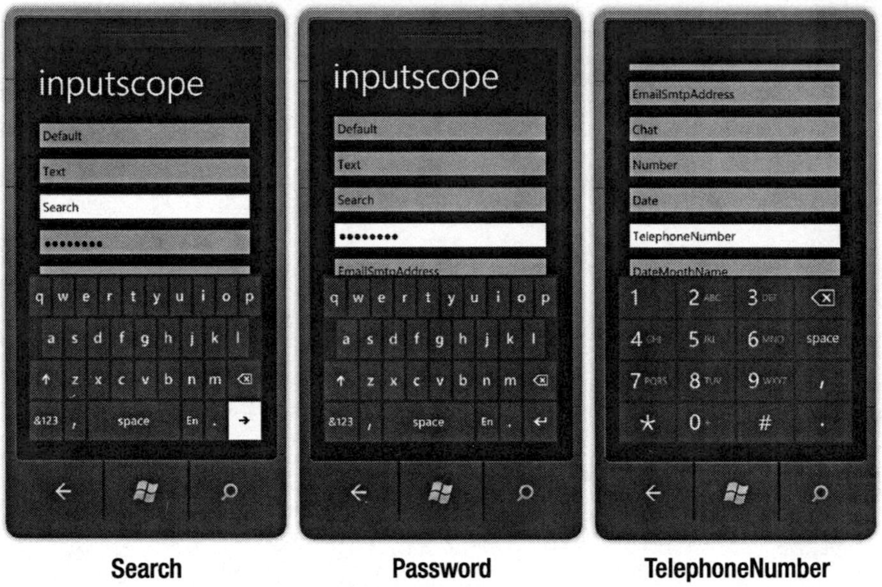

Figure 3–3. *Search, Password, and TelephoneNumber InputScope customizations*

Configuring an InputScope of Search turns the Enter key into a GO key with the idea that the user enters a search keyword and then clicks Enter to kick off a search. Password is not actually an InputScope. It is a custom TextBox class named PasswordBox that automatically hides data entry as the user types. An InputScope of TelephoneNumber brings up a phone keypad. As you can see, all of these could come in handy as you develop your application UI and optimize input for the end user. Table 3–1 lists the available InputScope options and their descriptions, reprinted here for your convenience from the Windows Phone 7 documentation.

Table 3–1. *Available InputScope Options*

Input Scope	Description
AddressCity	The text input pattern for a city address.
AddressCountryName	The text input pattern for the name of a country/region.
AddressCountryShortName	The text input pattern for the abbreviated name of a country/region.
AddressStateOrProvince	The text input pattern for a state or province.
AddressStreet	The text input pattern for a street address.

Input Scope	Description
AlphanumericFullWidth	The text input pattern for alphanumeric full-width characters (East-Asian languages only).
AlphanumericHalfWidth	The text input pattern for alphanumeric half-width characters (East-Asian languages only).
Chat	The SIP layout for text messaging, which recognizes pre-defined abbreviations. Supported only in Silverlight for Windows Phone.
CurrencyAmount	The text input pattern for amount of currency.
CurrencyAmountAndSymbol	The text input pattern for amount and symbol of currency.
CurrencyChinese	The text input pattern for Chinese currency.
Date	The text input pattern for a calendar date.
DateDay	The text input pattern for the numeric day in a calendar date.
DateDayName	The text input pattern for the name of the day in a calendar date.
DateMonth	The text input pattern for the numeric month in a calendar date.
DateMonthName	The text input pattern for the name of the month in a calendar date.
DateYear	The text input pattern for the year in a calendar date.
Default	The default handling of input commands.
Digits	The text input pattern for digits.
EmailNameOrAddress	The SIP layout for an e-mail name or address. Supported only in Silverlight for Windows Phone.
EmailSmtpAddress	The text input pattern for a Simple Mail Transfer Protocol (SMTP) e-mail address.
EmailUserName	The text input pattern for an e-mail user name.
FileName	The text input pattern for a file name.
FullFilePath	The text input pattern for the full path of a file.
Hanja	The text input pattern for Hanja characters (Korean characters).

Input Scope	Description
Hiragana	The text input pattern for the Hiragana writing system (a Japanese syllabary).
KatakanaFullWidth	The text input pattern for full-width Katakana characters (a Japanese syllabary).
KatakanaHalfWidth	The text input pattern for half-width Katakana characters (a Japanese syllabary).
LogOnName	The text input pattern for a log on name.
Maps	The SIP layout for entering a map location. Supported only in Silverlight for Windows Phone.
NameOrPhoneNumber	The SIP layout for SMS To field. Supported only in Silverlight for Windows Phone.
Number	The text input pattern for a number.
NumberFullWidth	The text input pattern for a full-width number.
OneChar	The text input pattern for one character.
Password	The text input pattern for a password.
PersonalFullName	The text input pattern for a person's full name.
PersonalGivenName	The text input pattern for a person's given name.
PersonalMiddleName	The text input pattern for a person's middle name.
PersonalNamePrefix	The text input pattern for the prefix of a person's name.
PersonalNameSuffix	The text input pattern for the suffix of a person's name.
PersonalSurname	The text input pattern for a person's surname.
PhraseList	The text input pattern for a phrase list.
PostalAddress	The text input pattern for a postal address.
PostalCode	The text input pattern for a postal code.
RegularExpression	The text input pattern for a regular expression.

Input Scope	Description
Search	The SIP layout for a search query. Supported only in Silverlight for Windows Phone.
Srgs	The text input pattern for the Speech Recognition Grammar Specification (SRGS).
TelephoneAreaCode	The text input pattern for a telephone area code.
TelephoneCountryCode	The text input pattern for a telephone country/region code.
TelephoneLocalNumber	The text input pattern for a telephone local number.
TelephoneNumber	The text input pattern for a telephone number.
Text	The software input panel (SIP) layout for standard text input. Supported only in Silverlight for Windows Phone.
Time	The text input pattern for the time.
TimeHour	The text input pattern for the hour of the time.
TimeMinorSec	The text input pattern for the minutes or seconds of time.
Url	The text input pattern for a Uniform Resource Locator (URL).
Xml	The text input pattern for XML.

Let's now shift gears and explore the available keyboard events.

Keyboard Events

There are two keyboard events available on the TextBox, as well as pretty much any other object that inherits from UIElement: the KeyDown and KeyUp events. Both events have a KeyEventArgs class in its parameters that provides access to the Key and PlatformKeyCode values native to the platform. It also provides access to the OriginalSource property that represents the control that raised the Keyboard event, as well as a Handled member to indicate that the key has been processed.

This completes our discussion of keyboard events. In general, typing should be minimized in a mobile application for the reasons listed previously, i.e., small screen, small keyboard, and so on. Mobile devices are optimized for touch input, especially modern devices with highly responsive capacitive touch screens that do not require a stylus. Let's now focus on touch input.

Touch Input

Most modern mobile devices that have touch screens do not require a stylus, which was necessary for resistive touch-based screens. Modern mobile devices are capacitive touch and respond very well to touch with a finger.

Windows Phone 7 supports up to four multi-touch contact points for XNA Framework development. Silverlight for Windows Phone supports two multi-touch contact points. As part of the platform, there is a touch driver and gesture engine under the covers that provides a consistent detection capability across hardware device OEMs and across applications.

As mentioned previously, Silverlight for Windows Phone 7 is based on Silverlight 3. The Windows Phone product team took the Silverlight 3 controls and APIs and optimized the controls for performance, for look and feel via control templates and styles and for input. The next section covers single-point touch as it relates to the controls optimized for Windows Phone 7.

Single-Point Touch

When a user clicks a Button control, TextBox control, ListBox control and the like on Windows Phone 7, it is single-point touch. For consistency, single-point touch events are translated to the Mouse events that you are familiar with when programming desktop Silverlight, Windows Forms, or other application frameworks. For example, touching a button appears as a Click event. Tapping to type text in a TextBox or touch a TextBlock control fires a MouseEnter, a MouseLeftButtonDown, a MouseLeftButtonUp, and a MouseLeave event.

The Chapter 3 SinglePointTouch project TextControlsMouseEventsPage.xaml page shows these events firing when you interact with the TextBox and TextBlock controls. You will notice when testing on a device that sometimes multiple MouseEnter/MouseLeave pairs can fire. You can also see multiple MouseMove events fire as well as a result of small movements in your finger when interacting with the controls. It's something to consider when using these events with touch, as opposed to mouse clicks on the desktop, and why discrete events like listening for click or gestures is recommended except when discrete touch points are required. Figure 3–4 shows the UI with the mouse events trace.

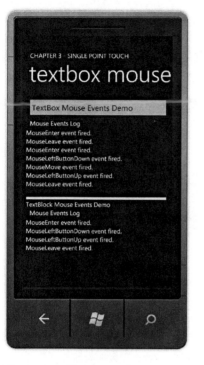

***Figure 3–4.** Text controls mouse events demo*

Listing 3–1 shows the TextControslMouseEventPage.xaml code file with the XAML markup.

***Listing 3–1.** WMAppManifest.xml Configuration File*

```
<phone:PhoneApplicationPage
  x:Class="SinglePointTouch.Pages.TextBoxMouseEventPage"
  xmlns="http://schemas.microsoft.com/winfx/2006/xaml/presentation"
  xmlns:x="http://schemas.microsoft.com/winfx/2006/xaml"
  xmlns:phone="clr-namespace:Microsoft.Phone.Controls;assembly=Microsoft.Phone"
  xmlns:shell="clr-namespace:Microsoft.Phone.Shell;assembly=Microsoft.Phone"
  xmlns:d="http://schemas.microsoft.com/expression/blend/2008"
  xmlns:mc="http://schemas.openxmlformats.org/markup-compatibility/2006"
  FontFamily="{StaticResource PhoneFontFamilyNormal}"
  FontSize="{StaticResource PhoneFontSizeNormal}"
  Foreground="{StaticResource PhoneForegroundBrush}"
  SupportedOrientations="Portrait" Orientation="Portrait"
  mc:Ignorable="d" d:DesignHeight="768" d:DesignWidth="480"
  shell:SystemTray.IsVisible="True">

  <!--LayoutRoot is the root grid where all page content is placed-->
  <Grid x:Name="LayoutRoot" Background="Transparent">
    <Grid.RowDefinitions>
      <RowDefinition Height="Auto"/>
      <RowDefinition Height="*"/>
```

```xml
        </Grid.RowDefinitions>

        <!--TitlePanel contains the name of the application and page title-->
        <StackPanel x:Name="TitlePanel" Grid.Row="0" Margin="12,17,0,28">
          <TextBlock x:Name="ApplicationTitle" Text="CHAPTER 3 - SINGLE POINT TOUCH"
                     Style="{StaticResource PhoneTextNormalStyle}"/>
          <TextBlock x:Name="PageTitle" Text="textbox mouse events" Margin="9,-7,0,0"
                     Style="{StaticResource PhoneTextTitle1Style}"/>
        </StackPanel>
        <!--ContentPanel - place additional content here-->
        <Grid x:Name="ContentPanel" Grid.Row="1" Margin="12,0,12,0">
          <StackPanel Orientation="Vertical">
            <TextBox HorizontalAlignment="Left" x:Name="MouseEventsTextBox"
              Text="TextBox Mouse Events Demo" Width="460" Height="72"
              MouseEnter="MouseEventsTextBox_MouseEnter"
              MouseLeave="MouseEventsTextBox_MouseLeave"
              MouseLeftButtonDown="MouseEventsTextBox_MouseLeftButtonDown"
              MouseLeftButtonUp="MouseEventsTextBox_MouseLeftButtonUp"
              MouseMove="MouseEventsTextBox_MouseMove"
              MouseWheel="MouseEventsTextBox_MouseWheel" />
            <TextBlock Height="30" HorizontalAlignment="Left" Margin="12,0,0,0"
                       x:Name="MouseEventStatusText" Text="Mouse Events Log"
                       Width="438" />
            <ListBox Height="217" x:Name="MouseEventLogListBox" />
            <Rectangle Fill="#FFF4F4F5" Height="10" Stroke="Black" Margin="0,0,6,0"/>
            <TextBlock TextWrapping="Wrap" Text="TextBlock Mouse Events Demo"
              Margin="0" Name="TextBlockMouseEventsDemo"
              MouseEnter="TextBlockMouseEventsDemo_MouseEnter"
              MouseLeave="TextBlockMouseEventsDemo_MouseLeave"
              MouseLeftButtonDown="TextBlockMouseEventsDemo_MouseLeftButtonDown"
              MouseLeftButtonUp="TextBlockMouseEventsDemo_MouseLeftButtonUp"
              MouseMove="TextBlockMouseEventsDemo_MouseMove"
              MouseWheel="TextBlockMouseEventsDemo_MouseWheel" />
            <TextBlock Height="30" HorizontalAlignment="Left" Margin="12,0,0,0"
              x:Name="MouseEventStatusTextBlock" Text="Mouse Events Log"
              Width="438" />
            <ListBox Height="220" x:Name="MouseEventLogListBox2" />
          </StackPanel>
        </Grid>
    </Grid>
</phone:PhoneApplicationPage>
```

In Listing 3–1, you can see the event handler assignments like this one assigning an event handler to the MouseEnter event for the MouseEventsTextBox object

```
MouseEnter="MouseEventsTextBox_MouseEnter"
```

The code-behind file has the related event handlers that simply write a text message to the MouseEventLogListBox like this one

```csharp
private void MouseEventsTextBox_MouseEnter(object sender, MouseEventArgs e)
{
  MouseEventLogListBox.Items.Add("MouseEnter event fired.");
}
```

Now that we have covered the mouse events, we will next look at how to use the mouse events for raw touch.

Raw Touch with Mouse Events

In addition to indicating a "click" or touch even, mouse events can be used for raw touch. An example of raw touch is drawing with your finger, where you need individual touch locations. What enables raw touch with mouse events is the MouseEventArgs class passed into the mouse events. The following are the key properties of the MouseEventArgs class:

- **GetPosition(UIElement relativeTo):** Gets the position of the mouse event in relation to the passed in object. Returns a Point object.

- **OriginalSource:** Provides a reference to the object that raised the event.

- **StylusDevice:** Returns a StylusDevice object that includes the set of stylus points associated with the input.

The StylusDevice object contains a GetStylusPoints method that returns a StylusPointsCollection that we can draw an object onscreen to represent user touches. The StylusPoint class is enhanced over the Point class with the StylusPoint.PressureFactor property. Because PressureFactor is a float, we can assign it to the Opacity property of the object we draw onscreen to represent touches such that the Opacity indicates whether it is a light or heavy press on the screen. So a light pressure press will have a lower opacity when drawn on screen.

In the next couple of sections we will build a mini finger drawing application that includes multi-color selection, ListBox customizations, animations, the application bar, and basic drawing functionality.

Setting Up the Basic UI

Add a Windows Phone Portrait Page new item to the SinglePointTouch project. Uncomment the sample ApplicationBar code at the bottom of the page. We will use the ApplicationBar to implement commands to clear the drawing canvas, set the touch object size, and so on.

At the top we set the title and subtitle for the page. In the default ContentPanel Grid object, we add a Canvas object. On top of the Canvas object is a Rectangle that receives the mouse events. We take advantage of absolute positioning in the Canvas object to place the objects that represent user touches using X and Y coordinates provided by StylusPoint objects. The following is a XAML snippet of the TitlePanel and ContentPanel:

```
<!--TitlePanel contains the name of the application and page title-->
<StackPanel x:Name="TitlePanel" Grid.Row="0" Margin="12,17,0,28">
  <TextBlock x:Name="ApplicationTitle" Text="CHAPTER 3 - SinglePointTouch"
           Style="{StaticResource PhoneTextNormalStyle}"/>
  <TextBlock x:Name="PageTitle" Text="finger painting" Margin="9,-7,0,0"
           Style="{StaticResource PhoneTextTitle1Style}"/>
</StackPanel>

<!--ContentPanel - place additional content here-->
<Grid x:Name="ContentPanel" Grid.Row="1" Margin="24,0,0,0">
  <Canvas x:Name="DrawCanvas"  >
    <Rectangle Fill="White"  Stroke="Black"
        MouseMove="Rectangle_MouseMove" Width="456" Height="535"  />
  </Canvas>
```

```
</Grid>
```

The following is the Rectangle_MouseMove event handler on the Rectangle object and related helper method:

```
private void Rectangle_MouseMove(object sender, MouseEventArgs e)
{
  foreach (StylusPoint p in e.StylusDevice.GetStylusPoints(DrawCanvas))
  {
    Ellipse ellipse = new Ellipse();
    ellipse.SetValue(Canvas.LeftProperty, p.X);
    ellipse.SetValue(Canvas.TopProperty, p.Y);
    ellipse.Opacity = p.PressureFactor;
    ellipse.Width = 20d;
    ellipse.Height = 20d;
    ellipse.IsHitTestVisible = false;
    ellipse.Stroke = new SolidColorBrush(Colors.Black);
    ellipse.Fill = new SolidColorBrush(Colors.Black);
    DrawCanvas.Children.Add(ellipse);
  }
}
```

The application uses the MouseMove event and the StylusPointsCollection to draw small Ellipse objects to the screen as you drag the mouse on the emulator or finger on a device across the screen. Figure 3–5 shows the UI in action.

Figure 3–5. *Basic finger paining UI*

Finger painting without multiple colors is boring. Let's add a ListBox and populate it with the built-in System.Windows.Media.Colors collection so that the user can select an item and change the "finger paint" color. We first create a couple of classes to encapsulate the System.Windows.Media.Colors collection since we cannot data bind directly to it. See Listing 3–2.

Listing 3–2. The ColorClass Code File

```
public class ColorClass
{
  public Brush ColorBrush { get; set; }
  public String ColorName { get; set; }
}
```

It contains a Brush to represent the RGB values for the color and a text name for the color. We need a collection of ColorClass objects to bind to. Listing 3–3 has the simple class that generates a collection of ColorClass objects.

Listing 3–3. The ColorsClass Code File

```
public class ColorsClass
{
  List<ColorClass> _colors;
  public ColorsClass()
  {
    _colors = new List<ColorClass>();
    _colors.Add(new ColorClass() {
      ColorBrush = new SolidColorBrush(Colors.Blue), ColorName = "Blue" });
    _colors.Add(new ColorClass() {
      ColorBrush = new SolidColorBrush(Colors.Brown), ColorName = "Brown"});
    _colors.Add(new ColorClass() {
      ColorBrush = new SolidColorBrush(Colors.Cyan), ColorName = "Cyan"});
    _colors.Add(new ColorClass() {
      ColorBrush = new SolidColorBrush(Colors.DarkGray),
      ColorName = "DarkGray"});
    _colors.Add(new ColorClass() {
      ColorBrush = new SolidColorBrush(Colors.Gray), ColorName = "Gray"});
    _colors.Add(new ColorClass() {
      ColorBrush = new SolidColorBrush(Colors.Green), ColorName = "Green"});
    _colors.Add(new ColorClass() {
      ColorBrush = new SolidColorBrush(Colors.LightGray),
      ColorName = "LightGray" });
    _colors.Add(new ColorClass() {
      ColorBrush = new SolidColorBrush(Colors.Magenta),
      ColorName = "Magenta" });
    _colors.Add(new ColorClass() {
      ColorBrush = new SolidColorBrush(Colors.Orange), ColorName="Orange"});
    _colors.Add(new ColorClass() {
      ColorBrush = new SolidColorBrush(Colors.Purple), ColorName="Purple"});
    _colors.Add(new ColorClass() {
      ColorBrush = new SolidColorBrush(Colors.Red), ColorName = "Red"});
    _colors.Add(new ColorClass() {
      ColorBrush = new SolidColorBrush(Colors.White), ColorName = "White"});
    _colors.Add(new ColorClass() {
      ColorBrush = new SolidColorBrush(Colors.Yellow), ColorName = "Yellow"});
    _colors.Add(new ColorClass() {
```

```
      ColorBrush = new SolidColorBrush(Colors.Black), ColorName = "Black"});
  }

  public List<ColorClass> ColorsCollection
  {
    get { return _colors; }
  }
}
```

All of the work is done in the constructor using abbreviated syntax to create the collection. Data bind the ColorListBox.ItemsSource to the ColorsClass.ColorsCollection either manually in Visual Studio or with Expression Blend. By default the ColorListBox scrolls vertically. To have the ColorListBox scroll horizontally, right-click on the ColorListBox in Expression Blend and select Edit Additional Templates ➤ Edit Layout of Items (ItemsPanel), Edit a Copy…to edit the template. Drop a StackPanel on to the root ItemsPanelTemplate object. Configure the StackPanel to have Orientation set to Horizontal and that's it: the ColorListBox will scroll horizontally. The last bit of customization is to create an ItemTemplate for ColorListBox. ColorListBox.ItemsSource data binds to the collection. The ItemTemplate has that as its context, so the ItemTemplate data binds to individual records. The following is the ItemTemplate:

```xml
<DataTemplate x:Key="FingerPaintingColorTemplate">
  <StackPanel Orientation="Vertical">
    <Rectangle Fill="{Binding ColorBrush}" HorizontalAlignment="Left"
      Height="95" Stroke="Black" VerticalAlignment="Top" Width="95" Margin="4,4,4,0"/>
    <TextBlock HorizontalAlignment="Center" TextWrapping="Wrap"
      Text="{Binding ColorName}" VerticalAlignment="Center" Margin="0"/>
  </StackPanel>
</DataTemplate>
```

The ColorListBox DataTemplate consists of a Rectangle that displays the color based on the ColorClass.ColorBrush property and a TextBlock that displays the name of the color based on the ColorClass.ColorName property. Figure 3–6 shows the resulting work.

Figure 3–6. Finger painting UI with ColorListBox

In PhoneApplicationPage_Loaded, set the SelectedIndex on ColorListBox so that a color is always selected.. The drawing code is updated to obtain the ColorListBox.SelectedItem object in order to set the brush color for the Ellipse.

```
private void Rectangle_MouseMove(object sender, MouseEventArgs e)
{
  foreach (StylusPoint p in e.StylusDevice.GetStylusPoints(DrawCanvas))
  {
    Ellipse ellipse = new Ellipse();
    ellipse.SetValue(Canvas.LeftProperty, p.X);
    ellipse.SetValue(Canvas.TopProperty, p.Y);
    ellipse.Opacity = p.PressureFactor;
    ellipse.Width = 20d;
    ellipse.Height = 20d;
    ellipse.IsHitTestVisible = false;
    ellipse.Stroke = ((ColorClass)ColorListBox.SelectedItem).ColorBrush;
    ellipse.Fill = ((ColorClass)ColorListBox.SelectedItem).ColorBrush;
    DrawCanvas.Children.Add(ellipse);
  }
}
```

The application will now allow finger painting using the selected color in the ColorListBox. In the next section we will expand the painting functionality in the application.

Expand Painting Functionality

Let's now add additional painting functionality to make the application more usable, such as to clear the drawing surface, increase the touch pencil size, decrease the touch pencil size, show/hide the color palate to change drawing color, and to set the background for the image. Here is how the UI is set up:

- **Clear:** Erase the drawing surface (trashcan icon).

- **Touch color:** Shows the color palate to set the drawing color (edit pencil icon).

- **Pencil size:** Increases pencil size (plus sign icon).

- **Pencil size:** Decreases pencil size (minus sign icon).

- **Set background color menu item:** Shows the color palate to set the background color.

In Expression Blend, edit the Application Bar to provide four application bar icons and one menu item. Expression Blend provides access to the built-in icons, as shown in Figure 3–7.

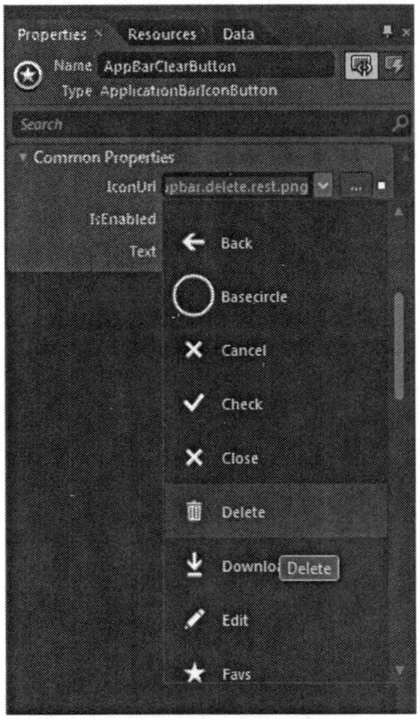

***Figure 3–7.** Finger painting UI with ColorListBox*

Once the application bar icons and menu item are configured visually in Blend, set the ColorListBox control's Visibility to Visibility.Collapsed so that it is only visible when needed. We switch over to Visual Studio to add the event handlers in XAML for the Application Bar button icons and menu item. Listings 3–4 and 3–5 have the full source code of the mini-application.

Listing 3–4. The FingerPaintingPageMouseEvents.xaml Code File

```
<phone:PhoneApplicationPage
  xmlns="http://schemas.microsoft.com/winfx/2006/xaml/presentation"
  xmlns:x="http://schemas.microsoft.com/winfx/2006/xaml"
  xmlns:phone="clr-namespace:Microsoft.Phone.Controls;assembly=Microsoft.Phone"
  xmlns:shell="clr-namespace:Microsoft.Phone.Shell;assembly=Microsoft.Phone"
  xmlns:d="http://schemas.microsoft.com/expression/blend/2008"
  xmlns:mc="http://schemas.openxmlformats.org/markup-compatibility/2006"
  xmlns:SinglePointTouch="clr-namespace:SinglePointTouch"
  x:Class="SinglePointTouch.Pages.FingerPaintingPageMouseEvents"
  SupportedOrientations="Portrait" Orientation="Portrait"
  mc:Ignorable="d" d:DesignHeight="696" d:DesignWidth="480"
  shell:SystemTray.IsVisible="True" Loaded="PhoneApplicationPage_Loaded">
  <phone:PhoneApplicationPage.Resources>
    <SinglePointTouch:ColorsClass x:Key="ColorsClassDataSource"
      d:IsDataSource="True"/>
    <DataTemplate x:Key="FingerPaintingColorTemplate">
      <StackPanel Orientation="Vertical">
        <Rectangle Fill="{Binding ColorBrush}" HorizontalAlignment="Left"
          Height="95" Stroke="Black" VerticalAlignment="Top" Width="95"
          Margin="4,4,4,0"/>
        <TextBlock HorizontalAlignment="Center" TextWrapping="Wrap"
          Text="{Binding ColorName}" VerticalAlignment="Center" Margin="0"/>
      </StackPanel>
    </DataTemplate>
    <ItemsPanelTemplate x:Key="FingerPaintingColorsListBoxItemsPanel">
      <StackPanel Orientation="Horizontal"/>
    </ItemsPanelTemplate>
  </phone:PhoneApplicationPage.Resources>

  <phone:PhoneApplicationPage.ApplicationBar>
    <shell:ApplicationBar IsVisible="True" IsMenuEnabled="True">
      <shell:ApplicationBarIconButton x:Name="AppBarClearButton"
        IconUri="/icons/appbar.delete.rest.png" Text="clear"
        Click="AppBarClearButton_Click" />
      <shell:ApplicationBarIconButton x:Name="AppBarChangeTouchColorButton"
        IconUri="/icons/appbar.edit.rest.png" Text="touch color"
        Click="AppBarChangeTouchColor_Click"/>
      <shell:ApplicationBarIconButton x:Name="AppBarIncreaseButton"
        IconUri="/icons/appbar.add.rest.png" Text="pencil size"
        Click="AppBarIncreaseButton_Click"/>
      <shell:ApplicationBarIconButton x:Name="AppBarDecreaseButton"
        IconUri="/icons/appbar.minus.rest.png" Text="pencil size"
        Click="AppBarDecreaseButton_Click"/>
      <shell:ApplicationBar.MenuItems>
        <shell:ApplicationBarMenuItem  Text="Set Background Color"
          x:Name="SetBackgroundColorMenuItem"
          Click="SetBackgroundColorMenuItem_Click" />
      </shell:ApplicationBar.MenuItems>
    </shell:ApplicationBar>
  </phone:PhoneApplicationPage.ApplicationBar>

  <phone:PhoneApplicationPage.FontFamily>
```

```xml
      <StaticResource ResourceKey="PhoneFontFamilyNormal"/>
    </phone:PhoneApplicationPage.FontFamily>
    <phone:PhoneApplicationPage.FontSize>
      <StaticResource ResourceKey="PhoneFontSizeNormal"/>
    </phone:PhoneApplicationPage.FontSize>
    <phone:PhoneApplicationPage.Foreground>
      <StaticResource ResourceKey="PhoneForegroundBrush"/>
    </phone:PhoneApplicationPage.Foreground>
    <Grid x:Name="LayoutRoot" Background="Transparent" DataContext=
        "{Binding Source={StaticResource ColorsClassDataSource}}" >
      <Grid.RowDefinitions>
        <RowDefinition Height="Auto"/>
        <RowDefinition Height="*"/>
      </Grid.RowDefinitions>

      <!--TitlePanel contains the name of the application and page title-->
      <StackPanel x:Name="TitlePanel" Grid.Row="0" Margin="12,17,0,28">
        <TextBlock x:Name="ApplicationTitle" Text="CHAPTER 3 - SinglePointTouch"
                   Style="{StaticResource PhoneTextNormalStyle}"/>
        <TextBlock x:Name="PageTitle" Text="finger painting" Margin="9,-7,0,0"
                   Style="{StaticResource PhoneTextTitle1Style}"/>
      </StackPanel>

      <!--ContentPanel - place additional content here-->
      <Grid x:Name="ContentPanel" Grid.Row="1" Margin="24,0,0,0">
        <Canvas x:Name="DrawCanvas"  >
                  <Rectangle Fill="White"  Stroke="Black" Name="BlankRectangle"
                       MouseMove="Rectangle_MouseMove" Width="456" Height="535"  />
        </Canvas>
        <ListBox x:Name="ColorListBox" Margin="0"
          ScrollViewer.HorizontalScrollBarVisibility="Auto"
          ScrollViewer.VerticalScrollBarVisibility="Disabled"
          ItemsPanel="{StaticResource FingerPaintingColorsListBoxItemsPanel}"
          VerticalAlignment="Top" ItemsSource="{Binding ColorsCollection}"
          ItemTemplate="{StaticResource FingerPaintingColorTemplate}"
          Background="Black" SelectedIndex="-1" HorizontalAlignment="Right"
          Width="456" RenderTransformOrigin="0.5,0.5"
          SelectionChanged="ColorListBox_SelectionChanged" Visibility="Collapsed">
        </ListBox>
      </Grid>
    </Grid>
</phone:PhoneApplicationPage>
```

Listing 3–5. *The FingerPaintingPageMouseEvents.xaml.cs Code File*

```csharp
using System;
using System.Windows;
using System.Windows.Controls;
using System.Windows.Input;
using System.Windows.Media;
using System.Windows.Shapes;
using System.Windows.Threading;
using Microsoft.Phone.Controls;
```

```
namespace SinglePointTouch.Pages
{
  public partial class FingerPaintingPageMouseEvents : PhoneApplicationPage
  {
    private Rectangle _backgroundRectangle;
    private double _touchRadius = 20d;
    private bool ColorBackgroundMode = false;
    private int TouchPaintingSelectedColorIndex;

    public FingerPaintingPageMouseEvents()
    {
      InitializeComponent();

      _backgroundRectangle = BlankRectangle;
    }

    private void Rectangle_MouseMove(object sender, MouseEventArgs e)
    {
      foreach (StylusPoint p in e.StylusDevice.GetStylusPoints(DrawCanvas))
      {
        Ellipse ellipse = new Ellipse();
        ellipse.SetValue(Canvas.LeftProperty, p.X);
        ellipse.SetValue(Canvas.TopProperty, p.Y);
        ellipse.Opacity = p.PressureFactor;
        ellipse.Width = _touchRadius;
        ellipse.Height = _touchRadius;
        ellipse.IsHitTestVisible = false;
        ellipse.Stroke = ((ColorClass)ColorListBox.SelectedItem).ColorBrush;
        ellipse.Fill = ((ColorClass)ColorListBox.SelectedItem).ColorBrush;
        DrawCanvas.Children.Add(ellipse);
      }
    }

    private void PhoneApplicationPage_Loaded(object sender, RoutedEventArgs e)
    {
      ColorListBox.SelectedIndex = 0;

      //Setup memory tracking timer
      DispatcherTimer DebugMemoryTimer = new DispatcherTimer();
      DebugMemoryTimer.Interval = new TimeSpan(0, 0, 0, 0, 5000);
      DebugMemoryTimer.Tick += DebugMemoryInfo_Tick;
      DebugMemoryTimer.Start();
    }

    // Track memory Info
    void DebugMemoryInfo_Tick(object sender, EventArgs e)
    {
      //GC.GetTotalMemory(true);
      long deviceTotalMemory =
        (long)Microsoft.Phone.Info.DeviceExtendedProperties.GetValue(
        "DeviceTotalMemory");
      long applicationCurrentMemoryUsage =
        (long)Microsoft.Phone.Info.DeviceExtendedProperties.GetValue(
        "ApplicationCurrentMemoryUsage");
```

```
  long applicationPeakMemoryUsage =
   (long)Microsoft.Phone.Info.DeviceExtendedProperties.GetValue(
   "ApplicationPeakMemoryUsage");

  System.Diagnostics.Debug.WriteLine("--> " +
    DateTime.Now.ToLongTimeString());
  System.Diagnostics.Debug.WriteLine("--> Device Total : " +
    deviceTotalMemory.ToString());
  System.Diagnostics.Debug.WriteLine("--> App Current : " +
    applicationCurrentMemoryUsage.ToString());
  System.Diagnostics.Debug.WriteLine("--> App Peak : " +
    applicationPeakMemoryUsage.ToString());
}

private void AppBarClearButton_Click(object sender, EventArgs e)
{
  DrawCanvas.Children.Clear();
  DrawCanvas.Children.Add(BlankRectangle);
  BlankRectangle.Fill = new SolidColorBrush(Colors.White);
}

private void AppBarIncreaseButton_Click(object sender, EventArgs e)
{
  if (_touchRadius <= 30d)
  {
    _touchRadius += 5;
  }
}

private void AppBarDecreaseButton_Click(object sender, EventArgs e)
{
  if (_touchRadius > 20d)
  {
    _touchRadius -= 5;
  }
}

private void SetBackgroundColorMenuItem_Click(object sender, EventArgs e)
{
  ColorListBox.Visibility = Visibility.Visible;
  ColorBackgroundMode = true;
  TouchPaintingSelectedColorIndex = ColorListBox.SelectedIndex;
}

private void ColorListBox_SelectionChanged(object sender,
  SelectionChangedEventArgs e)
{
  ColorListBox.Visibility = Visibility.Collapsed;
  if (ColorBackgroundMode == true)
  {
    _backgroundRectangle.Fill =
      ((ColorClass)ColorListBox.SelectedItem).ColorBrush;
    ColorBackgroundMode = false;
    ColorListBox.SelectedIndex = TouchPaintingSelectedColorIndex;
```

```
      }
    }

    private void AppBarChangeTouchColor_Click(object sender, EventArgs e)
    {
      ColorListBox.Visibility = Visibility.Visible;
    }
  }
}
```

In Listing 3–5 there is memory-tracking code to help analyze memory consumption that I cover in the next section.

Analyzing Memory

In Listing 3–5 there is an event handler named DebugMemoryInfo_Tick, as well as code in the PhoneApplicationPage_Loaded method to fire the Tick event for a DispatcherTimer object named TrackMemoryTimer. The DebugMemoryInfo_Tick event handler generates this text to the Output window in Visual Studio when the finger painting page is launched in the SinglePointTouch project.

```
--> 7:14:50 PM
--> Device Total : 497618944
--> App Current : 11014144
--> App Peak : 12492800
```

Next, draw a sample image, such as that shown in Figure 3–8.

Figure 3–8. Finger painting sample image

What follows is the resulting memory consumption:

```
--> 7:14:36 AM
--> Device Total : 390012928
--> App Current : 24748032
--> App Peak : 24748032
```

The emulator has essentially unlimited memory so consuming almost 250MB of RAM runs fine. You could finger paint a similar image on a physical device with 512MB, and it would be fine as well. However, for certification in AppHub, applications need to stay under 90MB to pass. This is because on a device with 256MB of RAM, consuming more than that could impact performance.

Tracking memory using this script or something similar is a very important aspect of performance tuning WP7 applications, especially when testing on the emulator that essentially has unlimited resources.

■ **Tip** Applications can momentarily go over 90MB and not crash, so don't panic if your application peaks over 90MB, but settles in below 90MB.

The reason the finger painting application consumes memory is that it is a purely vector-based drawing consisting of Ellipse objects. The Ellipse objects can yield an impressionistic effect with careful drawing but it does result in high memory consumption. As a user moves the mouse, new Ellipse objects are drawn to screen. When drawing over an area that is already colored, the old color is still present underneath in Ellipse objects. Options to investigate are to use Silverlight geometry primitives instead of Ellipse objects. Another option to reduce memory consumption is to use the WritableBitmap class to "burn" the objects into the background as a way to collapse the vector objects into simple raster bitmaps.

The Mouse and Touch events are familiar to developers and easy to work with; however, they should only be used when absolutely necessary, such as when you need individual touch points. The MSDN documentation has a section titled "Performance Considerations in Applications for Windows Phone" available here

```
http://msdn.microsoft.com/en-us/library/ff967560(v=VS.92).aspx
```

This white paper has a section titled "User Input" that recommends using Manipulation Events instead of mouse and touch events or performance and compatibility reasons for all scenarios other than when you need individual points. This chapter covers gestures and manipulation events next as part of multi-point touch.

Multi-Point Touch

As mentioned previously, Silverlight applications are generally based on the control framework and single touch when interacting with controls. There are parts of applications that may require multi-touch. Windows Phone 7 supports up to four touch points, which are available to both Silverlight- and XNA Framework-based applications. Examples of multi-touch in Silverlight would be image manipulation, zooming in or out on a news article to adjust the font, and so on.

In the XNA Framework, multi-touch is essential, since game-based user experiences are generally highly customized. One example of multi-touch in the XNA Framework are having one thumb manipulating a virtual accelerator and the other thumb manipulating a virtual brake in a driving game. Another example is one thumb manipulating a virtual joystick and the other thumb touching buttons to jump or shoot.

Controls

A couple of controls that are part of the Windows Phone 7 development platform include support for multi-touch. The WebBrowser control supports pinch/zoom and pan gestures. Another control that has built-in support for multi-touch is the Bing Maps control, which also supports pinch/zoom and pan gestures.

The other control that is more generic than the WebBrowser and Bing Maps controls is the ScrollViewer panel control, which supports flick and pan gestures for contained content. The ScrollViewer project in the Chapter 3 solution demonstrates the ScrollViewer Control. Once the solution is created, drag a ScrollViewer control onto the ContentPanel Grid control in Expression Blend. Reset the Height and Width on the Image control to Auto. Also reset layout on the ScrollViewer so that it fills the ContentPanel.

Drag an Image control onto the ScrollViewer control. Set the Source property of the Image control to point to the France.jpg image in the images folder of the ScrollViewer solution. Set the Stretch property on the Image control to None so that it expands beyond the screen bounds to full size. On the containing ScrollViewer control, set the HorizontalScrollBarVisibility property to Auto from Disabled. We want to be able to pan and flick the image in all directions.

Once layout is configured property for the controls as detailed in the previous paragraphs, we are ready to test. When you run the application, you can see that you get pan and flick gestures "for free," provided by the ScrollViewer control. In the next couple of sections I cover multi-touch programming, gestures, and manipulation events.

Raw Touch with Touch.FrameReported

The mouse events covered in the previous section may work fine for many cases, but may feel a bit clunky. In this section we will implement the finger-painting application using Touch.FrameReported for more fine-grained raw touch development.

We start with a copy of the previous finger painting application but change the Page class from FingerPaintingPageMouseEvents to FingerPaintingPageTouchEvents to prevent compilation errors with duplicate names. We keep both pages in the SinglePointTouch project, though System.Windows.Input.Touch supports multi-touch, which is an advantage over the mouse events. The next step is to remove the MouseMove event handler from the Rectangle and comment out the Rectangle_MouseMove event handler in the code behind.

In the PhoneApplicationPage_Loaded event, wire-up the FrameReported event like this

```
System.Windows.Input.Touch.FrameReported += new TouchFrameEventHandler(Touch_FrameReported);
```

To prevent exceptions when navigating back and forth to the page, the event is disconnected in the unload event here

```
private void PhoneApplicationPage_Unloaded(object sender, RoutedEventArgs e)
{
  System.Windows.Input.Touch.FrameReported -= Touch_FrameReported;
}
```

The Touch_FrameReported event is where the touch action happens and directly replaces the Rectangle_MouseMove event from the previous example. The FrameReported event TouchFrameEventArgs class provides a rich set of properties to provide fine-grained control over touch development. Table 3–2 provides a summary of its properties and events.

Table 3–2. Available InputScope Options

Member	Description
GetPrimaryTouchPoint	Returns the primary or first finger touch point for the reported frame as a TouchPoint class value.
GetTouchPoints	Returns a collection of all of the TouchPoint class objects from the reported frame.
SuspendMousePromotionUntilTouchUp	Disables promoting the low-level touch events from becoming mouse events. Useful if you want to override mouse event behavior in an application.
Timestamp	Determines how much time has passed between touch events.

Unlike with the mouse events StylusPoint class, the TouchPoint class does not support PressureFactor values, so Opacity is not varied by pressure. The TouchPoint class does support a Size value for the touch action but the size resolves to a very small value regardless of whether drawing with a small finger or larger finger, making the Size value less useful. The following is the final Touch_FrameReported event handler:

```
void Touch_FrameReported(object sender, TouchFrameEventArgs e)
{
  foreach (TouchPoint p in e.GetTouchPoints(DrawCanvas))
  {
    if ((InDrawingMode) && (p.Action == TouchAction.Move))
    {
      Ellipse ellipse = new Ellipse();
      ellipse.SetValue(Canvas.LeftProperty, p.Position.X);
      ellipse.SetValue(Canvas.TopProperty, p.Position.Y);
      ellipse.Width = _touchRadius;
      ellipse.Height = _touchRadius;
      ellipse.IsHitTestVisible = false;
      ellipse.Stroke = ((ColorClass)ColorListBox.SelectedItem).ColorBrush;
      ellipse.Fill = ((ColorClass)ColorListBox.SelectedItem).ColorBrush;
      DrawCanvas.Children.Add(ellipse);
    }
  }
}
```

Notice that this code has an additional check on the Boolean variable InDrawingMode. The value of InDrawingMode is set to false when showing the color selector ColorListBox. This is because the Touch.FrameReported event fires no matter what control has focus. So without additional checks, selecting or scrolling colors would generate additional touch events on the DrawCanvas Canvas object. Raw touch with Touch.FrameReported is truly raw touch processing.

The mouse events have a nice benefit over Touch.FrameReported. The mouse events generate StylusPoint objects, which include a PressureFactor value instead of the TouchPoint objects for Touch.FrameReported. This allows varying the Opacity, for a better drawing experience. However, for other touch-related programming where Gestures or Manipulations cannot provide needed functionality, raw touch with Touch.FrameReported is recommended over mouse events

Multi-Touch with Raw Touch

One capability that Touch.FrameReported provides over mouse events is multi-touch capabilities via the TouchPoint class. The TouchPoint class has the following two members that allow tracking of state and history.

- **Action:** Identifies whether the touch action is Down, Move, or Up.

- **TouchDevice:** Contains an ID that represents the "finger" as it moves about the screen.

With these two properties it is possible to track the state of the touch as well as associated history as the user moves their finger around the screen. The MultiTouchwithRawTouch project is a simple program that tracks up to four touch actions by a user. Essentially you can place four fingers on the screen and watch the Rectangle objects follow your fingers on the screen. The XAML for the project is a generic page that has Rectangle objects dynamically added to a Canvas panel added to the default ContentPanel Grid. Listing 3–6 contains the source code for the code-behind file.

Listing 3–6. MultiTouchwithRawTouch MainPage.xaml.cs Code File

```
using System.Collections.Generic;
using System.Linq;
using System.Windows;
using System.Windows.Controls;
using System.Windows.Input;
using System.Windows.Media;
using System.Windows.Shapes;
using Microsoft.Phone.Controls;

namespace MultiTouchwithRawTouch
{
  public partial class MainPage : PhoneApplicationPage
  {
    List<TrackedTouchPoint> trackedTouchPoints = new List<TrackedTouchPoint>();

    // Constructor
    public MainPage()
    {
      InitializeComponent();

      Touch.FrameReported += new TouchFrameEventHandler(Touch_FrameReported);
    }

    void Touch_FrameReported(object sender, TouchFrameEventArgs e)
    {
      foreach (TouchPoint tp in e.GetTouchPoints(DrawCanvas))
      {
        tp.TouchDevice.
        TrackedTouchPoint ttp = null;
        var query = from point in trackedTouchPoints
                    where point.ID == tp.TouchDevice.Id
```

```
                  select point;
    if (query.Count() != 0)
      ttp = query.First();

    switch (tp.Action)
    {
      case TouchAction.Down: ttp = new TrackedTouchPoint();
        ttp.ID = tp.TouchDevice.Id;
        if (trackedTouchPoints.Count == 0)
        {
          ttp.IsPrimary = true;
          DrawCanvas.Children.Clear();
        }
        trackedTouchPoints.Add(ttp);
        ttp.Position = tp.Position;
        ttp.Draw(DrawCanvas);
        break;

      case TouchAction.Up: ttp.UnDraw(DrawCanvas);
        trackedTouchPoints.Remove(ttp);
        break;
      default:
        ttp.Position = tp.Position;
        ttp.Draw(DrawCanvas);
        break;
    }
  }
  CleanUp(e.GetTouchPoints(DrawCanvas));
}

private void CleanUp(TouchPointCollection tpc)
{
  List<int> ToDelete = new List<int>();
  foreach (TrackedTouchPoint ttp in trackedTouchPoints)
  {
    var query = from point in tpc
                where point.TouchDevice.Id == ttp.ID
                select point;
    if (query.Count() == 0)
      ToDelete.Add(ttp.ID);
  }

  foreach (int i in ToDelete)
  {
    var query = from point in trackedTouchPoints
                where point.ID == i
                select point;
    if (query.Count() != 0)
      trackedTouchPoints.Remove(query.First());
  }
  if (trackedTouchPoints.Count == 0)
  {
    DrawCanvas.Children.Clear();
  }
```

```
    }
  }
  class TrackedTouchPoint
  {
    public TrackedTouchPoint()
    {
      Rect = new Rectangle() { Height = 50, Width = 50 };
      Position = new Point(0, 0);
      IsPrimary = false;
      BrushColor = new SolidColorBrush(Colors.Yellow);
    }

    private Rectangle Rect { get; set; }

    public int ID { get; set; }

    public Brush BrushColor
    {
      set
      {
        Rect.Fill = value;
      }
    }
    public Point Position { get; set; }

    public bool IsPrimary { get; set; }

    public void Draw(Canvas canvas)
    {
      if (IsPrimary)
        BrushColor = new SolidColorBrush(Colors.Blue);

      Rect.SetValue(Canvas.LeftProperty, Position.X);
      Rect.SetValue(Canvas.TopProperty, Position.Y);
      if (Rect.Parent == null)
        canvas.Children.Add(Rect);
    }

    public void UnDraw(Canvas canvas)
    {
      canvas.Children.Remove(Rect);
    }
  }
}
```

Raw touch with Touch.FrameReported gives full access to every touch event; however, it is cumbersome to work with when you just need to detect gestures or a set of gestures. For mutli-touch programming Touch.FrameReported is not recommended. The next couple of sections cover gesture detection in both the XNA Framework and Silverlight as well as manipulations, which are recommended for multi-touch.

Programming with Gestures

A gesture is a one or two finger action that is a pre-defined touch interaction. Gestures on Windows Phone 7 are similar to gestures that are defined on Windows 7, iPhone, Android, or pretty much any other touch device. What makes gestures useful is their consistency, which means that they should not be altered or "enhanced" in a way that will confuse users.

I cover single-touch and raw touch in the previous section titled "Single-Point Touch," but I did not speak to it in terms of gestures. Single-touch gestures consist of the following interactions:

- **Tap:** Select an object in a ListBox, touch to click a button, or text to navigate to another screen.

- **Double Tap:** Successive taps in a row that happen with a time duration such as one second and are therefore recognized as a double-tap, not two single-tap gestures.

- **Pan:** Use a single feature to move an object across the screen.

- **Flick:** Similar to a pan gesture except that the finger moves quickly across the screen, acceleration is detected, and the object moves with inertia relative to the amount of acceleration applied.

- **Touch and Hold:** Touch on an area of screen for a period of time, say a second, and a touch and hold gesture is detected. Used to open context menus.

The two-finger gestures are Pinch and Stretch. The pinch gesture consists of placing two fingers on the screen and moving them closer. Pinch is used to zoom out as well as to make an object smaller. The Stretch gesture consists of placing two fingers on the screen and moving them further away. Stretch is used to zoom in as well as to make an object larger. In the next two subsections I cover how to support gestures in Windows Phone 7 Applications.

Multi-Touch with XNA Framework Libraries

The XNA Framework on Windows Phone 7 includes the `Microsoft.Xna.Framework.Input.Touch` namespace. This is a non-graphical, non-rendering namespace, so it can be leveraged in both Silverlight and XNA Game Studio. The primary class for the namespace is the `TouchPanel` static class, which receives touch input that is automatically interpreted into a gesture for developers.

To process gestures, developers call `TouchPanel.IsGestureAvailable` to determine if a Gesture is pending. If one is, developers then call TouchPanel.ReadGesture. The `Microsoft.Xna.Framework.Input.Touch` namespace includes an enumeration named GestureType that identifies the supported gestures, DoubleTap, Flick, FreeDrag, HorizontalDrag, VerticalDrag, Hold, Pinch, and Tap.

The Chapter 3 project `GesturesTouchPanelXNA` demonstrates how simple it is to use the `TouchPanel` class to determine gestures. In the `Initialize()` method of Game1.cs, the code enables all possible gestures.

```
TouchPanel.EnabledGestures = GestureType.DoubleTap | GestureType.Flick |
   GestureType.FreeDrag | GestureType.Hold | GestureType.HorizontalDrag |
   GestureType.None | GestureType.Pinch | GestureType.PinchComplete |
   GestureType.Tap | GestureType.VerticalDrag | GestureType.DragComplete;
```

We want to draw text to the screen in the XNA Framework project so we right-click on the GesturesTouchPanelXNAContent Content project and select Add ➤ New Item…and then select Sprite Font. You can edit the FontName tag to be a different font name as long as you have rights to redistribute the font. It is changed to Pescadero because that is one of the fonts available for redistribution via XNA Game

Studio. For more details on font redistribution, visit http://msdn.microsoft.com/en-us/library/bb447673.aspx. The project declares a SpriteFont object named spriteFontSegoeUIMono to represent the font.

In the LoadContent() method of Game1.cs, this code loads the font and defines a position in the middle of the screen to draw the font.

```
spriteFontSegoeUIMono = Content.Load<SpriteFont>("Segoe UI Mono");
spriteFontDrawLocation = new Vector2(graphics.GraphicsDevice.Viewport.Width / 2,
  graphics.GraphicsDevice.Viewport.Height / 2);
```

In the Update() method, here is the code to check for a gesture:

```
if (TouchPanel.IsGestureAvailable)
{
  gestureSample = TouchPanel.ReadGesture();
  gestureInfo = gestureSample.GestureType.ToString();
}
```

The gestureInfo variable is printed to the screen using the imported font with these lines of code in the Draw() method.

```
spriteBatch.Begin();
// Draw gesture info
string output = "Last Gesture: " + gestureInfo;

// Find the center of the string to center the text when outputted
Vector2 FontOrigin = spriteFontSegoeUIMono.MeasureString(output) / 2;
// Draw the string
spriteBatch.DrawString(spriteFontSegoeUIMono, output, spriteFontDrawLocation,
  Color.LightGreen,0, FontOrigin, 1.0f, SpriteEffects.None, 0.5f);
spriteBatch.End();
```

Run the application on a device and gesture on the screen to see the gesture recognized and the name of the gesture action drawn onscreen. Now that we have an easy way to detect a gesture, let's use it to do something useful.

The GestureSample class provides six properties to provide useful information regarding the gesture, GestureType, Timestamp, Position, Position2, Delta, and Delta2. You know what GestureType does from the discussion in the preceding paragraphs. Timestamp indicates the time of the gesture sample reading. The Timestamp values are continuous for readings to they can be subtracted to determine how much time passed between readings. The other four values are Vector2 values related to the position of the finger on the screen. Position represents the first finger. Position2 represents the second finger if a two-finger gesture. The Delta and Delta2 values are like Timestamp, in that they indicate the changes in finger position relative to the last finger position, not between fingers if a multi-touch gesture. Table 3–3 relates gestures to the applicable fields with relevant notes.

Table 3–3. Gestures and Applicable GestureSample Members

Gesture	Applicable Members	Notes
Tap	Position	
DoubleTap	Position	
Hold	Position	
FreeDrag	Position, Delta	
VerticalDrag Position, Delta	Delta values are constrained to the direction of movement, either vertical (X=0) or horizontal (Y=0).	
HorizontalDrag	Position, Delta	
DragComplete	N/A	All vector2 values set to zero.
Flick	Delta	The Delta member represents flick speed (and direction) as pixels per second.
Pinch	Position, Position2, Delta, Delta2	Position/Delta represent the first finger. Position2/Delta2 represents the second finger. Negative values indicate the Pinch gesture is moving fingers closer together.
PinchCompete	N/A	All vector2 values set to zero.

Debug info is added to write out the data from the GestureSample instance named gestureSample to help with development. The following is an example from the beginning of a Pinch gesture:

```
gesture Type:      Pinch
gesture Timestamp: 03:27:37.3210000
gesture Position:  {X:425.2747 Y:287.3394}
gesture Position2: {X:523.077 Y:366.6055}
gesture Delta:     {X:0 Y:0}
gesture Delta2:    {X:0 Y:0}
```

A short expanding Pinch gesture results in about 30 gesture samples over just less than half a second, providing a rich set of data to apply to objects as a result of user touches. Run the sample and perform gestures on blank portions of the screen to see how position and delta values change.

To make the sample more interesting stickman figure manipulation is added to the GesturesTouchPanelXNA project. The stickman figure responds to Hold, Flick, Drag, and Pinch gestures. Figure 3–9 shows the simple UI but you will want to run this on a device to try out the supported gestures.

Figure 3–9. Multi-Touch with the XNA Framework UI

If you tap and hold (Hold GestureType) on the stickman, the figure rotates 90 degrees. If the stickman is flicked (Flick GestureType), the stickman will bounce around the screen and will eventually slow down. Tap on the stickman to stop movement. Finally, drag (FreeDrag GestureType) to slide the stickman around the screen.

There is a little bit of XNA Framework development in the sample to create a basic GameObject class to represent the stickman sprite. This keeps the game code clean without using a bunch of member variables to track state in the Game1.cs file. Listing 3–7 shows the GameObject class.

Listing 3–7. GameObject.cs Code File

```
using Microsoft.Xna.Framework;
using Microsoft.Xna.Framework.Graphics;

namespace GesturesTouchPanelXNA
{
  class GameObject
  {
    private const float _minScale = .4f;
    private const float _maxScale = 6f;
    private const float _friction = .7f;
    private const float _bounceVelocity = .9f;


    private float _scale = 1f;
    private Vector2 _velocity;
    private Vector2 _position;

    public GameObject(Texture2D gameObjectTexture)
    {
      Rotation = 0f;
      Position = Vector2.Zero;
      SpriteTexture = gameObjectTexture;
      Center = new Vector2(SpriteTexture.Width / 2, SpriteTexture.Height / 2);
      Velocity = Vector2.Zero;
      TintColor = Color.White;
      Selected = false;
```

```
        }

        public Texture2D SpriteTexture { get; set; }
        public Vector2 Center { get; set; }
        public float Rotation { get; set; }
        public Rectangle TouchArea { get; set; }
        public Color TintColor { get; set; }
        public bool Selected { get; set; }
        public float Scale
        {
          get { return _scale; }
          set
          {
            _scale = MathHelper.Clamp(value, _minScale, _maxScale);
          }
        }
        public Vector2 Position
        { get { return _position; }
          set { _position = value ; } //Move position to Center.
        }
        public Vector2 Velocity
        {
          get {return _velocity;}
          set { _velocity = value; }
        }

        public Rectangle BoundingBox
        {
          get
          {
            Rectangle rect =
              new Rectangle((int)(Position.X - SpriteTexture.Width / 2 * Scale),
              (int)(Position.Y - SpriteTexture.Height / 2 * Scale),
              (int)(SpriteTexture.Width * Scale),
              (int)(SpriteTexture.Height * Scale));
              //Increase the touch target a bit
              rect.Inflate(10, 10);
            return rect;
          }
        }

        public void Update(GameTime gameTime, Rectangle displayBounds)
        {
          //apply scale for pinch / zoom gesture
          float halfWidth = (SpriteTexture.Width * Scale) / 2f;
          float halfHeight = (SpriteTexture.Height * Scale) / 2f;

          // apply friction to slow down movement for simple physics when flicked
          Velocity *= 1f - (_friction * (float)gameTime.ElapsedGameTime.TotalSeconds);

          // Calculate position
          //position = velocity * time
          //TotalSeconds is the amount of time since last update in seconds
          Position += Velocity * (float)gameTime.ElapsedGameTime.TotalSeconds;
```

```
     // Apply "bounce" if sprite approaches screen bounds
     if (Position.Y < displayBounds.Top + halfHeight)
     {
       _position.Y = displayBounds.Top + halfHeight;
       _velocity.Y *= -_bounceVelocity;
     }
     if (Position.Y > displayBounds.Bottom - halfHeight)
     {
       _position.Y = displayBounds.Bottom - halfHeight;
       _velocity.Y *= -_bounceVelocity;
     } if (Position.X < displayBounds.Left + halfWidth)
     {
       _position.X = displayBounds.Left + halfWidth;
       _velocity.X *= -_bounceVelocity;
     }

     if (Position.X > displayBounds.Right - halfWidth)
     {
       _position.X = displayBounds.Right - halfWidth;
       _velocity.X *= -_bounceVelocity;
     }
   }
 }

 public void Draw(SpriteBatch spriteBatch)
 {
   spriteBatch.Draw(SpriteTexture, Position, null, TintColor, Rotation,
     Center,Scale,
     SpriteEffects.None,0);
 }
 }
}
```

The vast majority of the GameObject class is basic math calculations for checking screen boundaries, velocity, position, and so on. The one item to point out is the handy MathHelper static class that includes numerous helpful methods. The Clamp method is used to limit the zooming via the Pinch GestureType to be between a min and max scale value.

The other interesting code is the ProcessTouchInput() method in Game1.cs that is called in the Update() method. The method checks for touches first in order to determine if the stickman was touched on screen. To perform the check, each touch is converted to a Point object mapped into the screen coordinates. Next, we create a Rectangle object that encapsulates the stickman. The Rectangle.Contains method is passed in the Point object that represents the touch to determine if the touch was within the bounding box of the stickman. If the Point object is within the bounds of the Rectangle object, Selected is set to true on the StickMan sprite and gestures are applied. Otherwise, if a gesture is performed outside of the stickman, the gesture info is displayed to the screen as before but the StickMan sprite is not affected. The following is the code to determine selection:

```
TouchCollection touches = TouchPanel.GetState();
if ((touches.Count > 0) && (touches[0].State == TouchLocationState.Pressed))
{
  // map touch to a Point object to hit test
  Point touchPoint = new Point((int)touches[0].Position.X,
                               (int)touches[0].Position.Y);
```

```
  if (StickManGameObject.BoundingBox.Contains(touchPoint))
  {
    StickManGameObject.Selected = true;
    StickManGameObject.Velocity = Vector2.Zero;
  }
}
```

A switch statement is added to the `while (TouchPanel.IsGestureAvailable)` loop. As a `GestureType` is identified, it is applied to the `StrawMan` sprite. The switch statement is shown in Listing 3–8.

Listing 3–8. ProcessInput Method GestureType Switch Statement

```
if (StickManGameObject.Selected)
{
  switch (gestureSample.GestureType)
  {
    case GestureType.Hold:
      StickManGameObject.Rotation += MathHelper.Pi;
      break;
    case GestureType.FreeDrag:
      StickManGameObject.Position += gestureSample.Delta;
      break;
    case GestureType.Flick:
      StickManGameObject.Velocity = gestureSample.Delta;
      break;
    case GestureType.Pinch:
      Vector2 FirstFingerCurrentPosition = gestureSample.Position;
      Vector2 SecondFingerCurrentPosition = gestureSample.Position2;
      Vector2 FirstFingerPreviousPosition = FirstFingerCurrentPosition -
            gestureSample.Delta;
      Vector2 SecondFingerPreviousPosition = SecondFingerCurrentPosition -
            gestureSample.Delta2;
      //Calculate distance between fingers for the current and
      //previous finger positions.  Use it as a ration to
      //scale object.  Can have positive and negative scale.
      float CurentPositionFingerDistance = Vector2.Distance(
        FirstFingerCurrentPosition, SecondFingerCurrentPosition);
      float PreviousPositionFingerDistance = Vector2.Distance(
        FirstFingerPreviousPosition, SecondFingerPreviousPosition);

      float zoomDelta = (CurentPositionFingerDistance -
                        PreviousPositionFingerDistance) * .03f;
      StickManGameObject.Scale += zoomDelta;
      break;
  }
}
```

For the `GestureType.Hold` gesture, the StickMan's `Rotation` property on the sprite is altered by `MathHelper.PiOver2` radians, which is equal to 90 degrees. For the `GestureType.FreeDrag` gesture, the StickMan's `Position` property is updated by the Delta value, which is a `Vector2` in the direction and magnitude of movement since the last time a gesture sample was provided. For `GestureType.Flick`, the StickMan's `Velociy` is updated by the Delta as well, which in this case represents a flick speed that is added.

The `GestureType.Pinch` gesture requires a bit more calculation, but it is fairly straightforward. Essentially, the distance between fingers in screen coordinates is calculated for the current finger position and previous finger position. The differences are used to calculate scale factor. Increasing finger distance is a positive scale factor. Decreasing finger distance is a negative scale factor. If the distance greatly increases (either to be bigger or smaller), that determines the size of the scale factor.

Touch input and Gestures are a key component to game development for Windows Phone 7. This section covered a lot of ground from gesture recognition to applying gestures to a game object, taking advantage of the gesture capabilities available in the XNA Framework libraries. We will now cover how to work with gestures in Silverlight.

Multi-Touch with Silverlight

We can take the information above regarding XNA Framework multi-touch and apply it to Silverlight. Because Silverlight and XNA Framework share the same application model, you can share non-drawing libraries across programming models. This is demonstrated in the GesturesTouchPanelSilverlight project. To get started, add a reference to the Microsoft.Xna.Framework and Microsoft.Xna.Framework.Input.Touch namespaces.

In the MainPage() constructor in MainPage.xaml.cs, add the following code to enable Gestures, just as before:

```
TouchPanel.EnabledGestures = GestureType.DoubleTap | GestureType.Flick |
        GestureType.FreeDrag | GestureType.Hold | GestureType.HorizontalDrag |
        GestureType.None | GestureType.Pinch | GestureType.PinchComplete |
        GestureType.Tap | GestureType.VerticalDrag | GestureType.DragComplete;
```

In XNA Game Studio, the game loop Update method is called 30 times a second so it is a single convenient place to capture touch input. In Silverlight there isn't a game loop. A polling loop could be simulated with a DispatcherTimer that fires every 1000/30 milliseconds. This is the cleanest approach, because it exactly simulates how the XNA Framework works.

Another method is to hook into the mouse or manipulation events. I cover the manipulation events in the next section so we use the mouse events instead. This will work fine most of the time, but some gesture events fire in MouseLeftButtonDown and MouseButtonUp as well as MouseMove so you have to be careful if it causes you a bug if you are just tracking events in MouseMove, and so on. The following is the code to capture gesture events in Silverlight mouse events:

```
private void PhoneApplicationPage_MouseLeftButtonDown(object sender, MouseButtonEventArgs e)
{
  while (TouchPanel.IsGestureAvailable)
  {
    GestureActionsListBox.Items.Add("LeftBtnDown
"+TouchPanel.ReadGesture().GestureType.ToString());

  }
}

private void PhoneApplicationPage_MouseLeftButtonUp(object sender, MouseButtonEventArgs e)
{
  while (TouchPanel.IsGestureAvailable)
  {
    GestureActionsListBox.Items.Add("LeftBtnUp " +
TouchPanel.ReadGesture().GestureType.ToString());
  }
}

private void PhoneApplicationPage_MouseMove(object sender, MouseEventArgs e)
{
```

```
    while (TouchPanel.IsGestureAvailable)
    {
      GestureActionsListBox.Items.Add("MouseMove " +
TouchPanel.ReadGesture().GestureType.ToString());
    }
}
```

Once the gestures are detected in the mouse events, you can perform similar programming using a Canvas panel as with the XNA Framework ample to react to gestures. One additional item to consider when comparing the XNA Framework and Silverlight is the coordinate system. In the XNA Framework, all objects are absolutely positioned relative to the upper left hand corner so the math to calculate position is straightforward. In Silverlight, objects can be placed within containers. For example, a Rectangle can have margin top and left margin of 10,10, but be contained within a Grid that has margin of 100,100 relative to the screen so coordinate mapping is necessary to translate the touch location to an actual control position.

Another method to detect gestures in Silverlight is available within the Silverlight for Windows Phone Toolkit at Silverlight.codeplex.com. The toolkit includes the GestureService/GestureListener components to detect gestures, so you will want to download the toolkit to test out the sample

Once the Silverlight for Windows Phone Toolkit is installed, browse to the toolkit library and add a reference. On my system it is located here: C:\Program Files (x86)\Microsoft SDKs\Windows Phone\v7.0\Toolkit\Nov10\Bin. The GesturesSilverlightToolkit project demonstrates how to use the GestureListener control. The toolkit library is added as a reference and made available in MainPage.xaml via an xml namespace import:

```
xmlns:toolkit="clr-namespace:Microsoft.Phone.Controls;assembly=↵
Microsoft.Phone.Controls.Toolkit"
```

A Rectangle object containing a GestureListener control is added to the ContentPanel Grid:

```
<toolkit:GestureService.GestureListener>
  <toolkit:GestureListener />
</toolkit:GestureService.GestureListener>
```

Figure 3–10 shows the events available on the GestureListener.

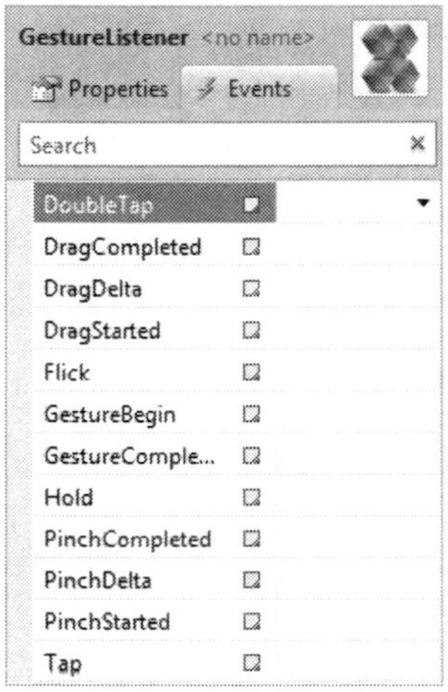

Figure 3–10. GestureListener events

An event handler is added for all the possible supported gestures, Tap, DoubleTap, Drag, Flick, TapAndHold, and Pinch to the GesturesSilverlightToolkit project to allow you to explore the events. Figure 3–11 shows the test UI.

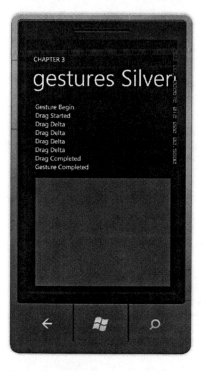

Figure 3–11. Multi-Touch with the XNA Framework UI

An important item to note, each event has unique EventArgs to provide the information developers need to apply the gesture to objects. As an example, the FlickGestureEventArgs class includes Angle, Direction, GetPosition, Handled, HorizontalVelocity, and VerticalVelocity members. The properties are more tailored toward Silverlight development, which may simplify gesture processing over using the XNA Framework libraries.

This concludes the discussion of gesture processing. The next section covers manipulation events.

Programming with Manipulation Events

Manipulations permit more complex interactions. They have two primary characteristics: Manipulations consists of multiple gestures that appear to happen simultaneously. The other characteristic is that manipulations consist of a set of transforms resulting from the user touch actions. The Manipulation events are very helpful because they interpret the user touch interaction into a set of transforms like translate and scale that you as the developer can apply to objects onscreen.

Windows Presentation Foundation 4.0 introduced Manipulation events to provide a high-level touch programming model that simplifies touch programming when compared to using low-level raw touch input. A subset of the manipulation events is available in Silverlight for Windows Phone 7 with some differences. WPF manipulation events support translation, scaling, and rotation. Silverlight for Windows Phone does not include rotation.

Manipulation events do not distinguish between fingers. The events interpret finger movement into translation and scaling as well as an indication of velocity to implement physics.

Windows Phone 7 includes three manipulation events: `ManipulationStarted`, `ManipulationDelta`, and `ManipulationCompleted` defined on the `UIElement` base class. Each manipulation event includes a custom `EventArgs` class with the following members in common:

- **e.OriginalSource:** The original object that raised the event.

- **e.ManipulationContainer:** The container object or panel that defines the coordinate system for the manipulation. This property will stay consistent through all three events.

- **e.ManipulationOrigin:** The point from which the manipulation originated. Indicates the location of the finger relative to the `ManipulationContainer` object. For two-finger manipulations, the `ManipulationOrigin` represents roughly the center point between the two fingers.

The events include unique `EventArgs` members as well, listed in the following:

- **ManipulationStarted:** The `ManipulationStartedEventArgs` class includes a `Complete` method that completes the manipulation without inertia, and a `Handled` property to indicate that the routed event is handled so that other controls don't attempt to handle the event again.

- **ManipulationDelta:** The `ManipulationDeltaEventArgs` class includes a `Complete` method. The `IsInertial` method indicates whether the Delta events is occurring during inertia. Other properties are `DeltaManipulation` and `CumulativeManipulation`, which represent the discrete (delta) and cumulative changes since `ManipulationStarted` resulting from the manipulation. The other `EventArgs` property is `Velocities`, which indicates the most recent rate of change for the manipulation.

- **ManipulationCompleted:** The `ManipulationCompletedEventArgs` include a `FinalVelocities` and `TotalManipulation` properties. It also includes a `Handled` and `IsInertial` properties.

As we saw before with gesture development there is one "started" event followed by zero or more `ManipulationDelta` events, and then a `ManipulationCompleted` "completed" event. To test manipulations, we created the `ManipulationEvents` project using the `StickMan` sprite from the `GesturesTouchPanelXNA` project. Figure 3–12 shows the UI.

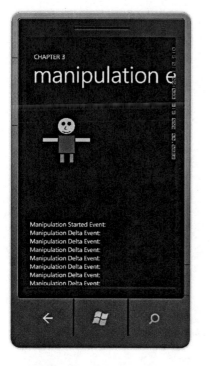

Figure 3–12. Manipulations test app UI

The project implements drag and scale via the ManipulationsDelta event. Here is the code for the ManipulationsDelta event.

```
private void StickManImage_ManipulationDelta(object sender,
  ManipulationDeltaEventArgs e)
{
  ReportEvent("Manipulation Delta Event: ");
  Image image = sender as Image;
  CompositeTransform compositeTransform =
    image.RenderTransform as CompositeTransform;

  if ((e.DeltaManipulation.Scale.X > 0) || (e.DeltaManipulation.Scale.Y > 0))
  {
    double ScaleValue = Math.Max(e.DeltaManipulation.Scale.X,
      e.DeltaManipulation.Scale.Y);
    System.Diagnostics.Debug.WriteLine("Scale Value: " +
      ScaleValue.ToString());

    //Limit how large
    if ((compositeTransform.ScaleX <= 4d) || (ScaleValue < 1d))
    {
      compositeTransform.ScaleX *= ScaleValue;
      compositeTransform.ScaleY *= ScaleValue;
    }
```

```
}
System.Diagnostics.Debug.WriteLine("compositeTransform.ScaleX: " +
  compositeTransform.ScaleX);
System.Diagnostics.Debug.WriteLine("compositeTransform.ScaleY: " +
  compositeTransform.ScaleY);

compositeTransform.TranslateX += e.DeltaManipulation.Translation.X;
compositeTransform.TranslateY += e.DeltaManipulation.Translation.Y;
e.Handled = true;
}
```

The code modifies a CompositeTransform based on the DeltaManipulation values, Scale for Pinch gestures and Translation for movement. The CompositeTransform is declared in the XAML for the StickMan Image tag, as shown in the following:

```
<Image x:Name="StickManImage" Source="/images/StickMan.png"
  ManipulationCompleted="StickManImage_ManipulationCompleted"
  ManipulationDelta="StickManImage_ManipulationDelta"
  ManipulationStarted="StickManImage_ManipulationStarted">
  <Image.RenderTransform>
    <CompositeTransform />
  </Image.RenderTransform>
</Image>
```

The Silverlight for Windows Phone Toolkit GestureListener control is the preferred method for detecting gestures in Silverlight for Windows Phone. Manipulation events should be a second or third choice if for some reason the GestureListener or XNA Framework libraries do not suit your needs. For non-gesture detection multi-touch development, the manipulation events are recommended. Let's now shift gears to discuss other forms of application input on Windows Phone 7.

Accelerometer

As far as fun goes, the accelerometer can be an entertaining and engaging method of input, especially for game development with XNA Game Studio or Silverlight. We all have seen the car racing games on mobile phone or mobile gaming devices where the user is tilting the device like a steering wheel. The next section covers how to work with the Accelerometer.

Understanding How It Works

The Accelerometer sensor detects acceleration in all three axis's, X, Y, Z to form a 3D vector. You may wonder in what direction and magnitude does the vector point? Collect a few accelerometer readings using this line of code

```
    System.Diagnostics.Debug.WriteLine(AccelerometerHelper↲
.Current2DAcceleration.ToString());
```

The following are a few samples from the Output window when debugging:

```
{X:0.351 Y:-0.002 Z:0.949} (Magnatude is approximately 1.02)
{X:0.401 Y:0.044 Z:0.984} (Magnatude is approximately 1.06)
{X:0.378 Y:0.04 Z:1.023} (Magnatude is approximately 1.09)
{X:0.386 Y:0.022 Z:0.992} (Magnatude is approximately 1.06)
{X:0.409 Y:0.03 Z:0.992} (Magnatude is approximately 1.07)
```

You can calculate the magnitude of the vector using the Pythagorean Theorem, which is the $Sqrt(X^2+Y^2+Z^2)$ = magnitude of the vector. The value should be about one but as you can see from the above samples, it can vary by location or could possibly be an error deviation. Either way, this is why applications like a level suggest that you calibrate the level against a known flat surface before using the virtual level.

If you run the application in the emulator, this reading is returned every time: {X:0 Y:0 Z:-1}. Holding the phone flat in my unsteady hand yields similar values with Z near one and X, and Y near zero.

```
{X:0.039 Y:0.072 Z:-1.019}
{X:0.069 Y:0.099 Z:-1.047}
{X:0.012 Y:0.056 Z:-1.008}
{X:0.016 Y:0.068 Z:-1.019}
```

This suggests that the vector is oriented to point towards the center of the earth, which for the above readings is the bottom of the phone or a negative Z when the phone is lying flat on its back. Flipping the phone in my hand yields the following values:

```
{X:-0.043 Y:0.08 Z:1.019}
{X:-0.069 Y:0.111 Z:1.093}
{X:-0.069 Y:0.099 Z:1.093}
{X:-0.039 Y:0.107 Z:1.031}
```

This time the vector is pointing out from the glass toward the ground, because the phone is lying face down. This information is useful if you need to determine how the phone is oriented in the users hand when say taking a photograph.

Figure 3–13 shows the accelerometer coordinate system. This is important because developers must translate readings into the coordinate system for the application.

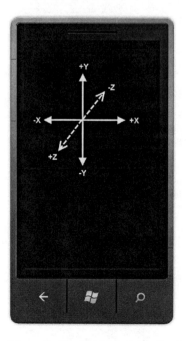

Figure 3–13. Accelorometer fixed coordinate system

As an example, in the XNA Framework, the default 2D coordinate system has positive Y going down, not up, so you cannot just take the Y component of acceleration and apply it to the Y value for a game object in 2D XNA.

■ **Note** The default coordinate system for 3D in the XNA Framework has positive Y going up. Chapter 8 covers 3D XNA Game Studio development.

With this background in hand, the next section covers development with the accelerometer sensor.

Programming with the Accelerometer

Accessing the Accelerometer sensor is pretty straightforward. We start with an XNA project, adding a reference to the Microsoft.Devices.Sensors assembly, and declaring instance of the Accelerometer class. In the Game1.Initialize() method, create an instance of the Accelerometer and call the Start() method to generate readings.

■ **Note** Turn off the Accelerometer if not needed to save battery power.

Create an event handler for ReadingChanged as well. The following is the code to create the event handler:

```
accelerometer = new Accelerometer();
accelerometer.Start();
accelerometer.ReadingChanged +=
  new EventHandler<AccelerometerReadingEventArgs>(accelerometer_ReadingChanged);
```

The accelerometer_ReadingChanged event handler event arguments AccelerometerReadingEventArgs class exposes acceleration in three dimensions via the X, Y, and Z member variables of type double. There is also a TimeStamp variable to allow measurement of acceleration changes over time.

A private member Vector3 variable named AccelerometerTemp is added to the Game1 class to collect the reading so that the code in the event handler does not have to new up a Vector3 each time a reading is collected. We create a helper static class named AccelerometerHelper that takes the accelerometer reading and assigns it to a Vector3 property named Current3DAcceleration. The following is the ReadingChanged event handler:

```
private Vector3 AccelerometerTemp = new Vector3();
void accelerometer_ReadingChanged(object sender, AccelerometerReadingEventArgs e)
{
  //
  AccelerometerTemp.X = (float)e.X;
  AccelerometerTemp.Y = (float)e.Y;
  AccelerometerTemp.Z = (float)e.Z;

  AccelerometerHelper.Current3DAcceleration  = AccelerometerTemp;
  AccelerometerHelper.CurrentTimeStamp = e.Timestamp;
}
```

The AccelerometerHelper class takes the Vector3 and parses the values up in the "setter" function for the Current3DAcceleration property into the class members listed in Figure 3–14.

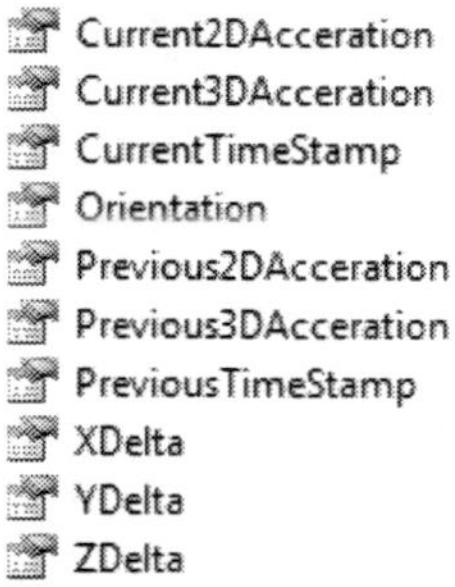

Current2DAcceration
Current3DAcceration
CurrentTimeStamp
Orientation
Previous2DAcceration
Previous3DAcceration
PreviousTimeStamp
XDelta
YDelta
ZDelta

Figure 3–14. AccelerometerHelper class members

Most of the code in the AccelerometerHelper class is properties and private member variables to hold values. Private backing variables are optional with the {get ; set ;} construct in C# but we use them here in order for all other member variables to be derived from just setting the Current3DAcceleration property. Listing 3–9 has the code for the AccelerometerHelper class.

Listing 3–9. AccelerometerHelper Class Code File

```
using System;
using System.Collections.Generic;
using System.Linq;
using System.Text;
using Microsoft.Xna.Framework;

namespace AccelerometerInputXNA
{
  static public class  AccelerometerHelper
  {
    static private Vector3 _current3DAcceleration;
    static public Vector3 Current3DAcceleration
    {
      get
      {
        return _current3DAcceleration;
      }
      set
      {
        //Set previous to "old" current 3D acceleration
        _previous3DAcceleration = _current3DAcceleration;

        //Update current 3D acceleration
        //Take into account screen orientation
        //when assigning values
        switch (Orientation)
        {
          case DisplayOrientation.LandscapeLeft:
            _current3DAcceleration.X = -value.Y;
```

```
            _current3DAcceleration.Y = -value.X;
            _current3DAcceleration.Z = -value.Z;
            break;
        case DisplayOrientation.LandscapeRight:
            _current3DAcceleration.X = value.Y;
            _current3DAcceleration.Y = value.X;
            _current3DAcceleration.Z = value.Z;
            break;
        case DisplayOrientation.Portrait:
            _current3DAcceleration.X = value.X;
            _current3DAcceleration.Y = value.Y;
            _current3DAcceleration.Z = value.Z;
            break;
    }

    //Update current 2D acceleration
    _current2DAcceleration.X = _current3DAcceleration.X;
    _current2DAcceleration.Y = _current3DAcceleration.Y;
    //Update previous 2D acceleration
    _previous2DAcceleration.X = _previous3DAcceleration.X;
    _previous2DAcceleration.Y = _previous3DAcceleration.Y;
    //Update deltas
    _xDelta = _current3DAcceleration.X - _previous3DAcceleration.X;
    _yDelta = _current3DAcceleration.Y - _previous3DAcceleration.Y;
    _zDelta = _current3DAcceleration.Z - _previous3DAcceleration.Z;
    }
}

static private Vector2 _current2DAcceleration;
static public Vector2 Current2DAcceleration
{
  get
  {
    return _current2DAcceleration;
  }
}

static private DateTimeOffset _currentTimeStamp;
static public DateTimeOffset CurrentTimeStamp
    {
  get
  {
    return _currentTimeStamp;
  }
  set
  {
    _previousTimeStamp = _currentTimeStamp;
    _currentTimeStamp = value;
  }
}

static private Vector3 _previous3DAcceleration;
static public Vector3 Previous3DAcceleration
{ get { return _previous3DAcceleration; } }
```

```
        static private Vector2 _previous2DAcceleration;
        static public Vector2 Previous2DAcceleration
        { get { return _previous2DAcceleration; } }

        static private DateTimeOffset _previousTimeStamp;
        static public DateTimeOffset PreviousTimeStamp
        { get { return _previousTimeStamp; } }

        static private double _xDelta ;
        static public double XDelta { get { return _xDelta;} }

        static private double _yDelta;
        static public double YDelta { get { return _yDelta; } }

        static private double _zDelta;
        static public double ZDelta { get { return _zDelta; } }

        public static DisplayOrientation Orientation { get; set; }
    }
}
```

Notice in the setter function for the Current3DAcceleration property, there is a switch statement that flips the sign as needed based on device orientation, whether landscape left or landscape right, because the accelerometer coordinate system is fixed. This ensures that behavior is consistent when the XNA Framework flips the screen based on how the user is holding the device

To test the helper class, we copy over the GameObject class and assets, StickMan and the font, from the GesturesTouchPanelXNA project as well as the code to load up the assets and draw on the screen. The gesture code is not copied over since the input for this project is the Accelerometer. As before, the Game1.Update() method in the game loop is the place to handle input and apply it to objects. This line of code is added to the Update method to apply acceleration to the StickMan GameObject instance:

StickManGameObject.Velocity += AccelerometerHelper.Current2DAcceleration;

Run the application and the application behaves as expected: tilt the phone left, and the StickMan slides left, and vice versa when holding the phone in landscape orientation. If you tilt the phone up far enough, the screen flips to either DisplayOrientation.LandscapeLeft or DisplayOrientation.LandscapeRight and the behavior remains consistent.

The main issue with this calculation of just adding the Current2DAcceleration to the StickMan's velocity results in a very slow acceleration. This can be easily remedied by scaling the value like this

StickManGameObject.Velocity +=30* AccelerometerHelper.Current2DAcceleration;

The UI "feels" much better with this value and is more fun to interact with. Depending on the game object's desired behavior, you could create a ratchet effect by having fixed positions when the accelerometer values are between discrete values instead of the smooth application of accelerometer values to position in this code sample.

The Accelerometer sensor works equally well in Silverlight. The difference is mapping Accelerometer changes to X/Y position values directly (instead of applying Vectors) using a CompositeTransform object just like what was done in the Silverlight sample with Manipulations in the previous section on multi-touch. Next up is the Location sensor.

Location

The location sensor is a very useful capability, given that mobile devices are generally on the go with their owner. Location provides context for applications that can make life easier on the user by automatically adjusting for the user's current location. A great example is the Search button on the phone. Enter or speak a keyword and click search. The local tab finds relevant items nearby. So a search for "Starbucks" gives the user exactly what they want on the local tab---which café is closest.

Understanding How It Works

The location sensor is a service that can use cell tower locations, wireless access point locations, and GPS to determine a user's location with varying degree of accuracy and power consumption.

Determining location with GPS is highly accurate, but it takes a while to spin up the GPS, and it consumes relatively more battery. Determining location using cell tower location is very fast, doesn't consume additional battery, but may not be accurate depending on how many cell towers are in range and their relative distance from each other in relation to the phone. Determining location with wireless access points can be accurate depending on how many wireless access points are in range and their relative position. If only one wireless access point is available location data will have a large error ring. Turning on Wi-Fi can consume additional battery power as well.

Programming with Location

You may try to guess that the Location namespace is in the `Microsoft.Devices.Sensors` namespace, but that would not be correct. It is located in the `System.Device.Location` namespace. The primary class for location is the `GeoCoordinateWatcher` class with the following class members:

- **DesiredAccuracy:** Can have a value of `GeoPositionAccuracy.Default` or `GeoPositionAccuracy.High`. The latter value forces the use of GPS, which can delay readings and consume battery. Use with care.

- **MovementThreshold:** This has a type of double. It indicates how far you have to move in order to generate a location reading in meters.

- **Permission:** Level of access to the location service.

- **Position:** Latest position obtained from location service.

- **PositionChanged:** Event that fires when a new position is available.

- **Start:** Starts location data acquisition from the location service.

- **Status:** Current status of the location service.

- **StatusChanged:** Event that fires when the status of the location changes.

- **Stop:** Stops location data acquisition from the location service.

- **TryStart:** Attempts to start location data acquisition with a timeout parameter passed in. The method returns false if the timeout expires before data is acquired. This call is synchronous and will block the thread it is called on – call on a background thread.

For this section topic on forward for the rest of the chapter, we start a new solution named Ch03_HandlingInput_Part2. The sample in that solution for this section is titled LocationSensorSilverlight. In the MainPage() constructor for the LocationSensorSilverlight project, the LocationService is instantiated and events for PositionChanged and StatusChanged are wired up. Here is the code:

```
LocationService = new GeoCoordinateWatcher();
LocationService.PositionChanged +=
  new EventHandler<GeoPositionChangedEventArgs<GeoCoordinate>>
    (LocationSensor_PositionChanged);

LocationService.StatusChanged +=
  new EventHandler<GeoPositionStatusChangedEventArgs>
    (LocationSensor_StatusChanged);
```

The rest of the application is just UI to display the LocationService information. The code uses the Bing Maps Map object to center the map on the user's current location. Here is the event handler to plot and zoom in on the map a bit:

```
private void PlotLocation_Click(object sender, EventArgs e)
{
  BingMap.Center = LocationService.Position.Location;
  BingMap.ZoomLevel = 15;
}
```

For more information we cover the Bing Maps control in detail in Chapter 5, but the most important property for the Map control is to set the CredentialsProvider key in XAML.

■ **Note** Obtain a free CredentialsProvider developer key from the Bing Maps account management web site located at www.bingmapsportal.com.

The UI implements the Application Bar to start and stop the Location Service as well as plot current location. The Application Bar also has a menu item to change the location accuracy. It is not possible to change accuracy after instantiating the GeoCoordinateWatcher variable. You have to instantiate a new GeoCoordinateWatcher variable and wire-up the event handlers again. Here is the code that handles this:

```
private void SetAccuracy_Click(object sender, EventArgs e)
{
  if (LocationService.DesiredAccuracy == GeoPositionAccuracy.Default)
    if (MessageBox.Show(
      "Current Accuracy is Default.  Change accuracy to High?"
      +"This may take some time and will consume additional battery power.",
      "Change Location Accuracy", MessageBoxButton.OKCancel)
      == MessageBoxResult.OK)
    {
      LocationService.Dispose();
      LocationService = new GeoCoordinateWatcher(GeoPositionAccuracy.High);
      LocationService.PositionChanged +=
    new EventHandler<GeoPositionChangedEventArgs<GeoCoordinate>>
      (LocationSensor_PositionChanged);
```

```
    LocationService.StatusChanged +=
      new EventHandler<GeoPositionStatusChangedEventArgs>
        (LocationSensor_StatusChanged);
    }
  else
    if (MessageBox.Show(
      "Current Accuracy is High.  Change accuracy to Default?"+
      "This wll be faster but will reduce accuracy.",
      "Change Location Accuracy", MessageBoxButton.OKCancel)
      == MessageBoxResult.OK)
    {
      LocationService.Dispose();
      LocationService =
        new GeoCoordinateWatcher(GeoPositionAccuracy.Default);
      LocationService.PositionChanged +=
    new EventHandler<GeoPositionChangedEventArgs<GeoCoordinate>>
      (LocationSensor_PositionChanged);

      LocationService.StatusChanged +=
        new EventHandler<GeoPositionStatusChangedEventArgs>
          (LocationSensor_StatusChanged);
        }
}
```

The XAML for the MainPage class implements a simple status panel that displays Location Service data. The code also uses the Silverlight Toolkit GestureListener to allow the user to drag the status panel over the map. Here is the markup:

```
<Border x:Name="LocationStatusPanel" HorizontalAlignment="Left"  VerticalAlignment="Top"
  Background="#96000000" Padding="2" >
  <toolkit:GestureService.GestureListener>
    <toolkit:GestureListener  DragDelta="GestureListener_DragDelta"/>
  </toolkit:GestureService.GestureListener>
  <Border.RenderTransform>
    <CompositeTransform/>
  </Border.RenderTransform>
    <StackPanel Orientation="Horizontal" Width="200" >
…Xaml for TextBoxes here.
    </StackPanel>
</Border>
```

Here is the GestureListener_DragDelta event handler code that repositions based on the user dragging the status panel.

```
private void GestureListener_DragDelta(object sender, DragDeltaGestureEventArgs e)
{
  Border border = sender as Border;
  CompositeTransform compositeTransform = border.RenderTransform as CompositeTransform;
  compositeTransform.TranslateX += e.HorizontalChange;
  compositeTransform.TranslateY += e.VerticalChange;
  e.Handled = true;
}
```

This concludes the overview of the Location Service available for Windows Phone 7. The next section covers how to capture Microphone input and play it back.

Microphone Input

The XNA Framework libraries make the Microphone available programmatically to applications. Add a reference to Microsoft.Xna.Framework assembly and a using clause for the Microsoft.Xna.Framework.Audio. The class of interest is the Microphone class that provides access to available microphones on the device.

The audio produced by the Microphone is 16-bit raw PCM. The audio can be played using the SoundEffect object without issue. To play recorded audio in a MediaElement control, the raw audio needs to be put into a .wmv file format.

For the sample project named MicrophoneWithSilverlight in the Ch03_HandlingInput_Part2 solution file the code uses the SoundEffect object to playback the audio.

In order to work with the microphone, some boilerplate XNA Framework code is required. Visit here for more info:

http://forums.create.msdn.com/forums/p/56995/347982.aspx

App.xaml.cs is modified to include the XNAAsyncDispatcher class and add an instance to this.ApplicationLifetimeObjects. With the boiler code in place, the application builds out a simple UI to record, stop, and play microphone audio. A slider is configured as a pitch selector so that you make your voice sound like Darth Vader or a Chipmunk. Figure 3–15 shows the UI.

Figure 3–15. *Microphone with Silverlight*

Listing 3–10 shows the source code.

Listing 3–10. MainPage.xaml.cs Code File

```csharp
using System;
using System.IO;
using System.Windows;
using Microsoft.Phone.Controls;
using Microsoft.Xna.Framework.Audio;

namespace MicrophoneWithSilverlight
{
  public partial class MainPage : PhoneApplicationPage
  {
    Microphone microphone = Microphone.Default;
    MemoryStream audioStream;

    // Constructor
    public MainPage()
    {
      InitializeComponent();

      microphone.BufferReady +=
        new EventHandler<EventArgs>(microphone_BufferReady);
      SoundEffect.MasterVolume = 1.0f;

      MicrophoneStatus.Text = microphone.State.ToString();
    }

    void microphone_BufferReady(object sender, EventArgs e)
    {
      byte[] audioBuffer = new byte[1024];
      int bytesRead = 0;

      while ((bytesRead = microphone.GetData(audioBuffer, 0, audioBuffer.Length)) > 0)
        audioStream.Write(audioBuffer, 0, bytesRead);

      MicrophoneStatus.Text = microphone.State.ToString();
    }

    private void recordButton_Click(object sender, RoutedEventArgs e)
    {
      if (microphone != null)
        microphone.Stop();

      audioStream = new MemoryStream();

      microphone.Start();
      MicrophoneStatus.Text = microphone.State.ToString();
    }

    private void stopRecordingButton_Click(object sender, RoutedEventArgs e)
    {
      if (microphone.State != MicrophoneState.Stopped)
        microphone.Stop();
```

```
        audioStream.Position = 0;
        MicrophoneStatus.Text = microphone.State.ToString();
    }

    private void playButton_Click(object sender, RoutedEventArgs e)
    {
      SoundEffect recordedAudio =
        new SoundEffect(audioStream.ToArray(), microphone.SampleRate,
          AudioChannels.Mono);

      recordedAudio.Play(1f, (float)pitchSlider.Value, 0f);
    }
  }
}
```

With the `Microphone` class, developers can create fun applications that allow a user to record and playback recorded audio with pitch modifications.

Camera Input

There is at least one camera on every Windows Phone 7 device with a minimum of five megapixels in resolution. The camera on Windows Phone 7 is accessible to developers. Developers can programmatically capture a photo but not video in the current release. It is implemented via the `CameraCaptureTask` in the `Microsoft.Phone.Tasks` namespace. I cover tasks and choosers in Chapter 4 in detail but wanted to mention it here as a possible input to an application.

Other Inputs

It is worth mentioning that the Compass, Proximity Sensor, Light Sensor hardware are present in every Windows Phone 7 device but these inputs are not available via the current SDK. Hopefully a future version of the SDK will make these inputs available to developers.

In this chapter, we explored user input for both Silverlight and XNA Game Studio across a wide range of inputs including touch, multi-touch, accelerometer, location, and Microphone. In the next chapter I will dive in to the programming model for Windows Phone.

Conclusion

In the last chapter I covered Silverlight output. In this chapter I covered input for both Silverlight and XNA Game Studio, covering text input and the value of InputScope. I next moved on to touch and multi-touch, covering the range of APIs available to developers, and I covered accelerometer input for both Silverlight and the XNA Framework. The last sections focused on Location, fun with the Microphone, and Camera input for capturing images. With the overview in Chapter 1, rendering in Chapter 2, and input in Chapter 3 out of the way, I next dive deep into the application programming model in Chapter 4.

Windows Phone 7 Programming Model

In the previous chapter, we covered handing input in a Windows Phone 7 application, and in Chapter 2, we covered rendering UI. With the fundamentals covered for input and output, let's now take a closer look at the Windows Phone 7 programming model.

In this chapter, we start first with covering the APIs available on Windows Phone 7 to obtain information either about the device or the user. Next we cover the tasks and choosers APIs that enable a Windows Phone 7 application to interact with other software components on the phone, such as the web browser from within the application.

We next cover asynchronous programming, which is fundamental when building real Silverlight applications for Windows Phone, as well as in desktop Silverlight. We quickly follow with a discussion of services programming, data persistence, and Windows Azure.

We next cover Windows Phone 7 Application lifecycle Management, otherwise known as tombstoning. This is a critical concept that will be a constant consideration. We will demonstrate how and when it plays a role with application development.

The final major topic of this chapter will be Windows Phone 7 application architecture. It is a question that developers invariably come to when building or porting an application to a new technology: how should I organize my application? We cover Model-View-ViewModel (MVVM) and pick an open source helper library that helps deal with complexities with MVVM and application development. Now let's jump into our first topic of page navigation.

Device Information

Developers need to understand the state of a device in order to provide the best experience for end users, such as letting the user know when a large download is about to begin and asking if the user would like to switch to a wireless or Ethernet connection via USB.

In this section, we cover the different pieces of device status and information that are available via the Windows Phone 7 APIs, including User Identifiers, Device Identifiers, Network Status, and Device capabilities. The Chapter 4 project DeviceInfo demonstrates these APIs in action.

Most of the code for device information is simply a matter of displaying string-based properties so the only code listed in this section is for network availability info below. Otherwise, please refer to the DeviceInfo project in the source code for additional detail. The next subsection starts with user and device identification first.

Identifying Unique Users

There is a properties class for user information available in this release of Windows Phone 7, which is contained in the Microsoft.Phone.Info.dll. It supports exactly one value, Anonymous Identifier ANID, which can be used to identify the user. Here is the full namespace, class, and method calls to obtain a user identifier:

```
Microsoft.Phone.Info.UserExtendedProperties.GetValue("ANID")
Microsoft.Phone.Info.UserExtendedProperties.TryGetValue("ANID")
```

How unique is this ID? It identifies the user with the same value, even if the user owns multiple phones. This value is persisted across reboots. Even if you factory-reset the phone, but configure it with the same Live ID, you will get the same value for the ANID property.

▪ **Note** The ANID property returns an empty string in the emulator.

Using this property requires the user identity capability and the ID_CAP_IDENTITY_DEVICE entry in the Capabilities section of WMAppManifest.xml for the application. If an application uses this class, the user will be alerted that the application requires this capability in the Windows Phone marketplace. You should only use this capability if your application absolutely needs it, and if it provides direct benefit to the user in some fashion. For example, if it makes it possible to store and retrieve from the cloud settings and data tied to the ID. Developers should mention the benefit in the application description; otherwise, users may be less inclined to download your application.

Device Information

There is a separate properties class for device information in Microsoft.Phone.Info.dll called DeviceExtendedProperties. It provides the ability to uniquely identify a device. Unlike the UserExtendedProperties class, the DeviceExtendedProperties class supports more than one value. The method call is the same as for the user property:

```
Microsoft.Phone.Info.DeviceExtendedProperties.GetValue()
Microsoft.Phone.Info.DeviceExtendedProperties.TryGetValue()
```

Table 4–1 lists the possible values that can be passed into the above method calls.

Table 4–1. Possible DeviceExtendedProperites Values

Value	Description
DeviceManufacturer	The name of the manufacturer of the device. A different value may be used across different devices from the same manufacturer, or it may be empty.
DeviceName	The name of the device. There are no rules enforced on naming and it may be empty.
DeviceUniqueID	Uniquely identify the device.

Value	Description
DeviceFirmwareVersion	The device manufacture's firmware version, which is different from the OS version. This value may be empty. It is recommended that the value be parsed as a System.Version structure, but it is not mandatory.
DeviceHardwareVersion	The device manufacture's hardware version running on the device. This value may be empty. It is recommended that the value be parsed as a System.Version structure, but it is not mandatory.
DeviceTotalMemory	Device's physical RAM size in bytes. It will be less than the actual amount of device memory. Most devices currently shipping have either 256MB or 512MB bytes of RAM.
ApplicationCurrentMemoryUsage	The running application's current memory usage in bytes. Developers need to track this value closely.
ApplicationPeakMemoryUsage	The running application's peak memory usage in bytes, which is another item that developers need to track closely.

The last two memory reporting items are very important to track. In Chapter 3 we mentioned using a DispatcherTimer and an event handler to track the values in the Visual Studio Output Tool Window, shown in Listing 4–1

Listing 4–1. Sample Tick Event to Record Debug Info

```
void DebugMemoryInfo_Tick(object sender, EventArgs e)
{
  //GC.GetTotalMemory(true);
  long deviceTotalMemory =
  (long)Microsoft.Phone.Info.DeviceExtendedProperties.GetValue(
  "DeviceTotalMemory");
  long applicationCurrentMemoryUsage =
  (long)Microsoft.Phone.Info.DeviceExtendedProperties.GetValue(
  "ApplicationCurrentMemoryUsage");
  long applicationPeakMemoryUsage =
  (long)Microsoft.Phone.Info.DeviceExtendedProperties.GetValue(
  "ApplicationPeakMemoryUsage");

  System.Diagnostics.Debug.WriteLine("--> " +
    DateTime.Now.ToLongTimeString());
  System.Diagnostics.Debug.WriteLine("--> Device Total : " +
    deviceTotalMemory.ToString("#,#", CultureInfo.InvariantCulture));
  System.Diagnostics.Debug.WriteLine("--> App Current : " +
    applicationCurrentMemoryUsage. ToString("#,#", CultureInfo.InvariantCulture));
  System.Diagnostics.Debug.WriteLine("--> App Peak : " +
    applicationPeakMemoryUsage. ToString("#,#", CultureInfo.InvariantCulture));
}
```

Certification requirements dictate that memory usage remain under 90MB, because the OS will shut down applications that are memory hogs. Applications can temporarily go over 90MB and not fail certification in some cases, such as if the application is transitioning pages and one page is going out of memory and another is loading data structures for display. In general, with memory constrained-devices, it is important to efficiently allocate memory to maximize performance. This is true for any mobile device application, regardless of the operating system, and it is something that makes mobile development a fun challenge: squeezing out every little bit of performance possible!

In Table 4–1 the DeviceUniqueID value will uniquely identify a device across all installed applications, even if the phone is updated with a new operating system version. This ID should not be used to identify users, because it is tied to the device, not the user

■ **Note** Accessing DeviceUniqueID in the emulator returns false for TryGetValue.

If your application can use the DeviceUniqueID in a way that benefits the user, you should use it; be sure, however, to mention why you use it in the application description, so that the user understands the benefit. Otherwise, cautious users may shy away of downloading your application.

System Environment Information

The System.Environment class provides the following information on the current environment via its properties:

- CurrentDirectory.

- HasShutdownStarted.

- OSVersion (includes and Platform and Version properties. The Version has additional properties of Build, Major, Minor, and Revision).

- TickCount (Since last reboot).

- Version. (CLR Version).

The next section starts with a very important topic when you are building mobile applications that depend on data in the cloud: current network status.

Network Status

Mobile applications must be thoughtful in using phone resources, such as data connectivity, and offer the user information when using the data connection. The Windows Phone 7 namespace Microsoft.Phone.Net.NetworkInformation provides the NetworkInterface object with the following two useful static members:

- NetworkInterface .GetIsNetworkAvailable method

- NetworkInterface .NetworkInterfaceType property

The GetIsNetworkAvailable method returns true or false. The NetworkInterface property stores a value from the Microsoft.Phone.Net.NetworkInformation.NetworkInterfaceType enumeration. Table 4–2 lists the common values in which most developers will be interested. You can find the full list at

http://msdn.microsoft.com/en-us/library/microsoft.phone.net.networkinformation
.networkinterfacetype(VS.92).aspx

Table 4–2. NetworkInterfaceType Enumeration Common Values

Enumeration Value	Description
None	No interface exists to provide access to the Internet.
Ethernet	The network interface is of type Ethernet. When connected via Zune and the PC, this is the value that is returned.
MobileBroadbandGSM	This is the value returned when connected over a wireless GSM network. (AT&T or T-Mobile in the U.S. and most of the world.)
MobileBraodbandCdma	This is the value returned when connected over a wireless CDMA network. (Verizon and Sprint in the U.S. and other regions of the world.)
Wireless80211	The network interface is a wireless LAN connection.

One item to note is that, when connected to the PC without Zune running, the network connection will return either MobileBroadband or Wirless80211 if a connection is available over those protocols. Zune must be running when connected to the PC in order to have an Ethernet connection.

You may be tempted to poll network status on a background thread, but that would not be battery efficient. Instead, the code can subscribe to the System.Net.NetworkInformation.NetworkChange.NetworkAddressChanged static event. The System.Net.NetworkInformation namespace also includes a NetworkInterface class, so you will need to disambiguate namespaces.

In the DeviceInfo project, we add two TextBlock controls and two TextBox controls to store network availability and connection type, storing network availability status in the NetworkAvailableTextbox control, and network connection type in the NetworkConnectionTextbox control. Listing 4–2 has the code from the DeviceInfo project that performs network detection.

Listing 4–2. Network Detection Method

```
#region Network Status Check
private void SetupNetworkStatusCheck()
{
  NetworkChange.NetworkAddressChanged +=
    new NetworkAddressChangedEventHandler
        (NetworkChange_NetworkAddressChanged);
  //Initialize values
  NetworkAvailableTextBlock.Text =
    PhoneNetworkApi.NetworkInterface.GetIsNetworkAvailable().ToString();
  NetworkConnectionTextBlock.Text =
    PhoneNetworkApi.NetworkInterface.NetworkInterfaceType.ToString();
}
```

```
void NetworkChange_NetworkAddressChanged(object sender, EventArgs e)
{
  NetworkAvailableTextBlock.Text =
    PhoneNetworkApi.NetworkInterface.GetIsNetworkAvailable().ToString();
  NetworkConnectionTextBlock.Text =
    PhoneNetworkApi.NetworkInterface.NetworkInterfaceType.ToString();
}
#endregion
```

This code requires the following two using statements for these namespaces:

```
using System.Net.NetworkInformation;
using PhoneNetworkApi = Microsoft.Phone.Net.NetworkInformation;
```

The code uses a namespace alias to disambiguate between the two namespaces for the NetworkInterface class that is present in both namespaces, though the Phone version includes the NetworkInterfaceType property. Figure 4–1 shows the UI displaying device and network info that we have covered in the previous sections.

Figure 4–1. Windows Phone 7 device information and network status

System Tray

The system tray appears at the top of the screen in portrait mode. Figure 4–2 is a clip from the Windows Phone 7 Design Template file named StatusBar_PSD.psd, which shows possible status information.

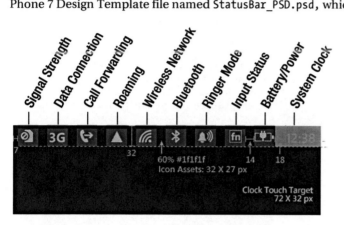

Figure 4–2. *Windows Phone 7 system tray indicators*

The Windows Phone 7 development guidelines recommend leaving the System Tray visible within applications, because it shows useful information without having to force the user to exit the application. The system tray does take up a little bit of screen real estate, so for games and media players, it makes sense to disable the System Tray.

The system tray can be disabled on a page-by-page basis by editing the phone:PhoneApplicationPage element and setting shell:SystemTray.IsVisible to False.

This concludes our discussion of device information. Next up is application data persistence using isolated storage on Windows Phone 7.

Marketplace Status and Trial Mode

Windows Phone 7 supports building a single application that includes both trial and full functionality. The Microsoft.Phone.Marketplace.LicenseInformation class provides has one method named IsTrial() that the application can use to determine if the application has been fully purchased or is in trial mode.

As a developer, you get to determine what is the right trial experience for your application. For a game, it might be a certain number of tries or just the first level. For an application, it might be filtering to a subset of information, display advertising, or lack of personalization.

Application developers in Silverlight can use the MarketplaceDetailTask class to display the purchase experience. The MarketplaceDetailTask is discussed below in the Tasks section covering launchers and choosers.

For XNA Game Studio developers, the Microsoft.Xna.Framework.GamerServices.Guide class has a method named IsTrialMode to get current license information. Developers call Guide.ShowMarketplace to display the purchase experience. The Guide.SimulateTrialMode property allows developer to test their game under trial mode conditions. We cover XNA Frameworkdevelopment in more detail in Chapter 7 and 8.

■ **Tip** Trial mode is a great way to encourage end users to try out your application, enjoy it, and purchase the full version. If you plan to sell your application, implement and test trial mode.

Silverlight developers may be wondering how they can simulate trial mode. The good news is that Silverlight developers can also use the `Microsoft.Xna.Framework.GamerServices.Guide` class and the `SimulateTrialMode` property. Set it to `true` to permit testing trial mode functionality.

When testing trial mode by setting SimulateTrialMode to true, a call to `Guide.IsTrialMode` returns the current value of `SimulateTrialMode`. Calling `Guide.ShowMarketplace` simulates making a purchase.

■ **Caution** You must set `SimulateTrialMode` to `false` in release code. Place the code that sets it to true in `#if` `DEBUG` to ensure it is not available in a released application submitted to Marketplace.

In this section, we covered how to identify users, the device, network status, and application trial mode status for Windows Phone 7. In the next section, we move to the next major topic of settings and data storage in isolated storage.

Application Data Persistence

Saving data to the file system is a necessity for most real applications. On Windows Phone 7, each application can access an isolated file system to read and write data that is only accessible to that application. This means that applications cannot share data with each other via the file system. It also means that one application cannot access or overwrite data from another application in the file system.

There are several namespaces related to data persistence that are available on Windows Phone 7. These namespaces include the following:

- **System.IO:** Provides access to base `Stream`, `StreamWriter,` and `StreamReader` classes.

- **System.IO.IsolatedStorage:** Provides access to Isolated Storage.

- **System.Runtime.Serialization:** Must add a reference to System.Runtime.Serialization assembly.

- **System.Xml:** Provides access to `XMLReader` stream class, as well as other core XML related classes.

- **System.Xml.Linq:** Must add a reference to System.Xml.Linq assembly. Provides access to XDocument class for XML manipulation as well as LINQ language constructs.

- **System.Xml.Serialization:** Provides access to XML serialization attributes that you can apply to .NET classes.

If you are a .NET developer, most of these look familiar, as they are the standard .NET classes related to serializing .NET objects, as well as reading and writing data to the file system. The one exception is possibly System.IO.IsolatedStorage, which is available via Silverlight on the desktop and also on Windows Phone 7. Isolated Storage represents the physical file system made available via the IsolatedStorage classes.

Unlike with Silverlight for the Web, there isn't an Isolated Storage quota on Windows Phone 7; however, it is recommended to not exceed two Gigabytes of data for an application if you are to be a good citizen and not abuse available space. Also, applications should make users aware of estimated file space requirements and try to give an option to delete data if needed. Keeping the user informed and in control is paramount.

The System.IO.IsolatedStorage namespace provides two possible methods to access the file system. The first is a key-value pair of type string-object where the key is a string and the value is of type object available in the static class IsolatedStorageSettings via its single property named ApplicationSettings. The Dictionary class stores object values, so essentially any class that can be serialized can be stored in the IsolatedStorageSettings.ApplicationSettings object. It is not limited to just simple values.

The other method to access the file system is via file and folder management using the IsolatedStorageFile static class. The method that provides access to the application's file system area is the GetUserStoreForApplication() method. With a reference to the user store in hand, you can create files to serialize objects to the file system.

The next two sections cover the sample code details for this section. The first example covers basic isolated storage operations, and the second example covers object persistence and serialization.

Basic File IO

In the Chapter 4 solution DataPersistence project is a MainPage page that has a menu to three additional pages, the first named BasicIsoStorage.xaml. Figure 4–3 has the UI.

Figure 4–3. DataPersistence BasicIsoStorage UI

The UI has several controls that store fake settings and data values. The sample uses both the ApplicationSettings object and an IsolatedStorageFileStream object to store and retrieve the values.

■ **Note** All of the data could persist within the ApplicationSettings object, but the sample shows how to work with the IsolatedStorageFileStream to prepare for more complex scenarios.

The code is straightforward Dictionary object access and file IO. See Listing 4–3.

Listing 4–3. BasicIsoStorage.xaml.cs Code File

```
using System;
using System.IO;
using System.IO.IsolatedStorage;
using Microsoft.Phone.Controls;

namespace DataPersistence.pages
{
  public partial class BasicIsoStorage : PhoneApplicationPage
  {
    private const string fileName = "notes.dat";

    public BasicIsoStorage()
    {
      InitializeComponent();
    }

    private void saveAppBarIcon_Click(object sender, EventArgs e)
    {
      SaveData();
    }

    private void loadAppBarIcon_Click(object sender, EventArgs e)
    {
      LoadData();
    }

    private void LoadData()
    {
      //Load "settings"
      if (IsolatedStorageSettings.ApplicationSettings.Contains("EnablePush"))
        enableNotifications.IsChecked =
          (bool)IsolatedStorageSettings.ApplicationSettings["EnablePush"];
      if (IsolatedStorageSettings.ApplicationSettings.Contains("FavColor"))
        colorListBox.SelectedIndex =
          (int)IsolatedStorageSettings.ApplicationSettings["FavColor"];
      if (IsolatedStorageSettings.ApplicationSettings.Contains("NickName"))
        nicknameTextBox.Text =
          (string)IsolatedStorageSettings.ApplicationSettings["NickName"];
```

```
    //Load "notes" text to file
    using (IsolatedStorageFile isf = IsolatedStorageFile.GetUserStoreForApplication())
    {
      if (isf.FileExists(fileName))
      {
        using (IsolatedStorageFileStream fs =
          isf.OpenFile(fileName, System.IO.FileMode.Open))
        {
          using (StreamReader reader = new StreamReader(fs))
          {
            notesTextBox.Text = reader.ReadToEnd();
            reader.Close();
          }
        }
      }
    }

}

private void SaveData()
{
  //Save "settings"
  IsolatedStorageSettings.ApplicationSettings["EnablePush"] =
    enableNotifications.IsChecked;
  IsolatedStorageSettings.ApplicationSettings["FavColor"] =
    colorListBox.SelectedIndex;
  IsolatedStorageSettings.ApplicationSettings["NickName"] =
    nicknameTextBox.Text;

  //Save "notes" text to file
  using (IsolatedStorageFile isf = IsolatedStorageFile.GetUserStoreForApplication())
  {
    using (IsolatedStorageFileStream fs =
      isf.OpenFile(fileName, System.IO.FileMode.Create))
    {
      using (StreamWriter writer = new StreamWriter(fs))
      {
        writer.Write(notesTextBox.Text);
        writer.Flush();
        writer.Close();
      }
    }
  }
  }
  }
 }
}
```

There are two application bar icons to load and save data. Loading data is a matter of checking that a key exists using ApplicationSettings.Contains, and then accessing the value via the key. The ApplicationSettings class is of type Dictionary that takes a key value of type String and stores the passed-in class as a type of Object. This permits you to pass any class into a Dictionary object, since all classes inherit from type Object. You must, however, type convert the retrieved object to the original type. Otherwise a runtime error will occur.

Loading the "Notes" TextBox data checks that the file exists and just reads the data using a StreamReader object. You may be tempted to put the filename into the StreamReader constructor directly. This will result in a code security access violation if you do. The only valid constructor parameter for an instance of StreamReader or StreamWriter is an object of type IsolatedStorageFile.

Saving the data is very similar code to loading the data. Note the use of the using construct for all objects that have a Dispose method. The following is the pseudocode:

```
Using (TextReader textReader = new StreamReader(streamResourceInfo.Stream)  // create
  isntance
{
//…code that leverages the instance….
}//Disposed called automatically when the block is exited
```

■ **Note** Only .NET objects that have handles to non-managed objects like a physical file handle have Dispose methods in .NET.

The using clause ensures that Dispose is called and that unmanaged resources are released. Otherwise, memory will not be freed immediately, and the runtime memory load will slowly increase until either Garbage Collection occurs or until the memory threshold limit is exceeded, and the app fails or until the application exits. Now that we've covered the basic isolated storage operations , we move on next to object persistence.

Object Persistence

In the previous section, we demonstrated how to store and retrieve individual values. In this section, we add some realism by serializing objects instead of individual values. The ObjectSerialization.xaml sample starts with almost the same UI and values as the BasicIsoStorage sample, but this time the controls data bind to a sample class named AppClass, as shown in Listing 4–4.

Listing 4–4. AppClass.cs Code File

```
using System.Xml.Serialization;

namespace DataPersistence
{
  [XmlRootAttribute("AppClass")]
  public class AppClass
  {
    public AppClass()
    {
      FavoriteColor = -1;
    }

    //Settings
    [XmlElement]
    public bool EnablePushNotifications { get; set; }

    [XmlElement]
```

```
    public int FavoriteColor { get; set; }

    [XmlElement]
    public string NickName { get; set; }

    //Data
    [XmlElement]
    public string Notes { get; set; }
  }
}
```

The sample AppClass class that we serialize in this example includes attributes from the System.Xml.Serialization namespace to provide support for serializing the object to the file system. The MSDN documentation covers all of the possible XML serialization attribute values:

http://msdn.microsoft.com/en-us/library/83y7df3e(v=VS.100).aspx

Configuring the data binding with Blend using sample data based on the AppClass is straightforward, as demonstrated in Chapter 2. A sample data source is added to the project that is based on the .NET AppClass class. This facilitates design-time data binding without causing issues at run-time.

In order to save and load the data, the code-behind for ObjectSerialization.xaml has modified Save and Load methods that serialize and deserialize an instance of the AppClass object, and configures it as the DataContext for the LayoutRoot Grid object. The following are the modified methods:

```
private void LoadData()
{
  using (IsolatedStorageFile isf = IsolatedStorageFile.GetUserStoreForApplication())
  {
    if (isf.FileExists(fileName))
    {
      using (IsolatedStorageFileStream fs =
        isf.OpenFile(fileName, System.IO.FileMode.Open))
      {
        XmlSerializer serializer = new XmlSerializer(typeof(AppClass));
        LayoutRoot.DataContext = (AppClass)serializer.Deserialize(fs);
      }
    }
  }
}


private void SaveData()
{
  using (IsolatedStorageFile isf = IsolatedStorageFile.GetUserStoreForApplication())
  {
    using (IsolatedStorageFileStream fs =
      isf.OpenFile(fileName, System.IO.FileMode.Create))
    {
      XmlSerializer xs = new XmlSerializer(typeof(AppClass));
      xs.Serialize(fs, ((AppClass)LayoutRoot.DataContext));
    }
  }
}
```

The serialization attributes attached to the `AppClass` object tell the `XmlSerializer` object how to read and write the class in Xml format. From there, the rest of the code in `SaveData` and `LoadData` methods is boilerplated, isolated storage file I/O, as in the previous sample.

The samples in this section exposed data management issues when you run the sample application to test the samples. If you navigate away from the sample, such as going to the Start screen, and then navigate back, the UI resets to what it is at startup. The data that was displayed is not preserved. Serializing out UI objects and settings is a critically important requirement for Windows Phone 7 applications. The concepts covered in this section lay the groundwork for the section titled Application Life Cycle Management.

In that section, application and data architecture is discussed, such that the data can be made to appear to be preserved, and to the user it will appear that the application was waiting in the background for the user to return to it. Before jumping there, we cover launchers and choosers first in the next section.

Tasks

Windows Phone 7 third-party applications run in a sandbox that is isolated from other third-party applications, as well as from the underlying operating system and hardware, except where APIs are surfaced.

One of the primary namespaces where a developer can integrate with the hardware and software platform is the `Microsoft.Phone.Tasks` namespace. The namespaces consists of launchers and choosers. The following are the launchers:

- `EmailComposeTask`
- `MarketplaceDetailTask`
- `MarketplaceHubTask`
- `MarketplaceReviewTask`
- `MarketplaceSearchTask`
- `MediaPlayerLauncher`
- `PhoneCallTask`
- `SearchTask`
- `SMSComposeTask`
- `WebBrowserTask`

Here are the choosers:

- `CameraCaptureTask`
- `EmailAddressChooserTask`
- `PhoneNumberChooserTask`
- `PhotoChooserTask`
- `SaveEmailAddressTask`
- `SavePhoneNumberTask`

Many of the launchers and choosers must be tested on a device, because the emulator does not include the full Windows Phone user experience with e-mail accounts, marketplace, and the like.

Most of the tasks in the Chapter 4 solution LaunchersAndChoosers sample project are launched directly by clicking on the name. Some open another page due to additional configuration options, or to show how the task can be fully utilized. We describe each launcher and chooser in the following section.

Debugging Launchers and Choosers

When debugging many of the launchers and choosers, the connection to Zune may prevent the application from running. To debug your application, you must use the WPConnect tool that was made available in the Windows Phone Developer Tools October and January updates. Here is a link:

http://create.msdn.com/en-us/home/getting_started

Once installed, the WPConnect tool is located here on my machine:

C:\Program Files (x86)\Microsoft SDKs\Windows Phone\v7.0\Tools\WPConnect

To use the tool, run Visual Studio 2010 and connect a device to your PC via the Zune client. Once connected, close Zune and run WPConnect via a command prompt. It will display a message that the device is connected. If you disconnect the device from the cable, you will have to repeat the process. Figure 4–4 shows a few runs just to show how easy it is to enable debugging when testing media such as the pictures hub or the MediaPlayerLauncher task.

Figure 4–4. WPConnect tool in action

Launchers

Launchers display UI to send the user to another part of the phone's functionality. When the user clicks the Back hardware button, he or she is returned to your application. Launchers are "fire and forget" in that they do not return information back to the application.

EmailComposeTask

The EmailComposeTask class allows the user to send e-mail from an application. You can configure the To, Cc, Subject, and Body of the e-mail message via properties. It is not possible to attach a file to the e-mail. Also, the Body property takes a string of text, so formatting such as HTML formatting the e-mail message is not supported. Listing 4–5 has the code for the EmailComposeTask sample.

Listing 4–5. EmailComposeTask Code

```
private void textBlock1_MouseLeftButtonUp(object sender, MouseButtonEventArgs e)
{
  //cause an exception and then send an error report.
  try
  {
    int num1 = 3;
    int num2 = 3;
    int num3 = num1 / (num1 - num2);
  }
  catch (Exception err)
  {
    EmailComposeTask task = new EmailComposeTask();
    task.To = "support@WP7isv.com";
    task.Subject = "Customer Error Report";
    //Size StringBuilder appropriately
    StringBuilder builder;
    if (null == err.InnerException)
      builder = new StringBuilder(600);
    else //need space for InnerException
      builder = new StringBuilder(1200);
    builder.AppendLine("Please tell us what you were doing when the problem occurred.\n\n\n");
    builder.AppendLine("EXCEPTION DETAILS:");
    builder.Append("message:");
    builder.AppendLine(err.Message);
    builder.AppendLine("");
    builder.Append("stack trace:");
    builder.AppendLine(err.StackTrace);
    if (null != err.InnerException)
    {
      builder.AppendLine("");
      builder.AppendLine("");
      builder.AppendLine("inner exception:");
      builder.Append("inner exception message:");
      builder.AppendLine(err.InnerException.Message);
      builder.AppendLine("");
      builder.Append("inner exception stack trace:");
      builder.AppendLine(err.InnerException.StackTrace);
    }
    task.Body = builder.ToString();
    task.Show();
  }
```

MarketplaceHubTask

The MarketplaceHubTask class launches into the Marketplace Hub. The only parameter is ContentType, which determines whether the application view or music view of the Marketplace is displayed. The following is the code to show the music view:

```
private void MarketplaceHubTask2_MouseLeftButtonDown(object sender, MouseButtonEventArgs e)
{
  marketplaceHubTask = new MarketplaceHubTask();
  marketplaceHubTask.ContentType = MarketplaceContentType.Music;
  marketplaceHubTask.Show();
}
```

There are no return properties or events. This task simply shows the marketplace hub, and allows the user to interact with the hub and then return back to the application by clicking the Back hardware button.

MarketplaceSearchTask

The MarketplaceSearchTask also has a ContentType property to filter by either Applications or Music. It also has a SearchTerms property to pass in search terms to kick off the search. The following is the code to kick off search:

```
private void MarketplaceSearchTask_MouseLeftButtonDown(object sender, MouseButtonEventArgs e)
{
  MarketplaceSearchTask marketplaceSearchTask = new MarketplaceSearchTask();
  marketplaceSearchTask.ContentType = MarketplaceContentType.Music;
  marketplaceSearchTask.SearchTerms = "driving music";
  marketplaceSearchTask.Show();
}
```

Figure 4–5 shows the task displayed after calling the Show() method.

Figure 4–5. MarketplaceSearchTask in action

MarketplaceDetailTask

The MarketplaceDetailTask class displays the marketplace details page for an application, which allows you to purchase the currently running application if it is in trial mode. You can also show the marketplace details for your other applications so you can promote them. The property that determines which application to show details for is the ContentIdentifier property, which is the product ID for the application found in marketplace when an application is certified.

■ **Tip** Leave the property null if you wish to display the marketplace details for the currently running application.

The product ID is generated when an application is submitted to marketplace, so if you have a family of applications that you wish to cross-promote, you can simply plug in the product ID for each application to display the marketplace details page. Here is the code:

```
private void MarketplaceDetailTask_MouseLeftButtonDown(object sender, MouseButtonEventArgs e)
{
  MarketplaceDetailTask marketplaceDetailTask = new MarketplaceDetailTask();
  marketplaceDetailTask.ContentType = MarketplaceContentType.Applications;
  //AppID for the youtube application
  marketplaceDetailTask.ContentIdentifier = "dcbb1ac6-a89a-df11-a490-00237de2db9e";
  marketplaceDetailTask.Show();
}
```

MarketplaceReviewTask

The marketplace review task allows you to display the marketplace review page for your application from within the application itself. This is a convenient way to encourage users to provide a review of your application. This task does not include a ContentIdentifier property, meaning that you can only display the review page for the currently running application. Here is the code:

```
private void MarketplaceReviewTask_MouseLeftButtonDown(object sender, MouseButtonEventArgs e)
{
  MarketplaceReviewTask marketplaceReviewTask = new MarketplaceReviewTask();
  marketplaceReviewTask.Show();
}
```

MediaPlayerLauncher

The MediaPlayerLauncher class has three properties of interest. The Control's property identifies which media player buttons to display. You can pick MediaPlaybackControls.All for full media controls, or you can use the bitwise "or" operator to combinea custom set of playback controls. The MediaPlayerLauncher has a property named Location that lets the player know how to resolve the URL if the media is located in isolated storage, or as part of the application's xap file. The most important property is the Media property where you set the URL for the media location. Here is code to play a Channel 9 video:

```
private void MediaPlayerLauncher_MouseLeftButtonDown(object sender, MouseButtonEventArgs e)
{
  MediaPlayerLauncher mediaPlayerLauncher = new MediaPlayerLauncher();
  mediaPlayerLauncher.Controls = MediaPlaybackControls.FastForward |
    MediaPlaybackControls.Pause | MediaPlaybackControls.Rewind |
    MediaPlaybackControls.Skip | MediaPlaybackControls.Stop;
  mediaPlayerLauncher.Location = MediaLocationType.Data;
  mediaPlayerLauncher.Media = new Uri("http://files.ch9.ms/ch9/f2c3/b59b6efb-3c70-4bc2-b3ff-
9e650007f2c3/wp7ces_high_ch9.mp4");
  mediaPlayerLauncher.Show();
}
```

PhoneCallTask

The PhoneCallTask class has two properties: DisplayName and PhoneNunber. When the PhoneCallTask.Show() method is called, a dialog box is displayed that says, "Dial DisplayName at PhoneNumber." Here is the code to dial a phone number with the user's consent:

```
private void PhoneCallTask_MouseLeftButtonDown(object sender, MouseButtonEventArgs e)
{
  PhoneCallTask phoneCallTask = new PhoneCallTask();
```

```
    phoneCallTask.DisplayName = "Rob Cameron";
    phoneCallTask.PhoneNumber = "555-555-1111";
    phoneCallTask.Show();
}
```

SearchTask

The SearchTask class performs the same search as pushing the hardware Search button. It has a SearchQuery property to pass a search string for the search. Here is the code for the SearchTask:

```
private void SearchTask_MouseLeftButtonDown(object sender, MouseButtonEventArgs e)
{
    SearchTask searchTask = new SearchTask();
    searchTask.SearchQuery = "driving music";
    searchTask.Show();
}
```

SMSComposeTask

The SmsComposeTask class sends an SMS based on the configured properties: the To property and the Body property. Calling the Show() method brings up the SMS application on the phone with the SMS ready to go. Note that the user can decide not to send. As with other launchers, there is no way to determine whether a user cancels or goes through with the action. Here is the code:

```
private void SMSComposeTask_MouseLeftButtonDown(object sender, MouseButtonEventArgs e)
{
    Microsoft.Phone.Tasks.SmsComposeTask smsComposeTask = new SmsComposeTask();
    smsComposeTask.To = "555-555-5555";
    smsComposeTask.Body = "Meet me for pizza.";
    smsComposeTask.Show();
}
```

WebBrowserTask

The WebBrowserTask class opens the full browser experience based on the configured property, URL, which takes a string. Here is the code:

```
private void WebBrowserTask_MouseLeftButtonDown(object sender, MouseButtonEventArgs e)
{
    WebBrowserTask webBrowserTask = new WebBrowserTask();
    webBrowserTask.URL = "http://create.msdn.com";
    webBrowserTask.Show();
}
```

There is a known issue that if you try running this code under the debugger, it quite often displays the web browser with a blank URL. Sometimes if you click in the address bar and then click outside of the address bar, it starts working. Running the code normally without the debugger seems to work much better.

■ **Note** Microsoft announced at Mobile World Conference in February 2011 that Internet Explorer 9 with support for HTML5 will be added to Windows Phone 7 later in 2011.

Choosers

While the launchers are fire-and-forget, choosers return information back to the application, such as an image from the camera, a phone number, or e-mail address. As with the launchers, users can cancel the action; however, the application will know if the action was canceled. If the action is not canceled, the information will be returned to the application with the user's consent.

Choosers have a Show( ) method like with launchers but choosers also have a Completed event where data is returned. Developers wire-up the Completed event in order to process the returned values.

CameraCaptureTask

This task allows the user to take a picture. The task returns a stream to the taken photo. One potential "got'cha" with this task is that you cannot invoke the camera on a device while syncing with Zune, because a photo is media, and media interaction is not allowed while synching with Zune. This is another example of where the WPConnect tool comes in handy. Because the sample is a little more involved, it has its own page for a UI. Listing 4–6 shows the code.

Listing 4–6. CameraTaskPage.xaml.cs Code File

```
using System;
using System.IO;
using System.IO.IsolatedStorage;
using System.Windows;
using System.Windows.Media.Imaging;
using Microsoft.Phone.Controls;
using Microsoft.Phone.Tasks;

namespace LaunchersAndChoosers.TaskPages
{
  public partial class CameraTaskPage : PhoneApplicationPage
  {
    private CameraCaptureTask cameraTask;
    private BitmapImage capturedImage;
    string fileName = "capturedimage.jpg";

    public CameraTaskPage()
    {
      InitializeComponent();

      cameraTask = new CameraCaptureTask();
      capturedImage = new BitmapImage();

      cameraTask.Completed += new EventHandler<PhotoResult>(cameraTask_Completed);
      PreviewImage.Source = capturedImage;
    }
```

```csharp
void cameraTask_Completed(object sender, PhotoResult e)
{
  if ((null == e.Error) && (null != e.ChosenPhoto))
    capturedImage.SetSource(e.ChosenPhoto);
  else
  {
    MessageBox.Show(e.Error.Message);
  }
}

private void TakePictureButton_Click(object sender, EventArgs e)
{
  cameraTask.Show();
}

private void SavePictureButton_Click(object sender, EventArgs e)
{
  WriteableBitmap bmp = new WriteableBitmap(capturedImage);

  using (IsolatedStorageFile iso = IsolatedStorageFile.GetUserStoreForApplication())
  {
    using (IsolatedStorageFileStream fs =
      iso.OpenFile(fileName, System.IO.FileMode.Create))
    {
      bmp.SaveJpeg(fs, bmp.PixelWidth, bmp.PixelHeight, 0, 100);
      savedImage.Source = bmp;
    }
  }
}
```

The sample application shows the CameraCaptureTask Chooser to take a picture. Once the user accepts the picture, the image is displayed in the bottom Image object. When the user clicks the Save Application bar button, the sample saves the image to isolated storage and displays the image in the UI in the top Image object.

EmailAddressChooserTask

The EmailAddressChooserTask class allows the user to pick an e-mail for an application action, such as sharing a link or other information in the application. The task shows the phone UI with a list of contacts to choose once the Show() method is called.

The e-mail address is made available in the Completed event. It could be used as part of launching the EmailComposeTask. Here is the code:

```csharp
private void EmailAddressChooserTask_MouseLeftButtonDown(object sender,
 MouseButtonEventArgs e)
{
  EmailAddressChooserTask emailAddressChooserTask = new EmailAddressChooserTask();
  emailAddressChooserTask.Completed += new EventHandler<EmailResult>
(emailAddressChooserTask_Completed);
  emailAddressChooserTask.Show();
```

```
}

void emailAddressChooserTask_Completed(object sender, EmailResult e)
{
  if ((null == e.Error) && (TaskResult.OK == e.TaskResult))
  {
    MessageBox.Show("Email Address Returned is: " + e.Email);
  }
}
```

PhoneNumberChooserTask

The PhoneNumberChooserTask class allows the user to pick a phone number for an application action, such as to open the PhoneCallTask launcher. The task shows the phone UI with a list of contacts to choose once the Show() method is called. The phone number is made available in the Completed event. Here is the code:

```
private void PhoneNumberChooserTask_MouseLeftButtonDown(object sender, MouseButtonEventArgs e)
{
  PhoneNumberChooserTask phoneNumberChooserTask = new PhoneNumberChooserTask();
  phoneNumberChooserTask.Completed += new EventHandler<PhoneNumberResult>↩
(phoneNumberChooserTask_Completed);
  phoneNumberChooserTask.Show();
}

void phoneNumberChooserTask_Completed(object sender, PhoneNumberResult e)
{
  if ((null == e.Error) && (TaskResult.OK == e.TaskResult))
  {
    MessageBox.Show("Phone number returned is: " + e.PhoneNumber);
  }
}
```

PhotoChooserTask

The PhotoChooserTask class is very similar to the CameraCaptureTask, in that it returns a photo image. The PhotoChooserTask has a property named ShowCamera to give the user an option of choosing an existing photo or capturing a new photo. After calling the Show() method to launch the UI, the Completed event fires when the user is done, and the picture is loaded into an Image control in the UI. Here is the code:

```
private void PhotoChooserTask_MouseLeftButtonDown(object sender, MouseButtonEventArgs e)
{
  PhotoChooserTask photoChoserTask = new PhotoChooserTask();
  photoChoserTask.ShowCamera = true;
  photoChoserTask.Completed += new EventHandler<PhotoResult>(photoChoserTask_Completed);
  photoChoserTask.Show();
}

private BitmapImage capturedImage;
void photoChoserTask_Completed(object sender, PhotoResult e)
{
  if ((null == e.Error) && (TaskResult.OK == e.TaskResult))
```

```
  {
    capturedImage = new BitmapImage();
    capturedImage.SetSource(e.ChosenPhoto);
    ChosenPhotoImage.Source = capturedImage;
  }
}
```

SaveEmailAddressTask

The SaveEmailAddressTask class shows the built-in contacts application. It allows the code to save the provided e-mail address to a new or existing contact via the Email property. Use the Completed event to determine whether an error occurred and that the task completed successfully. Here is the code:

```
private void SaveEmailAdressTask_MouseLeftButtonDown(object sender, MouseButtonEventArgs e)
{
  SaveEmailAddressTask saveEmailAddressTask = new SaveEmailAddressTask();
  saveEmailAddressTask.Completed += new EventHandler<TaskEventArgs>↩
(saveEmailAddressTask_Completed);
  saveEmailAddressTask.Email = "email@domain.com";
  MessageBox.Show("Saving this email: " + saveEmailAddressTask.Email);
  saveEmailAddressTask.Show();
}

void saveEmailAddressTask_Completed(object sender, TaskEventArgs e)
{
  if ((null == e.Error) && (TaskResult.OK == e.TaskResult))
  {
    MessageBox.Show("Email address saved");
  }
}
```

SavePhoneNumberTask

The SavePhoneNumberTask works very similarly to the SaveEmailAddressTask, except that it passes in a phone number instead of an e-mail address. Here is the code:

```
private void SavePhoneNumberTask_MouseLeftButtonDown(object sender, MouseButtonEventArgs e)
{
  SavePhoneNumberTask savePhoneNumberTask = new SavePhoneNumberTask();
  savePhoneNumberTask.Completed += new EventHandler<TaskEventArgs>↩
(savePhoneNumberTask_Completed);
  savePhoneNumberTask.PhoneNumber = "555-555-5555";
  MessageBox.Show("Saving this phone number: " + savePhoneNumberTask.PhoneNumber);
  savePhoneNumberTask.Show();
}

void savePhoneNumberTask_Completed(object sender, TaskEventArgs e)
{
  if ((null == e.Error) && (TaskResult.OK == e.TaskResult))
  {
    MessageBox.Show("Phonc number saved");
  }
}
```

Web Browser Control

The WebBrowser control is not a task, but it is related to the web browser task, so it makes sense to cover it here. The WebBrowser control is much more programmable than the WebBrowserTask covered in the previous section on Launchers.

The WebBrowser control can be embedded within the XAML of an application, so the content appears more integrated with the application itself. It is still a full browser, so you can navigate away from content if following hyperlinks, but you can configure how it behaves. The following is a list of the WebBrowser control class members to help guide capabilities:

- **Base:** Sets the base directory in isolated storage that is used to resolve relative URLs.

- **CacheMode:** Determines whether content should be cached when possible.

- **InvokeScript:** Executes a function in the script for the currently loaded content.

- **IsScriptEnabled:** Set to true to enable scripting. Applies to the next document navigated to, not the current document.

- **LoadCompleted:** Event fires when the content is fully loaded. Permits having a loading animation.

- **Navigate:** Navigates the browser control to the provided URI. Two overloads with the second taking post data and additional headers.

- **Navigated:** Fires after successful navigation.

- **Navigating:** Fires when browser is navigating

- **NavigateToString:** Allows loading the provided HTML string into the browser.

- **ScriptNotify:** Fires when JavaScript calls window.external.Notify(<data>).

The WebBrowserControl project sample in the Chapter 4 solution exercises the WebBrowser control with two pages. The first sample page demonstrates basic use. The second sample page demonstrates scripting interoperability between Silverlight and the hosted HTML code.

Basic WebBrowser Control Sample

In the BasicWebBrowserControlPage.xaml, there is a WebBrowser control, a TextBox to enter a URL, and a load button in the application bar. There is also a semi-transparent Rectangle to demonstrate transparency support in the WebBrowser control.

The project includes a simple animation named AnimateGreenRect that spins and animates the size of the green Rectangle while loading content into the WebBrowser control. The Storyboard object is built using Expression Blend. First a keyframe is added at 0 seconds with the configured position. The yellow timeline indicator is slid over to 500ms and another keyframe is added by clicking the small circle with a plus sign in the Object and Timeline window as shown in Figure 4–6.

Figure 4–6. Creating the animation

With the yellow timeline indicator over the second keyframe, move over to the Properties window and expand the Transform section. Select the Rotate tab and set the Angle property to 180 degrees. Next, select the Scale tab and set X and Y to .5. Click on the name of the Storyboard at the top of the Object and Timeline window to select the newly created Storyboard and move over to the Properties window. Check the AutoReverse checkbox and set the RepeatBehavior to Forever.

It takes just a little bit of code to wire-up playing the animation while loading the web page. Listing 4–7 has the code.

Listing 4–7. BasicWebBrowserControlPage.xaml.cs Code File

```
public partial class BasicWebBrowserControlPage : PhoneApplicationPage
  {
    public BasicWebBrowscrControlPage()
    {
      InitializeComponent();
```

```
        webBrowserControl.LoadCompleted += new
          System.Windows.Navigation.LoadCompletedEventHandler(webBrowserControl_LoadCompleted);
        webBrowserControl.Navigating += new
          EventHandler<NavigatingEventArgs>(webBrowserControl_Navigating);
    }

    void webBrowserControl_Navigating(object sender, NavigatingEventArgs e)
    {
        System.Diagnostics.Debug.WriteLine(e.Uri);
    }

    private void loadUrlAppBarButton_Click(object sender, EventArgs e)
    {
        AnimateGreenRect.Begin();
        webBrowserControl.Navigate(new Uri(WebAddressTextBox.Text));
    }

    void webBrowserControl_LoadCompleted(object sender, System.Windows.Navigation⏎
.NavigationEventArgs e)
    {
        AnimateGreenRect.Stop();
    }
}
```

You can hook into the various events available listed above in XAML as we have done previously. Using the += syntax, Visual Studio will automatically generate the correct event handler just by hitting the tab key to generate it:

```
webBrowserControl.Navigating += new
  EventHandler<NavigatingEventArgs>(webBrowserControl_Navigating);
```

An important capability of the WebBrowser control is to load HTML fragments using the WebBrowser.NavigateToString() method. Another important capability is the WebBrowser.Base property allows relative URLs for items such as images to be loaded locally. Caching items to the file system can save download time and bandwidth for the user, improving overall application performance. The next section covers interacting with the HTML content via scripting.

WebBrowser Control Scripting Sample

The WebBrowser control supports HTML, CSS, and JavaScript. To support JavaScript, set the IsScriptEnabled property to true in XAML or in the code-behind. The WebBrowserControlScriptingPage.xaml sample contains a WebBrowser control that is loaded with an HTML page stored in the xap as content. The HTML page contains two JavaScript script functions; one that sets the content on a DIV, the other script sets the source to an IMG tag in the HTML. Listing 4–8 has the HTML file that is stored in the xap as content.

Listing 4–8. The content.html Code File

```
<html>
<head>
  <title>Test Script</title>
  <script type="text/javascript">

    function PassData(data) {
```

```
      content1.innerHTML = data;
    }

    function SetImageSource(source) {
      image1.src = source;
    }
    <style type="text/css">
    body {
      font-family: "Segoe WP";
      font-size: medium;
      color: #FFFFFF;
      background-color: #000000;
    }
  </script>
</head>
<body>
  <h3>
    Page Loaded</h3>
  <img alt="image goes here" src="" id="image1" />
  <h4>
    Text appears below:</h4>
  <div id="content1">
  </div>
</body>
</html>
```

You can see the two JavaScript functions in Listing 4–5 as well as the div and image that are updated by the functions. The HTML file has a little bit of formatting to help the HTML file blend in with the UI. The style was creating using the Visual Studio Manage Styles dialog box by clicking the new style button. You can see the styling in the CSS style applied to the HTML BODY tag. The style does the following:

- Sets the font to match the Windows Phone 7 font (Segoe WP)

- Font Size to medi and a foreground color of White

- Set the background color to Black

When using the WebBrowser control, try to have the content blend into the UI with styling. Windows Phone 7 supports two themes, light and dark, so you should dynamically apply styles based on the theming, which you will see is not difficult to do via the scripting bridge.

The WebBrowser Control supports invoking script. Listing 4–9 has the code-behind file where the Silverlight code calls the two scripts.

Listing 4–9. The WebBrowserControlScriptingPage.xaml.cs Code File

```
using System;
using System.IO;
using System.IO.IsolatedStorage;
using System.Windows;
using Microsoft.Phone.Controls;

namespace WebBrowserControl.pages
{
  public partial class WebBrowserControlScriptingPage : PhoneApplicationPage
  {
```

```csharp
public WebBrowserControlScriptingPage()
{
  InitializeComponent();
  Loaded += new RoutedEventHandler(WebBrowserControlScriptingPage_Loaded);
}

void WebBrowserControlScriptingPage_Loaded(object sender, RoutedEventArgs e)
{
  SetUpWebBrowserControlContent();
  webBrowserControl.Base = "home";
  webBrowserControl.Navigate(new Uri("content.html", UriKind.Relative));
}

private void SetUpWebBrowserControlContent()
{
  //Copy content out of xap and into isolated storage
  using (IsolatedStorageFile isf =
          IsolatedStorageFile.GetUserStoreForApplication())
  {
    //if (!isf.DirectoryExists("home"))
    //{
    isf.CreateDirectory("home");
    //create base html file
    using (IsolatedStorageFileStream fs =
      isf.OpenFile("home/content.html", System.IO.FileMode.Create))
    {
      byte[] buffer = new byte[256];
      int count = 0;
      Stream resourceStream =
        Application.GetResourceStream(
                new Uri("html/content.html", UriKind.Relative)).Stream;
      count = resourceStream.Read(buffer, 0, 256);
      while (count > 0)
      {
        fs.Write(buffer, 0, count);
        count = resourceStream.Read(buffer, 0, 256);
      }
    }
    //Create Image directory
    isf.CreateDirectory("home/images");
    //Create image file
    using (IsolatedStorageFileStream fs =
      isf.OpenFile("home/images/image.jpg", System.IO.FileMode.Create))
    {
      byte[] buffer = new byte[256];
      int count = 0;
      Stream resourceStream = Application.GetResourceStream(
        new Uri("images/image.jpg", UriKind.Relative)).Stream;
      count = resourceStream.Read(buffer, 0, 256);
      while (count > 0)
      {
        fs.Write(buffer, 0, count);
        count = resourceStream.Read(buffer, 0, 256);
      }
```

```
      }
    }
  }

  private void loadUrlAppBarButton_Click(object sender, EventArgs e)
  {
    //Invoke script
    webBrowserControl.InvokeScript(
        "PassData", "This is the data.  Hello from Silverlight.");
    webBrowserControl.InvokeScript(
        "SetImageSource", "images/image.jpg");
  }
 }
}
```

The InvokeScript method on the WebBrowser control takes the name of the JavaScript method and a string array for parameters. When the refresh button is clicked, the loadUrlAppBarButton_Click shown in Listing 4–9 event fires resulting in the UI shown in Figure 4–7.

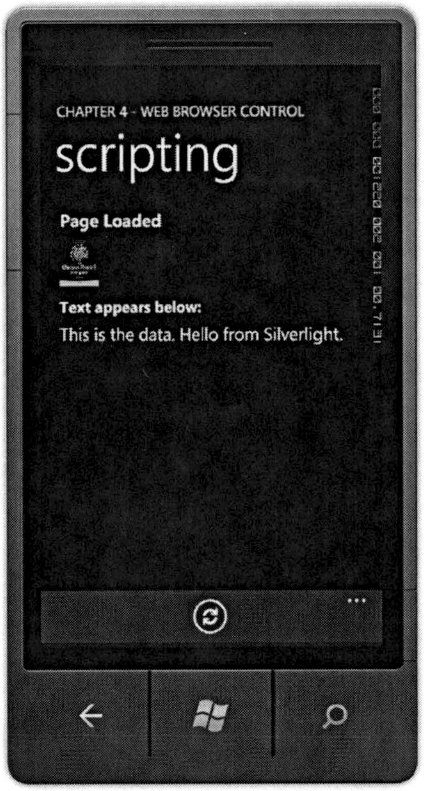

Figure 4–7. WebBrowser control scripting page

Asynchronous Programming

This section covers asynchronous programming, which is the preferred method do to work in Silverlight. Asynchronous programming is preferred, because it takes work off of the UI thread, which should be a priority in order to maximize UI performance for animation and transitions.

Rendering performance can be improved two ways: pushing work from the UI thread to the Render thread and pushing work such as processing remote data to a separate background thread. We cover various ways to push work off of the UI thread in this section.

Background Threads

You can use the standard .NET multithreading class `Thread.Start` and `ThreadPool.QueueUserWorkItem` to perform background work that writes data to isolated storage, and it will work fine. If you try to access the XAML from the standard classes without taking extra steps, it will throw an exception. Silverlight includes classes that make it easier to perform background work that interacts with the user interface.

Fire and Forget Background Processing

The `Dispatcher` class offers a safe way to call a method that updates the UI asynchronously from a background thread by providing services for managing the queue of work items for a thread. Both the `Dispatcher` and the `BackgroundWorker` classes can perform work on a separate thread. The `BackgroundWorker` class supports progress reporting and cancellation, which we cover in detail in the next section. The `Dispatcher` class is useful when you need a simple way to queue up background work without progress reporting or cancellation.

You can create a delegate and then user `Dispatcher.BeginInvoke` to fire the delegate, which then updates the UI. As an example, if you have a TextBlock named `TextBlock1` that you need to update from a background thread, obtain the `Dispatcher` from that control and perform the update. Here is an example of using C# lambda syntax (=>).

```
TextBlock1.Dispatcher.BeginInvoke(() =>
  {
    TextBlock1.Text = "Data Updated";
  };
```

You can call `Dispatcher.CheckAccess` to determine if the calling thread is on the same thread as the control or the UI thread. Use `BeginInvoke` it if returns false. It is recommended to obtain the `Dispatcher` instance from the control closest to the controls being updated. So if multiple controls need to be updated and they are contained in a `Grid` panel, obtain the Dispatcher from the `Grid`.

Our sample for this section will retrieve an xml file from the services project named WcfRemoteServices that is part of the Chapter 4 solution. Remote services are covered in detail in the section titled "Connecting Windows Phone to Services and Feeds" later in this chapter. A file named ApressBooks.xml is added to the AsynchronousProgramming project. This XML file contains a simple xml schema with a few book titles in it. Here is one record from the XML file:

```
<ApressBook>
  <ID>4</ID>
  <ISBN>1-4302-2435-5</ISBN>
  <Author>Jit Ghosh and Rob Cameron</Author>
  <Title>Silverlight Recipes: A Problem-Solution Approach, Second Edition</Title>
  <Description>Silverlight Recipes: A Problem-Solution Approach, Second Edition is your↵
practical
```

companion to developing rich, interactive web applications with Microsoft's latest↵
technology.
```
</Description>
  <DatePublished>2010-07-15T00:00:00</DatePublished>
  <NumPages>1056</NumPages>
  <Price>$49.99</Price>
</ApressBook>
```

The UI for the DispatcherPage.xaml contains a ListBox with an ItemTemplate to display the above data and an application bar with one button to load the data. When the button is clicked, the LoadDataAppBarButton_Click event handler spins up a WebRequest object that points to the local developer web server from the WcfRemoteServices Project to retrieve the XML file. Here is the code snippet for the application bar button event handler:

```
private void LoadDataAppBarButton_Click(object sender, EventArgs e)
{
  Uri location =
      new Uri("http://localhost:9090/xml/ApressBooks.xml", UriKind.Absolute);
  WebRequest request = HttpWebRequest.Create(location);
  request.BeginGetResponse(
      new AsyncCallback(this.RetrieveXmlCompleted), request);
}
```

All remote service calls MUST be executed asynchronously, so the callback function named RetrieveXmlCompleted is where the results are actually returned to the application. Here is the RetrieveXmlCompleted method:

```
void RetrieveXmlCompleted(IAsyncResult ar)
{
  List<ApressBook> _apressBookList;
  HttpWebRequest request = ar.AsyncState as HttpWebRequest;
  WebResponse response = request.EndGetResponse(ar);
  Stream responseStream = response.GetResponseStream();
  using (StreamReader streamreader = new StreamReader(responseStream))
  {
    XDocument xDoc = XDocument.Load(streamreader);
    _apressBookList =
    (from b in xDoc.Descendants("ApressBook")
      select new ApressBook()
      {
        Author = b.Element("Author").Value,
        Title = b.Element("Title").Value,
        ISBN = b.Element("ISBN").Value,
        Description = b.Element("Description").Value,
        PublishedDate = Convert.ToDateTime(b.Element("DatePublished").Value),
        NumberOfPages = b.Element("NumPages").Value,
        Price = b.Element("Price").Value,
        ID = b.Element("ID").Value
      }).ToList();
  }
  //Could use Anonymous delegate (does same as below line of code)
  // BooksListBox.Dispatcher.BeginInvoke(
  //   delegate()
  //   {
  //     DataBindListBox(_apressBookList);
```

```
// }
// );
//Use C# 3.0 Lambda
BooksListBox.Dispatcher.BeginInvoke(() => DataBindListBox(_apressBookList));
}
```

The xml file is received and then loaded into an XDocument object for some basic Linq to XML manipulation to turn it into a collection of APressBook .NET objects. Once that little bit of work is completed, the collection needs to be pushed back to the UI thread. This is where the BooksListBox.Dispatcher is finally used to fire the DataBindListBox method to perform the data binding.

The previous code snippet includes an alternative method of passing the _apressBookList to the UI thread and databind. It could be reduced further to the following:

```
BooksListBox.Dispatcher.BeginInvoke(() =>
{
  BooksListBox.ItemsSource = _apressBookList;
});
```

To test the Dispatcher using WebRequest, both the WCFRemoteServices project and the AsynchronousProgramming project must be running. Right-click on the Ch04_WP7ProgrammingModel Solution and configure it to have multiple startup projects, as shown in Figure 4–8.

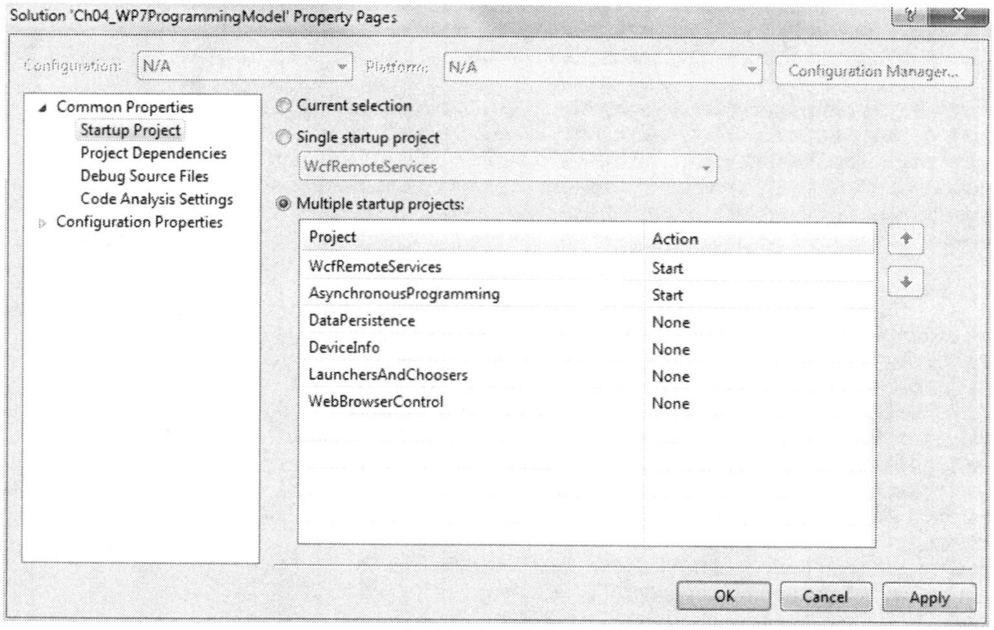

Figure 4–8. *WebBrowser control scripting page*

If you still want to use standard .NET Framework threading, You can call SynchronizationContext.Current to get the current DispatcherSynchronizationContext, assign it to a member variable on the Page, and call Post(method, data) to fire the event back on the UI thread. Calling Send(method, data) instead of Post will make a synchronous call, which you should avoid doing if possible as it could affect UI performance.

Supporting Progress Reporting and Cancellation

For long running processes, having the ability to cancel work as well as show work progress is necessary for a good user experience. A convenient class that provides a level of abstraction as well as progress updates is the System.ComponentModel.BackgroundWorker class. The BackgroundWorker class lets you indicate operation progress, completion, and cancellation in the Silverlight UI. For example, you can check whether the background operation is completed or canceled and display a message to the user.

The Chapter 4 sample AsynchronousProgramming project test page named BackgroundWorkerPage.xaml explores the BackgroundWorker class. To use a background worker thread, declare an instance of the BackgroundWorker class at the class level, not within an event handler:

```
BackgroundWorker bw = new BackgroundWorker();
```

You can specify whether you want to allow cancellation and progress reporting by setting one or both of the WorkerSupportsCancellation and WorkerReportsProgress properties on the BackgroundWorker object to true. The next step is to create an event handler for the BackgroundWorker.DoWork event. This is where you put the code for the time-consuming operation. Within the DoWork event, check the CancellationPending property to see if the user clicked the Cancel button. You must set e.Cancel = true in DoWork so that WorkCompleted can check the value and finish correctly if the work was completed.

If the operation is not cancelled, call the ReportProgress method to pass a percentage complete value that is between 0 and 100. Doing this raises the ProgressChanged event on the BackgroundWorker object. The UI thread code can subscribe to the event and update the UI based on the progress. If you call the ReportProgress method when WorkerReportsProgress is set to false, an exception will occur. You can also pass in a value for the UserState parameter, which in this case is a string that is used to update the UI.

Once the work is completed successfully, pass the data back to the calling process by setting the e.Result property of the DoWorkerEventArgs object to the object or collection containing the data resulting from the work. The DoWorkerEventArgs.Result is of type object and can therefore be assigned any object or collection of objects. The value of the Result property can be read when the RunWorkerCompleted event is raised upon completion of the operation and the value can be safely assigned to UI object properties. Listing 4–10 shows the XAML modifications in the ContentPanel Grid.

Listing 4–10. The BackgroundWorkerPage.xaml ContentPanel XAML

```xaml
<Grid x:Name="ContentPanel" Grid.Row="1" Margin="12,0,12,0">
  <StackPanel Orientation="Vertical" d:LayoutOverrides="Height">
    <StackPanel x:Name="StatusStackPanel" Orientation="Vertical">
      <StackPanel Orientation="Horizontal" d:LayoutOverrides="Width">
        <TextBlock x:Name="processingStateTextBlock" TextWrapping="Wrap"
            VerticalAlignment="Top" Width="190" Margin="12,34,0,0"/>
        <Button x:Name="cancelButton" Content="Cancel Operation"
            VerticalAlignment="Top" Click="cancelButton_Click" Width="254" />
      </StackPanel>
      <ProgressBar x:Name="BookListDownloadProgress" Width="456"
                    HorizontalAlignment="Left" />
    </StackPanel>
    <ListBox x:Name="BooksListBox" ItemsSource="{Binding ApressBookList}"
      Height="523" ItemTemplate="{StaticResource BookListBoxDataTemplate}" />
  </StackPanel>
</Grid>
```

The StatusStackPanel container that has the status info is made visible when the work is started, and is then hidden since the work is completed. Figure 4–9 has the UI.

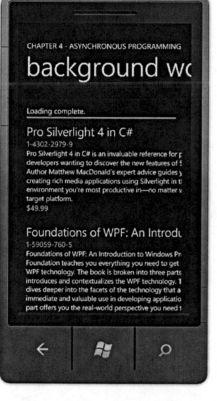

Figure 4–9. WebBrowser control scripting page

One additional wrinkle is that the code overrides OnNavigateFrom. If the BackgroundWorker thread is busy, the code cancels the operation, since the user navigated away. Listing 4–11 has the full source code.

Listing 4–11. The BackgroundWorkerPage.xaml.cs Code File

```csharp
using System.ComponentModel;
using System.Windows;
using Microsoft.Phone.Controls;

namespace AsynchronousProgramming.pages
{
  public partial class BackgroundWorkerPage : PhoneApplicationPage
  {
    private BackgroundWorker _worker = new BackgroundWorker();

    public BackgroundWorkerPage()
    {
      InitializeComponent();
```

```
    //Configure BackgroundWorker thread
    _worker.WorkerReportsProgress = true;
    _worker.WorkerSupportsCancellation = true;
    _worker.DoWork +=
      new DoWorkEventHandler(worker_DoWork);
    _worker.ProgressChanged +=
      new ProgressChangedEventHandler(worker_ProgressChanged);
    _worker.RunWorkerCompleted +=
      new RunWorkerCompletedEventHandler(worker_RunWorkerCompleted);

    //Kick off long running process
    //Make status visible
    _worker.RunWorkerAsync();
    StatusStackPanel.Visibility = Visibility.Visible;
}

protected override void OnNavigatedFrom(
                  System.Windows.Navigation.NavigationEventArgs e)
{
    //Cancel work if user navigates away
    if (_worker.IsBusy)
      _worker.CancelAsync();

    base.OnNavigatedFrom(e);
}

void worker_DoWork(object sender, DoWorkEventArgs e)
{
    ApressBooks books = new ApressBooks();
    books.LoadBooks();
    int progress;
    string state = "initializing...";
    //Do fake work to retrieve and process books
    for (int i = 1; i <= books.ApressBookList.Count;i++ )
    {
      if (_worker.CancellationPending == true)
      {
        e.Cancel = true;
        break;
      }
      else
      {
        progress = (int)System.Math.Round((double)i /
                    books.ApressBookList.Count * 100d);

        if ((progress > 15) && (progress < 90))
          state = "processing..." ;
        if (progress > 85)
          state = "finishing..." ;
        if (progress == 95)
          state = "Loading complete.";

        _worker.ReportProgress(progress, state);
        System.Threading.Thread.Sleep(250);
```

```
      }
    }
    e.Result = books;
  }

  void worker_ProgressChanged(object sender, ProgressChangedEventArgs e)
  {
    BookListDownloadProgress.Value = e.ProgressPercentage;
    processingStateTextBlock.Text = e.UserState as string;
  }


  void worker_RunWorkerCompleted(object sender, RunWorkerCompletedEventArgs e)
  {
    if (e.Cancelled == true)
      MessageBox.Show("Operation cancelled.","Cancelled",MessageBoxButton.OK);
    else
      LayoutRoot.DataContext = e.Result as ApressBooks;

    //Clean up status UI
    BookListDownloadProgress.Value = 0;
    processingStateTextBlock.Text = "";
    StatusStackPanel.Visibility = Visibility.Collapsed;
  }

  private void cancelButton_Click(object sender, RoutedEventArgs e)
  {
    _worker.CancelAsync();
  }
 }
}
```

Silverlight includes the standard .NET locking primitives, such as Monitor or lock, as well as the ManualResetEvent class where deadlocks can occur. A deadlock occurs when two threads each hold on to a resource while requesting the resource that the other thread is holding. A deadlock will cause the application to hang. It is easy to create a deadlock with two threads accessing the same resources in an application.

The BackgroundWorker class tries to prevent deadlocks or cross-thread invocations that could be unsafe.

Any exceptions that can occur must be caught within the background thread, because they will not be caught by the unhandled exception handler at the application level. If an exception occurs on the background thread, one option is to catch the exception and set Result to null as a signal that there was an error. Another option is to set a particular value to Result as a signal that a failure occurred.

Connecting Windows Phone to Services and Feeds

In this section, we cover the supported networking and service protocols available to Windows Phone 7 applications. These include Windows Communication Foundation (WCF), HttpWebRequest, and WebClient. Windows Communication Foundation is Microsoft's service development framework for SOAP, REST, and Feed-based services. HttpWebRequest and WebClient are straightforward HTTP request and response classes.

HttpWebRequest and WebClient

We demonstrated how to use HttpWebRequest earlier, when we discussed the Dispatcher and how it helps to marshal data back over to the UI thread. WebClient has similar functionality as HttpWebRequest and is fine for doing small amounts of work if preferred.

■ **Caution** One item to note is that WebClient primarily runs on the UI thread, which, as a Silverlight developer, you always want to avoid as much as possible. Use HttpWebRequest instead.

In Silverlight for Windows Phone 7, you can set the User-agent string and Headers for requests like using this syntax:

```
request.Headers.Add(HttpRequestHeader.UserAgent, "appname");
```

Windows Communication Foundation Support

In Chapter 1, we discussed how Silverlight for Windows Phone 7 relates to Silverlight 3 and Silverlight 4. Regarding WCF, Silverlight for Windows Phone 7 is based on Silverlight 3, supporting the WCF capabilities available in Silverlight 3, with some additions like the ability to set User-agent and Headers as noted earlier. WCF includes client-side libraries to call services and a server-side programming model to create services. You can use the WCF libraries to connect to services implemented in other programming models and languages, as long as it is a supported network and wire protocol.

There is a fair amount of networking capability available in Windows Phone 7 for Silverlight developers, including SOAP, REST, and Basic Authentication. With all of the code samples and blog posts on the Internet for Silverlight and the .NET Framework, it can be confusing to know exactly what is supported. This link includes information on what is not supported in Silverlight for Windows Phone 7 when compared to Silverlight 4 and the .NET Framework:

http://msdn.microsoft.com/en-us/library/ff637320(v=VS.95).aspx

Here is a summary of items that are *not* supported:

- New networking features available in Silverlight 4

- Custom WCF bindings

- Sockets

- WCF Data Services

- Duplex Communication over HTTP

- JSON Serialization (partial support is available using the DataContractJsonSerializer class)

- RSS and Atom Feeds

- Silverlight toolkit networking features

Focusing on what's supported, you can add a Service Reference in Visual Studio to access a SOAP or REST service. You can also generate a proxy class with the slsvcutil.exe utility, which we cover in the following section. You can include credentials via Basic Authentication; just don't forget to wrap the call in SSL.

Web Services

To have some data and services to work with, a new project solution named WcfRemoteServices is added to the Chapter 4 project. It is a WCF Service Application project type. When run, it launches the development web server to host the service. The project also includes an ADO.NET Entity Framework model to represent the AdventureWorks sample database available from Microsoft. The EF model is located in the model folder.-+

The database server used in the sample is SQL Server 2008 Express R2, which is available for free here:

www.microsoft.com/express/Database/

The sample database is available from CodePlex here:

http://msftdbprodsamples.codeplex.com/

The default Service1 WCF class is removed, and one service class is added to the project in the services folder named, AdventureWorks. To create the service, edit the corresponding IAdventureWorks Interface, and then implement the Interfaces in the AdventureWorks.svc class by editing the AdventureWorks.svc.cs file.

The service methods implement the Interfaces using LINQ queries against the AdventureWorksModel EF model. Listings 4–12 and 4–13 have the code for the Interface and concrete implementation of the AdventureWorks service.

Listing 4–12. The IAdventureWorks Interface for the SOAP WCF Service

```
using System;
using System.Collections.Generic;
using System.ServiceModel;
using WcfRemoteServices.model;
using System.Runtime.Serialization;

namespace WcfRemoteServices.services
{
  // NOTE: You can use the "Rename" command on the "Refactor" menu to change the
  //interface name "IProducts" in both code and config file together.
  [ServiceContract]
  public interface IAdventureWorks
  {
    [OperationContract]
    List<Product> FullProductList();

    [OperationContract]
    List<ProductCategory> ProductCategoryList();

    [OperationContract]
    List<ProductSubcategory> ProductSubcategoryList();

    [OperationContract]
    List<Product> GetProductsByCategory(Int32 CategoryID);
```

```csharp
    [OperationContract]
    List<Product> GetProductsBySubcategory(Int32 SubCategoryID);

    [OperationContract]
    int CheckInventory(Int32 ProductID);
    [OperationContract]
    List<Vendor> FullVendorList();

    VendorGeoLocation GetVendorAddress(Int32 VendorID);
  }

  [DataContract]
  public class VendorGeoLocation
  {
    [DataMember]
    public double Latitude { get; set; }

    [DataMember]
    public double Longitude { get; set; }
  }
}
```

Listing 4–13. The AdventureWorks.svc.cs Class Implementation for the WCF Service

```csharp
using System;
using System.Collections.Generic;
using System.ServiceModel;
using WcfRemoteServices.model;
using System.Runtime.Serialization;

namespace WcfRemoteServices.services
{
  // NOTE: You can use the "Rename" command on the "Refactor" menu to change the
  //interface name "IProducts" in both code and config file together.
  [ServiceContract]
  public interface IAdventureWorks
  {
    [OperationContract]
    List<Product> FullProductList();

    [OperationContract]
    List<ProductCategory> ProductCategoryList();

    [OperationContract]
    List<ProductSubcategory> ProductSubcategoryList();

    [OperationContract]
    List<Product> GetProductsByCategory(Int32 CategoryID);

    [OperationContract]
    List<Product> GetProductsBySubcategory(Int32 SubCategoryID);

    [OperationContract]
    int CheckInventory(Int32 ProductID);
```

```
    [OperationContract]
    List<Vendor> FullVendorList();

    VendorGeoLocation GetVendorAddress(Int32 VendorID);
}

[DataContract]
public class VendorGeoLocation
{
    [DataMember]
    public double Latitude { get; set; }

    [DataMember]
    public double Longitude { get; set; }
}
}
```

In the AdventureWorks service, the interface has a method named GetVendorAddress that uses the Bing Maps Geocode service to obtain a latitude and longitude. The developer environment is located here:

http://dev.virtualearth.net/webservices/v1/geocodeservice/geocodeservice.svc/mex

The staging environment is here:

http://staging.dev.virtualearth.net/webservices/v1/geocodeservice/geocodeservice.svc

The production environment is here:

http://dev.virtualearth.net/webservices/v1/geocodeservice/geocodeservice.svc

Once the WCF services are created, use the WCF Service Configuration Editor tool in the Visual Studio Tools menu to create the configuration for the services, which is located in the WcfRemoteServices Web.Config file. The most important item to keep in mind is that Silverlight for Windows Phone only supports basicHttpBinding and webHttpBinding. For security, Windows Phone 7 supports Basic Authentication for credentials (SSL always recommended if using Basic Authentication).

To access a remote service in Visual Studio 2010, you can generate a proxy class for the remote service using the Add Service Reference in the Windows Phone application as shown in Figure 4–10.

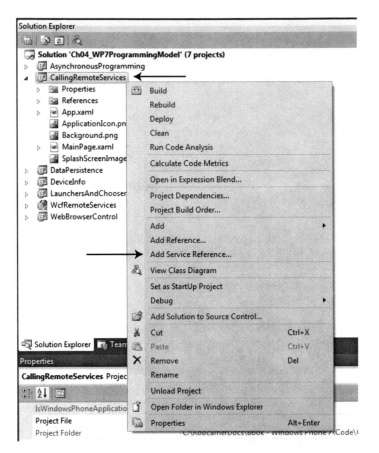

Figure 4–10. Add service reference menu

Silverlight includes a command-line tool for complete control when generating proxy classes. For Silverlight for Windows Phone 7, use the Silverlight 3 version of the tool called slsvcutil.exe, located at c:\Program Files (x86)\Microsoft SDKs\Silverlight\v3.0\Tools. The following is an example command-line for the two services we just created:

```
slsvcutil.exe http: //localhost:9090/services/AdventureWorks.svc↵
/out:c:\test\AdventureWorksProxy.cs
```

One advantage of using the command-line tool is that you can customize the proxy generation. For this sample, the slsvcutil.exe is used to generate the proxy class.

With the server-side service SOAP service created and the client proxy in hand, the WebServicePage.xaml page is customized to call the SOAP service. A ListBox control with an inline DataTemplate is added to the XAML of the WebServicePage.xaml page (see the following):

```
<ListBox x:Name="ProductsListBox" HorizontalAlignment="Left" VerticalAlignment="Top" >
  <ListBox.ItemTemplate>
    <DataTemplate>
      <StackPanel Margin="0,0,0,20">
```

```
        <TextBlock Text="{Binding Name}" Style="{StaticResource PhoneTextLargeStyle}" />
        <TextBlock Text="{Binding ProductNumber}" Style=↵
"{StaticResource PhoneTextSmallStyle}" />
        <TextBlock Text="{Binding ListPrice}" Style="{StaticResource PhoneTextAccentStyle}" />
      </StackPanel>
    </DataTemplate>
  </ListBox.ItemTemplate>
</ListBox>
```

Listing 4–14 has the code-behind file that calls the service asynchronously and then data binds the list box with the product info.

Listing 4–14. The WebServicePage.xaml.cs Code File

```
using Microsoft.Phone.Controls;

namespace CallingRemoteServices.pages
{
  public partial class WebServicePage : PhoneApplicationPage
  {
    public WebServicePage()
    {
      InitializeComponent();
    }

    private void PhoneApplicationPage_Loaded(object sender, RoutedEventArgs e)
    {
      AdventureWorksClient adventureWorksClient = new AdventureWorksClient();
      adventureWorksClient.FullProductListCompleted +=
        new EventHandler<FullProductListCompletedEventArgs>(
          adventureWorksClient_FullProductListCompleted);
      adventureWorksClient.FullProductListAsync();
    }

    void adventureWorksClient_FullProductListCompleted(
      object sender, FullProductListCompletedEventArgs e)
    {
      ProductsListBox.ItemsSource = e.Result;
    }
  }
}
```

When you run the sample, it takes a good 10 seconds to download and data bind the data, as it is a long list, but it demonstrates how to call a SOAP service in Windows Phone 7. Figure 4–11 has the UI.

Figure 4–11. WebServicePage.xaml in action

This concludes the demonstration on how to call SOAP web services. In the next section, we cover ADO.NET Data Services, and demonstrate accessing REST services with the OData client for Windows Phone 7.

REST+OData

We now switch to demonstrating how Windows Phone 7 can call REST services using an OData client. A new WCF Data Service item named AdventureWorksRestOData.svc is added to the WcfRemoteServices project and the class is edited to look like the following:

```
namespace WcfRemoteServices.services
{
  public class AdventureWorksREST : DataService<AdventureWorksEntities>
  {
    public static void InitializeService(DataServiceConfiguration config)
    {
            config.SetEntitySetAccessRule("*", EntitySetRights.All);
      config.DataServiceBehavior.MaxProtocolVersion = DataServiceProtocolVersion.V2;
```

```
        config.SetEntitySetPageSize("*", 20);
    }
  }
}
```

Notice that the DataService class also uses the AdventureWorksEntities Entity Framework model as the basis for which objects it makes available via REST. A similar URL is used to access the service:

```
http://localhost:9090/services/AdventureWorksRestOData.svc
```

To retrieve the Vendors list, append the text Vendors to the end of this URL. Other REST operations are supported as well, but that's all it takes to create the REST Service.

In the WP7 client project named CallingRemoteServices, a new page is added, named RestDataServicesODataPage.xaml, where the AdventureWorksREST service is called. We need to generate a client proxy class using the DataSvcUtil.exe available at this link:

```
http://odata.codeplex.com/releases/view/54698#DownloadId=161862
```

It works similarly to the slsvcutil.exe we looked at previously:

```
DataSvcUtil /uri:http://localhost:9090/services/AdventureWorksRestOData.svc
 /out:c:\test\AventureWorksREST.cs /language:CSharp
```

The generated class is added to the WP7 CallingRemoteServices project. There is one other item that we need to add to the project, which is a Windows Phone 7 version of the System.Data.Services.Client.dll. This assembly is also available at the CodePlex link, the same place where you download DataSvcUtil.exe. At this point, the project should compile without errors.

Essentially, we just created an OData Windows Phone 7 client to the REST services we created previously at the AdventureWorksRestOData.svc end point. We change the namespace in the AventureWorksRESTOData.cs to AdventureWorksModelOdataClient to ensure there are no name collisions. We add a using AdventureWorksModelOdataClient statement to RestDataServicesODataPage.xaml.cs.

Now that we have everything set up, we add a ListBox named VendorsListBox control to the ContentPanel Grid control in RestDataServicesODataPage XAML. We create a simple DataTemplate as well. Here is the XAML:

```
<ListBox.ItemTemplate>
  <DataTemplate>
    <StackPanel Margin="0,0,0,30">
      <TextBlock Text="{Binding Name}" />
      <TextBlock Text="{Binding AccountNumber}" />
      <StackPanel Orientation="Horizontal">
        <TextBlock Text="Credit Rating:" Margin="0,0,4,0"/>
        <TextBlock Text="{Binding CreditRating}" />
      </StackPanel>
    </StackPanel>
  </DataTemplate>
</ListBox.ItemTemplate>
</ListBox>
```

Listing 4–15 shows the code-behind for RestDataServicesOdataPage.xaml.

Listing 4–15. The RestDataServicesOdataPage.xaml.cs Code File

```
using System;
using System.Data.Services.Client;
using System.Windows;
using AdventureWorksModelOdataClient;
```

```
using Microsoft.Phone.Controls;

namespace CallingRemoteServices.pages
{
  public partial class RestDataServicesODataPage : PhoneApplicationPage
  {
    public RestDataServicesODataPage()
    {
      InitializeComponent();
    }

    private void PhoneApplicationPage_Loaded(object sender, RoutedEventArgs e)
    {
      AdventureWorksEntities context =
        new AdventureWorksEntities(
          new Uri("http://localhost:9090/services/AdventureWorksRestOData.svc"));

      DataServiceCollection<Vendor> vendors =
        new DataServiceCollection<Vendor>(context);
      //Add REST URL for collection
      VendorsListBox.ItemsSource = vendors;
      vendors.LoadAsync(new Uri("/Vendors", UriKind.Relative));
    }
  }
}
```

As you can see, it is pretty straightforward to connect to REST services with the OData client. You can support viewing collections of data, as well as inserting and deleting records. The sample named ODataClient_WinPhone7SampleApp.zip located at this link demonstrates viewing collections as well as inserting and deleting records:

http://odata.codeplex.com/releases/view/54698#DownloadId=161862

In the next section we cover accessing REST+JSON services directly.

Plain Old REST+JSON

There will be scenarios where you will build an application that connects to services created on non-Microsoft platforms that deliver JSON data over REST services. Another scenario is that you have a data-tier to retrieve data already created, and you just need to plug in that data-tier into a service that publishes the data via REST+JSON. This section provides an example of connecting to JSON data in those situations.

To have a completely fresh look at service creation for this scenario, another WCF Service Application project is added to the Chapter 4 solution named WcfRemoteServicesSimpleRestJSON. Use the refactoring capabilities in Visual Studio 2010 to change IService1 to IAdventureWorksRestJSON and to change the implementation from Service1 to AdventureWorksRestJSON. The IAdventureWorksRestJSON Interface is further modified to return rest data and it is provided a UriTemplate for the underlying GetVendors method. Listing 4–16 is the Interface IAdventureWorksRestJSON.

Listing 4–16. The IAdventureWorksRestJSON Interface Code File

```
using System.Collections.ObjectModel;
using System.ServiceModel;
using System.ServiceModel.Web;
```

```
using WcfRemoteServicesSimpleRestJSON.Models;

namespace WcfRemoteServicesSimpleRestJSON
{
  [ServiceContract]
  public interface IAdventureWorksRestJSON
  {
    [OperationContract]
    [WebGet(UriTemplate = "/Vendors",
      BodyStyle = WebMessageBodyStyle.Bare,
      ResponseFormat = WebMessageFormat.Json)]
    ObservableCollection<Vendor> GetVendors();

  }
}
```

Listing 4–17 provides the concrete implementation of the Interface.

Listing 4–17. The IAdventureWorksRestJSON Interface Code File

```
using WcfRemoteServicesSimpleRestJSON.Models;
using System.Collections.ObjectModel;

//TEST THE SERVICE: http://localhost:9191/AdventureWorksRestJSON.svc/Vendors

namespace WcfRemoteServicesSimpleRestJSON
{
  public class AdventureWorksRestJSON : IAdventureWorksRestJSON
  {

    public ObservableCollection<Vendor> GetVendors()
    {
      //Replace with real data layer here
      ObservableCollection<Vendor> vendors = new ObservableCollection<Vendor>()
      {
        new Vendor(){AccountNumber="111111", CreditRating=65,
          Name="Frabrikam Bikes" },
        new Vendor(){AccountNumber="222222", CreditRating=40,
          Name="Contoso Sports" },
        new Vendor(){AccountNumber="333333", CreditRating=30,
          Name="Duwamish Surfing Gear" },
      };

      return vendors;
    }

  }
}
```

The implementation simply creates an ObservableCollection of Vendor objects inline and returns the collection. Plug in your data layer here and using the refactoring capabilities to rename namespaces and classes in order to customize to your needs.

Using the refactoring capabilities in Visual Studio will automatically update the web.config that is in the project to match the new class names. Listing 4–18 shows the complete web.config file.

Listing 4–18. Web.config file for AdventureWorksRestJSON Service

```
    </system.web>
    <system.serviceModel>
      <behaviors>
        <serviceBehaviors>
          <behavior name="RestDataServiceBehavior">
            <serviceMetadata httpGetEnabled="true"  policyVersion="Policy15"/>
            <serviceDebug includeExceptionDetailInFaults="true" />
          </behavior>
        </serviceBehaviors>

        <endpointBehaviors>
          <behavior name="REST">
            <webHttp helpEnabled="true"/>
          </behavior>
        </endpointBehaviors>
      </behaviors>
      <services>
        <service behaviorConfiguration="RestDataServiceBehavior"
                 name="WcfRemoteServicesSimpleRestJSON.AdventureWorksRestJSON">
        <endpoint address="" behaviorConfiguration="REST" binding="webHttpBinding"
          contract="WcfRemoteServicesSimpleRestJSON.IAdventureWorksRestJSON" />
        <endpoint address="mex" binding="mexHttpBinding" name="RestDataMetaData"
          contract="IMetadataExchange" />
        </service>
      </services>
      <serviceHostingEnvironment multipleSiteBindingsEnabled="true" />

    </system.serviceModel>
    <system.webServer>
      <modules runAllManagedModulesForAllRequests="true" />
      <directoryBrowse enabled="true" />
    </system.webServer>
</configuration>
```

Notice the address attribute for the <endpoint> element under the <services> element. There are two endpoints configured for the service: one to return data with an attribute of address="" and the other to return metadata with an address="mex." These addresses are relative to where the service is hosted. In this case, the project is hosted in the file AdventureWorksRestJSON.svc, which is part of the URL where the service is hosted:

```
http://localhost:9191/AdventureWorksRestJSON.svc
```

The WcfRemoteServicesSimpleRestJSON project's Web tab defines where the project is hosted, such as the port number. Now that we have a functioning service, we add a label to MainPage.xaml in the CallingRemoteServices project that navigates to a new page named AdventureWorksRestJSONPage.xaml. Save the project and switch to Expression Blend to edit the page. Uncomment the application bar, and four application bar buttons are added. A ListBox named VendorsListBox is added to the ContentPanel Grid. Two buttons titled "Add" and "Delete" are added beneath the VendorsListBox. The sample demonstrates the following things:

- Application bar button to show the returned JSON

- Application bar button that retrieves the JSON, parses it into a collection, and then data binds with the VendorsListBox

- Application bar button to save the current object list to isolated storage

- Application bar button to load from isolated storage the saved object list

- The Add button adds a record to the collection displayed in the VendorsListBox

- The Delete button deletes the currently selected record in the VendorsListBox

To test calling the REST+JSON service the leftmost application bar button calls the service and displays the returned JSON in a MessageBox:

```
#region Get Raw JSON data
HttpWebRequest request;
private void GetRawJSONDataAppBarBtn_Click(object sender, EventArgs e)
{
  request = WebRequest.CreateHttp("http://localhost:9191/AdventureWorksRestJSON.svc/Vendors");
  request.BeginGetResponse(new AsyncCallback(ReceiveRawJSONData), null);
}

string returnedResult;
void ReceiveRawJSONData(IAsyncResult result)
{
  WebResponse response = request.EndGetResponse(result);
  using (StreamReader reader = new StreamReader(response.GetResponseStream()))
  {
    returnedResult = reader.ReadToEnd();
  }
  LayoutRoot.Dispatcher.BeginInvoke(() =>
  {
    MessageBox.Show(returnedResult);
  });
}
#endregion
```

Figure 4–12 displays the returned JSON when the leftmost application bar is clicked.

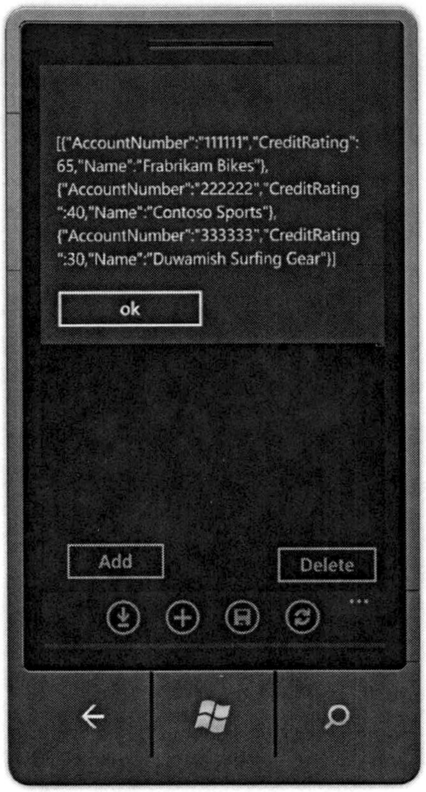

Figure 4–12. Raw JSON from the REST service

The application bar button second to the left makes the same web call, but this time it serializes the JSON into a collection of Vendor objects. Here is the code:

```
#region Retrieve Vendors Data
private void GetVendorsAppbarBtn_Click(object sender, EventArgs e)
{
  request = WebRequest.CreateHttp("http://localhost:9191/AdventureWorksRestJSON.svc/Vendors");
  request.BeginGetResponse(new AsyncCallback(GetVendors), null);
}

//add a reference to System.Servicemodel.web to get DataContractJsonSerializer
void GetVendors(IAsyncResult result)
{
  DataContractJsonSerializer ser = null;
  WebResponse response = request.EndGetResponse(result);
  ser = new DataContractJsonSerializer(typeof(ObservableCollection<Vendor>));
  DataStore.Instance.Vendors = ser.ReadObject(response.GetResponseStream()) as
ObservableCollection<Vendor>;
  VendorsListBox.Dispatcher.BeginInvoke(() =>
  {
```

```
      VendorsListBox.ItemsSource = DataStore.Instance.Vendors;
   });
}
#endregion
```

This code uses the DataContractJsonSerializer class to deserialize the JSON data into Vendor objects. A Lambda expression (the =>) is used to fire an anonymous delegate back on the UI thread to data bind the Vendors collection to the VendorsListBox. The anonymous delegate is represented by the block created by the braces.

JSON.NET is very popular in the dev community as an alternative JSON serializer to the DataContractJsonSerializer class. Many blog posts also claim that JSON.NET is faster at performing serialization over DataContractJsonSerialize. It also provides additional features, such as LINQ to JSON. Here is a link: http://json.codeplex.com/

In the previous code, you may have noticed the DataStore.Instance.Vendors object, which we will now explain. SQL Server Compact Edition, Microsoft's mobile database, is not currently available for Windows Phone 7. There are several third-party and open source solutions available to provide object persistence support, as well as an abstraction layer to hide boilerplate code. See Listing 4–19.

Listing 4–19. The DataStore and Vendor Class Code File

```csharp
using System;
using System.Collections.ObjectModel;
using System.ComponentModel;
using System.IO.IsolatedStorage;
using System.Runtime.Serialization;
using System.Runtime.Serialization.Json;

namespace RestJSON.DataModel
{
  sealed public class DataStore
  {
    //Declare suported collection types here
    public ObservableCollection<Vendor> Vendors { get; set; }

    //Provide a static read-only instance
    private static readonly DataStore instance = new DataStore();

    //Private Constructor for Singleton
    public DataStore() { }

    //The entry point into this Database
    public static DataStore Instance
    {
      get
      {
        return instance;
      }
    }

    //Deserialize ObservableCollection from JSON
    public T LoadCollection<T>(T collectionToLoad, string collectionName)
    {
      using (IsolatedStorageFile store =
             IsolatedStorageFile.GetUserStoreForApplication())
```

```csharp
    {
      if (store.FileExists(collectionName + ".txt"))
      {
        using (IsolatedStorageFileStream stream = store.OpenFile(
          collectionName + ".txt", System.IO.FileMode.Open))
        {
          DataContractJsonSerializer serializer =
            new DataContractJsonSerializer(typeof(T));
          return (T)serializer.ReadObject(stream);
        }
      }
      else
      {
        throw new Exception("Table not found");
      }
    }
}

//Serialize ObservableCollection to JSON
public void SaveCollection<T>(T collectionToSave, string collectionName)
{
  if (collectionToSave != null)
  {
    using (IsolatedStorageFile store =
          IsolatedStorageFile.GetUserStoreForApplication())
    {
      using (IsolatedStorageFileStream stream =
        store.CreateFile(collectionName + ".txt"))
      {
        DataContractJsonSerializer serializer =
          new DataContractJsonSerializer(typeof(T));
        serializer.WriteObject(stream, collectionToSave);
      }
    }
  }
}

//Delete ObservableCollection from Iso Storage
public void DeleteCollection(string tableName)
{
  using (IsolatedStorageFile store =
        IsolatedStorageFile.GetUserStoreForApplication())
  {
    if (store.FileExists(tableName + ".txt"))
    {
      store.DeleteFile(tableName + ".txt");
    }
  }
}
}

[DataContract()]
public class Vendor : INotifyPropertyChanged
{
```

```csharp
private string AccountNumberField;
private byte CreditRatingField;
private string NameField;

[DataMemberAttribute()]
public string AccountNumber
{
  get
  {
    return this.AccountNumberField;
  }
  set
  {
    this.AccountNumberField = value;
    NotifyPropertyChanged("AccountNumber");
  }
}

[DataMemberAttribute()]
public byte CreditRating
{
  get
  {
    return this.CreditRatingField;
  }
  set
  {
    this.CreditRatingField = value;
    NotifyPropertyChanged("CreditRating");
  }
}

[DataMemberAttribute()]
public string Name
{
  get
  {
    return this.NameField;
  }
  set
  {
    this.NameField = value;
    NotifyPropertyChanged("Name");
  }
}

public event PropertyChangedEventHandler PropertyChanged;
private void NotifyPropertyChanged(String propertyName)
{
  if (null != PropertyChanged)
  {
    PropertyChanged(this, new PropertyChangedEventArgs(propertyName));
  }
}
```

```
  }
}
```

The DataStore class shown in Listing 4–19 is not a lot of code, and it includes the Vendor class as well; but it provides a simple layer of abstraction that makes the code in the event handler much cleaner. Figure 4–13 shows the UI after the button second from the left is clicked.

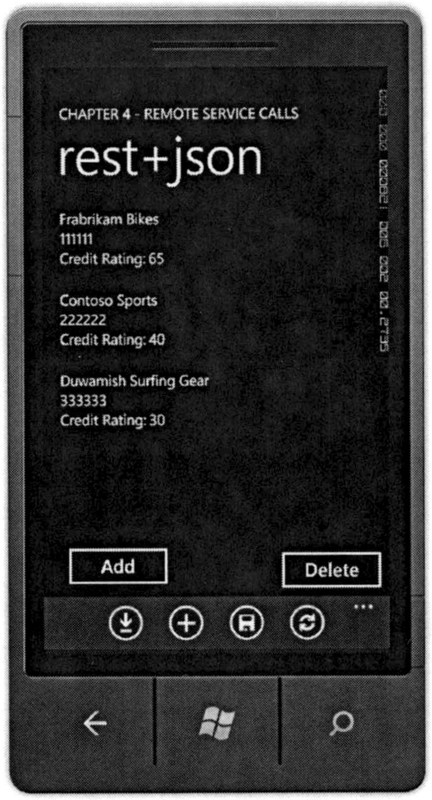

Figure 4–13. *Vendor" data databound to ListBox*

The last two buttons use the DataStore class to save to isolated storage and retrieve the data from isolated storage. Here are the event handlers:

```
private void SaveVendorsAppbarBtn_Click(object sender, EventArgs e)
{
  DataStore.Instance.SaveTable<ObservableCollection<Vendor>>(
    DataStore.Instance.Vendors, "Vendors");
}

private void LoadVendorsAppbarBtn_Click(object sender, EventArgs e)
{
  DataStore.Instance.Vendors =
```

```
    DataStore.Instance.LoadTable<ObservableCollection<Vendor>>(
    DataStore.Instance.Vendors, "Vendors");
  VendorsListBox.ItemsSource = DataStore.Instance.Vendors;
}
```

The Vendors save and load functionality turns into simple code with the help of the DataStore class. When the data is loaded into the VendorsListBox, save the data, click the Start hardware button, and then click the back button. The Resuming screen is displayed, and the data is not loaded. You can click the Load button to load the data from isolated storage and data bind it with the VendorsListBox. We cover how to manage application life cycle, also known as tombstoning, next.

The last two buttons in the UI are Add and Delete. Note that while the Vendors object collection that is part of the DataStore object is read-only, you can still add and remove objects from the collection. The read only modifier applies to the Vendors instance, not its underlying collection. The following is the code for the Add and Delete button:

```
private void addVendorButton_Click(object sender, RoutedEventArgs e)
{
  if (DataStore.Instance.Vendors != null)
  {
    DataStore.Instance.Vendors.Add(
    new Vendor()
    {
      AccountNumber = "555555",
      CreditRating = 45,
      Name = "Frabrikam Sports"
    });
  }
}

private void deleteButton_Click(object sender, RoutedEventArgs e)
{
  if (DataStore.Instance.Vendors != null)
  {
    DataStore.Instance.Vendors.Remove((Vendor)VendorsListBox.SelectedItem);
  }
}
```

The Add button is hard-coded to demonstrate how simple the operation is, but you could just as easily create a page with a set of controls that data bind to a new Vendor instance's properties and, upon clicking save, add the Vendor instance to the collection. The delete button removes the Vendor item selected in the VendorsListBox control from the underlying collection.

This concludes our discussion on connecting to remote services. Next up is the Bing Maps Control for Windows Phone 7, where we demonstrate adding pins to the map programmatically and via data binding to a collection.

Bing Maps Control

The Bing Maps control provides full mapping capabilities on Windows Phone 7. The control is optimized for mobile performance, including map tiles optimized for mobile bandwidth speeds.

The Bing Maps control fully supports Silverlight data binding for pushpin data with templates for plotting information. Users can pinch zoom the map, so it is not recommended to implement buttons for zooming in and out.

A new project named BingMapsControl is added to the Chapter 4 solution. A Bing Maps control is dropped into the ContentPanel Grid control, and two application bar buttons are enabled. The next three sections cover licensing, how to add a pin programmatically, and how to data bind to a collection of locations and plot on the Bing Maps control.

Licensing

As of this writing, the Bing Maps control is free to use for consumer-facing applications. This means if you are building a store locator, points of interest application, and so on that consumers would use, there is no licensing cost. To get started go to this URL to obtain an application key:

www.bingmapsportal.com

Set the Application Type to mobile for your mobile application. Next, set the key value in XAML, either directly or via data binding, for the CredentialProvider attribute:

```
<bing:Map Name=" TestBingMapsControl"
   CredentialsProvider="AppKeyGoesHere" />
```

It is really that simple to gain access to what is a very powerful Silverlight-based mapping control. The next two sections cover plotting data on the Bing Maps control.

Programmatically Add a Pin

There are many mobile scenarios where your application just needs to plot a single point, or a small number of points, and center the map on a point. In the BingMapsControl project's MainPage.xaml code file, the application bar is enabled. The left button plots a single point on the map by setting the location on a Pushpin object configured in the XAML. The following is the XAML for the Bing Maps Control:

```
<bing:Map Name="TestBingMapsControl"
  CredentialsProvider="…" >
  <bing:Pushpin x:Name="SinglePushpin" Visibility="Collapsed">
    <bing:Pushpin.Content>
      <Ellipse Width="25" Height="25" Fill="#FF00FF4A"/>
    </bing:Pushpin.Content>
  </bing:Pushpin>
</bing:Map>
```

Notice the <bing:Pushpin> object named SinglePushpin nested within the Map object. The Content property for the Pushpin is set to an Ellipse object. Notice that Visibility is set to Collapsed initially. All that's missing is a location.

The event handler for the left application bar button titled "add a pin" sets the position on the Pushpin object by name and then configures Visibility to Visible. Here is the code:

```
private void AddaPinAppBarBtn_Click(object sender, EventArgs e)
{
  //SinglePushpin is defined in XAML
  GeoCoordinate location = new GeoCoordinate(34d, -84d);
  SinglePushpin.Location = location;
  SinglePushpin.Visibility = Visibility.Visible;

  //Center and Zoom in on point
  TestBingMapsControl.Center = location;
  TestBingMapsControl.ZoomLevel = 11;
```

```
    //Turn on zoom bar for emulator testing
    TestBingMapsControl.ZoomBarVisibility = Visibility.Visible;
}
```

The Location property for the Pushpin object is set and Pushpin made visible. The Map control is also centered on the configured Location and zoomed in a bit. Figure 4–14 shows the results of clicking the application bar button.

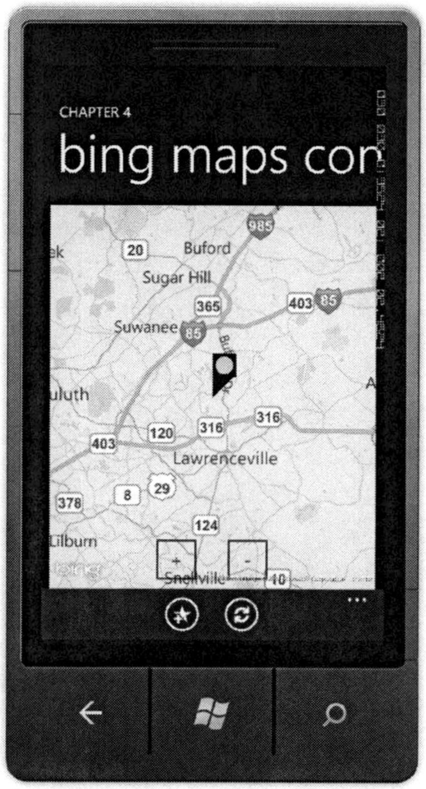

Figure 4–14. Plot a single Pushpin object

You could add another Pushpin object, and have one represent current location and the other represent desired location. Using Pushpin objects is a quick and easy way to get data on the Map control. For a large number of positions to plot, a MapItems control is recommended. We cover that in the next section.

Note that the zoom-in (+) and zoom-out (-) buttons are just there to ease development within the Emulator. You should have zoom-in and zoom-out buttons in a real application. The user should use pinch-zoom instead.

Data Bind to a Collection

In this section, we use the same MainPage.xaml and TestBingMapsControl Bing Maps control to plot a collection of points. A <bing:MapItemsControl> is nested within the TestBingMapsControl. The MapItemsControl represents a collection of points to plot on the Bing Maps control.

Two classes are added to the project: PushpinCollection and PlotPoint. The class PushpinCollection publishes a list of PlotPoint objects, and provides a method to initialize the collection. The PlotPoint class represents a point that is plotted, containing Quantity and Location properties. Quantity is what is displayed and Location represents where to plot the point. Listing 4–20 contains the source for the classes.

Listing 4–20. The PushpinCatalog and PlotPoints Classes

```
using System.Collections.Generic;
using System.Device.Location;

namespace BingMapsControl
{
  public class PushpinCollection
  {
    private List<PlotPoint> points;
    public List<PlotPoint> Points { get { return points; } }

    public void InitializePointsCollection()
    {
      //Generate sample data to plot
      points = new List<PlotPoint>()
      {
        new PlotPoint()
        { Quantity = 50,
          Location= new GeoCoordinate(35d, -86d)
        },
        new PlotPoint()
        { Quantity = 40,
          Location= new GeoCoordinate(33d, -85d)
        },
         new PlotPoint()
        { Quantity = 60,
          Location= new GeoCoordinate(34d, -83d)
        },
        new PlotPoint()
        { Quantity = 20,
          Location= new GeoCoordinate(40d, -120d)
        },
      };
    }
  }

  public class PlotPoint
  {
    public int Quantity { get; set; }
    public GeoCoordinate Location { get; set; }
  }
}
```

Expression Blend is used to data bind the MapItemsControl to the Points collection of the PushpinCatalog class. A DataTemplate is created to render the PlotPoint items into a customized Pushpin template. Listing 4–21 the XAML for the BingMapsControl project's MainPage.xaml page.

Listing 4–21. The BingMapsControl's MainPage.xaml

```xml
<phone:PhoneApplicationPage
    xmlns="http://schemas.microsoft.com/winfx/2006/xaml/presentation"
    xmlns:x="http://schemas.microsoft.com/winfx/2006/xaml"
    xmlns:phone="clr-namespace:Microsoft.Phone.Controls;assembly=Microsoft.Phone"
    xmlns:shell="clr-namespace:Microsoft.Phone.Shell;assembly=Microsoft.Phone"
    xmlns:d="http://schemas.microsoft.com/expression/blend/2008"
    xmlns:mc="http://schemas.openxmlformats.org/markup-compatibility/2006"
    xmlns:bing="clr-namespace:Microsoft.Phone.Controls.Maps;assembly=Microsoft↵
.Phone.Controls.Maps"
    xmlns:local="clr-namespace:BingMapsControl"
    x:Class="BingMapsControl.MainPage"
    mc:Ignorable="d" d:DesignWidth="480" d:DesignHeight="696"
    SupportedOrientations="Portrait" Orientation="Portrait"
    shell:SystemTray.IsVisible="True"
    >

  <phone:PhoneApplicationPage.Resources>
    <local:PushpinCollection x:Key="PushpinCollectionDataSource" d:IsDataSource="True"/>
    <DataTemplate x:Key="PlotPointDataTemplate">
      <Grid>
        <bing:Pushpin Location="{Binding Location}"
         ToolTipService.ToolTip="{Binding Quantity}" />
      </Grid>
    </DataTemplate>
  </phone:PhoneApplicationPage.Resources>
  <phone:PhoneApplicationPage.FontFamily>
    <StaticResource ResourceKey="PhoneFontFamilyNormal"/>
  </phone:PhoneApplicationPage.FontFamily>
  <phone:PhoneApplicationPage.FontSize>
    <StaticResource ResourceKey="PhoneFontSizeNormal"/>
  </phone:PhoneApplicationPage.FontSize>
  <phone:PhoneApplicationPage.Foreground>
    <StaticResource ResourceKey="PhoneForegroundBrush"/>
  </phone:PhoneApplicationPage.Foreground>
  <phone:PhoneApplicationPage.ApplicationBar>
    <shell:ApplicationBar IsVisible="True" IsMenuEnabled="True">
      <shell:ApplicationBarIconButton x:Name="AddaPinAppBarBtn"
              IconUri="/icons/appbar.favs.addto.rest.png"
              Text="add a pin" Click="AddaPinAppBarBtn_Click"/>
      <shell:ApplicationBarIconButton x:Name="DatabindAppBarBtn"
              IconUri="/icons/appbar.refresh.rest.png"
              Text="data bind" Click="DatabindAppBarBtn_Click"/>
    </shell:ApplicationBar>
  </phone:PhoneApplicationPage.ApplicationBar>

  <!--LayoutRoot is the root grid where all page content is placed-->
  <Grid x:Name="LayoutRoot" Background="Transparent"
    DataContext="{Binding Source={StaticResource PushpinCollectionDataSource}}">
```

```xml
<Grid.RowDefinitions>
  <RowDefinition Height="Auto"/>
  <RowDefinition Height="*"/>
</Grid.RowDefinitions>

<!--TitlePanel contains the name of the application and page title-->
<StackPanel x:Name="TitlePanel" Grid.Row="0" Margin="12,17,0,28">
  <TextBlock x:Name="ApplicationTitle" Text="CHAPTER 4"
          Style="{StaticResource PhoneTextNormalStyle}"/>
  <TextBlock x:Name="PageTitle" Text="bing maps control" Margin="9,-7,0,0"
             Style="{StaticResource PhoneTextTitle1Style}"/>
</StackPanel>

<!--ContentPanel - place additional content here-->
<Grid x:Name="ContentPanel" Grid.Row="1" Margin="12,0,12,0">
  <bing:Map x:Name="TestBingMapsControl"
    CredentialsProvider="your bing maps AppID goes here" >
    <bing:MapItemsControl Name="mapLayer"
       ItemTemplate="{StaticResource PlotPointDataTemplate}"
       ItemsSource="{Binding Points}"/>
    <bing:Pushpin x:Name="SinglePushpin" Visibility="Collapsed">
      <Ellipse Width="25" Height="25" Fill="#FF00FF4A"/>
    </bing:Pushpin>
  </bing:Map>
</Grid>
</Grid>
</phone:PhoneApplicationPage>
```

The following is the application bar button event handler that loads the Points collection:

```csharp
private void DatabindAppBarBtn_Click(object sender, EventArgs e)
{
  PushpinCollection collection = LayoutRoot.DataContext as PushpinCollection;
  if (collection != null)
    collection.InitializePointsCollection();
}
```

This code needs to grab the instance of the PushpinCollection that is configured as the DataContext of the LayoutRoot Grid object. See Figure 4–15.

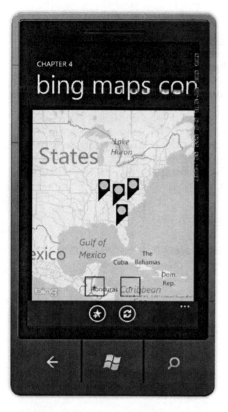

Figure 4–15. Plot a collection of points

Application Execution Model

Windows Phone 7 is not currently a multitasking operating system, which begs the question: how does the operating system handle application switching and state? In this section, the Windows Phone 7 application execution model is discussed in detail. We starts with an overview of the user experience, and then detail what happens under the hood. Finally the section explains how to manage application state within the available framework.

▦ **Note** Microsoft announced at Mobile World Conference in February 2011 that support for multi-tasking scenarios will be added to Windows Phone 7 later in 2011.

User Experience

If you have a Windows Phone 7 device, you are familiar with the navigation model. You know that the Start and the Back hardware button play an important role in the navigation model. The navigation model is similar to web browser navigation, which suggests that the phone maintains a back-stack of pages previously visited. Given that third-party applications do not multitask with other third-party applications in the current release, this brings up an intriguing question: what happens when you navigate back to a previous third-party application?

You probably noticed in previous examples that if you dynamically loaded data either via code or a remote service call, if you hit the Start button and then the Back button, the Resuming... screen is displayed and the application UI is rendered, but is missing the dynamic data. This happens because, while the operating system keeps a record in the back-stack of which apps have run previously, it does not maintain application state. Applications have a responsibility with the operating system to restore the application to its previous state.

Event Lifecycle

If you are a Windows Forms or WPF developer, you are familiar with these four events related to application life cycle:

- **Launching:** Application initially loads

- **Closing:** Application is excited by the user

- **Activated:** Application comes to the foreground

- **Deactivated:** Application loses focus

On Windows Phone 7, these events retain their general meaning, but with a twist. Launching and Closing work as expected. The Launching event fires upon initially launching the application. Closing fires upon exit.

The Deactivated event fires when the application loses focus when a hardware button is tapped, a phone call comes in, and so on. But the twist is that instead of continuing to run, the application is shut down, and an entry in the back-stack is made.

If the user navigates back to the application via the placeholder in the back-stack, the Activated event fires and the application resumes. Even though the application is no longer running when the Deactivated event fires, the Closing event does not fire. Same when the application launches upon resume in the Activated event; the Launching event does not fire.

For this section, the code for calling REST+JSON services in the CallingRemoteServices project is copied into this project to give us some interesting data to work with. We add additional code to log what is happening via the Visual Studio Output window using Debug.WriteLine, so as to not interfere with basic application functionality, but to let us know what is happening.

■ **Note** Configure both the WcfRemoteServicesSimpleRestJSON and AppExecutionModel projects as startup projects for the solution to ensure the service is running.

The application lifecycle events are not attached to the individual pages, like MainPage.xaml. Instead, the events are attached to the Application object directly via the

Microsoft.Phone.Shell.PhoneApplicationService class as part of the
Application.ApplicationLifetimObjects collection. The lifecycle events are already created for you
when you start a new project. In this project a few more events are added to the code:

- Application_Startup

- Application_Exit

- MainPage - PhoneApplicationPage_Loaded

- MainPage - PhoneApplicationPage_Unloaded

- MainPage - PhoneApplicationPage_BackKeyPress

The application uses Debug.WriteLine("") to log when in an event handler. Let's now run the
application, close the application, and then review the logged events in the Output Window.

```
In App constructor
In Application_Startup
In Application_Launching
In MainPage Constructor
In PhoneApplicationPage_Loaded
In PhoneApplicationPage_BackKeyPress
In Application_Closing
In Application_Exit
```

Let's next load the application, click the Start button, navigate back, and then hit the back button
again to exit the application.

```
In App constructor
In Application_Startup
In Application_Launching
In MainPage Constructor
In PhoneApplicationPage_Loaded
In Application_Deactivated
'taskhost.exe' (Managed): Loaded 'System.Runtime.Serialization.dll'
In Application_Exit
...navigate to Start screen,application tombstones, and then navigate back to application
In App constructor
In Application_Startup
In Application_Activated
In MainPage Constructor
In PhoneApplicationPage_Loaded
In PhoneApplicationPage_BackKeyPress
In Application_Closing
In Application_Exit
```

You can see that the Page and Application constructors and Page_Loaded fire every time, whether as
part of initial launch or when resuming from tombstoning. Same for Application_Exit. It fires whether
tombstoning or actually exiting the application. You will really want to understand this event cycle to
ensure that you place code in the appropriate event handler, depending on what's desired. The next
section discusses how to maintain state.

Managing State

Let's now add state management to the code copied from the AdventureWorksRestJSONPage page in the CallingRemoteServices project. First, let's generate random state in the App() constructor and store in a variable named randomState as a string. The state will be the current DateTime.Now value when the application is launched. It will be saved in Application_Deactivated, and restored in Application_Activated. The application will use Debug.WriteLine to log the state in App.xaml.cs. Here is the code to initialize state:

```
if (PhoneApplicationService.Current.StartupMode ==
    StartupMode.Launch)
{
  Debug.WriteLine("In App constructor");
  randomState = DateTime.Now.ToString();
  Debug.WriteLine("Random State: = " + randomState);
}
```

Notice that the code in App() to initialize state checks to ensure the application is Launching and not Activating. This is because the constructor is called in both cases as shown in the previous section.

The recommended location to store application state is in PhoneApplicationService.Current.State, which is of type IDictionary<string, object>. The "key" is a string, and the state is of type object, which means it can store any serializable object, including complex objects that contain objects. Here is the code to save in Application_Deactivated and restore in Application_Activated:

```
// Code to execute when the application is activated (brought to foreground)
// This code will not execute when the application is first launched
private void Application_Activated(object sender, ActivatedEventArgs e)
{
  Debug.WriteLine("Activating - load state");
  IDictionary<string, object> state =
    PhoneApplicationService.Current.State;
  if (state.ContainsKey("Random State"))
  {
    randomState = state["Random State"] as String;
  }
  Debug.WriteLine("Random State Restore - " + randomState);
  Debug.WriteLine("In Application_Activated");
}

// Code to execute when the application is deactivated (sent to background)
// This code will not execute when the application is closing
private void Application_Deactivated(object sender, DeactivatedEventArgs e)
{
  Debug.WriteLine("Deactivating - save state");
  IDictionary<string, object> state =
    PhoneApplicationService.Current.State;
  state["Random State"] = randomState;
  Debug.WriteLine("In Application_Deactivated");
}
```

The Application_Deactivated event adds the data to the State object. The Application_Activated event restores state, but first uses State.ContainsKey to make sure the state information is present before trying to retrieve the state using the key value.

■ **Caution** Applications have 10 seconds in both Application_Deactivated and Application_Activated to complete work. If saving or loading data goes beyond 10 seconds, the operating system will end the event handler.

The following is the data from the Output window after launching the app, clicking the Start button, and then the Back button:

```
In App constructor
Random State: = 1/24/2011 11:59:26 PM
In Application_Startup
In Application_Launching
In MainPage Constructor
In PhoneApplicationPage_Loaded
Deactivating - save state
In Application_Deactivated
In Application_Exit
In Application_Startup
Activating - load state
Random State Restore - 1/24/2011 11:59:26 PM
In Application_Activated
In MainPage Constructor
In PhoneApplicationPage_Loaded
In PhoneApplicationPage_BackKeyPress
In Application_Closing
In Application_Exit
```

As an alternative, you can handle state management at the page level. In many ways, this method makes more sense, because it is easier to restore the data as close to where it is needed, as opposed to restoring in App.xaml.cs and then passing it along. The code in MainPage.xaml.cs overrides the OnNavigatedFrom and OnNavigatedTo methods as shown here:

```
protected override void OnNavigatedFrom(
  System.Windows.Navigation.NavigationEventArgs e)
{
  base.OnNavigatedFrom(e);
  IDictionary<string, object> state = PhoneApplicationService.Current.State;
  state["Selected Item"] = VendorsListBox.SelectedIndex;
  DataStore.Instance.SaveCollection<ObservableCollection<Vendor>>(
    DataStore.Instance.Vendors, "Vendors");
}

protected override void OnNavigatedTo(
  System.Windows.Navigation.NavigationEventArgs e)
{
  base.OnNavigatedTo(e);
  if (PhoneApplicationService.Current.StartupMode ==
    StartupMode.Activate)
  {
    //Load data from isolated storage
    DataStore.Instance.Vendors =
    DataStore.Instance.LoadCollection<ObservableCollection<Vendor>>(
    DataStore.Instance.Vendors, "Vendors");
```

```
VendorsListBox.ItemsSource = DataStore.Instance.Vendors;
// The state bag for  temporary state
IDictionary<string, object> state =
  PhoneApplicationService.Current.State;
// See if the bag contains the selected item
if (state.ContainsKey("Selected Item"))
{
  //Set selected item on page
  VendorsListBox.SelectedIndex = (int)state["Selected Item"];
  //Scroll to selected item
  VendorsListBox.ScrollIntoView(
    VendorsListBox.Items[VendorsListBox.SelectedIndex]);
  }
 }
}
```

Notice that the code does not save the Vendors collection to the PhoneApplicationService.Current.State object. The application could do that, but it seems to make sense to persist the major data collections where they would normally be saved, as opposed to being temporary state. On the other hand, saving the selected item makes sense, because when the user returns to the application after resume, the user will expect to see the application state just as they left it.

When you run the application, retrieve it from the service and then tombstone it by clicking a hardware button; then click the Back button to resume. Notice that the data is restored, and the current item is selected in the VendorsListBox control. To the user, it is as if the application continued to run when it really hadn't.

Understanding and supporting good life-cycle management is critical to providing a robust user interface. With good state management, a user will not even notice that the application stopped running. While we demonstrated tombstoning and persisting data in the MainPage class, in Chapter 6 we pick up the programming model discussion again starting with how to architect Silverlight for Windows Phone 7 applications correctly to manage these scenarios.

Running Under Lock Screen

You can configure an application to run under the lock screen. This means that when the phone lock careen activates, the application continues to run in the foreground and is not tombstoned. This also means that the application continues to consume CPU and more importantly battery when running under the lock screen. Here is a link to the documentation:

http://msdn.microsoft.com/en-us/library/ff941090%28v=VS.92%29.aspx

There are some application scenarios in which running under the lock screen greatly enhances the user experience. An application that records GPS values while running under lock for a run tracker program is an excellent example.

It is pretty straightforward to implement running under the lock screen. Essentially configure ApplicationIdleDetectionMode to disabled in App.xaml.cs:

PhoneApplicationService.Current.ApplicationIdleDetectionMode = IdleDetectionMode.Disabled;

Handle the Application's RootFrame Obscured and UnObscured events. When the application is Obscured, execute code to reduce CPU cycles as much as possible to conserve battery. In the UnObscured event, restart application functionality to restore the application or game.

Conclusion

In this chapter we started by covering how to identify users, the device, network status, and application trial mode status for Windows Phone 7, and then investigated application data persistence with Isolated Storage. We next investigated platform integration by covering the launchers and choosers. This chapter also covered how to load HTML into the WebBrowser control, as well as how to call HTML script from Silverlight and how to call Silverlight methods from HTML script. The chapter moved on to cover the Bing Maps control and the Application Execution Model in detail. In the next chapter, we cover advanced user interface development.

CHAPTER 5

Windows Phone 7 Advanced UI Development

Building a great user interface for a professional application is challenging given all of the competing priorities, such as presenting data, interaction models, network connectivity, security, managing background tasks, and localization. It's important to build a rich application on a solid architecture that helps the different pieces work together.

This chapter delves more deeply into user interface development with Silverlight, covering a wide-range of topics. It builds on previous chapters, but especially on Chapter 2, which covered Silverlight user interface development. This chapter extends the topic of user interface development to include how to architect an application with separation of concerns without sacrificing support for tooling or ease of development.

This chapter starts with an introduction of the most prevalent application architecture model in Silverlight development, Model-View-ViewModel (MVVM), which provides excellent support for well-designed user interfaces with separation of concerns.

Next up is a section on the Silverlight for Windows Phone 7 Toolkit, covering the additional controls and capabilities. The section following is on creating transitions and interactivity in Expression Blend. The final section is on the Microsoft Advertising SDK, which provides an excellent vehicle to monetize applications.

The Model-View-ViewModel Architecture

The Model-View-ViewModel (MVVM) architecture originated when the Microsoft Windows Presentation Foundation (WPF) team were building the first version of Expression Blend. WPF is Microsoft's desktop XAML development model, and Expression Blend is written in WPF. MVVM is similar to other separation of concerns architectures, like the tried-and-true Model-View-Controller (MVC) model; however, MVVM is optimized to take advantage of XAML's rich data binding, data templates, commands, and event routing capabilities. The next section covers the architecture in more detail.

MVVM Overview

In this section, the MVVM pattern is defined to help you grasp how it works with XAML. If you are familiar with MVC, MVVM will look somewhat familiar to you – but it is much more than just MVC. MVVM relies heavily on XAML data binding capabilities to allow the UI to data bind to both data and commands. Figure 5–1 depicts the MVVM architecture.

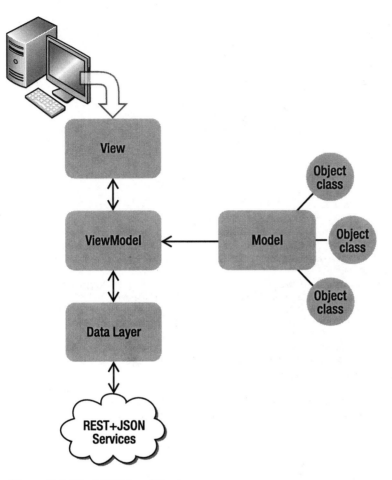

Figure 5–1. The MVVM architecture

In Chapter 4, there is a simple example that displays a list of fake Vendor data made available via JSON. The REST+JSON service project named, WcfRemoteServicesSimpleRestJSON, is added to the Chapter 5 solution. The BasicMVVM sample re-architects the AdventureWorksRestJSONPage.xaml page from the Chapter 4 CallingRemoteServices project to use MVVM in the Chapter 5 project named BasicMVVM.

The BasicMVVM and the WcfRemoteServicesSimpleRestJSON projects are configured as the startup project. Four folders are added to the project named Model, View, and ViewModel. The sections that follow cover the major components of MVVM in the BasicMVVM sample.

BasicMVVM - Model

The Model contains the building blocks of the application. It consists of the underlying data objects that are populated via a data access layer. Examples of Model classes are Customer, Store, Product, etc. When you create a class to represent an object in an application, it most likely belongs as part of the Model.

The Model sits behind the ViewModel. The View will data bind to lists of or individual objects based on classes in the Model.

To get started, copy over the Vendor class from the WcfRemoteServicesSimpleRestJSON services project to the BasicMVVM Models folder. The class implements the INotifyPropertyChanged interface to support data binding at the class level. The INotifyPropertyChanged interface ensures that changes to the underlying object are propagated to the UI and vice versa. See Listing 5–1 for the code.

Listing 5–1. Vendor Model Class Code File

```
using System;
using System.ComponentModel;
using System.Runtime.Serialization;

namespace BasicMVVM.Model
{
  //Copied from services project
  [DataContract()]
  public class Vendor : INotifyPropertyChanged
  {
    private string AccountNumberField;
    private byte CreditRatingField;
    private string NameField;

    [DataMemberAttribute()]
    public string AccountNumber
    {
      get
      {
        return this.AccountNumberField;
      }
      set
      {
        this.AccountNumberField = value;
        NotifyPropertyChanged("AccountNumber");
      }
    }

    [DataMemberAttribute()]
    public byte CreditRating
    {
      get
      {
        return this.CreditRatingField;
      }
      set
      {
        this.CreditRatingField = value;
        NotifyPropertyChanged("CreditRating");
      }
    }

    [DataMemberAttribute()]
    public string Name
    {
```

```
    get
    {
      return this.NameField;
    }
    set
    {
      this.NameField = value;
      NotifyPropertyChanged("Name");
    }
  }

  public event PropertyChangedEventHandler PropertyChanged;
  private void NotifyPropertyChanged(String propertyName)
  {
    if (null != PropertyChanged)
    {
      PropertyChanged(this, new PropertyChangedEventArgs(propertyName));
    }
  }
  }
 }
}
```

BasicMVVM - ViewModel

Mentioned above is the fact that the View or UI data binds to the ViewModel, suggesting that a ViewModel consists of the data containers for the application, which is correct. Lists of objects defined in the Model are created and managed by the ViewModel. In addition, the ViewModel consists of the majority of application logic as well.

Next create the VendorViewModel class. The VendorViewModel class in the BasicMVVM project supports the following four major features:

- Vendors specific business logic

- UI Databinding via INotifyPropertyChanged

- Design-time support

- REST+JSON data loading

The Vendor-specific business logic is pretty straightforward. It consists of a read-only collection of Vendor objects from the Model and two event handlers to add and remove Vendor objects from the collection. For a professional application, additional methods and business logic would be present but the implementation is the same.

■ **Note** While the VendorViewModel.Vendors collection is read-only – it has just a get property accessor – you can still add and remove Vendor objects in the collection. You just cannot assign a new collection to the property.

It is critical to implement INotifyPropertyChanged for data binding to work. Otherwise, changes are not propagated back to the UI, and vice versa. It is simple enough to do. Add an instance of the

PropertyChangedEventHandler class named PropertyChanged and a method that takes a property name as a string and then fires the PropertyChanged event instance.

To detect design-time, the System.ComponentModel.DesignerProperties class has a static bool property named IsInDesignTool that indicates whether the code is running in a design-time tool. The VendorViewModel constructor checks if an instance of the class is running at design-time. If at design-time, the constructor calls LoadSampleData method. Otherwise, at run-time, it calls LoadData, which invokes a remote REST+JSON service.

The last major functionality for the VendorsViewModel class is making the remote service call, which is covered in detail in Chapter 4. The interesting change for this scenario is that the service call and asynchronous callback live in the VendorsViewModel class, so the code does not have direct access to the View and the View UI elements like in Chapter 4. The callback cannot have code like the following:

```
vendorsListbox.Dispatcher.BeginInvoke(…);
```

The solution is to make the call using this line of code instead:

```
Deployment.Current.Dispatcher.BeginInvoke(..);
```

This code ensures that the correct Dispatcher instance is used to notify the UI that data changes occurred. The next challenge is that the callback function needs to update the Vendors collection property. Remember that the Vendors collection is a read-only collection, because we do not want external classes to be able to assign a new collection to it. We want the data to only come from the remote services. The code instead assigns the collection to the underlying _vendors collection private member variable.

The final issue is that the code still needs to notify the UI that data changes occurred, i.e. that the Vendors collection is loaded. Since the _vendors collection is updated directly, NotifyPropertyChanged("Vendors") is called in the anonymous delegate by BeginInvoke. Again, the code could make Vendors read/write and have a set accessor function like this but maintaining data integrity is preferred so the set function is commented out, as in the following:

```
set
{
  _vendors = value;
  NotifyPropertyChanged("Vendors");
}
```

Listing 5–2 has the full source code for review.

Listing 5–2. VendorViewModel Class Code File

```
using System;
using System.Collections.ObjectModel;
using System.ComponentModel;
using System.Linq;
using System.Net;
using System.Runtime.Serialization.Json;
using System.Windows;
using BasicMVVM.Model;

namespace BasicMVVM.ViewModel
{
  public class VendorViewModel : INotifyPropertyChanged
  {
    public VendorViewModel()
    {
      if (InDesignTime)
```

```csharp
        {
          LoadSampleData();
        }
        else
        {
          LoadData();
        }
      }

      #region Design-time support
      private bool InDesignTime
      {
        get
        {
          return DesignerProperties.IsInDesignTool;
        }
      }

      private void LoadSampleData()
      {
        _vendors = new ObservableCollection<Vendor>()
        {
          new Vendor(){AccountNumber="111111", CreditRating=65,
            Name="DesignTime - Fabrikam Bikes" },
          new Vendor(){AccountNumber="222222", CreditRating=40,
            Name="Contoso Sports" },
          new Vendor(){AccountNumber="333333", CreditRating=30,
            Name="Duwamish Surfing Gear" },
          new Vendor(){AccountNumber="444444", CreditRating=65,
            Name="Contoso Bikes" },
          new Vendor(){AccountNumber="555555", CreditRating=40,
            Name="Fabrikam Sports" },
          new Vendor(){AccountNumber="666666", CreditRating=30,
            Name="Duwamish Golf" },
          new Vendor(){AccountNumber="777777", CreditRating=65,
            Name="Fabrikam Sun Sports" },
          new Vendor(){AccountNumber="888888", CreditRating=40,
            Name="Contoso Lacross" },
          new Vendor(){AccountNumber="999999", CreditRating=30,
            Name="Duwamish Team Sports" },
        };
      }
      #endregion

      #region Vendors Data Load
      HttpWebRequest httpWebRequest;
      private void LoadData()
      {
        httpWebRequest = HttpWebRequest.CreateHttp("http://localhost:9191↵
/AdventureWorksRestJSON.svc/Vendors");
        httpWebRequest.BeginGetResponse(new AsyncCallback(GetVendors), null);
      }

    //add a reference to System.Servicemodel.web to get DataContractJsonSerializer
```

```csharp
    void GetVendors(IAsyncResult result)
    {
      HttpWebResponse response = httpWebRequest.EndGetResponse(result) as HttpWebResponse;
      DataContractJsonSerializer ser = new DataContractJsonSerializer↵
(typeof(ObservableCollection<Vendor>));
      _vendors = ser.ReadObject(response.GetResponseStream()) as ObservableCollection<Vendor>;
      //Vendors is read-only so cannot set directly
      //Must call NotifyPropertyChanged notifications on UI thread
      //to update the UI and have data binding work properly
      Deployment.Current.Dispatcher.BeginInvoke(() =>
      {
        NotifyPropertyChanged("Vendors");
      });
    }
    #endregion

    #region Vendors Business Logic
    private ObservableCollection<Vendor> _vendors;
    public ObservableCollection<Vendor> Vendors
    {
      get
      {
        return _vendors;
      }
      //set
      //{
      //    _vendors = value;
      //    NotifyPropertyChanged("Vendors");
      //}
    }

    public Vendor GetVendorByAccountNumber(string accountNumber)
    {
      var vendor = from v in _vendors
                   where v.AccountNumber == accountNumber
                   select v;

      return vendor.First<Vendor>();
    }

    public void AddVendor()
    {
      Vendors.Add(new Vendor()
      {
        AccountNumber = "111111",
        CreditRating = 65,
        Name = "Fabrikam Bikes - Added"
      });
    }

    public void RemoveVendor(object vendor)
    {
      if (null != vendor)
        Vendors.Remove((Vendor)vendor);
```

```
    }
    #endregion

    #region INotifyPropertyChanged interface members
    public event PropertyChangedEventHandler PropertyChanged;

    public void NotifyPropertyChanged(String property)
    {
      if (PropertyChanged != null)
      {
        PropertyChanged(this, new PropertyChangedEventArgs(property));
      }
    }
    #endregion
  }
}
```

The next section covers how to make the Model and ViewModel objects available to the UI.

BasicMVVM - View

The View is the actual XAML of an application. It is the mainpage.xaml file in a Silverlight project, and is what the user interacts with directly, presenting the underlying data and application logic. The View data binds to the ViewModel, which is covered in the previous section. The goal when building the view is to not have any code in the code-behind for the .xaml file, if possible. This means that all logic is in the ViewModel, which is non-visual, making it much more unit-testable. The other advantage of the separation of concerns here is that the design-team can focus on building out the View without interfering with business logic in event handlers. A View always has a reference to the ViewModel, because it data binds to it.

Remove the MainPage.xaml from the BasicMVVM project and add a new View (.xaml page) to the Views folder named VendorsView.xaml. Next, edit the WMAppManifest.xml file by changing the NavigationPage attribute to point to the new default task, as in the following:

```
<DefaultTask  Name ="_default" NavigationPage="Views/CustomersView.xaml"/>.
```

■ **Note** In general, the WMAppManifest.xml file should not be manually edited, but in this case it is required.

In Expression Blend, add a ListBox to VendorsView.xaml and configure the ItemsSource to data bind to the VendorViewModel.Vendors collection by clicking the Advanced Options button next to the ItemsSource property in the Expression Blend Properties window and selecting Data Binding... to bring up the Create Data Binding dialog. Click the +CLR Object button, select VendorViewModel, and then click OK.

■ **Tip** If the VendorViewModel class – or any .NET CLR class that you want to data bind – does not show up in the dialog box, make sure to compile the application. Static collections will not show either.

This generates a new Data Source named VendorViewModelDataSource in the left pane. Select Vendors in the right pane and then click OK. This configuration updates the XAML in three places. It adds a new resource to the VendorsView page, as in the following:

```
<phone:PhoneApplicationPage.Resources>
 <BasicMVVM_ViewModels:VendorViewModel
 x:Key="VendorViewModelDataSource" d:IsDataSource="True"/>
</phone:PhoneApplicationPage.Resources>
```

It configures LayoutRoot Grid's DataContext property to point to the VendorViewModel class:

```
DataContext="{Binding Source={StaticResource VendorViewModelDataSource}}"
```

Finally, the work in Expression Blend configures the vendorsListBox ItemsSource property to data bind to the VendorViewModel.Vendors collection like so ItemsSource="{Binding Vendors}."

One of the goals of MVVM and separating concerns is to make the View as "thin" as possible. WPF and Silverlight 4 have support for separating concerns by allowing UI element events like Click to data bind to methods on the ViewModel via Commanding and the ICommand interface. This means that instead of having event handlers in the code-behind for the view, everything is instead configured via data binding in XAML. Figure 5–2 shows the UI.

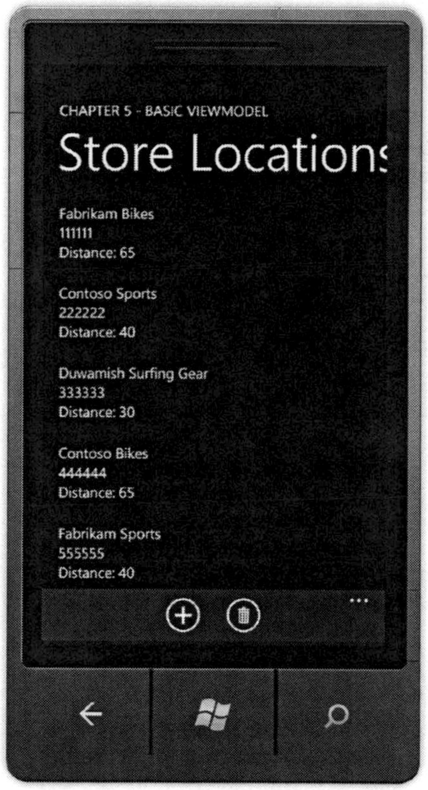

Figure 5–2. BasicMVVM running in the emulator

259

Silverlight for Windows Phone 7, which is based on Silverlight 3 plus some additional Silverlight 4 features like the WebBrowser control and offline DRM, does not have full support for Commanding. For the BasicMVVM sample, the VendorsView has two code-behind events to support adding and removing a Vendor, as in the following:

```
private void insertVendorAppBarBtn_Click(object sender, EventArgs e)
{
  VendorViewModel vm = LayoutRoot.DataContext as VendorViewModel;
  vm.AddVendor();
}

private void RemoveVendorAppBarBtn_Click(object sender, EventArgs e)
{
  VendorViewModel vm = LayoutRoot.DataContext as VendorViewModel;
  vm.RemoveVendor(vendorsListBox.SelectedItem);
}
```

Notice that the path to the underlying ViewModel is still via the instance of the VendorViewModel class that is data bound to the LayoutRoot Grid's DataContext property. It would be great to be able to avoid this type of code. Luckily, there are third-party, open-source frameworks that provide extensions to Silverlight that enable better support for MVVM, which we cover in the next section.

Pick a MVVM Helper SDK

Because Silverlight for Windows Phone 7 is based on Silverlight 3, it falls short of the MVVM capabilities available in Silverlight 4 and WPF, such as full Commanding support. Luckily, there are quite a few third-party MVVM frameworks available to choose from that provide Commanding support and more. The following lists a few in no particular order:

- Caliburn

- nRoute

- Composite Application Block/PRISM

- SilverlightFX

- GalaSoft's MVVM Light Toolkit

The major benefit that these frameworks have in varying degrees is increasing separation of concerns, unit testing support, and support for Commanding. You can find arguments for and against the available frameworks, so please investigate the available options. For this example, let's take MVVM Light Toolkit for a spin, as it is this author's opinion that MVVM Light provides a nice balance of power and simplicity that is a great fit for phone application development. Many others would suggest Caliburn instead for similar reasons. The most important thing is to pick a helper SDK, learn it, and use it.

GalaSoft MVVM Light Toolkit

For Windows Phone 7 development, my preference is GalaSoft's MVVM Light Toolkit. In my opinion it has the right combination of power and as the name says, lightness, for a mobile phone application.

■ **Tip** The MVVM Light Toolkit works across WPF and desktop Silverlight as well, which greatly aids in porting code to another screen such as a Windows Slate application.

The MVVM Light Toolkit is up to version 3 SP1. It was originally developed to address the Commanding shortfalls in Silverlight 2 and Silverlight 3 that I highlighted in the previous section when covering the BasicMVVM sample project. The MVVM Light Toolkit also includes customized Visual Studio 2010 templates to help you get started right away. First, download the MVVM Light Toolkit and follow the instructions at this page:

http://galasoft.ch/mvvm/getstarted/

If you like the MVVM Light toolkit, I encourage you to click the Donate button at the bottom of the above page, which goes towards the cost of running the site and the rest goes to charity. The source code is available in CodePlex here:

http://mvvmlight.codeplex.com/

Once you have the toolkit downloaded and installed, you can run the MVVMLightSample available in Chapter 5 to see it in action. The entire range of features of the MVVM Light Toolkit are not described end-to-end in this book, but the next couple of sections cover the features of MVVM Light used to migrate the BasicMVVM to MVVM Light.

MVVM Light Sample

In Visual Studio 2010, you can select File ➤ New Project, and click on Silverlight for Windows Phone to filter to the WP7 projects. Select MvvmLight (WP7) as the project template to get started. If you don't see that option, check to ensure that you installed the toolkit correctly before proceeding.

Once the project is created, run it and the screen in Figure 5–3 should appear, which indicates that all is configured correctly.

Figure 5–3. *Testing your MVVM Light installation*

The page title, subtitle, and text are all data bound to the `MainViewModel` class. Let's go through the architecture of MVVM Light works so that you have a basis as we migrate the `BasicMVVM` app to MVVM Light. After creating a new project, the project includes the default `App.xaml` and `MainPage.xaml` as well as the other items expected in a Silverlight for Windows Phone 7 application but with a couple of additions. There is an empty Model folder that we populate shortly. There is also a `ViewModel` folder that contains two `ViewModel` classes named `MainViewModel` and `ViewModelLocator`. I cover these in the next section.

ViewModelLocator

The `ViewModelLocator` class contains a reference to every `ViewModel` class in the project. This provides a centralized way to manage creation and allow XAML configuration via a single application resource. By default, in `App.xaml` a resource is added for the `ViewModelLocator` class. A namespace is added to the `<Application>` object that hosts the `PhoneApplicationFrame` that contains the XAML pages or View classes as they are navigated:

```
xmlns:vm="clr-namespace:MvvmLightSample.ViewModel"
```

The ViewModelLocator class is configured as an application level resource, as in the following:

```
<Application.Resources>
    <vm:ViewModelLocator x:Key="Locator"
                          d:IsDataSource="True" />
</Application.Resources>
```

This resource is available through the entire application, just like any other application-level resource, making the referenced ViewModel objects available now. Now we move on to explain how MainPage.xaml data binds to MainViewModel within this architecture. In the XAML, the <PhoneApplicationPage> element's DataContext property data binds to the Locator resource discussed above via this XAML code:

```
DataContext="{Binding Main, Source={StaticResource Locator}}"
```

The Path property for the Binding object is configured with the value of Main using the default syntax (it can also be written as Path=Main). This configuration makes an instance of the MainViewModel available within MainPage.xaml and allows the page title, sub-title, and text to data bind to properties available on the MainViewModel. Here's an example of one of the Application Title Bindings:

```
<TextBlock x:Name="ApplicationTitle"
    Text="{Binding ApplicationTitle}"
    Style="{StaticResource PhoneTextNormalStyle}" />
```

Listing 5–3 shows the default ViewModelLocator class.

Listing 5–3. Default ViewModelLocator Class Code File

```
namespace MvvmLightSample.ViewModel
{
  public class ViewModelLocator
  {
    private static MainViewModel _main;

    /// <summary>
    /// Initializes a new instance of the ViewModelLocator class.
    /// </summary>
    public ViewModelLocator()
    {
      //if (ViewModelBase.IsInDesignModeStatic)
      //{
      //    // Create design time view models
      //}
      //else
      //{
      //    // Create run time view models
      //}

      CreateMain();
    }

    /// <summary>
    /// Gets the Main property.
    /// </summary>
    public static MainViewModel MainStatic
    {
      get
      {
```

```csharp
        if (_main == null)
        {
          CreateMain();
        }

        return _main;
      }
    }

    /// <summary>
    /// Gets the Main property.
    /// </summary>
    [System.Diagnostics.CodeAnalysis.SuppressMessage("Microsoft.Performance",
        "CA1822:MarkMembersAsStatic",
        Justification =
        "This non-static member is needed for data binding purposes.")]
    public MainViewModel Main
    {
      get
      {
        return MainStatic;
      }
    }

    /// <summary>
    /// Provides a deterministic way to delete the Main property.
    /// </summary>
    public static void ClearMain()
    {
      _main.Cleanup();
      _main = null;
    }

    /// <summary>
    /// Provides a deterministic way to create the Main property.
    /// </summary>
    public static void CreateMain()
    {
      if (_main == null)
      {
        _main = new MainViewModel();
      }
    }

    /// <summary>
    /// Cleans up all the resources.
    /// </summary>
    public static void Cleanup()
    {
      ClearMain();
    }
  }
}
```

Notice in Listing 5–3 how the MainViewModel is made available. It is created in the ViewModelLocator constructor via a call to the CreateMain() method. There is also a ClearMain() method to provide a garbage collection safe way to clear the resource from memory, which is important on Windows Phone 7 with the goal of keeping application memory usage under 90MB for best performance.

The MainViewModel is available via a static property, which makes it more straightforward to find ViewModel objects by simply typing ViewModelLocator.MainStatic. MainStatic contains the reference to the MainViewModel object but for data binding purposes it must be a non-static variable. A second non-static property is declared named Main that can be configured in data binding. The Main property simply returns the static instance under the covers.

To add additional ViewModel objects, manually edit the ViewModelLocator class to include two properties for the additional ViewModel objects. There is a code snippet available to automate this process. Type mvvmlocatorproperty and tap the Tab key twice to quickly add the property using Visual Studio 2010's code snippet template UI. Essentially, type new values for the default and click the Tab key to move through the template to quickly add the property combination in the correct format.

MvvmLightSample – Model

The model class Vendor is copied from the BasicMVVM class. Edit the namespace at the top to be MVVMLightSample.Models so it makes sense for this project. A reference is added to System.Runtime.Serialization assembly. That's all that's required to add it to the MVVM Light Toolkit version.

MvvmLightSample – VendorsViewModel

The VendorsViewModel class is copied over from the BasicMVVM project, and the namespaces are fixed up for the MvvmLightSample project. To take advantage of as much of the framework as possible, replace INotifyPropertyChanged interface with the ViewModelBase class instead. Add a using clause for GalaSoft.MvvmLight. Remove the INotifyPropertyChanged PropertyChanged event and method from VendorsViweModel since we get it for free by inheriting from ViewModelBase class. Change NotifyPropertyChanged("") calls to base.RaisePropertyChanged("") to fix up compile errors.

Add a reference to Sytem.ServiceModel.Web to make the DataContractJsonSerializer class available within the VendorsViewModel. Remove the InDesignTime property and replace it with a call to GalaSoft.MvvmLight.IsInDesignMode instead. At this point, the migration is complete for the ViewModel.

MvvmLightSample – VendorsView

A new folder named View is added to the MVVMLightSample project, and the VendorsView.xaml page is copied from the BasicMVVM project to the MVVMLightSample view folder. Do a Find / Replace with BasicMVVM to replace it with MvvmLightSample with the "Look in" set to Current Project. That fixes up namespace references to compile the project successfully.

Next MainViewModel is modified to return a more appropriate page title and sub-title as well as string text for the Welcome message property, now configured to point to a StoreLocatorPage property. Clicking on that text will navigate you to the VendorsView.xaml page. Fix up the margins so that everything aligns at 24px on the left and then add a NavigateToPageAction behavior to the TextBlock containing the text Store Locator Page and configure it to point to the VendorsView page.

If you run the project, it works as before, but let's configure the VendorsView to take advantage of the MVVM Light toolkit capabilities. First, add a property combination to the ViewModelLocator via the mvvmlocatorproperty code snippet. By using the code snippet, it quickly generates this code for you in the ViewModelLocator class:

```
private static VendorViewModel _vendors;

/// <summary>
/// Gets the Vendors property.
/// </summary>
public static VendorViewModel VendorsStatic
{
  get
  {
    if (_vendors == null)
    {
      CreateVendors();
    }

    return _vendors;
  }
}

/// <summary>
/// Gets the Vendors property.
/// </summary>
[System.Diagnostics.CodeAnalysis.SuppressMessage("Microsoft.Performance",
    "CA1822:MarkMembersAsStatic",
    Justification = "This non-static member is needed for data binding purposes.")]
public VendorViewModel Vendors
{
  get
  {
    return VendorsStatic;
  }
}

/// <summary>
/// Provides a deterministic way to delete the Vendors property.
/// </summary>
public static void ClearVendors()
{
  _vendors.Cleanup();
  _vendors = null;
}

/// <summary>
/// Provides a deterministic way to create the Vendors property.
/// </summary>
public static void CreateVendors()
{
  if (_vendors == null)
  {
    _vendors = new VendorViewModel();
  }
}
```

As you can see, if you are not familiar with Visual Studio 2010 the code snippet is quite handy! One item to note is that the snippet adds another `Cleanup()` method so just copy `ClearVendors()` to the existing `Cleanup()` method and delete the one added.

Now that we have the `VendorsView` added to the `ViewModelLocator`, we can configure the `VendorsView` to data bind the MVVM Light Toolkit way using Expression Blend. First compile the project to make sure everything is up to date, and then remove the `DataContext` binding on the `LayoutRoot` `Grid`. Also remove the `VendorViewModelDataSource` from the `PhoneApplicationPage.Resources` section in the `VendorsView.xaml` file.

In Expression Blend, select the `PhoneApplicationPage` root item in the Objects and Timeline tool window. Find the `DataContext` property, click the Advanced Options… button, and select Data Binding… to bring up the Create Data Binding Dialog Window. Select the `Locator` data source and then select Vendors, as shown in Figure 5–4.

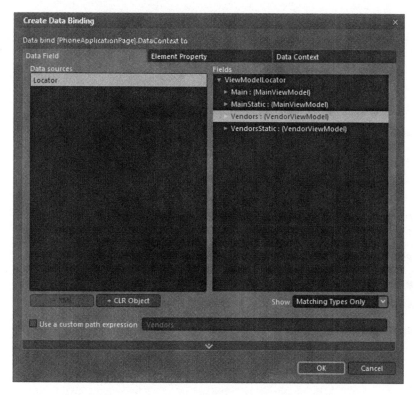

Figure 5–4. *Data bind DataContext to the VendorsViewModel*

Be sure to select the non-`static` property so the data binding work correctly. Run the application and navigate to the `VendorsView` and it displays the data as before. We still have the event handlers in the code-behind. In the next subsection the event handlers are removed and instead the application takes advantage Commanding support provided by the MVVM Light toolkit.

Commanding and RelayCommand

The MVVM Light Toolkit supports Commanding, or data binding events to ViewModel methods, via the RelayCommand and RelayCommand<T> classes. In the VendorViewModel class, two RelayCommand instances are added in a region named Commanding, one that is parameter-less and one that takes a parameter. Here is the declaration:

```
#region Commanding
public RelayCommand AddAVendorCommand
{
  get;
  private set;
}

public RelayCommand<Vendor> RemoveAVendorCommand
{
  get;
  private set;
}
#endregion
```

The commands are instantiated in the VendorViewModel() constructor in this code:

```
//Instantiate Commands
AddAVendorCommand = new RelayCommand(
  () => AddVendor());

RemoveAVendorCommand = new RelayCommand<Vendor>(
  param => RemoveVendor(param));
```

The RelayCommand objects bridge between the ViewModel methods and the UI events. RelayCommand has support for one parameter only so you need to pass more info, consider encapsulating into an object. Now it's time to data bind the commands in the UI. Currently the application uses the application bar to execute Add and Remove. Unfortunately the ApplicationBarIconButton class does not inherit from FrameworkElement so the ButtonBaseExtension cannot be attached to a DependencyObject. You can still call the relay in code behind as before. Here is an example from the sample:

```
private void insertVendorAppBarBtn_Click(object sender, EventArgs e)
{
  var vm = DataContext as VendorViewModel;
  if (vm != null)
  {
    vm.AddAVendorCommand.Execute(null);
  }
}
```

For this sample, the two Buttons are added so that we can demonstrate the EventToCommand Expression Blend behavior, as well as via the code-behind for the application bar buttons. In Expression Blend, switch to the Assets tab and select Behaviors to filter the list. Drag the EventToCommand behavior on to the Button objects and configure the correct command on each button. For the Remove Button, data bind the EventToCommand Command property to the RemoveAVendorCommand RelayCommand. Also data bind the CommandParameter for the Remove EventToCommand object to the vendorsListBox.SelectedItem method, which returns a Vendor object. Here is the resulting markup for Remove:

```
<Button x:Name="RemoveButton" Content="Remove" HorizontalAlignment="Right"
VerticalAlignment="Bottom" Margin="0,0,8,18">
```

```
<Custom:Interaction.Triggers>
  <Custom:EventTrigger EventName="Click">
    <GalaSoft_MvvmLight_Command:EventToCommand Command=
          "{Binding RemoveAVendorCommand, Mode=OneWay}"
      CommandParameter="{Binding SelectedItem, ElementName=vendorsListBox}"/>
  </Custom:EventTrigger>
</Custom:Interaction.Triggers>
</Button>
```

The RelayCommand class also supports CanExecute and CanExecuteChanged members as well to determine whether or not to enable or disable the element, in this case a Button object. The CanExecute method can be passed in to the constructor as a second parameter. Here's an example:

```
AddAVendorCommand = new RelayCommand(
  () => AddVendor(), () => CheckEnabled);
```

We have now completely migrated the sample over to MVVM. Listing 5–4 shows the source code for the updated VendorViewModel class.

Listing 5–4. Updated VendorViewModel Code File

```
using System;
using System.Collections.ObjectModel;
using System.Linq;
using System.Net;
using System.Runtime.Serialization.Json;
using System.Windows;
using GalaSoft.MvvmLight;
using GalaSoft.MvvmLight.Command;
using MvvmLightSample.Models;

namespace MvvmLightSample.ViewModel
{
  public class VendorViewModel : ViewModelBase
  {
    public VendorViewModel()
    {
      if (IsInDesignMode)
      {
        LoadSampleData();
      }
      else
      {
        LoadData();
      }

      //Instantiate Commands
      AddAVendorCommand = new RelayCommand(
        () => AddVendor());

      RemoveAVendorCommand = new RelayCommand<Vendor>(
        param => RemoveVendor(param));

    }
```

```csharp
#region Design-time support
private void LoadSampleData()
{
  _vendors = new ObservableCollection<Vendor>()
  {
    new Vendor(){AccountNumber="111111", CreditRating=65,
      Name="DesignTime - Fabrikam Bikes" },
    new Vendor(){AccountNumber="222222", CreditRating=40,
      Name="Contoso Sports" },
    new Vendor(){AccountNumber="333333", CreditRating=30,
      Name="Duwamish Surfing Gear" },
    new Vendor(){AccountNumber="444444", CreditRating=65,
      Name="Contoso Bikes" },
    new Vendor(){AccountNumber="555555", CreditRating=40,
      Name="Fabrikam Sports" },
    new Vendor(){AccountNumber="666666", CreditRating=30,
      Name="Duwamish Golf" },
    new Vendor(){AccountNumber="777777", CreditRating=65,
      Name="Fabrikam Sun Sports" },
    new Vendor(){AccountNumber="888888", CreditRating=40,
      Name="Contoso Lacross" },
    new Vendor(){AccountNumber="999999", CreditRating=30,
      Name="Duwamish Team Sports" },
  };
}
#endregion

#region Vendors Data Load
HttpWebRequest httpWebRequest;
private void LoadData()
{
  httpWebRequest =
HttpWebRequest.CreateHttp("http://localhost:9191/AdventureWorksRestJSON.svc/Vendors");
  httpWebRequest.BeginGetResponse(new AsyncCallback(GetVendors), null);
}

//add a reference to System.Servicemodel.web to get DataContractJsonSerializer
void GetVendors(IAsyncResult result)
{
  HttpWebResponse response = httpWebRequest.EndGetResponse(result) as HttpWebResponse;
  DataContractJsonSerializer ser = new
DataContractJsonSerializer(typeof(ObservableCollection<Vendor>));
  _vendors = ser.ReadObject(response.GetResponseStream()) as ObservableCollection<Vendor>;
  //Vendors is read-only so cannot set directly
  //Must call NotifyPropertyChanged notifications on UI thread
  //to update the UI and have data binding work properly
  Deployment.Current.Dispatcher.BeginInvoke(() =>
  {
    base.RaisePropertyChanged("Vendors");
  });
}
#endregion

#region Vendors Business Logic
```

```csharp
    private ObservableCollection<Vendor> _vendors;
    public ObservableCollection<Vendor> Vendors
    {
      get
      {
        return _vendors;
      }
      //set
      //{
      //  _vendors = value;
      //  NotifyPropertyChanged("Vendors");
      //}
    }

    public Vendor GetVendorByAccountNumber(string accountNumber)
    {
      var vendor = from v in _vendors
                   where v.AccountNumber == accountNumber
                   select v;

      return vendor.First<Vendor>();
    }

    public void AddVendor()
    {
      Vendors.Add(new Vendor()
      {
        AccountNumber = "111111",
        CreditRating = 65,
        Name = "Fabrikam Bikes - Added"
      });
    }

    public void RemoveVendor(object vendor)
    {
      if (null != vendor)
        Vendors.Remove((Vendor)vendor);
    }
    #endregion

    #region Commanding
    public RelayCommand AddAVendorCommand
    {
      get;
      private set;
    }

    public RelayCommand<Vendor> RemoveAVendorCommand
    {
      get;
      private set;
    }
    #endregion
  }
}
```

In the next couple of sections, I cover additional features of the MVVM Light Toolkit.

MVVM Light Messenger Class

The Messenger class provides a means to communicate within an application in a decoupled way. Classes can register to receive messages of different types. The message can be anything from simple values to complex objects. Likewise, messages can specify a target type that should receive the message for fined tuned control.

MVVM Light includes multiple message classes. The following is a list of possible messages from the docs:

- **MessageBase:** A simple message class, carrying optional information about the message's sender.

- **GenericMessage<T>:** A simple message with a Content property of type T.

- **NotificationMessage:** Used to send a notification (as a string) to a recipient. For example, define notifications as constants in a Notifications class, and then send Notifications.Save to recipients.

- **NotificationMessage<T>:** Same as the previous, but with a generic Content property. It can be used to pass a parameter to the recipient together with the notification.

- **NotificationMessageAction:** Sends a notification to a recipient and allows the recipient to call the sender back.

- **NotificationMessageAction<T>:** Sends a notification to a recipient and allows the recipient to call the sender back with a generic parameter.

- **DialogMessage:** Used to request that a recipient (typically a View) displays a dialog, and passes the result back to the caller (using a callback). The recipient can choose how to display the dialog, either with a standard MessageBox, with a custom popup, or something similar.

- **PropertyChangedMessage<T>:** Used to broadcast that a property changed in the message sender. Fulfills the same purpose as the PropertyChanged event, but in a decoupled manner.

The Messenger class provides a powerful means to pass data and notifications between application layers and within ViewModels in a decoupled way.

Silverlight for Windows Phone 7 Toolkit

The Silverlight Toolkit has been in existence for several years. The idea behind it is to be able to more frequently release control and other updates with full source code to developer's out-of-band from the normal product release cycle. The toolkit was extended to Windows Phone 7 with the initial release for phone in September 2010, with the latest update available as of this writing releasing mid-November 2010. It is available for download here:

http://silverlight.codeplex.com/

Installation and Overview

Installation is simply a matter of running the MSI and making the controls available in the Toolbox within Visual Studio 2010. Right-click on the Toolbox, select Choose Items…, and then put a check box next to controls you want to show up in the Toolbox. You can sort the controls alphabetically as well. The Silverlight for Windows Phone Toolkit includes several phone-specific controls that most developers will want to take advantage of to some degree listed in Table 5–1.

Table 5–1. Silverlight for Windows Phone 7 Toolkit Available Controls

Control Name	Description
GestureService/GestureListener	Enables rich gesture support for Silverlight applications.
ContextMenu	Enables a Tap-and-Hold action to bring up a Metro-style context menu.
DatePicker	A Metro-style DatePicker control.
TimePicker	A Metro-style TimePicker control.
ToggleSwitch	A Metro-style Toggle-button control.
WrapPanel	A phone-specific version of the Silverlight tried-and-true WrapPanel control.
AutoCompleteBox	A Metro-style auto-complete TextBox control.
ListPicker	A Metro-style DropDownList control.
LongListSelector	A turbo-charged ListBox control optimized for Windows Phone that also includes "Jump List" functionality.
PerformanceProgressBar	A custom progress bar control enhanced with better performance over the built-in progress bar.
Page Transitions	Set of transitions and animations. Covered in the next section.

The controls in Table 5–1 were frequently requested by developers during the beta-test phase of the Windows Phone Developer Tools. The product team created the toolkit to supplement the SDK to help match the built-in native UI controls look and feel.

■ **Note** GestureService and GestureListener are covered in Chapter 3.

The best way to proceed is to dive right in and show you how to put the controls to work within a sample project. Luckily, the Silverlight for Windows Phone 7 Toolkit includes a very robust sample that is included with the source code download titled "Silverlight for Windows Phone Toolkit Source & Sample – Nov 2010.zip" available here:

```
http://silverlight.codeplex.com/releases/view/55034
```

There isn't any documentation beyond the sample application so this section provides an overview of the available additional controls available in the toolkit. There is one additional sample project in the Chapter 5 solution that demonstrates how to data bind the WrapPanel control.

When you first run the sample app that ships with the source code available for download at the link I just gave you, it launches into a menu shown in Figure 5–5.

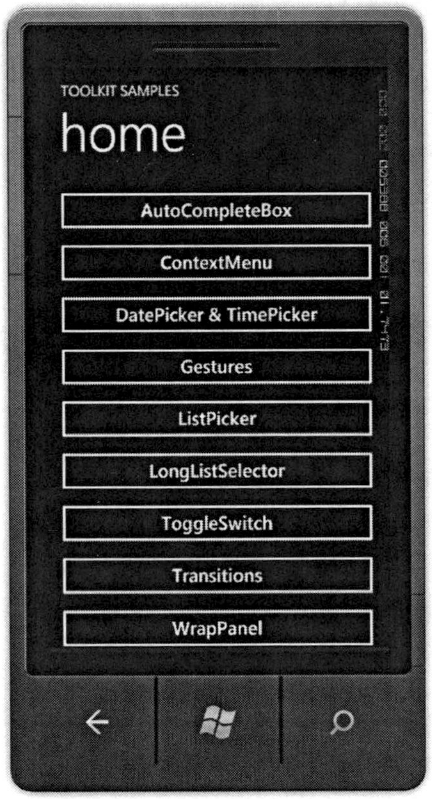

Figure 5–5. *Silverlight for Windows Phone Toolkit sample main menu*

Each control is covered in the sections that follow.

AutoCompleteBox Control

The `AutoCompleteBox` control allows a user to type letters, which brings up matches from the data source resource configured on the `ItemSource` attribute. Here is an example:

```
<toolkit:AutoCompleteBox VerticalAlignment="Top" ItemsSource="{StaticResource words}"↵
 Margin="0,12"/>
```

Figure 5–6 shows the `AutoCompleteBox` in action. The top `AutoCompleteBox` is configured with the above XAML.

Figure 5–6. *AutoCompleteBox in action*

The bottom `AutoCompleteBox` is configured with an `ItemTemplate` to display two lines of text:

```
<toolkit:AutoCompleteBox
    InputScope="Url"
    ItemsSource="{StaticResource websites}"
    Margin="0,12"
    ValueMemberPath="Item1">
    <toolkit:AutoCompleteBox.ItemTemplate>
        <DataTemplate>
            <StackPanel Margin="0,7">
                <TextBlock
                    Margin="8,0"
                    Text="{Binding Item1}"/>
```

```
<TextBlock
    FontSize="{StaticResource PhoneFontSizeNormal}"
    Foreground="#ff666666"
    Margin="8,-6,8,2"
    Text="{Binding Item2}"/>
        </StackPanel>
    </DataTemplate>
</toolkit:AutoCompleteBox.ItemTemplate>
</toolkit:AutoCompleteBox>
```

The words come from these resources configured in PhoneApplicationPage.Resources section:

```
<phone:PhoneApplicationPage.Resources>
    <data:LoremIpsum x:Key="words"/>
    <data:LoremIpsumWebsites x:Key="websites"/>
</phone:PhoneApplicationPage.Resources>
```

In the Data folder of the toolkit sample solution PhoneToolkitSample project, there are two classes, LoremIpsum.cs and LoremIpsumWebsites.cs, which generate a random collection of words in an IEnumerable collection. You can data bind to any collection of strings and display the values as the user types.

The AutoCompleteBox provides a great way to improve UI by populating text fields with most likely values, saving users from having to type.

ContextMenu Control

The ContextMenu control provides a user interaction unique to Windows Phone 7 with the tap-and-hold gesture. Figure 5–7 shows the test page within text hints on functionality, as well as results after tap-and-hold actions.

Figure 5–7. *ContextMenu control test page*

The ContextMenu control is bindable to ICommand objects, so it can work quite nicely with GalaSoft's MVVM support for Commanding allowing context menu items to invoke methods on the data bound ViewModel class.

DatePicker and TimePicker Controls

The DatePicker and TimePicker controls make it easy for users to pick date and time within a Windows Phone 7 application. Figure 5–8 shows the controls in action.

Figure 5–8. DatePicker & TimePicker controls in action

You can attach an event hander to the Click event and assign commands to the Command property. Here is example XAML for ICommand support:

```
<toolkit:ContextMenuService.ContextMenu>
    <toolkit:ContextMenu>
        <toolkit:MenuItem
        Header="Always-on item"
        Command="{Binding AlwaysCommand}"/>
        <toolkit:MenuItem
        Header="Intermittent item"
        Command="{Binding IntermittentCommand}"/>
        <toolkit:MenuItem
        Header="Always-on item with param"
```

```
            Command="{Binding AlwaysCommand}"
            CommandParameter="param1"/>
            <toolkit:MenuItem
            Header="Intermittent item with param"
            Command="{Binding IntermittentCommand}"
            CommandParameter="param2"/>
        </toolkit:ContextMenu>
    </toolkit:ContextMenuService.ContextMenu>
```

The controls are dependent on having the correct application bar icons in a folder named
Toolkit.Content. The icons are ApplicationBar.Cancel.png and ApplicationBar.Check.png and their
build action must be set to Content.

ListPicker Control

The ListPicker control provides a full-page, touch-friendly drop-down scrollable list to select an item.
Figure 5–9 shows the example.

Figure 5–9. ListPicker control in action

The ListPicker control can display a set of inline strings like this:

```
<toolkit:ListPicker Header="background">
    <sys:String>dark</sys:String>
    <sys:String>light</sys:String>
    <sys:String>dazzle</sys:String>
</toolkit:ListPicker>
```

The ListPicker control also has ItemSource and ItemTemplate attributes to support data binding and full customization of how items are displayed. Here is example XAML:

```
<toolkit:ListPicker ItemsSource="{Binding}" Header="accent color"
                 FullModeHeader="ACCENTS" CacheMode="BitmapCache">
    <toolkit:ListPicker.ItemTemplate>
        <DataTemplate>
            <StackPanel Orientation="Horizontal">
                <Rectangle Fill="{Binding}" Width="24" Height="24"/>
                <TextBlock Text="{Binding}" Margin="12 0 0 0"/>
            </StackPanel>
        </DataTemplate>
    </toolkit:ListPicker.ItemTemplate>
    <toolkit:ListPicker.FullModeItemTemplate>
        <DataTemplate>
            <StackPanel Orientation="Horizontal" Margin="16 21 0 20">
                <Rectangle Fill="{Binding}" Width="43" Height="43"/>
                <TextBlock Text="{Binding}" Margin="16 0 0 0" FontSize="43"
                         FontFamily="{StaticResource PhoneFontFamilyLight}"/>
            </StackPanel>
        </DataTemplate>
    </toolkit:ListPicker.FullModeItemTemplate>
</toolkit:ListPicker>
```

ToggleSwitch Control

The ToggleSwitch control configures a boolean value as On or Off. It can take a simple Header attribute for a text value to display across the top above the switch and current status as shown in the first two ToggleSwitch controls in Figure 5–10.

Figure 5–10. *The ToggleSwitch control*

The last ToggleSwitch control is much more customized than the first two. It includes a
ToggleSwitch.HeaderTemplate to adjust the Font for the header. The ToggleSwitch.ContentTemplate
customizes the ToggleSwitch status info on the left with additional detail. Simply embed a
<ContentControl Content="{Binding}"/> control inside of the ToggleSwitch.ContentTemplate to have
the On/Off status display correctly, as in the following:

```
<toolkit:ToggleSwitch Header="5:45 AM">
    <toolkit:ToggleSwitch.HeaderTemplate>
        <DataTemplate>
            <ContentControl FontSize="{StaticResource PhoneFontSizeLarge}"
                    Foreground="{StaticResource PhoneForegroundBrush}" Content="{Binding}"/>
        </DataTemplate>
    </toolkit:ToggleSwitch.HeaderTemplate>
    <toolkit:ToggleSwitch.ContentTemplate>
        <DataTemplate>
            <StackPanel>
                <StackPanel Orientation="Horizontal">
                    <TextBlock Text="Alarm: " FontSize="{StaticResource PhoneFontSizeSmall}"/>
                    <ContentControl HorizontalAlignment="Left"
```

```
                                  FontSize="{StaticResource PhoneFontSizeSmall}"
Content="{Binding}"/>
                </StackPanel>
                <TextBlock Text="every schoolday"
                           FontSize="{StaticResource PhoneFontSizeSmall}"
                           Foreground="{StaticResource PhoneSubtleBrush}"/>
            </StackPanel>
        </DataTemplate>
    </toolkit:ToggleSwitch.ContentTemplate>
</toolkit:ToggleSwitch>
```

WrapPanel Control

The WrapPanel control works very similarly to the same named control available in the desktop
Silverlight toolkit. It arranges child items left to right, row by row or top to bottom, column by column.
Figure 5–11 shows the UI.

Figure 5–11. The WrapPanel control

The WrapPanel control has a Children collection that allows you to add child items to the control via code, which is how the toolkit sample adds items. There may be situations in which you prefer to data bind to an ItemSource property and an ItemTemplate, like you can in the ListBox control. The WrapPanelDataBinding project sample in the Chapter 5 solution demonstrates how to do this.

You can use an ItemsControl to provide this functionality by changing the ItemsControl.ItemsPanel to a WrapPanel. Otherwise, data binding works just like with a ListBox. Here is the XAML markup:

```
<ItemsControl ItemsSource="{Binding Strings}">
  <ItemsControl.ItemsPanel>
    <ItemsPanelTemplate>
      <toolkit:WrapPanel ItemWidth="69"/>
    </ItemsPanelTemplate>
  </ItemsControl.ItemsPanel>
  <ItemsControl.ItemTemplate>
    <DataTemplate>
      <Grid Width="60" Height="60" Margin="4">
        <Rectangle Fill="#FF2A2AC8" Stroke="Black"/>
        <TextBlock
          Text="{Binding Text}" TextWrapping="Wrap"/>
      </Grid>
    </DataTemplate>
  </ItemsControl.ItemTemplate>
</ItemsControl>
```

The WrapPanelDataBinding project has a sample data source generated in Expression Blend to display random text over rectangles. The ItemsControl.ItemsSource points to the Strings collection in the sample data source. Figure 5–12 shows the output.

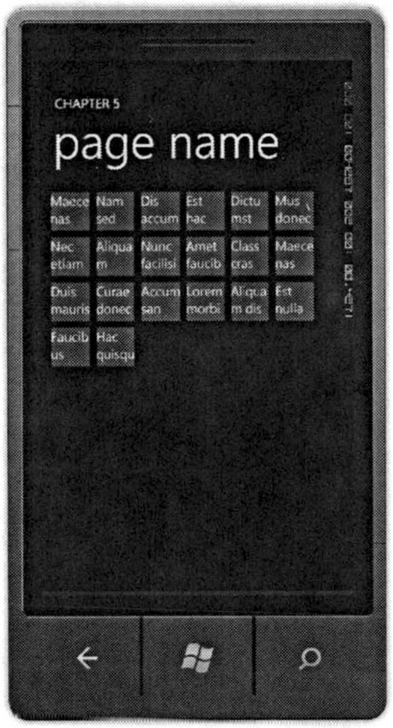

Figure 5–12. Data binding the WrapPanel control

A control that we won't dive into here is the PerformanceProgressBar control, which was added to the toolkit in February 2011. Using the control is pretty straightforward, as it models the functionality of the built-in Progressbar control. I mention it because you will want to use the toolkit PerformanceProgressBar to improve rendering performance in your Silverlight or Windows Phone applications.

LongListSelector Control

The LongListSelector control is the uber-ListBox control available for Windows Phone 7. It supports flat lists (like in a ListBox), but it can provide better performance than the standard ListBox control. Try it for your scenario. The LongListSelector control also supports grouped list, inline "more like these" buttons, and jump list UI.

Given the complexity and power of this control, the next couple sections describe its visual capabilities, key properties and methods, and coding approaches.

LongListSelector - IsFlatList

The quickest way to take advantage of the LongListSelector control's potential performance and list virtualization advantages is to replace existing ListBox controls with LongListSelector controls and set the attribute IsFlatList to True. When in IsFlatList=true mode, the UI looks just like a ListBox control though you can provide a header and footer to the list via the ListHeaderTemplate and ListFooterTemplate properties, as shown in Figure 5–13.

Figure 5–13. LongListSelector with header and footer

Listing 5–5 shows the XAML for the control and the three templates that are configured.

```
<phone:PhoneApplicationPage
```

Listing 5–5. LongListSelector XAML Markup File

```
    x:Class="LongListSelectorSample.pages.LongListSelectorPage2"
…<!—removed standard namespaces for clarity →
    SupportedOrientations="Portrait" Orientation="Portrait"
    mc:Ignorable="d" d:DesignHeight="768" d:DesignWidth="480"
    shell:SystemTray.IsVisible="True" Loaded="PhoneApplicationPage_Loaded"
    xmlns:toolkit="clr-namespace:Microsoft.Phone.Controls;assembly=↵
Microsoft.Phone.Controls.Toolkit">
  <phone:PhoneApplicationPage.Resources>
    <DataTemplate x:Key="ItemTemplate">
      <StackPanel Margin="0,0,0,20">
        <TextBlock Text="{Binding Name}"
                   Style="{StaticResource PhoneTextExtraLargeStyle}"/>
        <TextBlock Text="{Binding Description}"
                   Style="{StaticResource PhoneTextSmallStyle}"/>
        <TextBlock Text="{Binding Quantity}"
                   Style="{StaticResource PhoneTextAccentStyle}"/>
      </StackPanel>
    </DataTemplate>
    <DataTemplate x:Key="HeaderDataTemplate">
      <Border Background="#FF0027FF">
        <TextBlock TextWrapping="Wrap" Text="Chapter Five"
          HorizontalAlignment="Center" VerticalAlignment="Center"
          Style="{StaticResource PhoneTextLargeStyle}"/>
      </Border>
    </DataTemplate>
    <DataTemplate x:Key="FooterDataTemplate">
      <Border Background="#FF0027FF">
        <TextBlock TextWrapping="Wrap" Text="Advanced Silverlight UI"
          HorizontalAlignment="Center" VerticalAlignment="Center"
          Style="{StaticResource PhoneTextLargeStyle}"/>
      </Border>
    </DataTemplate>
  </phone:PhoneApplicationPage.Resources>
  <!--LayoutRoot is the root grid where all page content is placed-->
  <Grid x:Name="LayoutRoot" Background="Transparent"
    DataContext="{Binding Source={StaticResource longlistDataSource}}">
    <Grid.RowDefinitions>  <RowDefinition Height="Auto"/>
      <RowDefinition Height="*"/>  </Grid.RowDefinitions>
    <!--TitlePanel contains the name of the application and page title-->
    <StackPanel x:Name="TitlePanel" Grid.Row="0" Margin="12,17,0,28">
      <TextBlock x:Name="ApplicationTitle" Text="CHAPTER 5-LONGLISTSELECTORSAMPLE"
                 Style="{StaticResource PhoneTextNormalStyle}"/>
      <TextBlock x:Name="PageTitle" Text="longlistselector" Margin="9,-7,0,0"
                 Style="{StaticResource PhoneTextTitle1Style}"/>
    </StackPanel>
    <!--ContentPanel - place additional content here-->
    <Grid x:Name="ContentPanel" Grid.Row="1" Margin="12,0,12,0">
      <toolkit:LongListSelector IsFlatList="True"
```

```
        ItemTemplate="{StaticResource ItemTemplate}"
        ItemsSource="{Binding Collection}"
        ListHeaderTemplate="{StaticResource HeaderDataTemplate}"
        ListFooterTemplate="{StaticResource FooterDataTemplate}"/>
    </Grid>
  </Grid>
</phone:PhoneApplicationPage>
```

If you forget to set IsFlatList equal to True, it will generate an error when data bound to a flat list. This is because by default the LongListSelector control expects a data structure with a grouped set of items that permits the control to display the long list of content segmented by available groups.

LongListSelector via LINQ

The PhoneToolkit Sample Solution downloaded from CodePlex when you install the toolkit includes a page named LongListSelectorSample.xaml. This page demonstrates several ways a developer can implement grouping with the LongListSelector control. The UI for the LongListSelectorSample.xaml is a Pivot control with three PivotItem pages titled linq, code, and buddies. The LongListSelector implementation for the PivitItem titled linq has the following XAML:

```
<toolkit:LongListSelector x:Name="linqMovies" Background="Transparent"
    ListHeaderTemplate="{StaticResource movieListHeader}"
    GroupHeaderTemplate="{StaticResource movieGroupHeader}"
    GroupItemTemplate="{StaticResource groupItemHeader}"
    ItemTemplate="{StaticResource movieItemTemplate}">
</toolkit:LongListSelector>
```

Note that it does not implement a GroupFooterTemplate. The PivotItem page titled linq displays movie data via Category using LINQ to demonstrate how to group items in the correct format using LINQ. The item that is displayed in the LongListSelector for both the linq and code PivotItem pages is a Movie class that has fields like Title, Description, Year, etc. The movies are grouped by either Category, which is of type string. In the code-behind file, the LoadLinqMovies method creates a flat collection of movies with random data and then builds a LINQ to Object query to group the movies by category.

The LINQ query is dazzlingly simple, taking advantage of the built-in group by support in LINQ that is based on the IGrouping Interface. Here is the LoadLinqMovies method:

```
private void LoadLinqMovies()
{
    List<Movie> movies = new List<Movie>();

    for (int i = 0; i < 50; ++i)
    {
        movies.Add(Movie.CreateRandom());
    }

    var moviesByCategory = from movie in movies
                            group movie by movie.Category into c
                            orderby c.Key
                            select new PublicGrouping<string, Movie>(c);

    linqMovies.ItemsSource = moviesByCategory;
}
```

The class `PublicGrouping` implements the `IGrouping` Interface, which has this definition from metadata:

```
namespace System.Linq
{
  // Summary:
  //     Represents a collection of objects that have a common key.
  //
  // Type parameters:
  //   TKey:
  //     The type of the key of the System.Linq.IGrouping<TKey,TElement>.
  //
  //   TElement:
  //     The type of the values in the System.Linq.IGrouping<TKey,TElement>.
  public interface IGrouping<TKey, TElement> : IEnumerable<TElement>, IEnumerable
  {
    // Summary:
    //     Gets the key of the System.Linq.IGrouping<TKey,TElement>.
    //
    // Returns:
    //     The key of the System.Linq.IGrouping<TKey,TElement>.
    TKey Key { get; }
  }
}
```

An `IEnumerable` collection of `PublicGrouping` items is the output from the previous LINQ query:

```
var moviesByCategory = from movie in movies
                       group movie by movie.Category into c
                       orderby c.Key
                       select new PublicGrouping<string, Movie>(c);
```

The `PublicGrouping` class is generic: Here is the class declaration and constructor:

```
public class PublicGrouping<TKey, TElement> : IGrouping<TKey, TElement>
...
public PublicGrouping(IGrouping<TKey, TElement> internalGrouping)
{
    _internalGrouping = internalGrouping;
}
```

The LINQ query obtains the Enumerator from the LINQ Query, in this case the 'c' variable, which is defined as Category. Use the `PublicGrouping` class as a basis for your usage of the `LongListSelector` control.

Given the correctly formatted data structure, the `LongListSelector` class renders the UI in a grouped format. If you click on a group item, it displays a menu of available groups. Figure 5–14 shows the linq `PivotItem` in action, with the screenshot on the right showing the results of clicking the group item. Select a new group item like Comedy to jump to the portion of the list containing the Comedy movies.

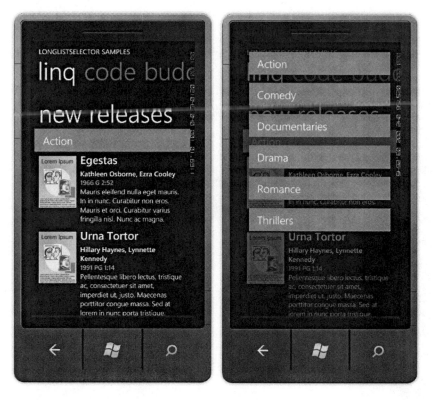

Figure 5–14. *LongListSelector using LINQ*

LongListSelector via Code

The code `PivotItem` in the `PhoneToolkit` project `LongListSelectorSample.xaml` page implements an additional feature with the `LongListSelector` control. The `GroupFooterTemplate` is modified to include a Button to display "more" of a particular category. Here is the XAML for the code `PivotItem` `LongListSelector` control:

```
<toolkit:LongListSelector x:Name="codeMovies" Background="Transparent"
            ItemsSource="{StaticResource movies}"
            ListHeaderTemplate="{StaticResource movieListHeader}"
            GroupHeaderTemplate="{StaticResource movieGroupHeader}"
            GroupItemTemplate="{StaticResource groupItemHeader}"
            ItemTemplate="{StaticResource movieItemTemplate}">
  <toolkit:LongListSelector.GroupFooterTemplate>
    <DataTemplate>
      <local:CommandButton DataContext="{Binding}" Content="{Binding GetMore}"
        Command="{StaticResource moreCommand}" CommandParameter="{Binding}"/>
    </DataTemplate>
  </toolkit:LongListSelector.GroupFooterTemplate>
</toolkit:LongListSelector>
```

Notice that the GroupFooterTemplate includes a DataTemplate with a CommandButton class instance, which is included in the sample code. The LongListSelector implementation on the code PivotItem does not use LINQ to generate the grouped item list. It binds to a StaticResource defined on the page named moreCommand, which is a class located in the MoviesByCategory.cs class file in the Data folder. More on that in a bit.

Also notice that ItemsSource data binds to a StaticResource named movies, which points to a class named MoviesByCategory located in the Data folder. The MoviesByCategory class is fairly simple. It obtains the Categories, and then randomly generates a set of fake objects for each Category using the MoviesInCategory class. It demonstrates how to create properly formatted groups in code and can provide a useful starter example.

The MoreCommand class implements the ICommand interface. The ICommand.Execute method adds additional random objects to the currently selected group that is passed in via a parameter. For a real implementation, some tracking is necessary to identify which records are already displayed so that the correct next set of records is retrieved, if present. Figure 5–15 shows the UI with the More Command button.

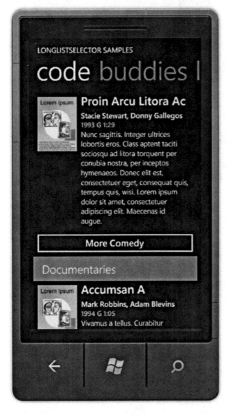

Figure 5–15. *LongListSelector with Command button displayed.*

The last PivotItem, named buddies, also generates a collection in code. It randomly generates a list of people names via the AllPeople class, sorts them, and then generates groups by the alphabet and related group of names starting with each letter in the PeopleByFirstName class. The GroupItemTemplate in this case is the alphabet as shown in Figure 5–16.

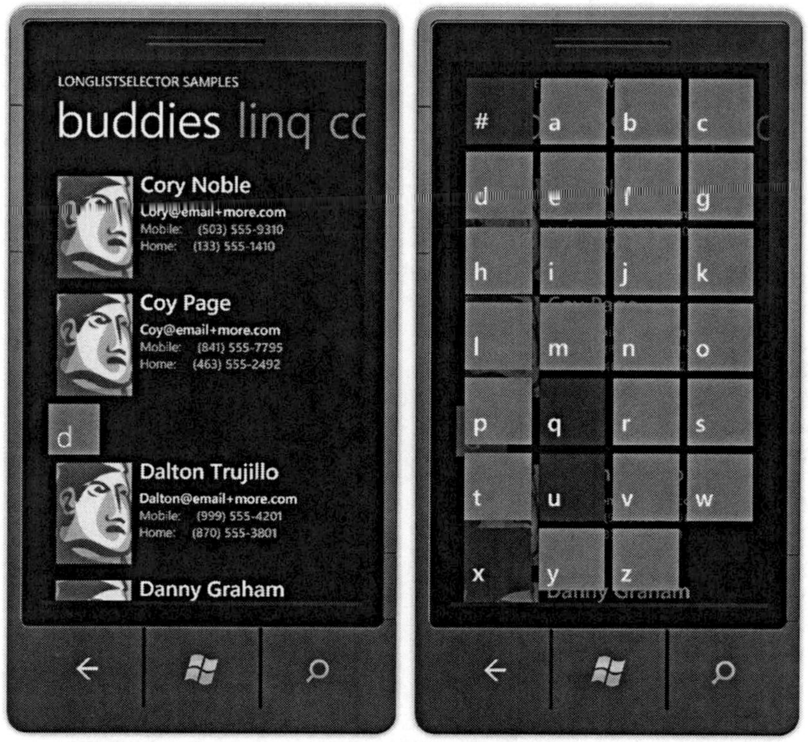

Figure 5–16. LongListSelector with alphabetized list

In this section, we performed an in-depth review of the LongListSelector control, because it provides rich and very much needed functionality for Windows Phone 7 applications that display lists of data. This section concludes the review of the Silverlight for Windows Phone 7 toolkit except for the transition animations, which we cover as part of the next section.

Creating Transitions and Interactivity

In previous sections, we used the NavigateToPageAction behavior to navigate from one page to another. In this section, I focus on how to create more interactivity with Expression Blend for page transitions, status changes, and orientation changes. We start with investigating how to add interactivity using the Silverlight for Windows Phone 7 Toolkit. We next focus on the Visual State Manager to create animations and transitions using a state-based management system.

Toolkit Page Transitions

The Silverlight for Windows Phone 7 toolkit enables transitions that match the built-in native transitions available in Windows Phone 7, allowing your application to have the same look and feel without a lot of work. It is very simple to make the transitions available within an application, which is demonstrated in the Chapter 5 project named `ToolkitTransitions`.

Sample Project

The `ToolkitTransitions` project has three XAML pages. `MainPage.xaml` navigates to `TestTransitionsPage.xaml`, which data binds to a collection of sample data. The sample data is present to make the transitions more obvious than with just a mostly blank screen. When an item is selected in the TestTransitionsPage.xaml's `sampleDataListBox`, the code in the `sampleDataListBox_SelectionChanged` event appends the index of the selected item to a query string and then navigates to `TestTransitionsPage2.xaml`. The `TestTransitionsPage2.xaml` page displays the full details of the selected item.

An extra page is added to the project beyond `MainPage.xaml` because transitions from the Silverlight for Windows Phone 7 toolkit do not override the standard application loading and exiting page transitions so we need another page to fully demonstrate the transitions. The page in the middle, `TestTransitionsPage.xaml`, will have the transitions configured on it to demonstrate the full navigating to and from page transition capabilities because it is not the default item or main page for the application.

To get started, first add a project reference to the `Microsoft.Phone.Controls.Toolkit` assembly. Next open the `App.xaml.cs` file and change this line of code in the `InitializePhoneApplication()` method:

```
RootFrame = new PhoneApplicationFrame();
```

to this line of code:

```
RootFrame = new Microsoft.Phone.Controls.TransitionFrame();
```

Next, add a second page named `toolkittransitionpage.xaml` to a pages folder. A `TextBlock` is added to `MainPage.xaml` and the `NavigateToPageAction` behavior is applied to the `TextBlock`, so that when it is touched, the `toolkittransitionpage.xaml` is displayed. Run the project and check to make sure the navigation from `MainPage` to the `toolkittranstiionpage.xaml` is working. It is working, but it still does not have a nice transition to the second page. Now you can add any transition within the application.

Configuring Transitions

There isn't any Expression Blend support for visually applying transitions via behaviors. You edit the XAML to apply transitions. For each page, you can define four types of transitions:

- **NavigationInTransition:** Applies when navigating to the current page, either via a forward navigation to the page or via clicking the Back button to navigate back to the page.

- **NavigationOutTransition:** Applies when the current page is navigating out to another page, either via forward navigation to another page or when clicking the Back button on the current page.

- **DatePickerPage:** Applies when the current page is navigating to a `DatePicker` control page.

- **TimePickerPage:** Applies when the current page is navigating to a `TimePicker` control page.

To add a transition in XAML, add a namespace reference to the toolkit:

```
xmlns:toolkit="clr-namespace:Microsoft.Phone.Controls;assembly=↵
Microsoft.Phone.Controls.Toolkit"
```

Next type `<toolkit:TransitionService` to bring up IntelliSense to show the four available transition types. Select `NavigationInTransition` and then close the tag to generate the ending element `</toolkit:TransitionService.NavigationInTransition>`. A warning appears "Property 'NavigationInTransition' does not have a value." and blue squiggly lines appear as shown in Figure 5–17.

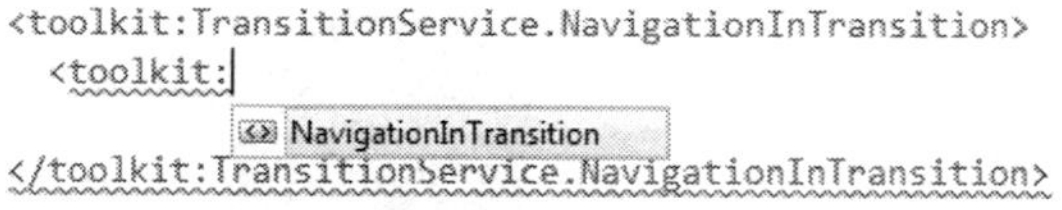

```
<toolkit:TransitionService.NavigationInTransition>
  <toolkit:|
        [▣] NavigationInTransition
</toolkit:TransitionService.NavigationInTransition>
```

Figure 5–17. *XAML Intellisense for* `NavigationInTransition`

The only option that displays is `toolkit:Navigation:InTransition`. Within that element you can add the following two additional elements:

- `NavigationInTransition.Backward`

- `NavigationInTransition.Forward`

Within the `.Backward` and `.Forward` transitions, you can configure one of four options, as shown in Figure 5–18.

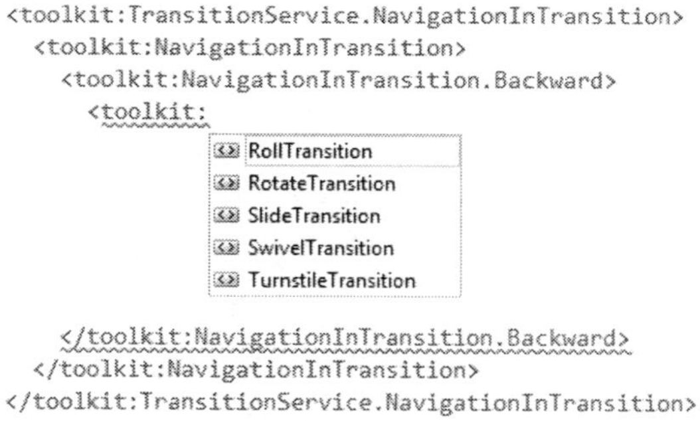

```
<toolkit:TransitionService.NavigationInTransition>
  <toolkit:NavigationInTransition>
    <toolkit:NavigationInTransition.Backward>
      <toolkit:
            [▣] RollTransition
            [▣] RotateTransition
            [▣] SlideTransition
            [▣] SwivelTransition
            [▣] TurnstileTransition

    </toolkit:NavigationInTransition.Backward>
  </toolkit:NavigationInTransition>
</toolkit:TransitionService.NavigationInTransition>
```

Figure 5–18. *XAML Intellisense for actual transition types*

We discuss the four possible transitions in detail in the next subsection. `NavigationOutTransition` also has a `.Backward` and `.Forward` option. Figure 5–19 describes the relationship for all four configurations.

Figure 5–19. Possible TransitionService Page navigation configurations

In Figure 5–19, all four transitions are configured on the middle page and have independent behavior depending on the relative navigation to the middle page. This is the same configuration as in the ToolkitTransitions sample project's TestTransitionsPage.xaml page where all four options are configured. Here is the XAML for the ToolkitTransitions sample transitions:

```
<toolkit:TransitionService.NavigationInTransition>
  <toolkit:NavigationInTransition>
    <toolkit:NavigationInTransition.Backward>
      <toolkit:RollTransition />
    </toolkit:NavigationInTransition.Backward>
    <toolkit:NavigationInTransition.Forward>
      <toolkit:RotateTransition  />
    </toolkit:NavigationInTransition.Forward>
  </toolkit:NavigationInTransition>
</toolkit:TransitionService.NavigationInTransition>
<toolkit:TransitionService.NavigationOutTransition>
  <toolkit:NavigationOutTransition>
    <toolkit:NavigationOutTransition.Backward>
      <toolkit:TurnstileTransition Mode="BackwardOut" />
    </toolkit:NavigationOutTransition.Backward>
    <toolkit:NavigationOutTransition.Forward>
      <toolkit:TurnstileTransition Mode="ForwardOut" />
    </toolkit:NavigationOutTransition.Forward>
  </toolkit:NavigationOutTransition>
</toolkit:TransitionService.NavigationOutTransition>
```

To help further explain, let's configure transitions on the page right. Since it is a "leaf" page without any additional forward navigation actions, only two transitions need to be configured. One for when the page is being navigated to and the other when on the page and the back button is touched and the page is navigated from. The two transitions are the forward "in" transition, NavigationInTransition.Forward, and the backward "out" transition, NavigationOutTransition.Backward. Here is the XAML:

```
<toolkit:TransitionService.NavigationInTransition>
  <toolkit:NavigationInTransition>
    <toolkit:NavigationInTransition.Forward>
      <toolkit:RotateTransition  />
    </toolkit:NavigationInTransition.Forward>
  </toolkit:NavigationInTransition>
</toolkit:TransitionService.NavigationInTransition>
<toolkit:TransitionService.NavigationOutTransition>
  <toolkit:NavigationOutTransition>
    <toolkit:NavigationOutTransition.Backward>
      <toolkit:TurnstileTransition Mode="BackwardOut" />
    </toolkit:NavigationOutTransition.Backward>
  </toolkit:NavigationOutTransition>
</toolkit:TransitionService.NavigationOutTransition>
```

Run the project in the emulator or, better yet, on a device where the transitions are more apparent. You will see that the transitions are "chained," meaning that the NavigationOutTranstion.Forward for page TestTransitionsPage.xaml does not override the NavigationIn.Forward for page TestTransitionsPage2.xaml. Instead, the transitions are chained. Again, this is more visible on a real device than in the emulator.

Transitions in Depth

We briefly mentioned above the four possible types of transitions that can be applied in any configuration, i.e., "in," "out," Forward, or Backward:

- RollTransition
- RotateTransition
- SlideTransition
- SwivelTransition
- TurnstileTransition

All of the transitions except the RollTransition take a Mode property that can have these values:

- BackwardIn
- BackwardOut
- ForwardIn
- ForwardOut

The Mode attribute allows you to tell the transition how it should appear based on whether it is a Forward "in" transition, and so on, so that it matches the native transitions correctly.

In addition to the Backward and Forward properties, the NavigationInTransition and NavigationOutTransition objects also have two events:

- BeginTransition
- EndTransition

These events allow you to hook into the transition at the Begin and End portion to perform actions such as data loading, unloading, and the like. Because these are events, you can use the MVVM Light Toolkit EventToCommand Behavior to bind the transition events to Commands declared in the ViewModel for your application.

Transitions and UI Elements

Transitions can be applied to any UI Element object. In the ToolkitTransitions project, click on the apply transition to rectangle TextBlock in MainPage.Xaml to load the corresponding page and click on the single application bar button. The Rectangle object will side down and fade in. The Rectangle is named targetRectangle and its Opacity is set to 0 in XAML:

```
private void ApplyTransitionAppBarBtn_Click(object sender, EventArgs e)
{
  RotateTransition rotateTransition =
    new RotateTransition { Mode = RotateTransitionMode.In180Clockwise};

  ITransition transition = rotateTransition.GetTransition(targetRectangle);

  transition.Completed +=
    (s, eventarg) => { transition.Stop(); targetRectangle.Opacity = 1; };

  transition.Begin();
}
```

You can of course simply create a Storyboard using Expression Blend and apply it to the Rectangle as well but this section demonstrates how to leverage the pre-existing animations available in the Silverlight for Windows Phone 7 toolkit. The next section describes how to create a transition based on a custom Storyboard object.

Custom Transitions

In this section I describe how to create a new transition class that leverages a custom Storyboard object. The steps are to implement the ITransition Interface with a custom class and implement another class that inherits from the TransitionElement base class. In the Chapter 5 Solution ToolkitTransitions project's MainPage.xaml, there is a TextBlock titled "custom transition that navigates to the CustomTransitionPage.xaml page. This page demonstrates a custom Transition.

The first step is to create a custom Storyboard animation that applies to the entire page named CustomPageTransitionStoryboard in Expression Blend. The CustomPageTransitionStoryboard uses translation to move the Page content from off-screen lower left sliding diagonally into place. The Storyboard is moved into the App.Resources section of App.xaml to make it globally available throughout the application.

Next create a class named TheTransition that implements ITransition, as shown in Listing 5–6

Listing 5–6. TheTransition Class

```
public class TheTransition : ITransition
{
  private Storyboard _storyboard;

  public TheTransition(Storyboard storyBoard)
  {
```

```
    _storyboard = storyBoard;
  }

  public void Begin()
  {
    _storyboard.Begin();
  }

  public event EventHandler Completed;

  public ClockState GetCurrentState()
  {
    return _storyboard.GetCurrentState();
  }

  public TimeSpan GetCurrentTime()
  {
    return _storyboard.GetCurrentTime();
  }

  public void Pause()
  {
    _storyboard.Pause();
  }

  public void Resume()
  {
    _storyboard.Resume();
  }

  public void Seek(TimeSpan offset)
  {
    _storyboard.Seek(offset);
  }

  public void SeekAlignedToLastTick(TimeSpan offset)
  {
    _storyboard.SeekAlignedToLastTick(offset);
  }

  public void SkipToFill()
  {
    _storyboard.SkipToFill();
  }

  public void Stop()
  {
    _storyboard.Stop();
  }
}
```

It is a pretty simple class that essentially wraps the Storyboard object. The class that is actually added in Xaml is named MyTransition, and is shown in Listing 5–7.

Listing 5–7. MyTransition Class

```
public class MyTransition : TransitionElement
{
  public override ITransition GetTransition(UIElement element)
  {
    Storyboard myStoryboard = App.Current.Resources["CustomPageTransitionStoryboard"] as
Storyboard;

    Storyboard.SetTarget(myStoryboard, element);

    return new TheTransition(myStoryboard);
  }
}
```

Notice how the MyTransition class obtains the Storyboard via the App.Current.Resources collection. In the CustomTransitionPage.xaml, a namespace named thisPage is added as is the custom transition:

```
xmlns:thisPage="clr-namespace:ToolkitTransitions.pages"
...
<toolkit:TransitionService.NavigationInTransition>
  <toolkit:NavigationInTransition>
    <toolkit:NavigationInTransition.Forward>
      <thisPage:MyTransition/>
    </toolkit:NavigationInTransition.Forward>
  </toolkit:NavigationInTransition>
</toolkit:TransitionService.NavigationInTransition>
```

Run the toolkitTransitions project to see the custom transition in action. It would make sense to add a Mode parameter to the MyTransitions class and then apply a custom Storyboard, depending on whether it is Backward, Forward, "in," or "out," but this sample demonstrates how to get started if you wish to create a custom transition.

This concludes coverage of the Silverlight for Windows Phone 7 Toolkit and how to create interactivity for page transitions. The next section demonstrates how to use the Visual State Manager to provide interactivity within a page.

Visual State Manager

The Visual State Manager (VSM) is a tool available within Expression Blend. It allows the developer / designer to visually define Visual State Groups that represent UI state for controls in that state, represented as a Storyboard. The best way to learn how to work with the VSM is by demonstration, most of which will be in Expression Blend.

Orientation Aware

This section demonstrates how to create an Orientation-aware application using the VSM. A new project named VSMVideoPlayer is added to the Chapter 5 solution based on the MVVMLight (WP7 Application project template. The project is customized to be a basic video player that can play a list of videos from a recent vacation – videos without ownership rights issues that I can use for this sample.

A Grid containing a MediaElement control named mediaPlayer is added to the ContentPanel Grid. Below the Grid containing the MediaElement, a ListBox named videosListBox is added and the Application Bar is enabled. The Application Bar is wired up to provide video controls for the mediaPlayer MediaElement.

A Model named Video is added to the Model folder and a collection of Video objects is added to the MainViewModel class. Finally three videos are added to a folder named Content and added to the project. Figure 5–20 shows the VSMVideoPlayer project in Expression Blend with the states tab opened.

Figure 5–20. VSMVideoPlayer and States Tab

The videosListBox is data bound to the Videos collection on the MainViewModel. The Grid containing the MediaElement is data bound to the SelectedItem of the videosListBox. The Source property for the mediaPlayer MediaElement is data bound to the Url property of the SelectedItem Video object. Run the project and when you select a video in the videosListBox it plays in the MediaElement. Listing 5–8 shows the XAML for the Content Grid and Application Bar from MainPage.xaml.

Listing 5–8. Content Grid and Application Bar Code

```
<Grid x:Name="ContentPanel" Grid.Row="1" Margin="12,0,12,0">
  <StackPanel d:LayoutOverrides="Width">
```

```xml
        <Grid Height="213" DataContext="{Binding SelectedItem, ElementName=videosListBox}">
            <MediaElement Source="{Binding Url}" Margin="5,9,7,-9" Name="mediaPlayer"
MediaFailed="mediaPlayer_MediaFailed" Stretch="UniformToFill" />
        </Grid>
        <ListBox x:Name="videosListBox" ItemsSource="{Binding Main.Videos}"
          Margin="12,24,0,0" ItemTemplate="{StaticResource VideoDataTemplate}" />
      </StackPanel>
    </Grid>
  </Grid>
  <phone:PhoneApplicationPage.ApplicationBar>
    <shell:ApplicationBar IsVisible="True" IsMenuEnabled="True">
      <shell:ApplicationBarIconButton x:Name="rewindAppBarBtn"
       IconUri="/icons/appbar.transport.rew.rest.png" Text="rewind"
       Click="rewindAppBarBtn_Click"/>
      <shell:ApplicationBarIconButton x:Name="stopAppBarBtn"
       IconUri="/icons/appbar.transport.pause.rest.png" Text="pause"
       Click="stopAppBarBtn_Click"/>
      <shell:ApplicationBarIconButton x:Name="playAppBarBtn"
       IconUri="/icons/appbar.transport.play.rest.png" Text="play"
       Click="playAppBarBtn_Click"/>
      <shell:ApplicationBarIconButton x:Name="ffAppBarBtn"
       IconUri="/icons/appbar.transport.ff.rest.png" Text="fastforward"
        Click="ffAppBarBtn_Click"/>
    </shell:ApplicationBar>
  </phone:PhoneApplicationPage.ApplicationBar>
```

Listing 5–9 shows the MainPage.xaml.cs code-behind file where the event handlers control the mediaPlayer MediaElement.

Listing 5–9. MainPage.xaml.cs Code File

```csharp
using Microsoft.Phone.Controls;
using System;
using System.Windows;

namespace VSMVideoPlayer
{
  public partial class MainPage : PhoneApplicationPage
  {
    // Constructor
    public MainPage()
    {
      InitializeComponent();
    }

    private void rewindAppBarBtn_Click(object sender, System.EventArgs e)
    {
      if (mediaPlayer.CanSeek)
      {
        mediaPlayer.Position = mediaPlayer.Position - new TimeSpan(0, 0, 5);
        mediaPlayer.Play();
      }
    }
```

```
private void stopAppBarBtn_Click(object sender, System.EventArgs e)
{
  mediaPlayer.Pause();
}

private void playAppBarBtn_Click(object sender, System.EventArgs e)
{

  mediaPlayer.Play();
}

private void ffAppBarBtn_Click(object sender, System.EventArgs e)
{

  if (mediaPlayer.CanSeek)
  {
    mediaPlayer.Position = mediaPlayer.Position + new TimeSpan(0, 0, 5);
    mediaPlayer.Play();
  }
}

private void mediaPlayer_MediaFailed(object sender,
  System.Windows.ExceptionRoutedEventArgs e)
{
  MessageBox.Show("Media Failed: " + e.ErrorException.Message);
}
}
}
```

The last item to highlight is that the SupportedOrientations attribute on the PhoneApplicationPage element in XAML is changed from Portrait to PortraitOrLandscape. This allows the page to respond to orientation changes via the PhoneApplicationPage.OrientationChanged event.

Now that everything is configured properly, let's configure the project to support a full-screen mode for video playback in Expression Blend. With the States tab opened in Expression Blend, the Add state group button creates a Visual State Group that can contain one or more Visual States. The Turn on transition preview button dynamically shows the changes when different states are selected at design time.

Click the Add state group button and name the Visual State Group "Orientations." Next, create an "Add state" button to create a Visual State for PortraitUp. Create another state named LandscapeRight. The VSM should look like Figure 5–21.

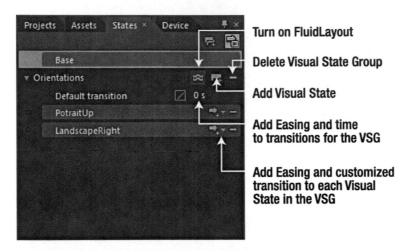

Figure 5–21. VSM with one State Group and two Visual States

Figure 5–21 also defines the UI available in the VSM to create states as well as customize the transitions. EasingFunctions provide for a more realistic animation flow. EasingFunctions are literally functions like quadratic, cubic, bounce, elastic, and so on. In general, EasingFunctions are available in Storyboards. Developers can create custom EasingFunctions as well. Think of an EasingFunction as altering the animation speed from a straight line to a curve, where sharp bends represent an increase in speed so that animations appear to better model real world movement with acceleration and bounce. Figure 5–22 shows the EasingFunction selector.

Figure 5–22. EasingFunction selector for Storyboards

The other buttons shown in Figure 5–22 are transition duration, which represents how long the animation should take in real time, regardless of EasingFunction, and a button to turn on FluidLayout. FluidLayout provides an engine that takes a look at the start state, the end state, and then creates a smooth animation between the states based on the selected EasingFunction. FluidLayout can help make animations created by non-designers look great. Now that we have the Blend functionality covered, let's create our states based on current orientation for the sample project.

Look at Figure 5–21, and you see a state at the top called "Base." When working in Blend previously, you may not have been aware, but this is the visual state that you were working in. "Base" represents the default or initial state. All other state modifications are referenced to the Base state.

■ **Tip** Be sure to select the Base state if you want to make modifications that apply across all states.

In Expression Blend, switch to Landscape in the Device tab and then switch back to the States tab. With the LandscapeRight Visual State selected, select the TitlePanel Grid and set Visibility to Collapsed and set Visibility to Collapsed for the videosListBox as well. For the Grid that contains the mediaPlayer MediaElement set the Height property on the Grid to 480px. The Objects and Timeline window indicates the changes visually in the timeline keyframe editor as shown in Figure 5–23.

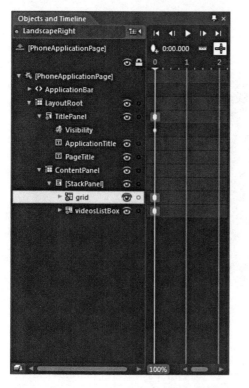

Figure 5–23. Object and Timeline window

When you run the application, it works as expected when flipped to LandscapeRight, as shown in Figure 5–24.

Figure 5–24. Project running in LandScapeRight orientation

If you switch the Emulator to LandscapeLeft, the UI remains as the Portrait layout, as shown in Figure 5–25.

Figure 5–25. Project running in LandScapeLeft orientation

You could build another state manually, but an easier option is to right-click on the LandscapeRight state, select Copy State To, and then select New State. Rename it LandscapeLeft, and that is all that's required to have both Landscape Orientation values display correctly.

The Visual State Manager provides a powerful tool to customize transitions and animations via a state-based mechanism. The next section covers the Microsoft Advertising SDK, which supports advertising revenue for both Silverlight and XNA Framework applications.

The Microsoft Advertising SDK

The Microsoft Advertising SDK provides mobile advertising support for Windows Phone 7. You are not required to use Microsoft's advertising SDK and associated advertising network. If you have an existing advertising network or an in-house creative and sales force, you can continue to use those resources for advertising revenue.

If you are new to mobile applications or simply want a fast and easy mobile advertising solution, the Microsoft Advertising SDK can get you up and running in about 20 minutes and about 50 lines of code. This is explained next.

Getting Started

While Windows Phone 7 is a new platform, Microsoft's advertising solution is not. With the world's first real-time bidding Mobile Ad Exchange with targeted advertising, multiple purchase models and leading resellers including Microsoft's sales force and large-scale adCenter marketplace you can tap into an existing advertising by simply downloading the Microsoft Advertising SDK here:

`http://advertising.microsoft.com/publisher`

or the direct link:

`http://go.microsoft.com/fwlink/?LinkId=198440`

Once you have the SDK installed, register on pubCenter at `https://pubcenter.microsoft.com` link as well to set up your advertising account. You create a software property where ads are displayed, create a mobile ad unit, and set up a targeting category. After registering in pubCenter, you will have an application ID and an Ad unit ID that you can use to request ads from the Microsoft Advertising Servers.

You can also try out the mobile advertising control without signing up to receive test ads, but you will soon want to take advantage of Microsoft's contextual advertising platform with over 20,000 advertisers and resellers to get paid.

Adding the Advertising Control

You can add the Advertising Control to the Visual Studio Toolbox by right-clicking the Toolbox window and selecting the Choose Items... option and clicking Browse... to this directory:

`C:\Program Files (x86)\Microsoft Advertising SDK for Windows Phone 7`

Select the Microsoft.Advertising.Mobile.UI.dll assembly and click OK. You can now drag the control onto your Silverlight UI to add advertising to a page. You can receive test ads using the test Application ID and test Ad Unit ID to get a feel for how the advertising works. There are three types of ads you can receive in your application summarized in Table 5–2.

Table 5–2. Advertising Types and Test Values

Ad Type	AdControl Size (width x height)	Test ApplicationId	TestAdUnitId
Text Ad	480 × 80	test_client	TextAd
XXL Image Banner 6-1	480 × 80	test_client	Image480_80
X-Large Image Banner 6-1	300 × 50	test_client	Image300_50

Even though there is support for a 300 × 50 ad size, it is recommended to always set the size of the AdControl instance to 480px wide by 80px height. For the X-Large Image Banner, the control will automatically size to display the full 300 × 50, centered at the center of the AdControl instance.

The AdControl also has a Location property to receive targeted ads by supplying a Latitude and Longitude value as a Location type. You can use a GeoCoordinateWatcher instance to collect location data as shown in Chapter 3 on input. The AdControl class supports the following events:

- **AdControlError:** Fires when there is a problem receiving or displaying an advertisement.

- **AdEngaged:** Fires when the user clicks the ad and the action dialog appears.

- **AdDisengaged:** Fires when the user clicks any button in the action dialog to dismiss the dialog.

- **NewAd:** Fires when a new advertisement is displayed. Can use to animate the AdControl to catch the user's attention.

AdControl in Silverlight

In this section, the AdControl is leveraged in a sample project named AdvertisingSLSample. For the Silverlight sample project, start with the Windows Phone Data bound Application project template so that you have some data to display. Next simply drag and drop the control at the bottom of the MainPage.xaml page, adjusting its settings so it just fits across the bottom of the screen.

It is recommended to place the AdControl at the top or bottom of a page. For the Panorama or Pivot controls, you can place the AdControl instance inside or over top of the Panorama or Pivot control. If placed inside either control, the ad will only display in a single pane. You can choose to have a unique ad on each pane if desired. To have the AdControl always visible, even when scrolling, place the instance outside of the Panorama control on top.

■ **Tip** It is not recommended to change the parent control of an AdControl instance at run time.

As you can see, the control is simple to configure. Here is the XAML for the configured ad control in the Silverlight AdvertisingSample project:

```
<my:AdControl  Height="80" HorizontalAlignment="Left" Margin="-12,527,0,0"
Name="adControl1" VerticalAlignment="Top" Width="480"
```

```
AdModel="Contextual" ApplicationId="test_client" AdUnitId="Image480_80" />
```

Figure 5–26 shows the control in action, using the test configuration in the previous XAML.

Figure 5–26. Advertising in a Silverlight application

We want to grab the user's attention when a new ad is available. One possible way to do that is to create an animation that indicates something happened, such as to make the control increase in size slightly and then return to its original size via a Storyboard animation.

In Expression Blend, create the AnimateAdControl Storyboard resource by clicking the New button in the Objects and Timeline window. Add a keyframe at zero time and then slide the yellow timeline over to 100 milliseconds. Click on the Transform section in the Properties window for the AdControl and switch to the Scale transform tab. Change X and Y to 1.1 from 1.Slide the yellow timeline bar to 200 miliseconds, right-click the first keyframe at zero seconds and then right-click and select paste.

Switch back to Visual Studio and create an event handler for the NewAd event on the adControl1 instance and then add this code:

```
AnimateAdControl.Begin();
```

For a multi-page application, it is recommended to unload the control when a page is unloaded to minimize resource consumption. This can be done in the PhoneApplicationPage.Unloaded event handler. Simply set the AdControl instance to null.

Although this chapter is focused on Silverlight UX, the next subsection covers how to add advertising support to a Windows Phone 7 XNA Framework-based game.

AdControl in the XNA Framework

Adding support for the AdControl in a Windows Phone 7 XNA Framework application is just as easy. Start by adding a reference to the Microsoft.Advertising.Mobile.Xna.dll assembly located in the `C:\Program Files (x86)\Microsoft Advertising SDK for Windows Phone 7\` directory in the Chapter 5 Solution AdvertisingXNASample project.

Next add a using `Microsoft.Advertising.Mobile.Xna;` statement to game1.cs. Next add an `AdManager` and `Ad` object are added as private members of the Game1 class:

```
AdManager adManager;
Ad bannerAd;
```

In the constructor for the Game1 class, instantiate the `adManager` and add it as a component to the `Game.Components` collection:

```
adManager = new AdManager(this, "test_client");
adManager.TestMode = true;
Components.Add(adManager);
```

Notice that the same application Id, `test_client`, is used as before for the testing functionality. Finally, we want to load an ad, which is done in the `LoadContent()` method where all game assets are generally loaded for most games.

```
bannerAd = adManager.CreateAd("Image300_50",
    new Rectangle(10, 390, GraphicsDevice.Viewport.Bounds.Width, 120),
    RotationMode.Manual, false);
```

That is all that is required to ad advertising to a Windows Phone 7 XNA Framework game. Figure 5–27 shows the results.

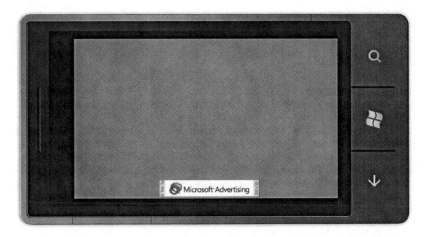

Figure 5–27. Test advertising in an XNA application

As you can see from this section, adding support for Advertising revenue to your applications is very straight-forward. For a free or trial application, advertising revenue is a great way to get paid for your hard work.

Conclusion

This chapter began with an overview of the Model-View-ViewModel pattern, which is the architecture to use in XAML based applications. We next moved on to covering one of the third-party MVVM frameworks that improve upon the built in support for MVVM when building property architected applications.

This was followed by a discussion of the Silverlight for Windows Phone toolkit, including coverage on all of the major controls including detailed coverage on the LongListSelector control as well as on page transitions. We then explained how to use the Visual State Manager in your applications to greatly simplify UI development.

The coverage on advertising concludes Chapter 5 on advanced user interface development. The next chapter covers advanced programming model topics that allow you to more deeply integrate with Windows Phone 7, leverage media, as well as other topics.

CHAPTER 6

■■■

Windows Phone 7 Advanced Programming Model

In this chapter, we cover additional topics related to the programming model. This is the final chapter on Silverlight for Windows Phone 7 development, so expect to see a variety of topics, including advanced data binding, encryption services, photo manipulation, video playback, and how to achieve deeper integration with Windows Phone for certain scenarios.

Advanced Data Binding

In this section, I cover how to access Syndicated Services like RSS feeds from Windows Phone 7, as well as advanced Model-View-ViewModel (MVVM) techniques to incorporate page navigation, showing progress, and lazy loading images. The last subsection covers the IValueConverter interface, which allows you to data bind any data type to just about any other data.

A sample project based on the MVVM Light project template named AdvancedDataBinding is added to the Chapter 6 solution. MVVM is leveraged for this example to demonstrate how to handle slightly additional complexity of separating concerns between the View and the ViewModel when dealing with more complex scenarios.

By default, the MainPage.xaml binds to the MainViewModel in the ViewModel folder. MainPage.xaml presents a menu of four items that navigate to individual pages corresponding to the sections that follow:

- Syndicated Services (/View/SyndicatedServices.xaml)

- Showing Progress (/View/ShowingProgress.xaml)

- Lazy Load Images (/View/LazyLoadImages.xaml)

- Data Bind to Anything (/View/DatabindToAnything.xaml)

MainPage.xaml consists of a ListBox databound to a collection of items that represent the above pages. Here is the XAML:

```
<ListBox x:Name="listBox1" Margin="24,0,0,0"
  ItemsSource="{Binding Pages}"
  ItemTemplate="{StaticResource PageItemTemplate}" />
```

In MainViewModel.cs, the ApplicationTitle and PageName properties are updated for the current project. A Pages property is added to MainViewModel class that is of type List<PageItemViewModel>:

```
public const string PagesPropertyName = "Pages";
private List<PageItemViewModel> _pages = null;
public List<PageItemViewModel> Pages
{
  get
  {
    return _pages;
  }

  protected set
  {
    if (_pages == value)
    {
      return;
    }

    var oldValue = _pages;
    _pages = value;

    // Update bindings, no broadcast
    RaisePropertyChanged(PagesPropertyName);
  }
}
```

The MainViewModel class has a method named LoadPageInfo(), which instantiates the Pages collection:

```
private void LoadPagesInfo()
{
  Pages = new List<PageItemViewModel>()
  {
    new PageItemViewModel(){PageTitle="syndicated services",
      PageUri=new Uri("/View/SyndicatedServices.xaml",UriKind.Relative)},
    new PageItemViewModel(){PageTitle="showing progress",
      PageUri=new Uri("/View/ShowingProgress.xaml",UriKind.Relative)},
    new PageItemViewModel(){PageTitle="lazy load images",
      PageUri=new Uri("/View/LazyLoadImages.xaml",UriKind.Relative)},
    new PageItemViewModel(){PageTitle="data binding to anything",
      PageUri=new Uri("/View/DatabindToAnything.xaml",UriKind.Relative)}
  };
}
```

Normally, the PageItem class would be a simple Model class; however, I made it a ViewModel class because of necessary support to allow data binding and navigation from a ListBox displaying the Pages data. When an item is selected in the ListBox shown in Figure 6–1, the application should navigate to the associated page. We don't want to write code to do this in the MainPage.xaml.cs code-behind file. Instead we take advantage of messaging and commanding support provided by the MVVM Light toolkit.

Figure 6–1. *AdvancedDataBinding MainPage.xaml UI*

The selected item in the ListBox on MainPage.xaml should perform navigation to the associated page pointed to by the selected item. This means that the Commanding support is required at the `PageItem` / `ItemTemplate` level, not at the `ListBox` level. To support this functionality, a ViewModel class named `PageItemViewModel` is added that supports GalaSoft Light Messaging and Commanding (see Chapter 5 for details on GalaSoft MVVM). Listing 6–1 shows the `PageItemViewModel`.

Listing 6–1. *PageItemViewModel Class File*

```
using System;
using GalaSoft.MvvmLight.Command;
using GalaSoft.MvvmLight.Messaging;
using GalaSoft.MvvmLight;
namespace AdvancedDataBinding.ViewModel
{
  public class PageItemViewModel : ViewModelBase
  {
    public PageItemViewModel()
    {
      //Wire up the NavigateToPageCommand RelayCommand to send the message
      //for the Uri of the page to navigate to.
      NavigateToPageCommand = new RelayCommand<Uri>(
```

```
      param => SendNavigationRequestMessage(param));
}

#region PageItem properties
public const string PageTitlePropertyName = "PageTitle";
private string _pageTitle = null;
public string PageTitle
{
  get
  {
    return _pageTitle;
  }
  set
  {
    if (_pageTitle == value)
    {
      return;
    }

    var oldValue = _pageTitle;
    _pageTitle = value;
    RaisePropertyChanged(PageTitlePropertyName);
  }
}


public const string PageUriPropertyName = "PageUri";
private Uri _pageUri = null;
public Uri PageUri
{
  get
  {
    return _pageUri;
  }
  set
  {
    if (_pageUri == value)
    {
      return;
    }

    var oldValue = _pageUri;
    _pageUri = value;

    // Update bindings, no broadcast
    RaisePropertyChanged(PageUriPropertyName);
  }
}
#endregion

#region Commanding and Messaging
public RelayCommand<Uri> NavigateToPageCommand
{
  get;
```

```
    private set;
  }

  protected void SendNavigationRequestMessage(Uri uri)
  {
    Messenger.Default.Send<Uri>(uri, "PageNavRequest");
  }
  #endregion
}
}
```

The PageItemViewModel class is broken up into two sections, one for the properties and the other for the Commanding and Messaging support. The PageItemViewModel class has two properties, PageTitle and PageUri. The PageUri points to the appropriate XAML file to navigate to for the PageTitle property value.

The Commanding and Messaging support is pretty simple code. The NavigateToPageCommand is what the MainPage.xaml View DataBinds to when the ListBoxItem is clicked via the MVVM Light EventToCommand Behavior. The NavigateToPageCommand RelayCommand<T> is connected to the MVVM Light Messaging infrastructure via this code in the PageItemViewModel constructor:

```
NavigateToPageCommand = new RelayCommand<Uri>(
  param => SendNavigationRequestMessage(param));
```

The NavigateToPageCommand takes an Uri and passes it to the SendNavigationRequestMessage. This is a bit of indirection, as the Uri property comes from the ListBox's template and then is sent back to the View via the MVVM Light Messaging infrastructure but it does promote decoupling of the UI from the ViewModel.

The MainPage.xaml View receives the message via this line of code added to the PhoneApplicationPage constructor and uses an inline Lambda statement to call the NavigationService:

```
Messenger.Default.Register<Uri>(
        this, "PageNavRequest",
        (uri) => NavigationService.Navigate(uri));
```

I mentioned earlier that the DataTemplate data binds to the NavigateToPageCommand. Here is the ItemTemplate="{StaticResource PageItemTemplate}" for the MainPage.ListBox control:

```xml
<DataTemplate x:Key="PageItemTemplate">
  <Grid Margin="0,15">
    <TextBlock Margin="0,0,1,0" TextWrapping="Wrap" Text="{Binding PageTitle}"
      d:LayoutOverrides="Width, Height" Style="{StaticResource PhoneTextLargeStyle}">
      <Custom:Interaction.Triggers>
        <Custom:EventTrigger EventName="MouseLeftButtonDown">
        <GalaSoft_MvvmLight_Command:EventToCommand Command="{Binding NavigateToPageCommand,
Mode=OneWay}" CommandParameter="{Binding PageUri}"/>
        </Custom:EventTrigger>
      </Custom:Interaction.Triggers>
    </TextBlock>
  </Grid>
</DataTemplate>
```

The EventToCommand behavior is dragged from the Assets | Behaviors section and is dropped on the TextBlock. Figure 6–2 shows the Properties window for the EventToCommand behavior.

Figure 6–2. *EventToCommand properties in Expression Blend*

In Figure 6–2, the Command value is databound to the NavigateToPageCommand property on the PageItemViewModel class. The CommandParameter is databound to PageUri property of the selected item from the MainViewModel Pages collection of type PageItemViewModel.

This was a detailed walkthrough of relatively simple functionality, but it demonstrates the powerful capabilities of MVVM Light's Commanding and Messaging infrastructure to support decoupling UI from the ViewModel via Silverlight's data binding framework.

The next section covers how to access syndicated services like RSS feeds from Windows Phone 7.

Syndicated Services

Silverlight 3 and later includes excellent support for easily consuming syndicated feeds like RSS, ATOM, and formatted data feeds. Unfortunately, the System.ServiceModel.Syndication.dll is not available in the Silverlight for Windows Phone 7 SDK. You can simply add a reference to the Silverlight 3 version of the assembly, but it is just as easy to use LINQ to XML to parse syndication feeds.

For the AdvancedDataBinding project, a page named SyndicatedServices.xaml is added to the View folder and a ViewModel named SyndicatedServicesViewModel is added to the ViewModel folder. The SyndicatedServicesViewModel is added to the ViewModelLocator class in the ViewModel folder.

Clicking the syndicated services label shown in Figure 6–3 navigates to the page. The page is configured with a ListBox named feedListBox and added to the ContentPanel in SyndicatedServices.xaml. The Application Bar is enabled to have a single button named LoadFeedAppBarBtn with a title of "load feed."

In the code, the Click event for the LoadFeedAppBarBtn Application Bar Button is wired up to fire an event that makes an HttpWebRequest to the Educational Resources feed from AppHub. Here is the code:

```
HttpWebRequest httpWebRequest;
private void LoadFeedAppBarBtn_Click(object sender, EventArgs c)
{
```

```
httpWebRequest = HttpWebRequest.CreateHttp(
  "http://public.create.msdn.com/Feeds/CcoFeeds.svc/CmsFeed?group=Education Catalog List");
httpWebRequest.BeginGetResponse(new AsyncCallback(ReceiveFeedData), null);
}
```

The ReceiveFeedData method has code to parse the response, load the data into an XDocument, and parse the feed into a collection of FeedItem objects that is databound to the feedListBox.ItemsSource property. Listing 6–2 has the FeedItem class.

Listing 6–2. FeedItem Class File

```
using System;

namespace AdvancedDataBinding
{
  public class FeedItem
  {
    public string Title { get; set; }

    public string Description { get; set; }

    public Uri Link { get; set; }
  }
}
```

Here is the code for the ReceiveFeedData method:

```
void ReceiveFeedData(IAsyncResult result)
{
  HttpWebResponse response = httpWebRequest.EndGetResponse(result) as HttpWebResponse;
  using (StreamReader reader = new StreamReader(response.GetResponseStream()))
  {
    XDocument doc = XDocument.Parse(reader.ReadToEnd());
    var items = from results in doc.Descendants("item")
                select new FeedItem
                {
                  Title = results.Element("title").Value.ToString(),
                  Link = new Uri(results.Element("link").Value.ToString(), UriKind.Absolute),
                  Description = results.Element("description").Value.ToString()
                };
    LayoutRoot.Dispatcher.BeginInvoke(() =>
    {
      feedListBox.ItemsSource = items;
    });
  }
}
```

As demonstrated in Chapter 4, the response is read into a StreamReader object and the feedListBox.Dispatcher is used to marshal the data over to the UI thread for assignment to the ItemsSource property. A simple DataTemplate is configured on feedListBox.ItemTemplate that binds to FeedItem object properties:

```
<ListBox.ItemTemplate>
  <DataTemplate>
    <StackPanel Margin="0,0,0,30">
```

```
    <TextBlock Text="{Binding Title}"  Margin="0,0,12,0" FontSize="24" FontFamily="Segoe WP
Semibold" />
    <TextBlock Text="{Binding Description}" />
    <HyperlinkButton  NavigateUri="{Binding Link}" FontFamily="Segoe WP SemiLight"
      TargetName="_blank"          FontSize="18.667" FontStyle="Italic"
      Content="More..." HorizontalAlignment="Left"/>
  </StackPanel>
 </DataTemplate>
</ListBox.ItemTemplate>
```

Figure 6–3 shows the UI when the Application Bar button is clicked.

Figure 6–3. *AppHub RSS feed parsed and loaded*

If you click More... it loads the URL for the content into the Web Browser. Clicking the back button takes you back to the page. Notice in Figure 6–3 that the Description is formatted as HTML. I can change the DataTemplate to have a WebBrowser control instead of a TextBlock but when I do this, the HTML does not render.

The WebBrowser control supports navigating to an HTML fragment using the NavigateToString Method, but it does not have a simple HTML property that we can data bind, too. We would rather not write a lot of code to data bind to the HTML fragment. When working in Silverlight, whenever a control is missing a property, you can always add it using XAML Attached properties. The goal is to have a simple

HTML property of type text for the HTML fragment from the feed that gets loaded via the
NavigateToString method. Listing 6–3 shows the attached property class.

Listing 6–3. WebBrowserHTMLProp Code File

```
public static class WebBrowserHTMLProp
{
  public static readonly DependencyProperty HtmlProperty =
    DependencyProperty.RegisterAttached(
      "Html", typeof(string), typeof(WebBrowserHTMLProp),
      new PropertyMetadata(OnHtmlPropChanged));

  public static string GetHtml(DependencyObject dependencyObject)
  {
    return (string)dependencyObject.GetValue(HtmlProperty);
  }

  public static void SetHtml(DependencyObject dependencyObject, string value)
  {
    dependencyObject.SetValue(HtmlProperty, value);
  }

  private static void OnHtmlPropChanged(DependencyObject dependencyObject,
    DependencyPropertyChangedEventArgs e)
  {
    var webBrowser = dependencyObject as WebBrowser;

    if (webBrowser == null)
      return;

    var html = e.NewValue.ToString();
    webBrowser.NavigateToString(html);
  }
}
```

It is mostly boilerplate code with the important code in the OnHtmlPropChanged method where the
HTML is loaded into the WebBrowser via NavigateToString. Unfortunately, because this code is part of the
DataTemplate, an error is thrown stating that "You cannot call WebBrowser methods until it is in the visual
tree." Because the DataTemplate is composited and then added to the Visual Tree, the Attached Property
does not help us here but it can assist in situations where the WebBrowser control is embedded into the
static XAML. Instead a TextBlock is placed within the DataTemplate. Figure 6–3 shows the output.
Clicking "More..." loads the link into IE Mobile.

An alternative approach for this feed would be to just display the Title in the ListBox and then
navigate to another page that displays the Description details in a WebBrowser control that is part of the
static XAML visual tree of the page.

In this section I covered how to load an RSS feed using LINQ to XML. We will explore adding
additional functionality for displaying feed data, showing progress, and lazy loading images in the
following sections.

Showing Progress

In this section, I demonstrate how to have your ViewModel drive UI, such as when to show progress bars
or not, via data binding. It is a quick example based on the previous example that downloads the

AppHub feed but the concept is very important to help you understand how to put more code into your ViewModels and less code in your View.

The SyndicatedServicesViewModel.cs code file is copied and renamed ShowProgressViewModel as well as the constructor. The new ShowProgressViewModel property is added to the ViewModelLocator just as before, and a new View named ShowingProgress.xaml is created and data bound to the ShowProgressViewModel. Run the project and it should work just as the previous sample.

A new Boolean property named ShowProgressBar is added to the ShowProgressViewModel class. The ShowProgressBar property is set to true just before the HttpWebRequest.CreateHttp method call in the ShowProgressViewModel .DownloadAppHubFeed method. The property must be modified on the UI thread so that data binding propagates to the UI and an error doesn't happen from cross-thread access:

```
public void DownloadAppHubFeed()
{
  Deployment.Current.Dispatcher.BeginInvoke(() =>
  {
    ShowProgressBar = true;
  });
  …
```

At the end of the ShowProgressViewModel.ReceiveFeedData method set ShowProgressBar to false. This completes the changes in the ViewModel. The progress bar should be enabled right before making the web call and then disabled once the new data is data binded to the UI. Again the property must be modified on the UI thread:

```
Deployment.Current.Dispatcher.BeginInvoke(() =>
{
  FeedItems = items.ToList<FeedItem>();
  //Artificial delay to test progress bar
  System.Threading.Thread.Sleep(3000);
  ShowProgressBar = false;
});
```

In the ShowProgress.xaml page, add a progress bar that applies to the width of the screen in the middle of the page. The progress bar should look like the native WP7 progress bar, otherwise known as "the flying dots." Luckily the Silverlight for Windows Phone Toolkit has been updated to include two new controls, TiltEffect and PerformanceProgressBar. Previously you had to create a customized version of the built-in progress bar in order to have good UI thread performance.

Once the latest Silverlight toolkit for WP7 is installed, add PerformanceProgressBar to the Toolbox window in Visual Studio and drag the control on to the ShowingProgress.xaml View. Switch over to Expression Blend and set the HorizontalAlignment to stretch and reset Margin to just a top Margin of 300. Next set the IndeterminateProperty to True and you can see the flying dots at design-time in Expression Blend. We only want to see the flying dots when loading data so let's data bind the LoadingDataPerfProgressBar's Indeterminate property to the ShowProgressViewModel.ShowProgressBar property. Here is the XAML for the PerformanceProgressBar from ShowingProgress.xaml:

```
<toolkit:PerformanceProgressBar x:Name="LoadingDataPerfProgressBar" Margin="0,300,0,0"
  VerticalAlignment="Top"  IsIndeterminate="{Binding ShowProgressBar}" />
```

By default, the data is obtained by ShowProgressViewModel when the application loads and the ShowProgressViewModel is created. We modify the constructor to not automatically call the DownloadAppHubFeed() method. The ShowingProgressView is modified to have an Application Bar button that manually downloads the feed. Clicking the Application Bar button will enable the progress bar, download the feed, and then disable the progress bar by calling the DownloadAppHubFeed() method. Figure 6–4 shows the flying dots in the emulator.

Figure 6–4. PerformanceProgressBar in action

This example demonstrates the power of Silverlight and its data binding infrastructure to allow the ViewModel non-visual class to drive the UI based on the applications current state. This technique is critical to effective MVVM development and can be extended to other data-driven UI to indicate state and display additional UI when needed.

Lazy Load Images

When developing for a mobile device with constrained networking and hardware capabilities relative to a desktop computer, you sometimes have to take additional steps beyond the "default" programming model. As an example, loading a ListBox with data and images from a remote server can peg the UI thread resulting in a poor user experience for scrolling and animations. Anytime work can be taken off of the UI thread is a win for performance.

A Silverlight for Windows Phone team member David Anson blogged here about a way to offload image loading to a background thread that results in much better UI performance:

```
http://blogs.msdn.com/b/delay/archive/2010/09/02/keep-a-low-profile-lowprofileimageloader-
helps-the-windows-phone-7-ui-thread-stay-responsive-by-loading-images-in-the-background.aspx
```

In the blog post, Dave introduces the LowProfileImageLoader class to address the very specific issue of loading lots of images from the web simultaneously. The LowProfileImageLoader slows the loading of images but the UI remains responsive as images are loaded because the UI thread is not slammed waiting for images to load and then data bind.

To test out the LowProfileImageLoader, let's work with the Netflix API. I picked this API because it has an interesting set of images (movie art) in a well-documented API. The API is available at developer.netflix.com.

▨ **Note** You must register an account to use the Netflix APIs at

`http://developer.netflix.com/member/register`.

We will use the OData Client Library for Windows Phone 7 that we covered in Chapter 4 to access the Netflix API. As before we add a reference to System.Data.Services.Client.dll. We use the DataSvcUtil.exe to generate a proxy class:

```
DataSvcUti.exe /uri:http://odata.netflix.com/Catalog/ /out:Netfli xOdataAPI.cs
/Version:2.0 /DataServiceCollection
```

Adding the DataServiceCollection option has the tool implement the INotifyPropertyChanged interface, which is important for change notification purposes. The OData access is wired into the LazyLoadViewModel.cs class, which is a copy of the ShowProgressViewModel:

```
public void DownloadNetflixTopTitles()
{
  Deployment.Current.Dispatcher.BeginInvoke(() =>
  {
    ShowProgressBar = true;
  });
  topMovieTitles = new DataServiceCollection<Title>(ODataContext);
  topMovieTitles.LoadCompleted +=
    new EventHandler<LoadCompletedEventArgs>(topMovieTitles_LoadCompleted);
  topMovieTitles.LoadAsync(new Uri("/Titles()",UriKind.Relative));

}

void topMovieTitles_LoadCompleted(object sender, LoadCompletedEventArgs e)
{
  Deployment.Current.Dispatcher.BeginInvoke(() =>
  {
    ShowProgressBar = false;
    TopMovieTitles = topMovieTitles;
  });
}
```

The LazyLoad.xaml View page is modified to include a ListBox with a simple DataTemplate that shows the movie title and image. Figure 6–5 shows the UI.

Figure 6–5. Netflix API top titles via OData

Not every movie title has box art, but many do. Let's now modify this application to use the LowProfileImageLoader class to asynchronously display the images. Download the source code at the blog post link above and grab the PhonePerformance.dll. Add a reference to it in the AdvancedDatabinding project and then add a namespace reference to LazyLoadImage.xaml:

```
xmlns:delay="clr-namespace:Delay;assembly=PhonePerformance"
```

Next update the NetflixTopTitleDataTemplate so that the image is not loaded from the built-in Source property but instead is loaded using this XAML:

```
<Image delay:LowProfileImageLoader.UriSource="{Binding BoxArt.SmallUrl}"
HorizontalAlignment="Left" Stretch="UniformToFill" Width="150"/>
```

The performance difference is much more obvious on a physical device over 3G, but as you can see it is pretty trivial to add support for the LowProfileImageLoader to see if it can help with any performance issues related to image loading in your applications.

Data Bind to Anything

There are situations where you need to data bind to a value and the value type or format does not quite line up with what you need. The IValueConverter interface allows your application to data bind to just about anything including data that does not match the type expected for a particular control.

As an example, let's say you have a field that takes values of either Yes or No. You could use a ListPicker but a CheckBox makes more sense since it is just two values. You can implement IValueConverter to convert true to a Yes value and No value to false (and vice versa) while still using standard data binding mechanisms.

In this section, we create a custom IValueConverter named HtmlToImageUriConverter. This very simple converter parses the AppHub Feed html, previously displayed as raw html text, into a URL that points to an image related to the content. The URL is extracted from the HTML. Listing 6–4 shows the code for the converter.

Listing 6–4. WebBrowserHTMLProp Code File

```
using System;
using System.Windows.Data;

namespace AdvancedDataBinding.Converters
{
  public class HtmlToImageUriConverter : IValueConverter
  {
    public object Convert(object value, Type targetType,
      object parameter, System.Globalization.CultureInfo culture)
    {
      string html = (string)value;
      string imageUrl = "";
      if (null != html)
      {
        string[] strings = html.Split('"');
        if (strings.Length > 3)
          imageUrl = strings[3].Trim();
      }
      return imageUrl;
    }

    public object ConvertBack(object value, Type targetType,
      object parameter, System.Globalization.CultureInfo culture)
    {
      throw new NotImplementedException();
    }
  }
}
```

The converter is somewhat brittle in that it depends on the URL value to be the fourth string when split, but one wouldn't expect the feed format to change very often, and it makes for an interesting sample. The converter is made available to the DatabindToAnything.xaml View via an xml namespace import:

```
xmlns:converters="clr-namespace:AdvancedDataBinding.Converters"
```

The converter is added as a resource in this XAML:

```
<phone:PhoneApplicationPage.Resources>
  <converters:HtmlToImageUriConverter x:Key="HtmlToImageConverter"/>
</phone:PhoneApplicationPage.Resources>
```

Applying the converter is a simple modification in XAML or visually in Expression Blend. Here is the updated ListBox DataTemplate:

```
<DataTemplate>
  <StackPanel Margin="0,0,0,30">
    <TextBlock Text="{Binding Title}" Margin="0,0,12,0" Style="{StaticResource
PhoneTextLargeStyle}" />
    <Image delay:LowProfileImageLoader.UriSource=
       "{Binding Description, Converter={StaticResource HtmlToImageConverter}}"
       Margin="0,6,0,4" Width="100" HorizontalAlignment="Left" />
    <HyperlinkButton NavigateUri="{Binding Link}" FontFamily="Segoe WP SemiLight"
TargetName="_blank"
       FontSize="18.667" FontStyle="Italic" Content="More..." HorizontalAlignment="Left"
Margin="-12,0,0,0"/>
  </StackPanel>
</DataTemplate>
```

The Binding.Converter parameter is configured to the added StaticResource to apply the converter for the Image object. Note that this sample also implements the LowProfileImageLoader for better performance as well as the PerformanceProgressBar to give better visual status to the user. Figure 6–6 shows the resulting output with a nice image instead of the raw HTML that was displayed previously.

Figure 6–6. AppHub feed with articles and corresponding images

In this section, data binding concepts are extended to more real world scenarios while also incorporating MVVM concepts. The next section provides a quick tour of available encryption services in Windows Phone 7.

Encryption Services

A mobile device no matter what operating system or platform is inherently insecure. A mobile device is not locked safely in a server room within a secure data center like a web server. A mobile device is easily misplaced or stolen. For just about any computing platform, loss of physical control is loss of security. Therefore, it is important to minimize storing sensitive data on a mobile device.

However, there are scenarios in which it is convenient to store sensitive data on a device. As an example, a user would never use a video player application that requires the user to memorize and enter a long key to unlock DRM'd content. It is a risk management challenge that weighs the benefits and inconvenience provided by any given security solution. This section in the MSDN documentation provides a detailed overview of balancing security with convenience:

`http://msdn.microsoft.com/en-us/library/ff402533(v=VS.92).aspx`

In the next few sections, I provide an overview of the capabilities available in the Windows Phone 7 platform.

Secure Sockets Layer

Many mobile applications transfer data to and from the server-side of a mobile application solution. In cases where sensitive data must be transported always use Secure Sockets Layer (SSL) to protect data in transit. This link lists SSL root certificates that ship on Windows Phone 7:

`http://msdn.microsoft.com/en-us/library/gg521150(v=VS.92).aspx`

Once sensitive data is on the device, use available encryption services on the platform to secure the data. Windows Phone 7 supports the following cryptographic algorithms:

- AES
- HMACSHA1
- HMACSHA256
- Rfc2898DeriveBytes
- SHA1
- SHA256

The next covers how to use these algorithms to securely store data on Windows Phone 7.

Securely Encrypting Data

We add a project named EncryptingData to the Chapter 6 solution based on the GalaSoft MVVM project template. The UI takes some data to encrypt, a password and salt to perform the encryption, and then a couple of TextBlocks to show the encrypted data as well as results from decrypting.

The Application Bar is enabled with four buttons:

- Encrypt Data
- Decrypt Data
- Save to Isolated Storage
- Load from Isolated Storage

All the UI data fields and event methods have corresponding properties on the MainViewModel class. The encryption operations are actually performed on MainViewModel properties with data binding bringing the results to the UI. Figure 6–7 shows the UI layout.

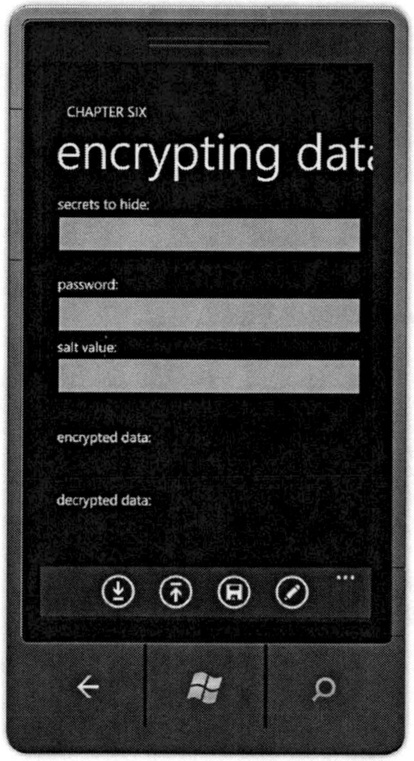

Figure 6–7. EncryptData project UI

The following using statements are added to the MainViewModel class to provide the necessary access for stream-based processing and encryption:

```
using System.IO;
using System.IO.IsolatedStorage;
using System.Security.Cryptography;
using System.Text;
```

In addition to the ViewModel data fields backing the UI MainPage.xaml View, four additional methods are added to MainViewModel:

- EncryptData

- DecryptData

- SaveEncryptedDataToIsolatedStorage

- LoadEncryptedDataFromIsolatedStorage

Each method performs the task described by the method name. These four methods are accessed via the Application Bar buttons in the View as shown in Listing 6–5.

Listing 6–5. MainPage.Xaml.cs Code File

```
using System.Windows;
using System.Windows.Controls;
using EncryptingData.ViewModel;
using Microsoft.Phone.Controls;

namespace EncryptingData
{
  public partial class MainPage : PhoneApplicationPage
  {
    MainViewModel vm;
    // Constructor
    public MainPage()
    {
      InitializeComponent();
      vm = this.DataContext as MainViewModel;
    }

    private void EncryptAppBarBtn_Click(object sender, System.EventArgs e)
    {
      vm.EncryptData();
    }

    private void DecryptAppBarBtn_Click(object sender, System.EventArgs e)
    {
      vm.DecryptData();
    }

    private void SaveIsoAppBarBtn_Click(object sender, System.EventArgs e)
    {
      vm.SaveEncryptedDataToIsolatedStorage();
    }

    private void LoadIsoAppBarBtn_Click(object sender, System.EventArgs e)
    {
      vm.LoadEncryptedDataFromIsolatedStorage();
    }

    private void PasswordBox_LostFocus(object sender,
      System.Windows.RoutedEventArgs e)
    {
      if (((PasswordBox)sender).Password.Length < 8)
        MessageBox.Show("Salt Value must be at least eight characters.",
```

```
                    "Minimum Length Error",MessageBoxButton.OK);
        }
    }
}
```

The four encryption related methods in MainViewModel code are shown in Listing 6–6.

Listing 6–6. *Methods from MainViewModel.cs Code File*

```csharp
public void EncryptData()
{
  using (AesManaged aes = new AesManaged())
  {
    Rfc2898DeriveBytes rfc2898 = new Rfc2898DeriveBytes(Password,
      Encoding.UTF8.GetBytes(SaltValue), 10000);
    aes.Key = rfc2898.GetBytes(32);
    aes.IV = rfc2898.GetBytes(16);
    using (MemoryStream memoryStream = new MemoryStream())
    {
      using (CryptoStream cryptoStream = new CryptoStream(memoryStream,
        aes.CreateEncryptor(), CryptoStreamMode.Write))
      {
        //Encrypt Data with created CryptoStream
        byte[] secret = Encoding.UTF8.GetBytes(DataToEncrypt);
        cryptoStream.Write(secret, 0, secret.Length);
        cryptoStream.FlushFinalBlock();
        aes.Clear();
        //Set values on UI thread
        Deployment.Current.Dispatcher.BeginInvoke(() =>
        {
          EncryptedData = Convert.ToBase64String(memoryStream.ToArray());
        });
      }
    }
  }
}

public void DecryptData()
{
  MemoryStream memoryStream = null;

  using (AesManaged aes = new AesManaged())
  {
    //Generate Key and IV values for decryption
    Rfc2898DeriveBytes rfc2898 = new Rfc2898DeriveBytes(Password,
Encoding.UTF8.GetBytes(SaltValue), 10000);
    aes.Key = rfc2898.GetBytes(32);
    aes.IV = rfc2898.GetBytes(16);

    using (memoryStream = new MemoryStream())
    {
      using (CryptoStream cryptoStream =
        new CryptoStream(memoryStream, aes.CreateDecryptor(),
                         CryptoStreamMode.Write))
```

```
            {
              //Decrypt Data
              byte[] secret = Convert.FromBase64String(EncryptedData);
              cryptoStream.Write(secret, 0, secret.Length);
              cryptoStream.FlushFinalBlock();
              byte[] decryptBytes = memoryStream.ToArray();
              aes.Clear();
              //Update values on UI thread
              Deployment.Current.Dispatcher.BeginInvoke(() =>
              {
                DecryptedData = Encoding.UTF8.GetString(decryptBytes, 0, decryptBytes.Length);
              });
            }
          }
        }
      }

      public void SaveEncryptedDataToIsolatedStorage()
      {
        //Save secret to Application Settings
        if (EncryptedData != "")
        {
          if (IsolatedStorageSettings.ApplicationSettings.Contains(StorageKeyName))
          {
            IsolatedStorageSettings.ApplicationSettings[StorageKeyName] =
              EncryptedData;
          }
          else
          {
            IsolatedStorageSettings.ApplicationSettings.Add(
              StorageKeyName, EncryptedData);
          }
        }
      }

      public void LoadEncryptedDataFromIsolatedStorage()
      {
        //Retrieve secret from Application Settings
        if (IsolatedStorageSettings.ApplicationSettings.Contains(StorageKeyName))
        {
          Deployment.Current.Dispatcher.BeginInvoke(() =>
          {
            EncryptedData =
              IsolatedStorageSettings.ApplicationSettings[StorageKeyName].ToString();
          });
        }
        else
        {
          Deployment.Current.Dispatcher.BeginInvoke(() =>
          {
            EncryptedData = "";
          });
        }
      }
```

The code generates a Key for AES based on the Password and Salt values provided by the user. The Rfc2898DeriveBytes class is used to generate the HMACSHA1 random number (iteration count of 1,000) for the AES Key and IV values. What's handy with implementing encryption via the ViewModel is that it is easily reusable. The MainViewModel class has zero dependencies on UI.

One other item to note is that this section demonstrates the only truly secure means to encrypt data, because it requires a password by the user. This is because the initial release of the Windows Phone Developer Tools does not include access to a secure key store. This is a frequently requested feature by developers so I would bet that it is one of the first features to be added to the next release of the tools.

Working with Images on Windows Phone 7

Windows Phone 7 supports BMP, TIF, GIF, JPEG, and PNG formats in general. However, from a development perspective JPG and PNG are supported for viewing in the Silverlight Image control. The JPG and PNG formats are recommended for displaying images within an application. JPG is preferred when the image will remain opaque. The PNG format supports transparency and is preferred for this scenario.

Images Classes

The Image control is the Silverlight class for displaying images in applications. A related Silverlight object that us very useful is the ImageBrush object. As an example, setting the background on a Panorama object is via an ImageBrush like this:

```
<controls:Panorama.Background>
  <ImageBrush  ImageSource="PanoramaBackground.png" Opacity="0.785" />
</controls:Panorama.Background>
```

Note that for the Opacity value to have an effect with an ImageBrush object, the image pointed to via the ImageSource property must be a .PNG file.

The BitmapImage is the utility class that provides the class for the Image.Source property. The BitmapImage supports the JPEG and PNG format. The BitmapImage has two constructors, one that takes a URI and the other that takes a Stream. You can set Image.Source via a BitmapImage without having to save the file to disk, which is better for performance.

The WriteableBitmap class is a versatile class that provides a BitmapSource that can be written to and updated. The WriteableBitmap class has properties to retrieve DPI, Format, Metadata, Palette, and Pixel size. The WriteableBitmap class provides methods to CopyPixels and to WritePixels into the WriteableBitmap. It is possible to generate an image within your application using the WriteableBitmap's constructor that takes a UIElement:

```
WriteableBitmap bmp =
new WriteableBitmap(element, transform)
```

The WriteableBitmap class allows you to generate images on the client when needed. One example would be if you need to add branding to an image or somehow modify it before rendering, such as when creating a music+video hub application, covered later in this chapter.

This is a short section highlighting key classes, properties, and capabilities when working with images. These classes are leveraged in the next couple of sections including the next section that demonstrates how to work with the media library on Windows Phone 7.

The Windows Phone 7 Media Library

The MediaLibrary class provides access to the media available on the device as part of the music+video hub and corresponding Zune service. So if a user rips their CD collection, purchases some music from Zune, and so on, and the content is available in the music+video hub on the device, the MediaLibrary class provides the ability to enumerate and index the content but you cannot add media content to the Media Library except for images, which can be added to the Pictures collection. If you download audio or video content in your application you can only save it to your application's isolated storage area.

The MediaLibrary class does not provide access to media content stored in individual third-party application's isolated storage area. Here is a list of the available media collections on Windows Phone 7:

- **Albums:** AlbumCollection class

- **Artists:** ArtistCollection class

- **Genres:** GenreCollection class

- **Pictures:** PictureCollection class

- **Playlists:** PlaylistCollection class

- **Songs:** SongCollection class

To gain access to the MediaLibrary class add a reference to the Microsoft.Xna.Framework assembly. The MediaLibrary class was originally available as part of the XNA Game Studio development environment for the Zune music player, and that is how it is made available on Windows Phone 7. Add a using clause for the Microsoft.Xna.Framework.Media namespace to get started.

■ **Note** To run this sample while debugging, shutdown Zune and run the WPConnect.exe tool from a command-line to enable debugging when accessing media content on a physical device.

The Chapter 6 sample code has a project named WorkingWithMediaLibrary to demonstrate how to access media content. The project is once again based on the MVVM Light SDK and data bound to the UI. This time we use a Panorama control as the main page with a background based on a photo from a recent vacation. There are four PanoramaItem panels:

- Albums

- Artists

- Playlists

- Songs

Each PanoramaItem includes a ListBox that data binds to a collection of these items. You might be tempted to do something like this for making the media available to the UI:

```
public AlbumCollection Albums
{
  get { return _mediaLibrary.Albums; }
}
```

Data binding to this property does not return any data. This is because there could be many artists, albums, and songs in a collection. Instead you must access each item via indexed access into the collection. To make the media items available, declare properties of type List<Album>, and so on, for each property just like with other samples.

The interesting aspect to this code sample is the method call that loads the data as shown in Listing 6-7.

Listing 6–7. MainViwModel Method that Populates the Media Collections

```
private void CreateDataCollections()
{
  Albums = new List<Album>();
  Album album = null;
  for (int i = 0; i < _mediaLibrary.Albums.Count;i++)
  {
    album = _mediaLibrary.Albums[i];
    Albums.Add(album);
  }

  Artists = new List<Artist>();
  Artist artist = null;
  for (int i = 0; i < _mediaLibrary.Artists.Count; i++)
  {
    artist = _mediaLibrary.Artists[i];
    Artists.Add(artist);
  }

  Songs = new List<Song>();
  Song song = null;
  for (int i = 0; i < _mediaLibrary.Songs.Count; i++)
  {
    song = _mediaLibrary.Songs[i];
    Songs.Add(song);
  }

  Playlists = new List<Playlist>();
  Playlist playlist = null;
  for (int i = 0; i < _mediaLibrary.Playlists.Count; i++)
  {
    playlist = _mediaLibrary.Playlists[i];
    Playlists.Add(playlist);
  }
}
```

You must access the media item by index into a local variable and then add it to the List<Artist> collections, as shown in Listing 6–7, for each media type in order to have an actual object reference. Note that adding the entire collection as in the sample can be risky from a memory consumption standpoint if the user has a large media collection.

The MediaLibrary.Albums collection has a reference to album art available but it is not directly published as a property on the Album object. The Album object does have a HaveArt property with a GetAlbumArt method. Remember from the previous sample that IValueConverter data converters allow you to data bind to anything. For this sample a simple data converter that creates a BitmapImage object to hold the image returned by the Album.GetAlbumArt() method call. The BitmapImage is then returned as the value for the Image.Source property to display the album art. Listing 6–8 shows the data converter.

Listing 6–8. AlbumArtConverter Code File

```
using System;
using System.Windows.Data;
using System.Windows.Media.Imaging;
using Microsoft.Xna.Framework.Media;

namespace WorkingWithMediaLibrary.Converters
{
  public class AlbumArtConverter : IValueConverter
  {
    public object Convert(object value, Type targetType, object parameter,
      System.Globalization.CultureInfo culture)
    {
      try
      {
        BitmapImage artImage = new BitmapImage();
        Album album = value as Album;
        if (album.HasArt)
        {
          artImage.SetSource(album.GetAlbumArt());
        }
        return artImage;
      }
      catch (Exception err)
      {
        return "";
      }
    }

    public object ConvertBack(object value, Type targetType, object parameter,
      System.Globalization.CultureInfo culture)
    {
      throw new NotImplementedException();
    }
  }
}
```

The last item to cover is that you can play songs or SongCollection objects via the
MediaPlayer.Play() method, which is covered in more detail below. Figure 6–8 shows the UI in the
emulator, which has just test data for a single album and a few songs so you will want to run on a real
device with a populated library.

Figure 6–8. WorkingWithMediaLibrary UI in the Emulator

This concludes our coverage of the Windows Phone 7 media library programmable API. Next up is how to create a Photo Extras application.

Building a Photo Extras Application

Developers always ask about ways to integrate with the underlying platform. This is especially true for a mobile device where mobile devices users want to perform actions with as little effort as possible. One popular use case is manipulating pictures taken with the built-in camera. Many applications allow photo manipulation directly on the device so integrating these application as much as possible to the Pictures Hub benefits the end-user.

Integrated experiences are a key differentiator for Windows Phone 7 and this is extended to developers as well. You can build applications that integrate with the Pictures hub such that your application can be launched directly from the Extras menu.

A Photos Extra application is accessible from within the Pictures hub Single Photo Viewer (SPV). When in the SPV, swipe up the Application Bar to expose the extras… menu item to launch a Photo Extra application to work on the currently displayed image. Note that images are the only media type that can be added to the Media Library, so once a Photos Extra performs its magic on an image, it can be saved back to the media library to be shared with others. Figure 6–9 shows the Photos Extra UI.

Figure 6–9. Photos Extra UI

The next section covers how to create a Photos Extra application.

Creating a Photos Extra App

This section covers how easy it is to integrate with the Pictures hub. Building a Photos Extra application includes the following two major steps:

- Creating the Extras.xml file

- Retrieving the selected photo

A new project named PhotosExtraApp is added to the Chapter 6 solution. We will turn this project into a Photos Extra App and use MVVM Light as part of the sample. We will take advantage of messaging to communicate between the image editing View named ImageEditorView.xaml and the backing ViewModel class named PictureEditingViewModel.cs. We also will use a few type converters as well. Fist we need to edit the project so that it shows up in the Photos Extra menu. The next section covers how to create the Extras.xml file.

Extras.xml File

The Extras.xml file is pretty easy to create. Here are its contents:

```
<Extras>
  <PhotosExtrasApplication>
    <Enabled>true</Enabled>
  </PhotosExtrasApplication>
</Extras>
```

Run the application to test that the WP7 Book Photos Extra is added to the Extras menu when in the Single Picture Viewer in the Pictures hub. When selected, the application just launches normally and doesn't present an editing mode but the test is successful with the application appearing in the menu. The next section covers how to capture the current picture.

Retrieving the Selected Photo

Retrieving the selected photo is performed in the OnNavigatedTo method override of the application. A set of parameters are passed in when the application is launched from the Single Photo Viewer in the Pictures hub. This allows the application to know when it is launched as a Photos Extra or when the application is simply launched from the application list or Start screen tile if pinned to the Start screen because no query parameters are present.

To retrieve the query parameters, you use the NavigationContext.QueryString property. The QueryString object is a Dictionary<string, string> object. Look for the pre-defined QueryString["token"] to know that the application was launched as a Photos Extra. Use the query value to also obtain a handle to the image.

To get started, we override OnNavigatedTo in Main.xaml.cs in order to capture the query string value to set the correct picture on PictureEditingViewModel.PictureToEdit property. Listing 6–9 has the code for PhotosExtraApp MainPage.xaml.cs.

Listing 6–9. PhotosExtraApp MainPage.xaml.cs Code File

```
using System;
using System.Collections.Generic;
using System.Windows.Controls;
using GalaSoft.MvvmLight.Messaging;
using Microsoft.Phone.Controls;
using Microsoft.Xna.Framework.Media;

namespace PhotosExtraApp
{
  public partial class MainPage : PhoneApplicationPage
  {
    // Constructor
    public MainPage()
    {
      InitializeComponent();
    }

    protected override void OnNavigatedTo(System.Windows.Navigation.NavigationEventArgs e)
    {
      base.OnNavigatedTo(e);
      //Process query string
      IDictionary<string, string> queryStrings = this.NavigationContext.QueryString;
      if (NavigationContext.QueryString.Count > 0 &&
        NavigationContext.QueryString.ContainsKey("token"))
      {
        MediaLibrary library = new MediaLibrary();
        Picture picture = library.GetPictureFromToken(queryStrings["token"]);
        //Remove this query string item so that when the user clicks
        //"back" from the ImageEditorView page the app doesn't loop back
        //over to the ImageEditorView in an endless loop of navigation because
        //the query string value is still present and picked up by
        //MainPage.OnNavigateTo each time...
        NavigationContext.QueryString.Remove("token");

        //Send Message with Picture object
        SetPictureAndNavigate(picture);
      }
```

```
    }

    private void ListBox_SelectionChanged(object sender,
System.Windows.Controls.SelectionChangedEventArgs e)
    {
        ListBox lb = sender as ListBox;
        SetPictureAndNavigate(lb.SelectedItem as Picture);
    }

    void SetPictureAndNavigate(Picture picture)
    {
        Messenger.Default.Send<Picture>(picture, "PictureToEdit");
        NavigationService.Navigate(new Uri("/ImageEditorView.xaml", UriKind.Relative));
    }
  }
}
```

The query string value for the token parameter is obtained and the
MediaLibrary.GetPictureFromToken method is called to obtain the correct image from the Picture hub.
The picture is passed to the SetPictureAndNavigate method shown in Listing 6–9. This same method is
called when an image is selected from the ListBox in MainPage.xaml via the ListBox_SelectionChanged
method also in Listing 6–9.

Notice in the SetPictureAndNavigate method, it uses the MVVM Light Messenger.Default.Send to
pass the picture as a message. The message is registered for and received in the
PictureEditingViewModel class constructor in this line of code:

```
Messenger.Default.Register<Picture>(
    this, "PictureToEdit",
    (picture) => { PictureToEdit = picture; });
```

The PictureEditorView.xamlView data binds to the PictureEditingViewModel so that the Image
control on that page can data bind to the PictureEditingViewModel.PictureToEdit property. This allows
the UI to data bind to a ViewModel without directly accessing the ViewModel by using MVVM Light
Toolkit Messaging.

Let's finish discussing the MainPage.xaml functionality before diving further into the picture edit
page. The ListBox in MainPage.xaml data binds to the List<Picture> Pictures property in the
MainViewModel class. The interesting part of the MainViewModel class is loading the images:

```
private void CreateDataCollections()
{
    Pictures = new List<Picture>();
    Picture picture = null;
    for (int i = 0; i < _mediaLibrary.Pictures.Count; i++)
    {
        picture = _mediaLibrary.Pictures[i];
        Pictures.Add(picture);
        if (i > 30)
            break;
    }
}
```

The CreateDataCollections method is hard coded to just load the first 30 pictures found into the
MainViewModel.Pictures property. Figure 6–10 shows the MainPage.xaml UI with sample images from
the Emulator rendered in a basic data template that shows the name, the image, and the album it is
from.

Figure 6–10. PhotosExtra main page UI

The ListBox data binds to the List<Picture> Pictures collection. The data template includes an Image control. It leverages a value converter named ImageSourceConverter that calls Picture.GetImage() and sets it on the Source property for the Image control in the Data Template. Picture.GetThumbnail would be a better choice for the ListBox template, because it is a small image but we use the same converter when displaying the image on the edit screen and GetImage returns the full image and so looks better when full screen.

MainPage.xaml only displays when launched from the App List. When an image is touched, it opens to the picture editing View named PictureEditorView.xaml. When launched from the Photos Extra menu with the QueryStrings value present, the application goes straight to the picture editing view as shown in Figure 6–11.

Figure 6–11. PhotosExtra picture editing UI

Notice that in both Figure 6–10 and Figure 6–11 that the name does not include the extension. The TextBlock data binds to the `Picture.Name` property that includes the extension but it is parsed out. This is accomplished by a simple value converter named `ImageNameConverter` that has a simple line of code to obtain just the name portion:

```
return ((string)value).Split('.')[0];
```

Notice also that in Figure 6–11, when the UI is in Landscape mode the text title disappears to maximize space for image viewing and editing. This is also achieved via a value converter. The TextBlock's Visibility property Element data binds to the `Orientation` of the Page. The value converter sets Visibility to `Collapsed` if the phone is in Landscape mode. Otherwise the TextBlock's `Visibility` is configured to `Visible`. The PictureEditorView data binds to the PictureEditingViewModel class shown in Listing 6–10.

Listing 6–10. PictureEditingViewModel.cs Code File

```
using System.IO;
using System.Windows.Media.Imaging;
using GalaSoft.MvvmLight;
using GalaSoft.MvvmLight.Command;
using GalaSoft.MvvmLight.Messaging;
using Microsoft.Xna.Framework.Media;
```

```
namespace PhotosExtraApp.ViewModel
{
  public class PictureEditingViewModel : ViewModelBase
  {
    private MediaLibrary mediaLibrary;

    public PictureEditingViewModel()
    {
      mediaLibrary = new MediaLibrary();

      //Register to receive message with picture object from Picture Hub
      //This message is sent from MainPage.xaml.cs in OnNavigateTo
      Messenger.Default.Register<Picture>(
       this, "PictureToEdit",
       (picture) => { PictureToEdit = picture; });

      //Instantiate Commands
      SaveImageCommand = new RelayCommand(
        () => SaveImage());

      SaveImageAsCommand = new RelayCommand<string>(
        param => SaveImageAs(param));

      RevertToSavedImageCommand = new RelayCommand(
        () => EditImage());
      EditImageCommand = new RelayCommand(
        () => RevertToSavedImage());
    }

    #region Image State
    public const string PictureToEditPropertyName = "PictureToEdit";
    private Picture _pictureToEdit = null;
    public Picture PictureToEdit
    {
      get
      {
        return _pictureToEdit;
      }

      set
      {
        if (_pictureToEdit == value)
        {
          return;
        }
        var oldValue = _pictureToEdit;
        _pictureToEdit = value;
        RaisePropertyChanged(PictureToEditPropertyName);
      }
    }


    public const string ModifiedPicturePropertyName = "ModifiedPicture";
    private WriteableBitmap _modifiedPicture = null;
```

```
public WriteableBitmap ModifiedPicture
{
  get { return _modifiedPicture; }
  set
  {
    if (_modifiedPicture == value)
    { return; }
    var oldValue = _modifiedPicture;
    _modifiedPicture = value;
    RaisePropertyChanged(ModifiedPicturePropertyName);
  }
}

//Property to data bind to for SaveAs input UI
//Used for SaveAs command
public const string ImageSaveAsNamePropertyName = "ImageSaveAsName";
private string _imageSaveAsName = null;
public string ImageSaveAsName
{
  get { return _imageSaveAsName;}
  set
  {
    if (_imageSaveAsName == value)
    { return; }
    var oldValue = _imageSaveAsName;
    _imageSaveAsName = value;
    RaisePropertyChanged(ImageSaveAsNamePropertyName);
  }
}

public const string ImageIsDirtyPropertyName = "ImageIsDirty";
private bool _imageIsDirety = false;
public bool ImageIsDirty
{
  get { return _imageIsDirety; }
  set
  {
    if (_imageIsDirety == value)
    { return; }

    var oldValue = _imageIsDirety;
    _imageIsDirety = value;
    RaisePropertyChanged(ImageIsDirtyPropertyName);
  }
}
#endregion

#region Image Actions for RelayCommand Objects
private void EditImage()
{
  //Editing, unsaved changes pending
  ImageIsDirty = true;
}
```

```csharp
//View must set the writable bitmap area
//prior to executing this command
//This Save action takes a new name
private void SaveImageAs(string saveAsName)
{
  using (MemoryStream jpegStream = new MemoryStream())
  {
    //Tell the UI to update the WriteableBitmap property
    Messenger.Default.Send<bool>(true, "UpdateWriteableBitmap");
    ModifiedPicture.SaveJpeg(jpegStream, ModifiedPicture.PixelWidth,
      ModifiedPicture.PixelHeight, 0, 100);
    //Update current Picture to reflect new modified image
    PictureToEdit = mediaLibrary.SavePicture(saveAsName, jpegStream);
    //Saved, not editing
    ImageIsDirty = false;
  };
}

//View must set the writable bitmap area
//prior to executing this command
//This save action overwrites existing image
private void SaveImage()
{
  using (MemoryStream jpegStream = new MemoryStream())
  {
    //Tell the UI to update the WriteableBitmap property
    Messenger.Default.Send<bool>(true, "UpdateWriteableBitmap");
    ModifiedPicture.SaveJpeg(jpegStream, ModifiedPicture.PixelWidth,
      ModifiedPicture.PixelHeight, 0, 100);
    //Update current Picture to reflect new modified image
    PictureToEdit = mediaLibrary.SavePicture(PictureToEdit.Name, jpegStream);
    //Saved, not editing
    ImageIsDirty = false;
  };
}

//PictureEditingView registers to receive this message
//It would clear out any edits at the UI level.
private void RevertToSavedImage()
{
  Messenger.Default.Send<bool>(true, "UndoImageChanges");
}
#endregion

#region Image Editing Commmands
public RelayCommand SaveImageCommand { get; private set; }
public RelayCommand<string> SaveImageAsCommand { get; private set; }
public RelayCommand EditImageCommand { get; private set; }
public RelayCommand RevertToSavedImageCommand { get; private set; }
#endregion
  }
}
```

The `PictureEditingViewModel` class has two primary data properties: `PictureToEdit` of type Picture and the `ModifiedPicture` of type `WriteableBitmap`. The idea is to display the selected picture to be modified in an `Image` control.

■ **Note** The sample doesn't actually modify the control, but you could enable drawing, etc., just like what was demonstrated in Chapter 2.

The user can then edit the image in the UI. The modifications under the covers would result in additional Silverlight controls added to the XAML with the Grid WritableBitMapSourceArea as the top-level parent. When the user clicks save, the Grid is passed into the `WriteableBitmap` to turn it into a bitmap image.

You can pass any `UIElement` into the `WriteableBitmap.Render` method and it will turn the element and its children into an image. In the `SaveImageCommand` (`SaveImage()`) and `SaveImageAsCommand` (`SaveImageAs()`) commands, a message is sent to the UI to update the `ModifiedPicture` property on the VM prior to saving. We could do this in a way without tying the View to the ViewModel via additional messages, but for our example this is sufficient.

The `PictureEditingViewModel` class also sends a message to the UI to ask the View to undo modifications to the image. Listing 6–11 has the PictureEditorView code-behind file.

Listing 6–11. PictureEditorView .xaml.cs Code File

```
using System.Windows.Controls;
using GalaSoft.MvvmLight.Messaging;
using Microsoft.Phone.Controls;
using PhotosExtraApp.ViewModel;

namespace PhotosExtraApp
{
  /// <summary>
  /// Description for ImageEditorView.
  /// </summary>
  public partial class PictureEditorView : PhoneApplicationPage
  {
    PictureEditingViewModel vm;
    /// <summary>
    /// Initializes a new instance of the ImageEditorView class.
    /// </summary>
    public PictureEditorView()
    {
      InitializeComponent();

      vm = DataContext as PictureEditingViewModel;

      //Register for message to undo changes
      Messenger.Default.Register<bool>(
        this, "UndoImageChanges",
        (param) => UndoImageChanges());

      Messenger.Default.Register<bool>(
```

```
        this, "UpdateWriteableBitmap",
        (param) => UpdateWriteableBitmap());
    }

    private void UpdateWriteableBitmap()
    {
      //Update WriteableBitmap so it is ready to save
      vm.ModifiedPicture.Render(WriteableBitmapSourceArea, null);
    }

    private void UndoImageChanges()
    {
      //Undo Image changes
      //Reset WriteableBitmapSourceArea Grid to just hold
      //the original image content only
      Image img = ImageToEdit;
      WriteableBitmapSourceArea.Children.Clear();
      WriteableBitmapSourceArea.Children.Add(img);
    }

    private void EditAppBarBtn_Click(object sender, System.EventArgs e)
    {
      vm.EditImageCommand.Execute(null);
    }

    private void saveAppBarBtn_Click(object sender, System.EventArgs e)
    {
      vm.SaveImageCommand.Execute(null);
    }

    private void SaveAsAppMenItem_Click(object sender, System.EventArgs e)
    {
      vm.SaveImageAsCommand.Execute(vm.ImageSaveAsName);
    }

    private void RevertToLastSaveMenuItem_Click(object sender, System.EventArgs e)
    {
      vm.RevertToSavedImageCommand.Execute(null);
    }
  }
}
```

This code walkthrough demonstrates how to set up all the infrastructure for a picture modifying Photos Extra application. It does not actually perform edits, that we leave to the enterprising reader to build the next great Photos Extra application.

Working with Video and Audio Media

So far, we have discussed working with the Media Library and the Picture hub with Photo Extras applications. In this section, we discuss video and audio media. As mentioned previously, Windows Phone 7 third-party applications cannot add media to the Media Library but third-party applications can add content to Isolated Storage in addition to playing video and audio content in memory.

In this section we cover supported codecs, playing video, audio, and DRM considerations within the context of the programming model.

Supported Codecs and Containers

Windows Phone 7 has extensive codec and container support as detailed at this link:

`http://msdn.microsoft.com/en-us/library/ff462087%28VS.92%29.aspx`

Container support for a variety of media includes WAV, MP3, WMA, 3GP, MP4, 3G2, M4A, WMV, M4V, 3G2, JPG, and PNG. Of note, GIF, BMP, and TIF are not supported in the Image control in Silverlight.

Decoder support is a long list at the above link, but of note support is available for MP3, WMA Standard v9, AAC-LC, HE-AAC v1, HE-AAC v2, AMR-NB, WMV (VC-1, WMV9) simple, main, and advanced. Also supported are MPEG-4 Part 2, Simple, Advanced Simple, MPEG-4 Part 10 Level 3.0 Baseline, Main, High, and H.263. There are specific requirements in terms of bitrate, constant bitrate vs. variable bitrate, as well as methods of playback, so check the above link when troubleshooting playback issues on a device to see if a capability or playback method is not correct.

Video and Audio in the Emulator

The emulator does not support all of the codecs supported on a device. Specifically, AAC-LC, HE-AAC v1, HE-AAC v2, AMR-NB, MPEG-4 Part 2 simple, MPEG-4 Part 2 advanced, MPEG-4 Part 10 level 3 baseline, main or high, and H.263 are all not supported.

The following codecs are supported but with caveats:

- WMV (VC-1, WMV9) – Simple Profile – Unsupported above 320 x 176 pixels.

- WMV (VC-1, WMV9) - Main Profile – Unsupported above 800 x 488 pixels.

- WMV (VC-1, WMV9) - Advanced Profile – Unsupported above 720 x 480 pixels.

When investigating video support for your content, it is recommended to test on a real device first to ensure that an accurate assessment is made.

Progressive Download Video

Progressive download is generally used for short form video, clips, music videos, and the like. The file is completely downloaded over HTP while playback begins immediately.

We create a project named WorkingWtihMedia in the Chapter 6 solution. The MainPage is a menu page to launch additional pages to test out functionality starting with testing progressive play back in the MediaPlayerLauncher, which was covered in Chapter 4 in the LaunchersAndChoosers sample.

Progressive Video with MediaPlayerLauncher

Silverlight supports both progressive and streaming video via the MediaElement control, but a simple way to play progressive non-DRM video is via the Microsoft.Phone.Tasks.MediaPlayerLauncher task. A page named MediaPlayeTask.xaml is added to the WorkingWithMedia project that has a single button titled play video.

```
private void textBlock1_MouseLeftButtonDown(object sender, MouseButtonEventArgs e)
{
  MediaPlayerLauncher mediaPlayerLauncher = new MediaPlayerLauncher();
  mediaPlayerLauncher.Controls = MediaPlaybackControls.FastForward |
    MediaPlaybackControls.Pause | MediaPlaybackControls.Rewind |
    MediaPlaybackControls.Skip | MediaPlaybackControls.Stop;
  mediaPlayerLauncher.Location = MediaLocationType.Data;
  mediaPlayerLauncher.Media = new
Uri("http://ecn.channel9.msdn.com/o9/ch9/8/9/6/6/3/5/WP7Xbox_ch9.mp4");
  mediaPlayerLauncher.Show();
}
```

As you can see, it is possible to configure what vcr controls are visible during playback. In the next section, we cover playing video with the MediaElement, which is pretty simple as well – but you will need to build up your own media player for best user experience. This is because the MediaElement is a blank canvas with a highly programmable API. By default, it does not have any media controls and the like. Unless you need specific functionality or want complete control over the playback UI the MediaPlayerLauncher task is easiest.

One situation where the MediaPlayerLauncher is not a good choice is with DRM'd content. I cover DRM'd video later in the chapter. The next section covers playing progressive video with the MediaElement control.

Progressive Video with MediaElement

The MediaElement is a very powerful control with a rich API to provide fined-grained control during playback with a rich event model. We create a simple example that hooks into the interesting events as well as displays values for video related properties.

A new page named MediaElement.xaml is added to the WorkingWithMedia project. A MediaElement control is added to the page. The application bar is enabled to host a play and pause button that will programmatically control the MediaElement control. Several TextBlocks are laid out to display values from various MediaElement properties as shown in Figure 6–12.

Figure 6–12. *MediaElement.xaml UI*

There are several interesting events available with the MediaElement control. Listing 6–12 shows the available media-related events.

Listing 6–12. *PictureEditorView .xaml.cs Code File*

```
using System;
using System.Windows;
using System.Windows.Threading;
using Microsoft.Phone.Controls;

namespace WorkingWithMedia.pages
{
  public partial class MediaElement : PhoneApplicationPage
  {
    public MediaElement()
    {
      InitializeComponent();
      DispatcherTimer timer = new DispatcherTimer();
      timer.Tick += new EventHandler(timer_Tick);
      timer.Interval = new TimeSpan(0, 0, 1);
      timer.Start();
```

```
}

void timer_Tick(object sender, EventArgs e)
{
  CanSeekTextBlock.Text = mediaPlayer.CanSeek.ToString();
  CanPauseTextBlock.Text = mediaPlayer.CanPause.ToString();
  DroppedFramesTextBlock.Text =
    mediaPlayer.DroppedFramesPerSecond.ToString();
}

private void mediaPlayer_MediaOpened(object sender, RoutedEventArgs e)
{
  mediaPlayer.Play();
}

private void mediaPlayer_MediaFailed(object sender,
  ExceptionRoutedEventArgs e)
{
  MessageBox.Show("Media Failed: " + e.ErrorException.Message);
}

private void mediaPlayer_MediaEnded(object sender, RoutedEventArgs e)
{

}

private void PlayAppBarBtn_Click(object sender, EventArgs e)
{
  mediaPlayer.Source =
    new Uri("http://ecn.channel9.msdn.com/o9/ch9/8/9/6/6/3/5/WP7Xbox_ch9.wmv",
      UriKind.Absolute);
}

private void PauseAppBarBtn_Click(object sender, EventArgs e)
{
  mediaPlayer.Pause();
}

private void mediaPlayer_CurrentStateChanged(object sender,
  RoutedEventArgs e)
{
  CurrentStateTextBlock.Text = mediaPlayer.CurrentState.ToString();
}

private void mediaPlayer_BufferingProgressChanged(object sender,
  RoutedEventArgs e)
{
  BufferingProgressTextBlock.Text = mediaPlayer.BufferingProgress.ToString();
}

private void mediaPlayer_DownloadProgressChanged(object sender,
  RoutedEventArgs e)
{
  DownloadProgressChangedTextBlock.Text = mediaPlayer.DownloadProgress.ToString();
```

```
      }
    }
}
```

Notice that clicking play doesn't start playback. Instead, it sets the Source property on the MediaElement control. If the video configured on the Source property is successfully opened, the MediaOpened event fires, which is where Play is actually called.

MediaStreamSource

For custom video delivery, you can use the MediaElement.SetSource() method in your code to specify the media to be played. One overload of SetSource() accepts a System.IO.Stream, which is suited for the scenario where you decide to acquire the media through some other mechanism rather than have the MediaElement handle the download. When you acquire the media file, you can create a Stream around it (using a more concrete type like System.IO.IsolatedStorage.IsolatedStorageFileStream) and pass it to SetSource().

The second overload of SetSource() accepts an instance of the System.Windows.Media.MediaStreamSource type. The MediaStreamSource type is actually a way to plug a video container file format into Silverlight, for which the MediaElement does not come with a built-in parser. Video container file formats and related specifications are complex topics, and consequently a treatment of MediaStreamSource implementations is beyond the scope of this book.

When the Source is set by either mechanism, for progressive download scenarios the MediaElement immediately starts to download the media. The MediaElement.DownloadProgressChanged event is raised repeatedly as the download progresses. The MediaElement.DownloadProgress property reports the download progress as a percentage value (actually a double between 0 and 1 that you can convert to percentage) that you can use to track and report the download progress in the DownloadProgressChanged event handler.

■ **Note** For more information on Silverlight and MediaStreamSource check out *Silverlight Recipes: A Problem-Solution Approach*, Second Edition: http://apress.com/book/view/1430230339.

Streaming Video

In addition to progressive download video, streaming video is another technique used to deliver media to a player. Streaming does not require downloading the media file locally, and it is well suited for scenarios involving either live or on-demand broadcasts to a large population of viewers.

Microsoft provides Smooth Streaming, an IIS Media Services extension that enables adaptive streaming of media to Silverlight and other clients over HTTP. Smooth Streaming provides a high-quality viewing experience that scales massively on content distribution networks, making true HD 1080p media experiences a reality.

Smooth Streaming is the productized version of technology first used by Microsoft to deliver on-demand video for the 2008 Summer Olympics at NBCOlympics.com. By dynamically monitoring both local bandwidth and video rendering performance, Smooth Streaming optimizes playback of content by switching video quality in real-time to match current network conditions resulting in a better viewing experience.

Smooth Streaming uses the simple but powerful concept of delivering small content fragments (typically two seconds worth of video) and verifying that each has arrived within the appropriate time and played back at the expected quality level. If one fragment does not meet these requirements, the next fragment delivered will be at a somewhat lower quality level. Conversely, when conditions allow it, the quality of subsequent fragments will be at a higher level if network conditions improve.

▓ **Note** For more information on IIS Smooth Streaming go to `http://learn.iis.net/page.aspx/558/getting-started-with-iis-smooth-streaming/`.

SmoothStreamingMediaElement

The `Microsoft.Web.Media.SmoothStreaming.SmoothStreamingMediaElement` is a customized version of the MediaElement that works directly with IIS Smooth Streaming technology. The SmoothStreamingMediaElement available in Windows Phone 7 is compatible with the IIS Smooth Streaming Client 1.1. Windows Phone 7 is a subset of the full client support. The phone icon in the API reference identifies members of classes in the Microsoft.Web.Media.SmoothStreaming namespace that are available for Windows Phone 7 development. Review the documentation at the following link:

`http://msdn.microsoft.com/en-us/library/microsoft.web.media.smoothstreaming(v=VS.90).aspx`

IIS Smooth Streaming combined with the SmoothStreamingMediaElement provide an incredibly powerful and flexible streaming capability with support for multiple video and audio tracks, multiple languages, subtitles, Timeline Markers, Fast Forward and Rewind, and metadata in tracks for "pop-up" information during playback for a rich media experience. Please refer to this link for details on capabilities:

`http://msdn.microsoft.com/en-us/library/ee958035(v=VS.90).aspx`

Silverlight Media Framework

The Silverlight Media Framework (SMF), or "smurf," is an open source CodePlex project that provides a robust, scalable customizable media player for IIS Smooth Streaming media delivery. The SMF builds on the core functionality of the Smooth Streaming Client (formerly known as the Smooth Streaming Player Development Kit) and adds a large number of additional features, including an extensibility API that allows developers to create plug-ins for the framework. The SMF also now includes full support for Windows Phone 7 so developers can incorporate high-end video playback experiences in their Windows Phone 7 applications. Please check out the SMF at this link:

`http://smf.codeplex.com/`

DRM

Most long form video, whether it be TV show episodes, movies, or live TV, has some form of Digital Rights Management (DRM). As the goal of DRM is to prevent illegal copying of digital content, securely storing licenses to content is of paramount concern.

Silverlight for Windows Phone 7 supports DRM via Microsoft PlayReady. Microsoft PlayReady is a platform independent DRM content access technology that is optimized for broad use across a range of devices. Microsoft PlayReady supports subscription, purchase, rental, and pay-per-view business models that can be applied to many digital content types and to a wide range of audio and video formats.

On Windows Phone 7, there is support for Microsoft PlayReady built into the platform including a secure key store for online and offline DRM key storage. After DRM media is accessed the first time, the license is stored offline enabling offline playback of DRM'd content.

A full discussion of DRM is beyond this book but here is a link for more information on Microsoft PlayReady technology:

www.microsoft.com/PlayReady/Default.mspx

When it comes to DRM protected content available via the Zune Service, either purchased or subscription, you can play that content within Silverlight applications using the MediaElement as well as the MediaPlayer available in the XNA Framework. License acquisition occurs behind the scenes with no additional work necessary by the developer. For content that is not owned by the end-user, you can use the MarketplaceDetailsTask to show UI that allows the user to purchase the content.

Audio Support

Because audio is critical to video playback, audio support is covered in pretty good detail in concert with what has been discussed above regarding video playback. However, in addition to the MediaElement and SmoothStreamingMediaElement, developers can play audio using the Microsoft.Xna.Framework.Media.MediaPlayer object. We demonstrated this in the Chapter 6 WorkingWithMediaLibrary project in this event handler from MainPanoramaPage.xaml.cs:

```
private void ListBox_SelectionChanged(object sender, SelectionChangedEventArgs e)
{
  object obj = (sender as ListBox).SelectedItem;
  MediaLibrary library = new MediaLibrary();
  try
  {
    switch (obj.GetType().ToString())
    {
      case "Microsoft.Xna.Framework.Media.Album": MediaPlayer.Play(((Album)(obj)).Songs);
break;
      case "Microsoft.Xna.Framework.Media.Song": MediaPlayer.Play((Song)(obj)); break;
      case "Microsoft.Xna.Framework.Media.Playlist":
MediaPlayer.Play(((Playlist)(obj)).Songs); break;
      case "Microsoft.Xna.Framework.Media.Artist": MediaPlayer.Play(((Artist)(obj)).Songs);
break;
    }
  }
  catch (Exception ex)
  {
    MessageBox.Show("Error: " + ex.Message);
  };
}
```

The MediaPlayer object can play by Album, Song, Playlist, and Artist, but only one of these items at a time. So, for example, for a custom play list you must provide one song at a time. The MediaPlayer object has two events that you can hook, MediaStateChanged and ActiveSongChanged. MediaStateChanged fires when state changes from Paused, Playing, or Stopped to another MediaState value. Here is a code example, not from a specific project but provided as reference:

```
public MainPage()
{
  InitializeComponent();
```

```
  MediaPlayer.MediaStateChanged += new EventHandler<EventArgs>(MediaPlayer_MediaStateChanged);
  MediaPlayer.ActiveSongChanged += new EventHandler<EventArgs>(MediaPlayer_ActiveSongChanged);
}

void MediaPlayer_ActiveSongChanged(object sender, EventArgs e)
{
  if (MediaPlayer.Queue.Count == 0)
  {
    //add a song to Play
    MediaPlayer.Play(nextSong);
  }
}

void MediaPlayer_MediaStateChanged(object sender, EventArgs e)
{
  switch (MediaPlayer.State)
  {
    case MediaState.Paused:
      break;
    case MediaState.Playing:
      break;
    case MediaState.Stopped:
      break;
  }
}
```

On a related note, you can prompt the user to purchase additional music using MarketplaceSearchTask and passing in a search string containing the artist, album, and song title. You can also use the WebBrowserTask and Zune Http links for content if you have the ID for the content. Here is an example:

```
WebBrowserTask task = new WebBrowserTask();
task.URL = HttpUtility.UrlEncode("http://social.zune.net/External/LaunchZuneProtocol.aspx?
                pathuri=navigate%3FalbumID%3Dd1935e06-0100-11db-89ca-0019b92a3933");
task.Show();
```

You can then use the MediaLibrary object covered above and demonstrated in the WorkingWithMediaLibrary project to find acquired content and show album art as well as purchase the media.

You might guess that the MarketplaceDetailsTask could also show the purchase UI but it is not supported in this release.

Building a music+videos Hub Application

Applications that play music or video can integrate more deeply into the Windows Phone 7 user experience. This helps to provide consistent quick access to content for the end user, while also allowing your application to surface content and the application itself within the music+videos hub in addition to the App List. Figure 6–13 shows the music+videos hub panorama for reference.

Figure 6–13. Microsoft Windows Phone 7 music+videos hub

The music+videos hub has an apps, history, and new section that a music or video application can integrate into for a richer user experience.

An application that calls the `Microsoft.Devices.MediaHistory` or `Microsoft.Devices.MediaHistoryItem` classes is considered as a Music + Videos hub application and will appear in the Marquee list in the hub when installed on the phone. When an application is submitted to the Windows Phone Marketplace, the marketplace detects that the application uses these classes and will automatically update the hub type to Music + Videos in the application's Windows Phone application manifest.

The Windows Phone 7 Certification Requirements Document covers music+videos hub application certification requirements in section 6.5. In this section, we build a sample music+videos hub application that you can use to guide you in building your own application that takes advantage of this integration point.

Additional Assets

As you can see in Figure 6–13 that shows the music+videos hub, applications and content are represented by tiles. Here are the rules for tiles:

- Tile images must be a .jpg image.

- The application title or logo must be present on each tile.

- The now playing tile must be 358 pixels x 358 pixels in size.

- Other tiles shown on the hub must be 173 pixels x 173 pixels in size.

- The Title property of the MediaHistoryItem class must be set to text that represents the content, such as a station name or video title.

We create two tiles to represent the videos, named `ParisVideoTile.jpg` and `tdfVideoTile.jpg`, to correspond to the videos of the Paris skyline video and Tour De France video. We also create two now playing tiles appropriately named `NowPlayingParisTile.jpg` and NowPlayingtdfTile.jpg.

All of the image tiles are passed into the `MediaHistoryItem`API as a `System.IO.Stream` object.

■ **Tip** In an application retrieving images from server-apis, use the `WriteableBitmap` class to create images that are branded to your application.

Testing music+videos Hub Applications

When an application is ingested into marketplace, marketplace detects if the application makes calls to the MediaHistory and MediaHistoryItem classes and updates the application manifest so that the application is ready for publishing. We cover how to work with these APIs in the next section.

You can test music+videos hub applications with Visual Studio and an actual device, but you must edit the manifest file manually. Set the HubType attribute on the `<App>` element to a value of 1 and be sure to disconnect from Zune when testing. The APIs will throw an exception if syncing with Zune.

Because the emulator does not ship with the full Windows Phone 7 experience (i.e., the music+videos hub is not available), it is not possible to test music+videos hub applications in the emulator in this release.

Debugging music+videos Hub Applications

There's a tool that allows Visual Studio 2010 to connect to a device without the Zune Client software running. This functionality is especially necessary for applications that play media because it is not possible to play media when connected to the Zune Client. It is also not possible to update music+videos hub items like the "History," "Now playing," and "New" sections while connected to Zune.

To enable debugging without the Zune client running, download the WPDTPTConnect tool available with the Zune Client in this directory: robcamer. The steps are as follows:

1. Connect the device.

2. Close the Zune software.

3. Run either the 32-bit or 64-bit version of the WPDTPTConnect tool from the command-line.

Disconnecting the device reverts back to normal Zune functionality with the device.

music+videos Hub Sample Application

We start with a Windows Phone Application project named `MusicPlusVideoHub` in the Chapter Six solution. We create a simple UI with two videos from a recent vacation to play as shown in Figure 6–14.

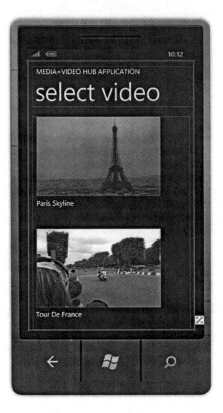

Figure 6–14. *MusicPlusVideoHub sample application*

We add another page to the application called VideoPlayerPage.xaml that contains a MediaElement where the content is actually played. When one of the thumbnails shown in Figure 6–14 is clicked, the associated video is passed as part of the query string and the application navigates to the VideoPlayerPage.xaml page to actually play the video. Here is the method handler for the top thumbnail image when touched or clicked:

```
private void PlayParisImage_MouseLeftButtonUp(object sender, MouseButtonEventArgs e)
{
  NavigationService.Navigate(new Uri(
    "/VideoPlayerPage.xaml?video=Paris",UriKind.Relative));
}
```

▨ **Note** The videos are royalty-free because the author recorded them, but the videos were shot with an old camera at 320 x 240, resulting in terrible quality on a high-resolution device like Windows Phone 7. But they are still useful to demonstrate the concepts.

The VideoPlayerPage.xaml page does not manifest any video playing UI as we are laser focused on just the code to create a music+videos hub application. Listing 6–13 has the code for VideoPlayerPage.xaml.cs.

Listing 6–13. Initial VideoPlayerPage.xaml.cs Code File

```
using System;
using System.Windows;
using Microsoft.Phone.Controls;

namespace MusicPlusVideoHub
{
  public partial class VideoPlayerPage : PhoneApplicationPage
  {
    public VideoPlayerPage()
    {
      InitializeComponent();
    }

    protected override void OnNavigatedTo(System.Windows.Navigation.NavigationEventArgs e)
    {
      VideoPlayer.Source = new
          Uri(@"/video/"+NavigationContext.QueryString["video"]+".wmv",UriKind.Relative);

      base.OnNavigatedTo(e);
    }

    private void VideoPlayer_MediaOpened(object sender, RoutedEventArgs e)
    {
      VideoPlayer.Play();
    }

    private void VideoPlayer_MediaFailed(object sender, ExceptionRoutedEventArgs e)
    {
      MessageBox.Show(e.ErrorException.Message);
    }
  }
}
```

In Listing 6–13, we process the query string with the video name in the OnNavigatedTo event handler. If the media is successfully opened we play it. If it fails to open the application displays a messagebox with the error message.

We now focus on modifying the code to become a music+videos hub application. From the Windows Phone 7 application certification requirements, the application needs to do these items:

- The application must update the "New" section of the music+videos hub when media is added to the device.

- The application must update the "Now playing" section of the music+videos hub when the application plays media.

- The application must update the "History" section of the music+videos hub when the application plays media.

- The application must launch the playback experience when the user taps on a hub tile in the "History" or "Now playing" area of the music+videos hub.

▓ **Note** The "Now playing" tile must update for each media item played, i.e., you cannot have one "Now playing" tile for the entire application or for a video series or an album.

Before proceeding, let's add a using clause for the Microsoft.Devices and System.IO namespaces to MainPage.xaml.cs and VideoPlayerPage.xaml.cs code files. The Microsoft.Devices provides access to the MediaHistory and MediaHistoryItem classes, which we use to update the "Now playing," "New," and "History" sections of the music+videos hub. We pass in the image tiles as a System.IO.Stream object.

Update the music+videos "New" Section

When the application acquires new content such as user-selected favorite radio stations or videos, it must update the "New" section in the music+videos hub for each content item individually. For our sample application, we add code to the MainPage.xaml.cs code file for the two media items available, a video of the Paris skyline and a short clip taken by the author at the 2010 Tour De France.

Add a call to the UpdateMusicPlusVideosHub_NewSection() method in the MainPage constructor. In this method we have the following code shown in Listing 6–14.

Listing 6–14. UpdateMusicPlusVideosHub_NewSection Method Code

```
StreamResourceInfo ParisTileStreamResource =
    Application.GetResourceStream(new Uri("images/hubTiles/ParisTile.jpg",
      UriKind.Relative));
//Create the MediaHistoryItem that has been newly aquired
MediaHistoryItem ParisVideoMediaHistoryItem = new MediaHistoryItem();
ParisVideoMediaHistoryItem.ImageStream = ParisTileStreamResource.Stream;
ParisVideoMediaHistoryItem.Source = "xap";
ParisVideoMediaHistoryItem.Title = "Paris Skyline Video";
//Set State for situation when navigating via click in Music+Videos Hub
ParisVideoMediaHistoryItem.PlayerContext.Add("videoHub", "Paris");
//This method call writes the history item to the 'New' section
MediaHistory.Instance.WriteAcquiredItem(ParisVideoMediaHistoryItem);

//NEW Tour De France Video
StreamResourceInfo tdfTileStreamResource =
Application.GetResourceStream(new Uri("images/hubTiles/TDFTile.jpg",
  UriKind.Relative));
//Create the MediaHistoryItem that has been newly aquired
MediaHistoryItem tdfVideoMediaHistoryItem = new MediaHistoryItem();
tdfVideoMediaHistoryItem.ImageStream = tdfTileStreamResource.Stream;
tdfVideoMediaHistoryItem.Source = "xap";
tdfVideoMediaHistoryItem.Title = "Tour De France Video";
//Set State for situation when navigating via click in Music+Videos Hub
tdfVideoMediaHistoryItem.PlayerContext.Add("videoHub", "TDF");
//This method call writes the history item to the 'New' section
MediaHistory.Instance.WriteAcquiredItem(tdfVideoMediaHistoryItem);
```

In the UpdateMusicPlusVideosHub_NewSection method code shown in Listing 6–14, we retrieve a stream that contains the desired image using Application.GetResourceStream. Since the images are stored as content in the XAP file, we simply pass in an Uri to the content based on the project folder structure. Images retrieved from server-side APIs work just as well and can be customized with a brand using the WriteableBitmap class as shown previously.

Once we have a stream to the image, we can create a MediaHistoryItem object. We assign the stream pointing to the tile image that we obtained via Application.GetResourceStream to the MediaHistoryItem.ImageStream property. According to IntelliSense, the MediaHistoryItem.Source property is not used but we set it to "xap." We set MediaHistoryItem.Title to the desired name of the object, "Paris Skyline Video" and "Tour De France Video" for our two videos.

The MediaHistoryItem class contains a dictionary of key/value pairs stored in the PlayerContext property. The values stored in the PlayerContext property are made available to the application when the item is touched in the music+videos hub in the OnNavigatedTo method of the XAML page configured as the DefaultTask for the application in WMAppManifest.xml. I cover how to leverage this information in the section titled "Implement Playback from music+videos hub" later in this chapter.

We add a key/value pair to the MediaHistoryItem.PlayerContext Dictionary object. For our simple application, we just need one value to be stored with the MediaHistoryItem. For a more complex implementation, multiple values may be stored in order to facilitate accessing the media content when the item is selected in the music+videos hub.

The last bit of code is to add the new media item to the "New" section of the music+videos hub by calling the MediaHistory.Instance.WriteAcquiredItem method and passing in our newly created MediaHistoryItem. The next two subsections covers the code added to the VideoPlayerPage.xaml file in order to update the "Now playing" and "History" sections.

Update the music+videos "Now playing" Section

In VideoPlayerPage.xaml.cs we follow the same process as we did in the previous section and create a MediaHistoryItem each time content is played in the UpdateMusicPlusVideoAppNowPlaying() method. This method is called when the media is successfully opened in the VideoPlayer_MediaOpened event where playback begins with a call to VideoPlayer.Play.

We create a MediaHistoryItem but with a few modifications. The tile image is different for "Now playing" in terms of size, which is 358 x 358 pixels square. The other change is that we add a different key/value pair to MediaHistoryItem.PlayerContext using a key name of "videoHub". This helps us distinguish between values passed within app versus a value made available as a result of clicking on an item in the music+videos hub.

As covered in the previous section, the MediaHistoryItem object makes the PlayerContext values available to the music+videos hub and passes those values back to the application upon activation. The last bit of code in the UpdateMusicPlusVideoAppNowPlaying() method is that we assign the newly created MediaHistoryItem to the MediaHistory.Instance.NowPlaying property.

Update the music+videos "History" Section

In VideoPlayerPage.xaml.cs we follow the same process as we did in the previous section and create a MediaHistoryItem each time content is played in the UpdateMusicPlusVideoAppHistory() method. This method is called when the media is successfully opened in the VideoPlayer_MediaOpened event where playback begins with a call to VideoPlayer.Play.

As before the code acquires an image, this time the same 173 x 173 pixel tile that we display in the "New" section of the music+videos hub. This image includes the book logo in the upper left corner so that the content is associated with the application. This method also adds the "videoHub" key to the PlayerContext as before:

```
VideoMediaHistoryItem.PlayerContext.Add("videoHub", video);
```

The other code that is different when adding an item to the music+videos "History" section is a call to MediaHistory.Instance.WriteRecentPlay() method where the code passes in the newly created MediaHistoryItem.

Implement Playback from music+videos Hub

According to the AppHub certification requirements, the play back experience should display when media associated with the application is selected in the music+videos hub. This helps to provide the seamless experience of selecting media and having it immediately start playing without having to find the media by navigating the application.

The application implements a simple scheme to provide this experience by passing in to the application an ID that identifies the correct video. In the sample application, either "Paris" or "TDF" are passed in to identify the correct video. This value is captured in the OnNavigatedTo event of the DefaultTask XAML page, which in this application is MainPage.xaml. Here is the code from MainPage.xaml.cs:

```
protected override void OnNavigatedTo(
  System.Windows.Navigation.NavigationEventArgs e)
{
  base.OnNavigatedTo(e);

  if (NavigationContext.QueryString.Count > 0 &&
    NavigationContext.QueryString.ContainsKey("videoHub"))
  {
    NavigationService.Navigate(new Uri("/VideoPlayerPage.xaml?video=" +
        NavigationContext.QueryString["videoHub"], UriKind.Relative));
    NavigationContext.QueryString.Remove("videoHub");
  }
}
```

In general, there are two reasons why the MainPage.OnNavigatedTo event will fire for a XAML page. It will fire as a result of normal application startup with the passed-in query values if launched from the music+video hub, or because the Mainpage.xaml was activated as a result of a "Back" navigation from the VideoPlayerPage as part of normal application back stack function. If it is activated as a result of selecting media in the music+videos hub, the QueryString Dictionary object will contain the videoHub key/value pair that was associated with the item when it was initially added to the hub.

In the OnNavigatedTo method, the code checks to see if there are any values available in the NavigationContext.QueryString dictionary. If there is, it indicates that the page was activated from the music+videos hub as part of application start up. If this is the case, the application navigates to the VideoPlayerPage.xaml file, passing in the video name. It also removes the videoHub key so that we don't enter an endless loop of navigating back and forth between MainPage.xaml and VideoPlayerPage.xaml.

This completes our implementation of a music+videos hub application. In the next section, we shift gears and cover remote media consumption.

Microsoft Push Notification Services

In this section we cover how Microsoft push notifications work, when to use notifications, and how to add push notifications to your application. First we start with an overview of how Microsoft push Notifications work.

Microsoft Push Notification Services (MPNS) provides a facility to connect your Windows Phone 7 application to the server without requiring continuous polling by the application. Polling works and is functional, but if an application is continuously polling and the server response is "nothing to download," the application is potentially consuming battery without any user benefit.

▓ **Note** Push notifications are not a new concept in the industry. Other platforms include push notification services as well.

Another challenge with polling is that Windows Phone 7 does not support multitasking for third-party applications running on the device. Therefore, for an application to poll for data it must remain in the foreground as the active application. While not letting any third-party application to drain the battery polling for data in the background helps to enhance the end-user experience, applications still need to be able to react to application data and status changes even when not running.

Raw Push Notification Description

Microsoft Push Notification Services raw push notifications sends the actual data to the application. You can use raw notifications in addition to tile and toast notifications to send information directly to your application. It can be up to 1kb in size. The idea is to send a toast that something has happened and then send a raw notification to the application so that it can display the corresponding data when the application is launched.

Toast Push Notification Description

Microsoft Push Notification Services allows an application to receive notifications that data has been updated or application status has changed even when the application is not running. When a toast notification is received, the user receives a "toast," which is a little pop-up across the top of the screen that the user can click on, resulting in launching your application. Figure 6–15 shows a sample toast notification from the MSDN documentation.

Figure 6–15. Example toast notification

The toast notification is system generated. It displays over any application running, whether the Start screen or running application. If the application that expects to receive the notification is running, the toast notification is not displayed, but because the application is already running, the application simply processes and displays the data directly.

An important user experience consideration is to use toast notifications sparingly and with flexible configuration settings to help the user tune which notifications they are interested in receiving. The reason why is because toast notifications are disruptive, appearing over top any running application, even an action game.

■ **Note** First party applications such as the phone dialer and other built-in applications can multitask with a running third-party application, as well as with other first-party applications.

Tile Notification

Another type of notification is a tile notification, which updates the application tile if, and only if, the user decided to pin your application's tile to the Windows Phone 7 Start screen. Tile notifications can consist of a value for the tile Title value, a Count value (between 1 and 99), as well as a 173 x 173 background image for the tile. There are not any additional customizations available but with a little bit of server-side work your application can dynamically generate custom images for the tile background, which we cover further down in the chapter.

How Microsoft Push Notifications Work

For MPNS to work by sending important data to the user's phone, it implies some sort of server-side component to the Windows Phone 7 application receiving the notification, which is correct. Essentially MPNS is a proxy between the server-side component of your solution and the Windows Phone 7 application component. Figure 6–16 provides a graphical representation of how MPNS works.

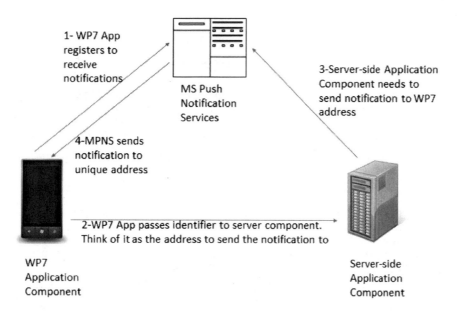

Figure 6–16. Microsoft Push Notification Services process flow

The user via their Windows Phone 7 phone initiates the request to MPNS. MPNS receives the request and passes a URI back to the application. The application then passes the URI to the server-side application component along with information on which notifications the user would like to receive such as scores for their favorite sports team.

The server-side component now has all the information it needs, the "address" to send the notification to via MPNS as well as the criteria the user has chosen for what notifications the user would like to receive.

Getting Started with Push Notifications

Note from Figure 6–16 that there is a server-side component that you must create in order to support push notifications. The server-side component performs the following two primary tasks:

- Receive registration requests and subscription criteria (i.e., send me a notification for breaking news regarding my favorite sports team) from the Windows Phone 7 application.

- Perform subscription matching and then send push notification requests to MPNS.

For all of the gory details on push notifications, I recommend reviewing the MSDN documentation to start:

`http://msdn.microsoft.com/en-us/library/ff402537(v=VS.92).aspx`

Also, there is a full set of Windows Phone 7 labs including labs on push notifications available here:

`www.microsoft.com/downloads/en/details.aspx?displaylang=en&FamilyID=ca23285f-bab8-47fa-b364-11553e076a9a`

For this section, I want to focus on the Windows Push Notification Server Side Helper Library created by the Microsoft evangelism team to assist developers quickly implement push notification services. The library supports sending all three push notification messages available, specifically Raw, Tile, and Toast. The library abstracts out the complexity of implementing push notifications to just a few lines of code for your application.

To get started, obtain a copy of the Push Notification Server Side Helper for WP7 "Recipe" from this link:

`http://create.msdn.com/en-us/education/catalog/article/pnhelp-wp7`

The sample code included with the download provides a very powerful example of how to work with the library it includes a "server" application as a Windows Presentation Foundation client. A real application could be a Windows Service or similar construct on other platforms.

What's great about the sample is that it demonstrates a dialog between the client and the server. For example, the client keeps the server aware of whether the user has pinned the application tile. Once the user has pinned the tile the server-side application is made aware and prepares to send tile updates. Even just switching tabs on the server-side WPF application results in UI updates via RAW notifications on the WP7 application. Run the sample to see it in action.

Updating Application Tile Without Push Notification Services

Microsoft has done research that indicates end-users like applications that support live tiles. It promotes "at a glance" information delivery, such as when the Outlook tile indicates the number of unread messages. As mentioned in the previous section, Microsoft Push Notification Services provides fine-grained control over tile updates for maximum personalization.

There are situations where an ISV develops an application that doesn't need full push notification functionality but the ISV would still like to support tile updates. Windows Phone 7 provides a client-side pull API that allows an application to update its pinned tile on a pre-defined basis of every hour, every day, or every week. No other update schedule is available. Delivery times will vary within the specified schedule meaning if an application registers for a tile update on a daily basis, the tile update can happen at any time within that time period. Still, this can provide a simple way to add a Live Tile to an application.

The API that provides this functionality is the `Microsoft.Phone.Shell.ShellTileSchedule` API. The API takes a URI to a web service or image located on a web site as well as an interval setting. Listing 6–15 shows the code.

Listing 6–15. ShellTileNotificationSample MainPage.xaml.cs

```
using System;
using Microsoft.Phone.Controls;
using Microsoft.Phone.Shell;

namespace ShellTileNotificationSample
{
  public partial class MainPage : PhoneApplicationPage
  {
    // Constructor
    public MainPage()
    {
      InitializeComponent();
    }
    //store as global variable so that the schedule
    //can be Started and Stopped.
    private ShellTileSchedule shellTileSchedule;
    private void StartShellTileAppBarBtn_Click(object sender, EventArgs e)
    {
      StartShellTileSchedule();
    }

    private void StartShellTileSchedule()
    {
      shellTileSchedule = new ShellTileSchedule();
      shellTileSchedule.Recurrence = UpdateRecurrence.Interval;
      shellTileSchedule.Interval = UpdateInterval.EveryHour;
      shellTileSchedule.StartTime = DateTime.Now;
      shellTileSchedule.RemoteImageUri =
        new Uri(@"http://apress.com/resource/bookcover/9781430232193?size=medium");
      shellTileSchedule.Start();
    }

    private void StopShellTileAppBarBtn_Click(object sender, EventArgs e)
    {
      if (shellTileSchedule != null)
        shellTileSchedule.Stop();
    }
  }
}
```

Create a private variable for the ShellTileSchedule instance so that you can stop it at a later time if the user decides for some reason to want to turn off Live Tile updates. In this example, two application bar buttons titled start and stop control the schedule. Once the tile is pinned it can take up the full interval time before it is updated.

Tile updates do not occur if the phone is in an idle state, meaning the screen is off or the lock screen is visible. As soon as the screen is on and unlocked the tile will update. Figure 6–17 shows the updated tile.

Figure 6–17. *Live tile update*

The image at the URI must be less than 80KB in size with a maximum download time of 15 seconds. If the API cannot download the image within 15 seconds three consecutive times the schedule will be removed.

You can have more than one ShellTileSchedule available in your application, although only one schedule can be active at a time. As an example, let's say you are building an application that provides news coverage for all 32 NFL football teams. You could create 32 URIs that are updated with team specific content and present a menu to the user that says something like "which team would you like to get live tile updates for?" Once the user selects a team, create the corresponding ShellTileSchedule to that team's URI, and voila! Customized live tile updates with just a few lines of code.

Localization

At launch, Windows Phone 7 supported the English, French, Italian, and German languages. Otherwise known as EFIGs. At Mobile World Congress 2011, Microsoft announced that more languages will be added in 2011. Supporting multiple languages can increase the market share for your application. Luckily Windows Phone 7 provides full localization support just as what is available in the full .NET Framework.

There is extensive documentation available on localization in .NET. Here is a link to the localization best practices for Windows Phone:

```
http://msdn.microsoft.com/en-us/library/ff967552(v=VS.92).aspx
```

This link describes how to build a localized application for Windows Phone:

```
http://msdn.microsoft.com/en-us/library/ff637520(VS.92).aspx
```

Conclusion

This chapter is the last chapter on Silverlight for Windows Phone development, and it covers a lot of ground. It starts off with a discussion of advanced data binding techniques, how to lazy load images for a ListBox, as well as how to data bind to any type using the IValueConverter interface.

Encryption Services available in Windows Phone 7 are covered as well, describing capabilities and precautions when it comes to securing data. The chapter shifts gears to a discussion of the Image classes and capabilities, as well as the MediaLibrary APIs.

The chapter moves on to covering two key integration capabilities, how to build a Photos Extra application as well as a music+video hub application. Along the way, the chapter covers audio and video support and capabilities.

Finally the chapter concludes with a discussion of Microsoft Push Notification Services and ends with a short overview on Localization, as there is broad coverage of localization in the .NET Framework MSDN documentation.

In the next two chapters, the book shifts gears, focusing exclusively on building 2D and 3D development with the XNA Framework.

CHAPTER 7

■ ■ ■

Building 2D Games with the XNA Framework

In this and the next chapter, we won't be covering Silverlight. These two chapters are 100 percent dedicated to game development with XNA Game Studio, which is a free Visual Studio add-on that ships with the Windows Phone Developer Tools.

If you jumped straight to this chapter in the book, first please review the extensive introduction to XNA Game Studio development in Chapter 1. Chapter 3 focuses on user input. It also contains several examples based on XNA Game Studio development related to touch and accelerometer input. In Chapter 6, we discussed how to work with the XNA Media Library APIs, playing music, displaying image art, and the like. I recommend reviewing those chapters prior to diving in here.

In general, it is impossible to cover the full range of game development in just two chapters, so we take an optimized approach that builds on existing samples available at Microsoft's AppHub website, which is located at `http://create.msdn.com`. There are quite a few samples based on the XNA Framework that we leverage in this chapter to jumpstart game development. Why reinvent a game screen or menu framework when there are tried and true samples that we can leverage while covering key concepts of game development?

■ **Note** The AppHub samples are available under the Microsoft Permissive License (Ms-PL) license, which you can download and review at `http://create.msdn.com/downloads/?id=15`.

I'm not a lawyer, so I won't provide an opinion on the license – but please do download and read it.

Xbox LIVE Gamer Services

A hot topic of interest to indie game developers is access to Xbox LIVE gamer services. Xbox LIVE gamer services provide matchmaking, Achievements, Leaderboards, etc. support to Xbox games. You can find more information here:

`http://msdn.microsoft.com/en-us/library/microsoft.xna.framework.gamerservices.aspx`

On Windows Phone 7, a subset of Xbox LIVE gamer services is available to Xbox LIVE publishers. Example Xbox Live game publishers are Microsoft Game Studios, Electronic Arts, and Gameloft. Generally, a game developer works with an existing Xbox LIVE game publisher to ship a game that includes Xbox LIVE gamer services. It is difficult for a new game developer to immediately become an Xbox LIVE game publisher. It is a high bar; just look at the names of existing publishers.

So for an indie game developer, create an awesome game or possibly a fully fleshed out concept as the first step to gain access to Xbox LIVE gamer services. The next step is to get your game in front of an existing Xbox LIVE game publisher. Microsoft Game Studios currently has an e-mail alias to which you can send proposals: wpgame@microsoft.com. The other way to get noticed is to submit your finished game to AppHub and climb the popularity charts. An existing proven success as an indie publisher will help you get noticed.

Don't lose hope if you have your heart set on Xbox LIVE gamer services. Initially, the services were not available to Xbox Indie game publishers as part of create.msdn.com, but the services were eventually made available to indie game publishers on big Xbox. One can hope that in the future more Xbox LIVE gamer services become available to indie developers on Windows Phone 7 as well.

In the next section we will begin a journey of taking the HelloXNA project from Chapter 1 and turn it into a full-fledged game with a menu system, score keeping, options, tombstone support, and the like – all of the things you need to consider when building a game for Windows Phone 7.

Alien Shooter

Back in Chapter 1, we covered XNA Game Studio development fundamentals in the HelloXNA sample. The sample covered game loop basics with a very simple UI that had a hero ship that shot a missile at the alien attacker ship. As you recall, XNA is not event driven. Rather, it checks status on objects and input (polls) in a type loop that tries to ensure that the screen is drawn at 30 frames/second. Frame rate can drop if a game spends too much time "thinking" when updating objects. Here is a summary of how this works:

```
while (Game.IsRunning)
{
  Update();  //Perform calculations, update objects, handle input
  Draw();  //Draw background, objects, effects
}
```

The HelloXNA sample isn't really much of a "game," because there wasn't any interactivity. It essentially loaded up content and initialized state in the Game.LoadContent method. The Update method did some screen bounds checking and reset objects when they flew off the screen, and then the objects were rendered in the Draw method. In the HelloXNA sample, you cannot move the hero ship and the one attacker appears on the screen at the same place. In this section we will turn it into a "real" game with a menu, score, movable hero ship, and more worthy opponents in the alien attackers.

In the next section, we turn the HelloXNA game into a real game in the Chapter 7 AlienShooter sample project. The AlienShooter game will include a main menu, options menu, and actual game play. We introduce a Game Management sample that provides a ScreenManager class, a Menu class, and GameScreen objects to manage game functions. The game is modularized into individual screen classes, so you can have a screen that shows the main menu, a screen that shows the options for the game, and so on, as well as a screen that actually handles game play. By following these best practices your game will have a professional look and feel as well as be more maintainable. In subsequent sections we cover how to add basic animations and effects to provide more interesting game play.

From Demo to Game

This section covers how to add the game management and screens to the AlienShooter sample project. We start by creating the Chapter 7 code solution with a project named AlienShooter based on the XNA Game Studio 4.0 Windows Phone 7 Game (4.0) project template. The best way to start creating a "real" game is to base it on the Game State Management sample, which includes a main menu, an options screen, some gameplay, and a pause menu. It displays a loading screen between menus and gameplay with a popup message box to confirm that a user intends to quit. You can download the sample here:

http://create.msdn.com/en-US/education/catalog/sample/game_state_management

---

■ **Tip** Right-click on the .zip and select "unblock" to ensure that security checks don't prevent you from being able to compile and run the application.

When you deploy the GameStateManagementSample (Phone) sample, notice that the game does not show up in the Games Hub, but is instead in the application list. The Genre attribute on the App element in the WMManifest.xml file determines where an application appears. The default is Genre="Apps.Normal" so that the application appears in the Application List. Change the genre attribute to Genre="Apps.Games" to have the game show up in the Games Hub.

Run the GameStateManagementSample (Phone) sample project to see the nice animations and transitions available with this sample. Let's get started by transitioning the AlienShooter sample to this format and then we will add in the code from Chapter 1's sample named HelloXNA. From there we will refactor to make the game interactive.

■ **Tip** Close the Toolbox tool window to give yourself more space when working with XNA Game Studio games since there aren't components relevant in the Toolbox tool window.

With both the AlienShooter and GameStateManagementSample (Phone) sample projects open, we first create two new folders in AlienShooter named Screens and GameManagement. Copy the contents of the ScreenManager folder in the GameStateManagementSample (Phone) sample project to the GameManagement folder in the AlienShooter project. Copy the Screens folder content to the Screens folder content in the AlienShooter project.

Once copied over, select the option to Show All Files at the top of the Solutions Tool Window in Visual Studio. The next step is to right-click on the files in Visual Studio and select Include In Project to add them to the AlienShooter project. Be sure to fix up the namespaces by changing them from GameStateManagement to AlienShooter.GameManagement for the GameManagement folder content and to AlienShooter.Screens for the Screens folder content. You will also need to add a using AlienShooter.GameManagement; statement to all of the code files in the Screens folder as well. After fixing everything up the application should compile without any errors or warnings.

Next open the GameStateManagementSample (Phone) Content project folder and copy over all of the content files to the AlienShooterContent project folder using Windows Explorer except for the Content.contentproj file. As before, select the option to Show All Files in Visual Studio 2010, and then include the files into the AlienShooterContent project folder. We decide to split the content between GameManagement content and actual game content. Create a new folder in the AlienShooterContent project named GameManagement and copy menufont.spritefont and blank.png into the AlienShooterContent project GameManagement folder. The rest of the content is related to game play, which we will eventually replace anyway.

Next we go through the GameStateManagementSample (Phone) project's Game1.cs and modify the AlienShooter Game1.cs to match the game state sample's Game.cs file. First, rename the Game1 class to

AlienShooterGame and rename the code file Game1.cs to AlienShooterGame.cs. You will notice right away that the default spriteBatch private variable is not present in the game state sample, which suggests that the Game1.Draw and Game1.Update methods must not perform any game logic in this code file. Instead, there is a private field variable named screenManager of type ScreenManager that is added. Add a using AlienShooter.GameManagement; statement to the top of AlienshooterGame.cs as well.

We next move to the Constructor AlienShooterGame() and modify it to match the game state sample's GameStateManagementGame constructor as shown in Listing 7–1.

Listing 7–1. AlienShooterGame Constructor

```
public AlienShooterGame()
{
  graphics = new GraphicsDeviceManager(this);
  Content.RootDirectory = "Content";
  TargetElapsedTime = TimeSpan.FromTicks(333333);

  // you can choose whether you want a landscape or portrait
  // game by using one of the two helper functions defined below
  InitializePortraitGraphics();
  // InitializeLandscapeGraphics();

  // Create the screen manager component.
  screenManager = new ScreenManager(this);

  Components.Add(screenManager);

  // attempt to deserialize the screen manager from disk. if that
  // fails, we add our default screens.
  if (!screenManager.DeserializeState())
  {
    // Activate the first screens.
    screenManager.AddScreen(new BackgroundScreen(), null);
    screenManager.AddScreen(new MainMenuScreen(), null);
  }
}
```

The code file defines two helper functions that set whether the game is a portrait or landscape game. Listing 7–2 has the code for the two helper functions.

Listing 7–2. Helper Functions to Configure Portrait or Landscape Game

```
private void InitializePortraitGraphics()
{
  graphics.PreferredBackBufferWidth = 480;
  graphics.PreferredBackBufferHeight = 800;
}

private void InitializeLandscapeGraphics()
{
  graphics.PreferredBackBufferWidth = 800;
  graphics.PreferredBackBufferHeight = 480;
}
```

The next bit of code in Listing 7–1 for the AlienShooterGame constructor creates the ScreenManager and then adds it to the Components collection for the Microsoft.Xna.Framework.Game base class.

Component classes inherit from the Microsoft.Xna.Framework.DrawableGameComponent class, which attempts to modularize game development by providing the ability to have objects Update and Draw themselves without forcing all of that logic into the default Game.Draw and Game.Update methods. The ScreenManager class inherits from DrawableGameComponent and handles all of the actual Draw and Update logic for the game. I cover the ScreenManager class in detail in just a bit, so let's continue updating our AlienShooterGame (formerly Game1.cs) code file to get our game up and running. The last section of the AlienShooterGame constructor attempts to load the ScreenManager instance from disk. If it cannot, it loads the default screens to start the game.

The code overrides Game.OnExiting to serialize game state to disk in this event handler to set up state for the next time the game launches.

```
protected override void OnExiting(object sender, System.EventArgs args)
{
  // serialize the screen manager whenever the game exits
  screenManager.SerializeState();

  base.OnExiting(sender, args);
}
```

Unlike in Chapter 1, where all of our code was packed into Game1.cs, AlienShooterGame.cs does not perform any code in Update or in Draw. For our new version of the application, we use the ScreenManager to do work for us so we remove the LoadContent, UnloadContent, and Update methods from AlienShooterGame.cs. We modify Game.Draw to set the background color to Color.Black from Color.CornflowerBlue but otherwise this completes our edits for this file.

In order to test our work, we need to modify where GameManagement content is loaded from because remember that we placed that content inside of a GameManagement folder in the AlienShooterContent project. Open up the ScreenManager class and find the LoadContent override. Modify the load locations like this:

```
font = content.Load<SpriteFont>("GameManagement/menufont");
blankTexture = content.Load<Texture2D>("GameManagement/blank");
```

Once the above edits are completed, test and run and the AlienShooter project should work just like the GameStateManagementSample (Phone) sample project with a bit of code and content reorganization under the covers. You can choose to follow these steps by hand in your project or simply grab the AlienShooter project and rename the namespaces, game class, and screen classes to match your application. In the next section we go through the Game Management related classes located in the GameManagement folder to help you understand what's going on under the covers so that you can further customize the game to meet your needs.

Game Management

The GameManagement folder contains three class files, GameScreen.cs, InputState.cs, and ScreenManager.cs. The ScreenManager class orchestrates loading GameScreen objects and transitions between GameScreen objects for you. The GameScreen abstract base class contains all of the underlying plumbing code to plug into the Game Management framework and is the base class for objects declared in the Screens folder. The InputState class collects Keyboard, Gamepad, and TouchPanel inputs. For Windows Phone 7, TouchPanel input is primary, though some devices support a keyboard as well. Figure 7–1 shows the class diagram for the Game Management classes.

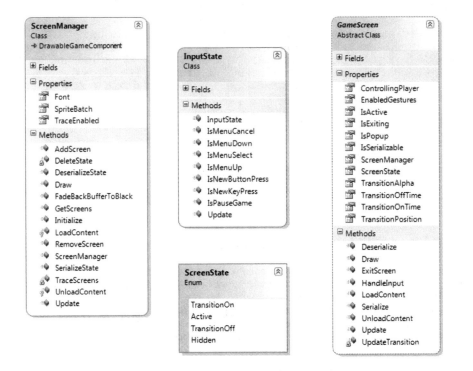

Figure 7–1. Game Management framework

The ScreenManager class is a DrawableGameComponent, while the GameScreen base class is not. The ScreenManager manages one or more screen classes that inherit from GameScreen. ScreenManager maintains a stack of screens, calls their Update and Draw methods at the appropriate times, and automatically routes input to the top most active screen.

You will notice that DrawableGameComponent looks very similar to the Game class. There are method overrides available for LoadContent, UnloadContent, Update, and Draw, much like the Game class. Under the covers the XNA Framework keeps the main Game class and available DrawableGameComponents in sync with respect to the Update and Draw methods, so that the developer can just focus on each individual component and screen.

In the ScreenManager.Draw and ScreenManager.Update methods, each screen is given an opportunity to process input, and either Update or Draw itself if it is the active screen. The ScreenManager's framework provides nice transition support for fade-in and fade-out of screens as the user navigates the game. If you like the way things work as is, you can just focus on your menu, options, game play screen, etc., and the framework takes care of the rest.

Screens and Menus

Now that we have covered the game management plumbing provided by the ScreenManager class, we will switch focus to the UX aspects of screens and menu. There are several screens in the project that were copied over from the Game Management sample that provide the starter UI. We go through these screens in this section.

The BackgroundScreen class sits behind all of the other menu screens. It draws a background image that remains fixed in place regardless of whatever transitions that other screens may implement. The content that is loaded is the background.png. Swap the background.png file with your default background image.

The MainMenuScreen class is the first screen that is loaded by the game. It displays the main menu items of Play and Options. The OptionsMenuScreen class is displayed over the main menu screen. It provides the user a chance to configure the game. Figure 7–2 shows the default Main Menu and Options Menu screens.

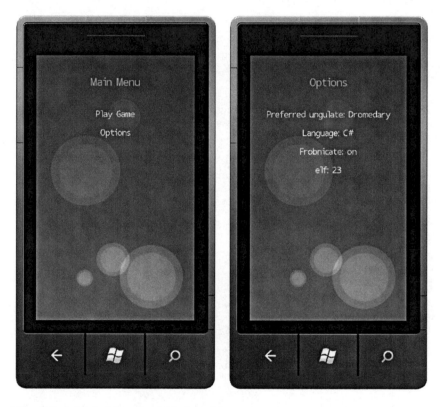

Figure 7–2. Main Menu and Options Menu

The menu items have a nice "Metro" transition when flying in and out. Individual menu items are still graphic items with additional logic to detect a touch and fire an event. The MenuEntry class provides menu item functionality. Here is the constructor for the OptionsMenuScreen class:

```
public OptionsMenuScreen()
    : base("Options")
{
    // Create our menu entries.
    ungulateMenuEntry = new MenuEntry(string.Empty);
```

```
        languageMenuEntry = new MenuEntry(string.Empty);
        frobnicateMenuEntry = new MenuEntry(string.Empty);
        elfMenuEntry = new MenuEntry(string.Empty);

        SetMenuEntryText();

        // Hook up menu event handlers.
        ungulateMenuEntry.Selected += UngulateMenuEntrySelected;
        languageMenuEntry.Selected += LanguageMenuEntrySelected;
        frobnicateMenuEntry.Selected += FrobnicateMenuEntrySelected;
        elfMenuEntry.Selected += ElfMenuEntrySelected;

        // Add entries to the menu.
        MenuEntries.Add(ungulateMenuEntry);
        MenuEntries.Add(languageMenuEntry);
        MenuEntries.Add(frobnicateMenuEntry);
        MenuEntries.Add(elfMenuEntry);
    }
```

The MenuEntries collection in the OptionsMenuScreen constructor is a protected member of the MenuScreen base class for the MainMenuScreen and OptionsMenuScreen classes. The MenuScreen.Draw and MenuScreen.Update methods measure and position menu entries for drawing to the screen. The MenuScreen class includes the sliding transitions logic for menu items in case you want to modify it.

Click on a menu item to view the transition to a new screen. The loading screen inherits from the GameScreen class coordinates transitions between the menu system and the game itself. Normally one screen will transition off at the same time as the next screen is transitioning on, but for larger transitions that can take a longer time to load their data; we want the menu system to be entirely gone before we start loading the game. This is done as follows:

- Tell all the existing screens to transition off.

- Activate a loading screen, which will transition on at the same time.

- The loading screen watches the state of the previous screens.

- When the loading screen sees they have finished transitioning off, it activates the real next screen, which may take a long time to load its data. The loading screen will be the only thing displayed while this load is taking place.

This concludes the overview of the Game Management ScreenManager, GameScreen, MenuScreen, and MenuEntry classes. In the next section we dive in and start to customize the template game for the AlienShooter game.

AlienShooter Game Structure

In this section, we begin customizing the game management starter project with content and game logic. We start by adding the content from the original game in Chapter 1 to AlienShooter. We copy over the Sprites and Textures folder and remove background.png, which is the generic XNA Framework sample image.

Content Project

When you create a new XNA project, it always creates two projects, one project for your game and the other for your content. The Content project provides compile-time processing for game assets, including detecting missing assets, asset conversion, compression, and pre-processing. The key component to the Content project is the Content Pipeline.

Content Pipeline

The content pipeline does the work of preparing assets for use within an XNA Framework game. Assets are processed in two steps. The first step is importing the content. For the majority of formats, XNA has Content Importer classes to convert content into a common intermediate format. The second step converts the imported content into a final compiled, compressed, format via a Content Processor.

Importing the Content

Importing content is as simple as adding new items to the Content project. In most cases, the content pipeline automatically detects the asset type and assigns the correct Content Importer and Content Processor. It is also possible to create custom Content Importer and Content Processor classes for assets not supported by the built-in classes.

In the Chapter 1 HelloXNA sample we demonstrate how to load content a single texture at a time using this code from the LoadContent method:

```
HeroShip = this.Content.Load<Texture2D>("Sprites/heroship");
SpaceShip = this.Content.Load<Texture2D>("Sprites/spaceship");
Missile = this.Content.Load<Texture2D>("Sprites/missile");
```

Each content item is loaded into a single texture. When drawn, each item requires its texture to be loaded by the GPU and rendered. The above items are drawn to the screen with these three lines of code in the Draw method:

```
spriteBatch.Draw(SpaceShip, SpaceShipPosition, Color.White);
spriteBatch.Draw(Missile, MissilePosition, Color.White);
spriteBatch.Draw(HeroShip, HeroShipPosition, Color.White);
```

Loading each texture is a performance hit for the GPU. A better way is to load a single texture that contains all of the images, and then just tell Draw which area of the texture to draw for that item. This type of texture is called a sprite sheet and is very common to use in game development, especially when creating sprite animation, which we will cover later in the chapter. There are two challenges with using sprite sheets: you have to take all of your individual images and mash them into a larger image, and you have to remember which part of the single large texture contains the particular image you want to draw to the screen.

Luckily AppHub comes to the rescue again with a ready-to-go custom Content Importer and Content Processor that can take a collection of images and automatically turn them into a single sprite sheet, solving the first challenge. For the complete background on the sample, download it here:

```
http://create.msdn.com/en-US/education/catalog/sample/sprite_sheet
```

The sample also includes a runtime class to include in your game named SpriteSheet, which allows either named or indexed access to images so that you do not have to remember the exact pixel location, solving the second challenge listed previously.

We implement the SpriteSheet sample in AlienShooter by copying over the SpriteSheetPipeline and SpriteSheetRuntime (Phone) projects from the AppHub SpriteSheetSample and adding them to the

Chapter 7 Solution. Right-click the References folder in the AlienShooterContent project, select Add Reference, choose the Projects tab, and select the SpriteSheetPipeline project. Next, right-click on the References folder in the AlienShooter project and select Add Reference, choose the Projects tab, and select the SpriteSheetRuntime (Phone) project.

In the AlienShooterContent project navigate to the Sprites folder and exclude from the project these assets: heroship.tga, missile.tga, and spaceship.tga. We don't want to add the textures twice, so they should not be included as individual assets any more. Next, right-click on the Sprites folder and select Add | New Item… and choose XML File with a name of AlienShooterSpriteSheet.xml. Listing 7–3 shows the edited XML file.

Listing 7–3. AlienShooterSpriteSheet.xml Sprite Sheet XML File

```xml
<?xml version="1.0" encoding="utf-8" ?>
<XnaContent>
  <Asset Type="System.String[]">
    <Item>Sprites/heroship.tga</Item>
    <Item>Sprites/missile.tga</Item>
    <Item>Sprites/spaceship.tga</Item>
  </Asset>
</XnaContent>
```

If you don't edit the file correctly, you will get a compile error if the SpriteSheetPipeline Content Processor cannot find an asset listed in the XML file. Notice in this example that the folder location is included relative to the AlienShooterContent project to correctly identify the asset location. Figure 7–3 shows the Solution tool window with the AlienShooterContent project expanded and the Properties dialog for the AlienShooterSpriteSheet.xml.

Notice in Figure 7–3 that the individual sprite images are hidden and not part of the project in the Sprites folder, though they need to be accessible in the file system to the SpriteSheetProcessor Content Processor so that it can turn them into a single sprite sheet. The only content that is part of the Sprites folder is the AlienShooterSpriteSheet.xml XML file. Also in Figure 7–3, notice that the custom SpriteSheetProcessor Content Processor is configured for the XML file. Let's now draw update the GamePlay screen to start to render our new AlienShooter assets. A using SpriteSheetRuntime statement is added to the top of the GamePlay.cs code file. Three new private fields are added at the top of the GamePlayScreen class:

```
SpriteSheet alienShooterSpriteSheet;
Texture2D backgroundTexture;
Rectangle screenRect;
```

The alienShooterSpriteSheet variable will let us render the entire sprite sheet to the screen for debug purposes. The backgroundTexture variable represents our game background as with the HelloXNA sample and the screenRect variable holds a variable that points to the Rectangle object that is the size of the draw area.

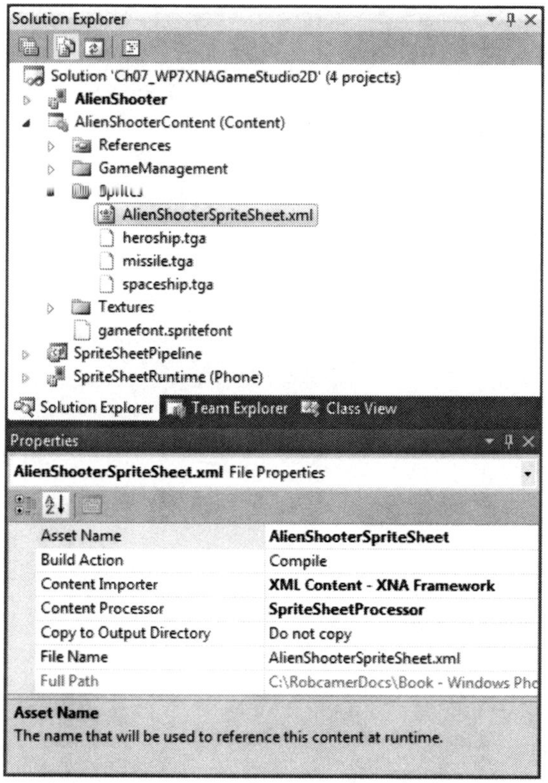

Figure 7–3. Solution and Content project after SpriteSheet modifications

The LoadContent method is updated to load the alienShooterSpriteSheet SpriteSheet and backgroundTexture Texture2D variables:

```
alienShooterSpriteSheet = content.Load<SpriteSheet>("Sprites/AlienShooterSpriteSheet");
backgroundTexture = content.Load<Texture2D>("Textures/background");
```

Most of the code in the Update and HandleInput methods is commented out since we no longer want the place holder code. The placeholder draw code is modified in the Draw method, and the following two additional items are added to draw the backgroundTexture and the alienShooterSpriteSheet to the screen:

```
spriteBatch.Begin();
//Draw background
spriteBatch.Draw(backgroundTexture, screenRect, Color.White);
//Draw Sprite Sheet
spriteBatch.Draw(alienShooterSpriteSheet.Texture,
  new Rectangle(screenRect.Width / 2, screenRect.Height / 2,
                alienShooterSpriteSheet.Texture.Width / 2,
                alienShooterSpriteSheet.Texture.Height / 2),
    Color.White);
spriteBatch.End();
```

Everything should compile and the game now shows AlienShooter assets on the GamePlayScreen, as shown in Figure 7–4.

Figure 7–4. *AlienShooter SpriteSheet and background textures*

Notice how tightly the Hero Spaceship, Missile, and Alien Ship are automatically packed in Figure 7–4 by the custom Content Processor. Just to close the loop, the code to draw an individual image from the AlienShooterSpriteSheet is very simple. Here is the code to just draw the Hero Spaceship at a point in the middle of the screen:

```
spriteBatch.Draw(alienShooterSpriteSheet.Texture,
    new Vector2((screenRect.Width / 2)-
            alienShooterSpriteSheet.SourceRectangle("heroship").Width / 2,
                (screenRect.Height / 2)-
            alienShooterSpriteSheet.SourceRectangle("heroship").Height / 2),
    alienShooterSpriteSheet.SourceRectangle("heroship"),
```

There is a verbose computation to create a Vector2 for the screen center minus the center of the Hero Ship, but otherwise it is the standard Draw(texture, Vector, SourceRectangle, Color) method. Notice how easy it is to identify the Rectangle on the alienShooterSpriteSheet where the Hero Ship resides. Just pass in the asset name and the SpriteSheet class will locate it. More on drawing later in the chapter, but I wanted to close out how to completely work with the SpriteSheet class.

When you download the SpriteSheet Sample from AppHub, it includes an example extension on how to add a compression option to the Content Processor. Unfortunately the extension does not work for the XNA Game Studio 4.0 Reach profile. It just works for the HiDef profile.

▦ **Tip** The "Reach" profile limits XNA Game Studio to a subset of functions supported on Windows Phone, Xbox, and Windows for maximum compatibility. The "HiDef" profile supports only Xbox and Windows. It includes support for custom HLSL shaders as well as additional features.

We dive into creating a more robust game below but first let's cover some of the other constructs for a real game such as displaying game status text and menus, which is covered in the next section.

Text and Menus

Displayed text, such as game status and menus, is an important component of game development. Users want a nice clean menu system to navigate. Game status is critical to game play; it makes the game interesting such as how much life is left, high score, rounds of ammunition available, and the like.

There are two methods to display text in the XNA Framework. The first is via the SpriteFont class. The SpriteFont class leverages the built in Font classes on your PC to create the font texture to display letter character images when rendered. The SpriteFont class is covered in the next section.

The other method to display text in the XNA Framework is with customized bitmap fonts. This method is more advanced, which means it is highly customizable but also requires additional work. To demonstrate working with fonts a new project named FontsSample is added to the Chapter 7 solution.

SpriteFont

The SpriteFont class takes a built in font and rasterizes it based on configuration parameters. To add a text Font for rendering in XNA Game Studio, right-click on the FontsSampleContent project and select Add ➤ Item… ➤ select Sprite Font, and enter a name. Usually, you name the Sprite Font item the same as the Font Name. If you include multiple sizes append the size to the end, which will make more sense in a bit.

While we take fonts for granted when working in Microsoft Word or in Outlook, fonts are licensed content. You must have redistribution rights to include a font in your game. Search the Web for "purchase fonts online" and quite a few sites show up. Some include free fonts with others for purchase.

Luckily XNA Game Studio 4.0 includes a set of OpenTypefonts you can use in your games. Figure 7–5 shows the fonts that are licensed by Microsoft for your use. The image is taken from the AppHub education catalog.

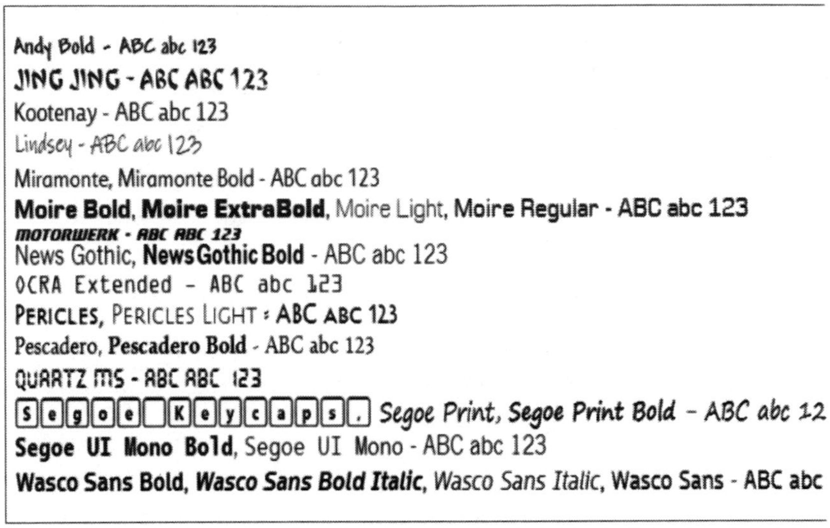

Figure 7–5. Fonts provided by XNA Game Studio for use in XNA framework games

For our sample, name the new Sprite Font item SegoeKeycaps24 and click Add. A new item named SegoeKeycaps16.spritefont is added to the FontSampleContent project. What may surprise you is that the SegoeKeycaps16.spritefont file is an XML file. Listing 7–4 shows the contents of the newly added file.

Listing 7–4. SpriteFont XML File Format

```xml
<?xml version="1.0" encoding="utf-8"?>
<XnaContent xmlns:Graphics="Microsoft.Xna.Framework.Content.Pipeline.Graphics">
  <Asset Type="Graphics:FontDescription">
    <FontName>Segoe UI Mono</FontName>
    <Size>14</Size>
    <Spacing>0</Spacing>
    <UseKerning>true</UseKerning>
    <Style>Regular</Style>
    <!-- <DefaultCharacter>*</DefaultCharacter> -->
    <CharacterRegions>
      <CharacterRegion>
        <Start>&#32;</Start>
        <End>&#126;</End>
      </CharacterRegion>
    </CharacterRegions>
  </Asset>
</XnaContent>
```

The XML file describes the parameters for what should be rendered when text is drawn using this SpriteFont. For our example, change the FontName element to Segoe Keycaps. Change the Size to 16 and leave everything else at the default values.

You can edit the Spacing element to increase the space between characters, as well as modify the UseKerning item to modify how the font is laid out. Kerning adjusts the spacing between characters to be more pleasing to the eye. An example of kerning is when a capital "W" overhangs a neighboring "e" slightly when typing the word "Well." Without kerning, letters do not overhang or underhang as the case may be. The Style element indicates whether it should be Regular, Bold, or Italic.

The last element to discuss is the CharacterRegions element. CharacterRegions element controls what letters are available in the font. The default range is 32 (ASCII space) to 126 (ASCHII '~'). This reduces the number of characters rasterized as part of the content import process.

To draw the SegoeKeycaps16 Sprite Font, add a new private member named segoeKeycaps16 of type SpriteFont to the Game1 class in the FontSample project. Next add this line of code to the Game1.LoadContent method.

```
segoeKeycaps16 = Content.Load<SpriteFont>("SegoeKeycaps16");
```

We used the SpriteBatch.Draw method to draw textures to the screen. The SpriteBatch.DrawString method has six overloads to provide flexibility in drawing text to the screen. Here are a couple of examples:

```
spriteBatch.DrawString(segoeKeycaps24, text, new Vector2(24, 130), Color.Yellow);

spriteBatch.DrawString(segoeKeycaps24, text, new Vector2(24, 450), Color.Orange,
    -.25f * (float)Math.PI, Vector2.Zero, 3, SpriteEffects.None, 0);
```

You can tinge the font color by adjusting the fourth parameter with a color value such as Color.Yellow. The second DrawString call above applies a –negative 45 degree rotation in the fifth parameter and a 300 percent scale in the sixth parameter, with an orange tinge applied to the Sprite Font. Another font is added to the project named Miramonte with Italics style and a few more DrawString calls are in the code but Figure 7–6 shows the results.

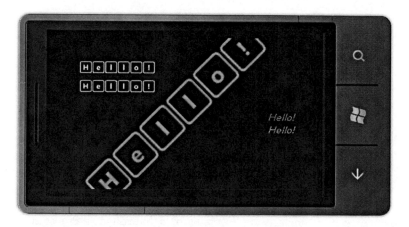

Figure 7–6. DrawString examples with the SpriteFont class

The scaled font renders pretty well but you can see some stretching in the letter "e" in Figure 7–6 that could be more obvious with other fonts. In the next section we cover how to create a bitmap font.

Bitmap Fonts

Bitmap fonts are not dependent on a built-in font. Instead, the fonts are loaded from a texture similar to what is shown in Figure 7–7.

Figure 7–7. *Bitmap font texture example*

The example in Figure 7–7was copied from MSDN by zooming in the browser by 200% and taking a screenshot, but you can create a custom bitmap font texture using any drawing program by following the conventions specified in the documentation.

The character order matters, with a space as the upper-left character. You can use a solid white or black background color for monochrome characters. In the previous example, black is used as the background color. Multicolored characters are supported with an alpha channel.

The space between characters must be filled with Magenta color (Red:255 Green:0 Blue:255 Alpha:255). The FontTextureProcessor class is applied to the texture instead of the default processor. The FontTextureProcessor will pack the characters in as close as possible so you don't have to worry about exact spacing between characters.

A new project named BitmapFontSample is added to the Chapter 7 solution. The bitmap font texture in Figure 7–7 is added to the BitmapFontSampleContent project with a name of BitmapFont.bmp. The Content Processor is configured to Sprite Font Texture - XNA Framework from the default of Texture - XNA Framework.

The SpriteFont class is still used as the member type for the bitmapFont object and the bitmap font is loaded in LoadContent just like for a regular SpriteFont content:

```
SpriteFont bitmapFont;
…//Load Content
bitmapFont = Content.Load<SpriteFont>("BitmapFont");
```

Drawing is the same as well with the DrawString method:

```
spriteBatch.Begin();
spriteBatch.DrawString(bitmapFont, text, new Vector2(24, 70), Color.White);
spriteBatch.End();
```

In summary, the primary differences when using a custom bitmap font is that you must draw out the characters correctly in the proper order and you configure the Content Processor to Sprite Font Texture - XNA Framework for the bitmap font texture.

MenuScreen Class

The MenuScreen class is part of the GameStateManagementSample (Phone) sample project. It is the base class for the MainMenu.cs and OptionsMenu.cs screen objects that are part of the AlienShooter game project.

The MenuScreen class takes advantage of a helper class named MenuEntry, which draws the text and publishes a Selected event. The MenuEntry class does not detect the touch. Instead, the MenuScreen does most of the work to draw, detect a touch, and associate the touch with the correct `MenuEntry` item. A good way to understand how this works is to look at the constructor for the `MainMenuScreen` class:

```
public MainMenuScreen()
    : base("Main Menu")
{
    // Create our menu entries.
    MenuEntry playGameMenuEntry = new MenuEntry("Play Game");
    MenuEntry optionsMenuEntry = new MenuEntry("Options");

    // Hook up menu event handlers.
    playGameMenuEntry.Selected += PlayGameMenuEntrySelected;
    optionsMenuEntry.Selected += OptionsMenuEntrySelected;

    // Add entries to the menu.
    MenuEntries.Add(playGameMenuEntry);
    MenuEntries.Add(optionsMenuEntry);
}
```

The `MainMenuScreen` class creates the menu entries and associates event handlers with the menu entries. The base class `MenuScreen` handles the animation and positioning. A developer can customize the animation and layout by modifying the base `MenuScreen` class.

One way to customize the menu screens is to change the Font in the `AlienShooterContent` project. Open the /GameManagement/menufont.spritefont file and change the FontName element to Quartz MS from Figure 7–5 and change the Size to 24. The font has a science fiction look to it, which suites a game named AlienShooter pretty well.

We also modify the `GamePlayScreen` class to have Score and Lives text across the top with a `SlateBlue` color background. This is achieved via the `SpriteBatch.DrawString` method as well as adjusting the background color to `SlateBlue` and drawing the `backgroundTexture` 34 pixels lower via the added `backgroundPosition` Vector2 object. Figure 7–8 shows both the updated menu screen and game play screen.

Figure 7–8. Updated Menu and Game screens for AlienShooter

When you run the project on a device, the animations and transitions look pretty nice. These can certainly be customized as well once you understand how to create animations and transitions in XNA Game Studio. We cover both topics in detail to create the actual game play.

AlienShooter Game Play

In this section we focus on building out the game. Remember in Chapter 1 that we drew all of the objects directly in the Game1.cs class. In this chapter we will build up an object hierarchy to add better organization to the game structure. We start with an explanation of how sprite animation works so that we can then encapsulate the work in a GameObject class.

Sprite Animation

In this section we cover spite animation, which is the technique that brings a 2D game to life. Sprite Animation is a matter of showing frames or individual sprites at set intervals to give the illusion of motion, no different than flipping a drawing book that has pictures of a stick man running. Each picture is static, but when drawn in the correct order with the right position, the stick man appears animated when flipping through the images.

A new project named SpriteAnimation is added to the Chapter 7 solution. Project references to the SpriteSheetRuntime and SpriteSheetPipeline are added to the SpriteAnimation and SpriteAnimationContent projects respectively in order to take advantage of the automatic Sprite Sheet creation and easy sprite access via file name within the Sprite Sheet without having to remember coordinates or the math to track frames.

The Sprite Sheet is created from the AlienShooter textures. For the hero ship, we want to add rocket engine exhaust animations as well as for the missile. For the alien spaceship, a bit of glow is added underneath that shimmers and some tilt to the left and right is added to the ship. To create these effects I fired up Paint.NET and created 10 sprites for each object, varying, the patterns enough to make cartoonish flame for the hero ship and missile as well as the glow and tilt for the spaceship. Figure 7–9 shows the individually edited sprite files in the file system.

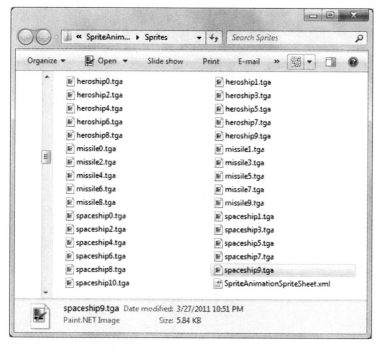

Figure 7–9. Individual sprite files

The files are added to the Sprite Sheet XML file as shown in Listing 7–5

Listing 7–5. SpriteAnimationSpriteSheet.xml Content File

```xml
<?xml version="1.0" encoding="utf-8" ?>
<XnaContent>
  <Asset Type="System.String[]">
    <Item>Sprites/heroship0.tga</Item>
    <Item>Sprites/heroship1.tga</Item>
    <Item>Sprites/heroship2.tga</Item>
    <Item>Sprites/heroship3.tga</Item>
    <Item>Sprites/heroship4.tga</Item>
    <Item>Sprites/heroship5.tga</Item>
```

```
        <Item>Sprites/heroship6.tga</Item>
        <Item>Sprites/heroship7.tga</Item>
        <Item>Sprites/heroship8.tga</Item>
        <Item>Sprites/heroship9.tga</Item>
        <Item>Sprites/spaceship0.tga</Item>
        <Item>Sprites/spaceship1.tga</Item>
        <Item>Sprites/spaceship2.tga</Item>
        <Item>Sprites/spaceship3.tga</Item>
        <Item>Sprites/spaceship4.tga</Item>
        <Item>Sprites/spaceship5.tga</Item>
        <Item>Sprites/spaceship6.tga</Item>
        <Item>Sprites/spaceship7.tga</Item>
        <Item>Sprites/spaceship8.tga</Item>
        <Item>Sprites/spaceship9.tga</Item>
        <Item>Sprites/missile0.tga</Item>
        <Item>Sprites/missile1.tga</Item>
        <Item>Sprites/missile2.tga</Item>
        <Item>Sprites/missile3.tga</Item>
        <Item>Sprites/missile4.tga</Item>
        <Item>Sprites/missile5.tga</Item>
        <Item>Sprites/missile6.tga</Item>
        <Item>Sprites/missile7.tga</Item>
        <Item>Sprites/missile8.tga</Item>
        <Item>Sprites/missile9.tga</Item>
    </Asset>
</XnaContent>
```

The Content Processor is configured to SpriteSheetProcessor, which instructs the Content Pipeline to collect the individual files and mash them together into a single texture, as shown in Figure 7–10.

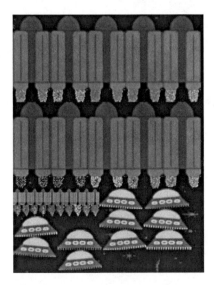

Figure 7–10. Generated textures

Personally, I would find it tedious to hand create a sprite texture, as shown in Figure 7–10 and prefer drawing individual images and letting the SpriteSheet sample code do the hard work for me. Once you see how easy it is to animate sprites using this method I think you will agree.

Drawing the frames so that it animates between the images is pretty straightforward. In the Game1 class for the SpriteAnimation sample, the following private fields are declared:

```
SpriteSheet SpriteAnimationSpriteSheet;
int spriteIndex = 0;
Rectangle screenRect;
TimeSpan timeToNextFrame = new TimeSpan();
TimeSpan frameTime = TimeSpan.FromMilliseconds(50d);
```

The spriteIndex variable is used to append a number from 0 to 9 to the sprite name of heroship, missile, and spaceship. Note in Figure 7–9 and Listing 7–5 how the sprite images are named. Incrementing spriteIndex steps over to the next sprite by name in Figure 7–10.

The timeToNextFrame field is used to sum elapsed time for the game. The frameTime field stores how often the spriteIndex should change over to the next frame. Here is the code from Game1.Update that performs this calculation:

```
protected override void Update(GameTime gameTime)
{
  // Allows the game to exit
  if (GamePad.GetState(PlayerIndex.One).Buttons.Back == ButtonState.Pressed)
    this.Exit();

  // TODO: Add your update logic here
  // Add elapsed game time between calls to Update
  // Once enough time has passed, i.e. timeToNextFrame > frameTime
  //increment sprite index.
  timeToNextFrame += gameTime.ElapsedGameTime;
  if (timeToNextFrame > frameTime)
  {
    if (spriteIndex < 9)
      spriteIndex++;
    else spriteIndex = 0;
      frameElapsedTime = TimeSpan.FromMilliseconds(0d);  }
  base.Update(gameTime);
}
```

Essentially, the frameTime variable is how long any given frame is displayed. If you want the frames to animate more slowly, increase the value of the frameTime variable, currently set to 50.

Drawing a frame is pretty straightforward as well. Here is the code to draw the center of the hero ship at the center of the screen:

```
spriteBatch.Draw(SpriteAnimationSpriteSheet.Texture,
  new Vector2((screenRect.Width / 3) -
        SpriteAnimationSpriteSheet.SourceRectangle("spaceship" +
spriteIndex.ToString()).Width / 2,
      (screenRect.Height / 3) -
        SpriteAnimationSpriteSheet.SourceRectangle("spaceship" +
spriteIndex.ToString()).Height / 2),
  SpriteAnimationSpriteSheet.SourceRectangle("spaceship" + spriteIndex.ToString()),
  Color.White);
```

The previous code takes the entire sprite sheet and uses this parameter for the source rectangle to select which sprite to draw:

```
SpriteAnimationSpriteSheet.SourceRectangle("spaceship" + spriteIndex.ToString())
```

You can only see the actual animation by running the code, but Figure 7–11 provides a snapshot.

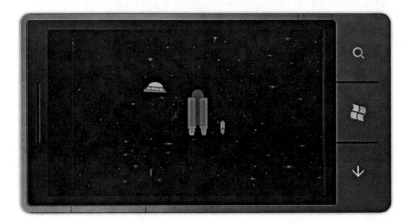

Figure 7–11. *Animated sprites*

We copy over all of the heroship, alienship, and missile images and SpriteSheet XML file to the AlienShooterContent content project's Sprites folder so that we can leverage the assets we created in our primary game.

Now that you understand how to animate sprites, we can move forward and create a GameObject class that handles the animation logic, as well as other object state allowing the code to focus more on game play and let the GameObject class handle rendering and state management.

Remember from our ScreenManager coverage that the actual game functionality exists in the GameplayScreen class. The rest of this chapter focuses on the code in the in the GameplayScreen class that manages the game objects as well as the game object code itself. The goal is that you come away with a solid understanding of how to go about creating your own games.

Game Object Class

We create a class named GameObject to be our base class for game assets, which includes the hero ship, the missiles, and the alien ships. The GameObject class handles the animation, Update, and Drawing for each object. We copied over the assets and sprite sheet logic from the SpriteAnimation sample project. Here is the GameObject constructor:

```
public GameObject(SpriteSheet loadedTexture, string spriteName, Rectangle screenRect)
{
  SpriteAnimationSpriteSheet = loadedTexture;
  SpriteCenter = new Vector2(
    SpriteAnimationSpriteSheet.SourceRectangle(spriteName + 0).Width / 2,
    SpriteAnimationSpriteSheet.SourceRectangle(spriteName + 0).Height / 2);
  //Used to access sprite in SpriteSheet
  //Assume starts at 0 so SpriteName+0 is first Sprite frame for animation
  //NumberOfAnimationFrames is how many sprite frames that are available
  SpriteName = spriteName;
  _screenRect = screenRect;
```

```
    //Default initialization
    FrameTime = TimeSpan.FromMilliseconds(100d);
    NumberOfAnimationFrames = 10;
    Position = Vector2.Zero;
    ElapsedFrameTime = TimeSpan.FromMilliseconds(0d);
    Velocity = Vector2.Zero;
    Rotation = 0f;
    Alive = false;
}
```

The constructor for GameObject takes the following parameters:

- SpriteSheet loadedTexture

- string spriteName

- Rectangle screenRect

Just as with the SpriteAnimation sample, all of the individual object frames are combined into a single texture shared by all of the objects, which is more efficient than loading individual textures and switching textures when rendering. The loadedTexture parameter represents the single texture and is passed in to the constructor. The spriteName parameter is used by the animation code so that the correct object frames can be found in the loadedTexture. This code assumes a naming convention starting at spriteName+0 through spriteName+NumberOfAnimationFrames, which is hard-coded to 10 frames for all objects. The screenRect parameter is used to check when objects collide with screen bounds.

Properties

The GameObject class has quite a few public properties declared that are used to animate the sprite and to hold information on Sprite such as the center point, position, velocity and rotation. Here are the declarations:

```
public SpriteSheet SpriteAnimationSpriteSheet { get; set; }
public string SpriteName { get; private set; }
public int NumberOfAnimationFrames { get; set; }
public TimeSpan FrameTime { get; set; }
public TimeSpan ElapsedFrameTime { get; set; }
public Vector2 SpriteCenter { get; set; }
public bool Alive { get; set; }
public Vector2 Position { get; set; }
public Vector2 Velocity { get; set; }
public float Rotation { get; set; }
```

There is an additional property related to collision detection that we will cover next.

Collision Detection

The BoundingRect property of type Rectangle is used to return the Rectangle area that contains the sprite on screen. This property is used for collision detection. If you have ever played a video game where the objects seemed to touch but nothing happen, it is a result of imperfect collision detection, as shown in Figure 7–12 where a regular shaped object, like a rectangle, is used to define the area of an irregularly shaped object.

Imperfect Collision Detection

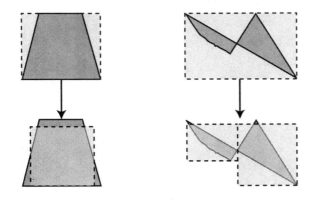

Figure 7–12. Bounding box collision detection

There are more than a few algorithms for sprite collision detection that can be found in books focused on the topic that range in accuracy from bounding rectangles to resource intensive point by point comparison. Probably the best answer lies somewhere in-between those extremes, such as using more than one bounding box or only performing point-by-point comparison on sides that could collide, and so on. For our purposes, we check for intersection using the BoundingRect property defined in GameObject:

```
public virtual Rectangle BoundingRect
{
  get
  {
    return new Rectangle((int)Position.X, (int)Position.Y,
      SpriteAnimationSpriteSheet.SourceRectangle(SpriteName + 0).Width,
      SpriteAnimationSpriteSheet.SourceRectangle(SpriteName + 0).Height);
  }
}
```

One trick to that you can use to adjust collision detection is to call the Inflate(horizontalAmount,verticalAmount) method to individually increase or decrease (with a negative value) the sides of the Rectangle to better match the object shape.

GameObject Methods

The rest of the GameObject class contain its individual methods to reset its position if the object flies off the screen, update the object state, and draw the object to screen. Methods are marked with the virtual keyword so that they can be overridden in inherited classes as needed:

```
public virtual void ResetGameObject()
{
  Position = Vector2.Zero;
  Velocity = Vector2.Zero;
  Alive = false;
```

```
}

public virtual void Update(GameTime GameTime)
{
  if (Alive)
  {
    Position += Velocity;
    //Check screen bounds
    if ((Position.X < 0) ||
        (Position.X > _screenRect.Width) ||
        (Position.Y < 0) ||
        (Position.Y > _screenRect.Height))
      ResetGameObject();
    //Update animation
    UpdateAnimation(GameTime);
  }
}

private void UpdateAnimation(GameTime gameTime)
{
  ElapsedFrameTime += gameTime.ElapsedGameTime;
  if (ElapsedFrameTime > FrameTime)
  {
    if (_spriteIndex < NumberOfAnimationFrames - 1)
      _spriteIndex++;
    else _spriteIndex = 0;
    ElapsedFrameTime = TimeSpan.FromMilliseconds(0d);
  }
}

public virtual void Draw(GameTime gameTime, SpriteBatch spriteBatch)
{
  if (Alive)
  {
    spriteBatch.Draw(SpriteAnimationSpriteSheet.Texture, Position - SpriteCenter,
      SpriteAnimationSpriteSheet.SourceRectangle(SpriteName + _spriteIndex.ToString()),
      Color.White);
  }
}
```

The ResetGameObject is called when an object is "destroyed" or flies off the screen. The method is pretty simple in just setting Position and Velocity to a zero vector and Alive to false.

The Update method checks to see if the object is Alive before updating Position by adding Velocity to it and then checking screen bounds. The Update method also calls the UpdateAnimation method, which leverages the code we developed in the SpriteAnimation sample. Finally, the Draw method simply applies the same logic we used in the SpriteAnimation sample to draw the correct frame to screen as part of the animation sequence.

Now that we have our base class out of the way, we move on to cover the enemy alien class and then move on to the user controlled hero ship and missile classes.

Enemy Class

The AlienGameObject class that represents the frenzied aliens is remarkably simple. The class inherits from the GameObject class and uses the inherited constructor with some modifications:

```
public AlienGameObject(SpriteSheet loadedTexture,
        string spriteName, Rectangle screenRect)
  : base(loadedTexture, spriteName, screenRect)
{
  Alive = true;
  ResetGameObject();
}
```

The Alive property is set to true because we want enemies to keep dropping. There is a customized ResetGameObject method that overrides the base class version as well:

```
public override void ResetGameObject()
{
  //Randomize animation
  _spriteIndex = (int)(randomNumber.NextDouble() * NumberOfAnimationFrames);
  //Randomize initial position
  Position = new Vector2(randomNumber.Next(_screenRect.Width), 35);

  //Apply default alien speed
  Velocity = new Vector2(randomNumber.Next(alienVelocityArc), alienSpeed);
  Alive = true;
}
```

The alien spaceship has a unique shape. For better collision detection we override the BoundingRect property and call Rectangle.Inflate(0,2); to inflate the Rectangle on the Y axis resulting in much better collision detection for this game:

```
public override Rectangle BoundingRect
{
  get
  {
    Rectangle rect = new Rectangle((int)Position.X, (int)Position.Y,
      SpriteAnimationSpriteSheet.SourceRectangle(SpriteName + 0).Width,
      SpriteAnimationSpriteSheet.SourceRectangle(SpriteName + 0).Height);
    rect.Inflate(0,20);
    return rect ;
  }
}
```

That's it to this class. All of the lively action is a result of the animation code handled by the base class and the ResetGameObject method. The ResetGameObject method does a couple of things:

- It starts the animation at a random index, so that the objects don't appear to be animating in sync, which would be boring.

- It randomly picks an 'X' value for the initial Position Vector2 to start the drop.

- Finally, it applies a random but very small 'X' value to the Velocity so that the alien space ships don't appear to just fall straight down.

Figure 7–13 shows an army of aliens invading.

Figure 7–13. Alien invasion

You will want to play on a real device to get a full sense of the game, but as you can see in Figure 7–13, the aliens strike different drop lines and fall fairly randomly for such little code. The animation code helps to keep things lively as well. In the next section, we cover the hero ship class, which takes accelerometer and touch input to move and fire missiles at the invasion.

Hero Ship Class

We create another class named UserGameObject that inherits from the GameObject class. This class represents the player, which is the Hero Ship in AlienShooter, which makes it unique to the other classes since it takes user input in the form of accelerometer and touch. The accelerometer input will move the ship left or right by tilting the phone. It has a window so that if the phone is relatively flat the ship does not move. Touching the screen will fire missiles.

User Input

By default, the Game Management sample does not include support for Accelerometer input. The GamePlayScreen class has a HandleInput method that takes a parameter of type InputState, which is a class that captures keyboard, controller, and touch input. It does not capture Accelerometer input by default. In the source code for the book, you will find a modified InputState class, as well as a new class named AccelerometerState, which is shown in Listing 7–6.

Listing 7–6. AccelerometerState Class File

```
public class AccelerometerState
{
  public double X;
  public double Y;
  public double Z;
  public DateTimeOffset Timestamp;
}
```

The modifications to the InputState class are pretty straightforward:

```
//robcamer - Add a private instance of AccelerometerState
public AccelerometerState CurrentAccelerometerState { get; private set; }
//robcamer - Add private field for the accelerometer
private Accelerometer accelerometer;
```

The constructor for the InputState class is modified to instantiate the previous two private variables, as well as add an event handler to the Accelerometer:

```
CurrentAccelerometerState = new AccelerometerState();
//Robcamer - initialize accelerometer
accelerometer = new Accelerometer();
accelerometer.ReadingChanged +=
  new System.EventHandler<AccelerometerReadingEventArgs>(accelerometer_ReadingChanged);
accelerometer.Start();
```

The values of CurrentAccelerometerState are updated in the accelerometer_ReadingChanged event handler:

```
void accelerometer_ReadingChanged(object sender, AccelerometerReadingEventArgs e)
{
  CurrentAccelerometerState.X = e.X;
  CurrentAccelerometerState.Y = e.Y;
  CurrentAccelerometerState.Y = e.Z;
  CurrentAccelerometerState.Timestamp = e.Timestamp;
}
```

Processing Input

Now that we have the modifications in place for the InputState class, two private fields related to user input are added to the UserGameObject class.

```
private AccelerometerState _accelerometerState;
private Vector2 _leftRightVector = new Vector2(5, 0);
```

The _accelerometerState and _leftRightVector fields are modified in the UserGameObject.HandleInput method.

```
public void HandleInput(InputState input)
{
  //Must check for TouchLocationState as wel as Count
  //Otherwise, FireMissile will be called twice
```

```
//Once for 'Pressed' and once for 'Released'
if ((input.TouchState.Count > 0) &&
   input.TouchState[0].State == TouchLocationState.Pressed)
{
  FireMissile();
}

_accelerometerState = input.CurrentAccelerometerState;
if (_accelerometerState.X > .1)
{
  Velocity = _leftRightVector;
}
if (_accelerometerState.X < -.1)
{
  Velocity = -_leftRightVector;
}
//near Zero tilt left or right so
//set velocity to zero
if ((_accelerometerState.X < .1) &&
   (_accelerometerState.X > -.1))
   Velocity = Vector2.Zero;
}
```

If the _accelerometerState X component is greater than .1, a positive or negative velocity is applied to the Velocity vector via the leftRightVector variable in the proper tilt direction. Likewise, if the user holds the phone close to neutral, Velocity is set to zero. If you don't like how it responds, play with the .1 value to see what feels good to you.

The other part of the HandleInput session is to detect if the screen is touched. Each touch fires to TouchState values, one for TouchLocationState.Pressed and one for TouchLocationState.Released. If the screen is touched the FireMissile method is fired.

The UserGameObject class manages a collection of Missile objects since they are closely associated with the hero ship:

```
public List<MissileGameObject> Missiles;
public int MaxNumberofMissiles;
```

The Missile related properties are public properties because the GameplayScreen will need to check collisions between missiles and enemy alien ships. Also, the number of available missiles could be adjusted dynamically as part of game play for a "blitz" mode, where the hero ship can fire more than three at a time as an example. The Missiles collection is instantiated in the UserGameObject constructor:

```
MaxNumberofMissiles = 3;
Missiles = new List<MissileGameObject>();
for (int i=0;i < MaxNumberofMissiles; i++)
  Missiles.Add(new MissileGameObject(loadedTexture,"missile",screenRect));
```

When the screen is touched, the FireMissile method code searches for an available missile. Only three are available by default, and sets the missile property to Alive and the Missile Position property to the same Position value for the hero ship / UserGameObject class. Note that once the Missile is set to Alive, it automatically starts moving based on the default logic implemented in the GameObject class.

UserGameObject Class Core Methods

The UserGameObject class overrides the Update method with custom code to position the spaceship correctly with user input. It also manages the Missiles collection by calling Update for missiles where Alive is true, i.e., they are in flight. Here is the UserGameObject.Update method:

```
public override void Update(GameTime gameTime)
{
  base.Update(gameTime);

  if (Position.X < SpriteCenter.X)
    Position = new Vector2(SpriteCenter.X,Position.Y);
  if (Position.X > (_screenRect.Width - SpriteCenter.X))
    Position = new Vector2(_screenRect.Width-SpriteCenter.X,Position.Y);


  for (int i = 0; i < MaxNumberofMissiles; i++)
  {
    if (Missiles[i].Alive == true)
      Missiles[i].Update(gameTime);
  }
}
```

The Draw method is overridden as well:

```
public override void Draw(GameTime gameTime, Microsoft.Xna.Framework.Graphics.SpriteBatch
spriteBatch)
{
  for (int i = 0; i < MaxNumberofMissiles; i++)
  {
    if (Missiles[i].Alive == true)
      Missiles[i].Draw(gameTime, spriteBatch);
  }
  base.Draw(gameTime, spriteBatch);
}
```

The Draw method checks to see if each Missile is Alive and then calls Draw for the Missile object. The last item in the UserGameObject class to cover is the LoadContent method. In this method, the ContentManager instance is passed in so that the UserGameObject can make a sound effect when a missile is fired from the hero ship. Here is the method:

```
public void LoadContent(ContentManager content)
{
  _missileLaunchSoundEffect =
               content.Load<SoundEffect>("SoundEffects/MissileLaunch");
}
```

Sound Effects

XNA Game Studio has very rich audio mixing capabilities to support Dolby quality sound. For our game the SoundEffect class provides a quick and easy way to play audio during a game with the Play method. We add three sound effects to the AlienShooterContent project in the SoundEffects folder:

- Explosion.wma

- HeroShipDamage.wma

- MissileLaunch.wma

One item to note is that I recorded the sounds using the Windows 7 Recorder tool, which generates a .wma file. When added to the Content project the XNA Framework automatically chose the Song - XNA Framework Content Processor. This format cannot be played by the SoundEffect class. Simply change the Content Processor to Sound Effect - XNA Framework and the audio plays fine.

Let's now move on to a discussion of the Missile class.

Missile Class

The Missile class pretty straightforward, shown in Listing 7–7.

Listing 7–7. Missile GameObject Class File

```
using System;
using System.Collections.Generic;
using System.Linq;
using System.Text;
using SpriteSheetRuntime;
using Microsoft.Xna.Framework;

namespace AlienShooter.GameObjects
{
  class MissileGameObject : GameObject
  {
    public MissileGameObject(SpriteSheet loadedTexture,
             string spriteName, Rectangle screenRect)
      : base(loadedTexture, spriteName, screenRect)
    {
      ResetGameObject();
    }

    public override void ResetGameObject()
    {
      Position = new Vector2(-SpriteCenter.X, _screenRect.Height + SpriteCenter.Y);
      Velocity = new Vector2(0,-5);
      Alive = false;
    }
  }
}
```

The next class we cover is the GameStatusBoard class.

Game Status Board Class

The GameStatusBoard class keeps track of and displays the score and lives available during the game. This class also plays sound effects when an enemy ship is destroyed and when the hero ship takes a hit from an enemy ship. The GameStatusBoard class also vibrates the phone when an alien ship hits the hero ship using the VibrateController class. Figure 7–14 shows the status board in action.

Figure 7–14. *Alien invasion status board*

In the following two sections, we cover keeping score and tracking lives functionality in the GameStatusBoard class.

Keeping Score

Each time a hero ship missile intercepts an alien space ship, 5 points are added to the GameStatusBoard.Score property. The Score property is modified in the GamePlay screen, which we cover later. Within the GameStatusBoard class, updating the score results in a SoundEffect.Play call for the Explosion.wma file:

```
public int Score
{
  get { return _score; }
  set
  {
    _score = value;
```

```
      _alienExplosionSoundEffect.Play();
   }
}
```

The GameStatusBoard.Update method has a switch statement to display a message based on current score:

```
switch (Score)
{
  case 50: _displayMessage = true;
    _message = "Nice Start!";
    break;
  case 60: _displayMessage = false;
    break;
  case 100: _displayMessage = true;
    _message = "Keep It Up!";
    break;
  case 120: _displayMessage = false;
    break;
  default: break;
}
```

When the _displayMessage field is true based on score, GameStatusBoard.Draw displays the message in the Status Board with this call:

```
if (_displayMessage)
  spriteBatch.DrawString(_gameFont, _message, new Vector2(175, 0),
    _livesTextColor);
```

That's it for score keeping. We next cover tracking hero ship lives and game over functionality.

Tracking Lives

Be default, when playing the Alien Shooter game, you get 3 lives to start. Each time an alien ship intersects the hero ship, a life is deducted. At 2 lives a message of "Warning!" is displayed. At 1 life, a message of "Danger!" is displayed. Finally, when zero lives are the state, a "Game Over!" message is displayed at top and in the middle of the screen. Also, each time a live is deducted, the phone is briefly vibrated. Here is the declaration and instantiation of the VibrateController class:

```
private VibrateController _vibrateController = VibrateController.Default;
private TimeSpan _vibrateTimeSpan = TimeSpan.FromMilliseconds(400);
```

Here is the Lives property where the sound is played and phone vibrated when the Lives property is modified:

```
public int Lives
{
  get { return _lives; }
  set
  {
    _lives = value;
    _heroShipDamageSoundEffect.Play();
    _vibrateController.Start( _vibrateTimeSpan);
  }
}
```

Here is the code from the GameStatusBoard.Update method that determines what message to display, and in what color:

```
switch (_lives)
{
  case 3: _livesTextColor = Color.LightGreen;
          break;
  case 2: _livesTextColor = Color.Yellow;
          _displayMessage = true;
          _message = "Waring!";
          break;
  case 1: _livesTextColor = Color.Red;
          _displayMessage = true;
          _message = "Danger!";
          break;
  case 0: _livesTextColor = Color.Red;
          _displayMessage = true;
          _message = "Game Over!";
          GameOver = true;
          break;
}
```

Here is the corresponding code from the GameStatusBoard.Draw method that determines when to display a message about the hero ship help on the screen:

```
if (_displayMessage)
  spriteBatch.DrawString(_gameFont, _message, new Vector2(175, 0),
    _livesTextColor);
if (GameOver)
  spriteBatch.DrawString(_gameFont, _message, new Vector2(175, 370),
    _livesTextColor);
```

Having an informative game status board is an important component of any game development effort. This section covered how simple it is to provide the basics. In the next section, we cover the overall logic in the GamePlayScreen class that pulls together all of the game objects we just covered.

Updated GameplayScreen Class

When you click "new game" in the main menu, the GameplayScreen is the screen that loads and the GameplayScreen class is where all of the game action occurs. The following sections cover how the GameplayScreen class manages the game objects, collision detection, and scoring.

GamePlay Screen Initialization

Now we are ready to modify the GameplayScreen class to manage the game objects. We declare the object instances needed:

```
//Game objects
GameStatusBoard statusBoard;
List<AlienGameObject> enemies;
int maxEnemies = 5;
UserGameObject heroShip;
int maxMissiles = 3;
```

```
//Indicates to draw game over frame;
bool drawGameOverFrame = false ;
```

The maxMissiles and maxEnemies variable are not a constant because we may want to change it dynamically during the game as part of the game play. Otherwise, one UserGameObject named heroShip and a List of AlienGameObjects are the other key components of the game. Another potential modification would be to increase the number of AlienGameObjects in the game as the score gets higher to make it more interesting. Otherwise a player will get bored if nothing changes.

Next we load and initialize assets in LoadContent():

```
public override void LoadContent()
{
  if (content == null)
    content = new ContentManager(ScreenManager.Game.Services, "Content");

  gameFont = content.Load<SpriteFont>("gamefont");
  alienShooterSpriteSheet = content.Load<SpriteSheet>("Sprites/AlienShooterSpriteSheet");
  backgroundTexture = content.Load<Texture2D>("Textures/background");
  backgroundPosition = new Vector2(0, 34);
  //Get a pointer to the entire screen Rectangle
  screenRect = ScreenManager.GraphicsDevice.Viewport.Bounds;

  //Initialize Enemies collection
  enemies = new List<AlienGameObject>();
  for (int i = 0; i < maxEnemies; i++)
  {
    enemies.Add(new AlienGameObject(alienShooterSpriteSheet, "spaceship", screenRect));
  }

  //Initialize Player Object
  heroShip = new UserGameObject(alienShooterSpriteSheet, "heroship", screenRect, maxMissiles);
  heroShip.Position = new Vector2(screenRect.Width / 2, 720);
  heroShip.LoadContent(content);

  //Initialize Status Board
  statusBoard = new GameStatusBoard(gameFont);
  statusBoard.LoadContent(content);

  // A real game would probably have more content than this sample, so
  // it would take longer to load. We simulate that by delaying for a
  // while, giving you a chance to admire the beautiful loading screen.
  Thread.Sleep(1000);

  // once the load has finished, we use ResetElapsedTime to tell the game's
  // timing mechanism that we have just finished a very long frame, and that
  // it should not try to catch up.
  ScreenManager.Game.ResetElapsedTime();
}
```

By breaking out our game assets into objects it greatly unclutters the code in GameplayScreen class. As an example, initializing the enemies object is a matter of passing in the texture information for the animations:

```
//Initialize Enemies collection
enemies = new List<AlienGameObject>();
```

```
for (int i = 0; i < maxEnemies; i++)
{
  enemies.Add(new AlienGameObject(alienShooterSpriteSheet, "spaceship", screenRect));
}
```

GameplayScreen Update and Draw Methods

Adding support for the heroShip and the AlienGameObject to the GameplayScreen.Update method is pretty straightforward now that we have nice objects that manage work for us:

```
public override void Update(GameTime gameTime, bool otherScreenHasFocus,
                                           bool coveredByOtherScreen)
{
  if (IsActive)
  {
    if (!statusBoard.GameOver)
    {
      CheckForCollisions();

      heroShip.Update(gameTime);
      statusBoard.Update(gameTime);

      for (int i = 0; i < maxEnemies; i++)
      {
        enemies[i].Update(gameTime);
      }
    }
  }
  base.Update(gameTime, otherScreenHasFocus, coveredByOtherScreen);
}
```

If StatusBoard.GameOver is not true, i.e. the hero ship has lives available, the game action continues. Otherwise, the code is straightforward, calling Update for each object. Notice the call to the CheckForCollisions method. We cover collision detection in the next sub section.

Adding support for user input is just as easy by adding a call to heroShip.HandleIpnut(input) just after the else in the GameplayScreen.HandleInput method. For the GameplayScreen.Draw method the Draw method is called for each object. If StatusBoard.GameOver is true, the Draw method is not called for the enemies any further and the game is over.

```
public override void Draw(GameTime gameTime)
{
  ScreenManager.GraphicsDevice.Clear(ClearOptions.Target,
                                     Color.SlateBlue, 0, 0);

  // Our player and enemy are both actually just text strings.
  SpriteBatch spriteBatch = ScreenManager.SpriteBatch;

  spriteBatch.Begin();
  //Draw Background
  spriteBatch.Draw(backgroundTexture, backgroundPosition, Color.White);
  //Draw Status Board
  statusBoard.Draw(gameTime, spriteBatch);
  //Draw Hero Ship
  heroShip.Draw(gameTime, spriteBatch);
```

```
  //Draw enemies
  if (!statusBoard.GameOver)
  {
    for (int i = 0; i < maxEnemies; i++)
    {
      enemies[i].Draw(gameTime, spriteBatch);
    }
  }
  spriteBatch.End();

  // If the game is transitioning on or off, fade it out to black.
  if (TransitionPosition > 0)
    ScreenManager.FadeBackBufferToBlack(1f - TransitionAlpha);
}
```

Collision Detection and Memory Management

In the GameplayScreen.Update method, there is a call to the CheckForCollisions method. This method detects collisions between inflight missiles and enemy alien ships (a score) as well as collisions between enemy alien ships and the hero ship (lose a life). Here is the code for the CheckForCollisions method:

```
private void CheckForCollisions()
{
  //Checking for two major collisions
  //1 - Has an in flight missile intersected an alien spaceship - score 5 pts
  for (int i = 0; i < heroShip.MaxNumberofMissiles; i++)
    if (heroShip.Missiles[i].Alive)
      for (int j = 0; j < maxEnemies; j++)
        if ((enemies[j].Alive) &&
            (enemies[j].BoundingRect.Intersects(heroShip.Missiles[i].BoundingRect)))
        {
          statusBoard.Score += 5;
          enemies[j].ResetGameObject();
          heroShip.Missiles[i].ResetGameObject();
        }
  //2 - Has an alien spaceship intersected the hero ship - deduct a life
  for (int j = 0; j < maxEnemies; j++)
    if ((enemies[j].Alive) && (enemies[j].Position.Y > 600) &&
        (enemies[j].BoundingRect.Intersects(heroShip.BoundingRect)))
    {
      statusBoard.Lives -= 1;
      for (int i = 0; i < maxEnemies; i++)
        enemies[i].ResetGameObject();
      for (int i = 0; i < heroShip.MaxNumberofMissiles; i++)
        heroShip.Missiles[i].ResetGameObject();
    }
}
```

For detecting a hit by a missile by an alien ship, each missile's bounding box must be compared with each enemy alien ship's bounding box. Same goes for detecting a collision between an enemy ship and the hero ship to lose a life. Each one must be compared every frame for the most part. This means that every time two objects are compared, which could be every frame, two new bounding boxes must be constructed. Remember the bounding box includes a position for the bounding box as well as height and width. Here is the code to return a bounding box in the GameObject base class as a refresher:

```
public virtual Rectangle BoundingRect
{
  get
  {
    return new Rectangle((int)Position.X, (int)Position.Y,
      SpriteAnimationSpriteSheet.SourceRectangle(SpriteName + 0).Width,
      SpriteAnimationSpriteSheet.SourceRectangle(SpriteName + 0).Height);
  }
}
```

In a mobile application you want to try to minimize memory allocations to reduce garbage collection activity. In a mobile game, it is especially important to watch memory allocations. As an example, when an enemy is destroyed by a hit, the AlienGameObject for that enemy has its Alive property set to false. We could instead set the object to null and then instantiate a new object but that just wastes CPU cycles on garbage collection.

Another way to minimize CPU cycles is to only do work if needed. Notice in the CheckforCollisions method that the if statements are structured to only perform work and get a BoundingRect when needed. As an example, an enemy alien ship can only intersect the hero ship after it has fallen about two/thirds of the way down the screen so a check is made to only perform the collision calculations if the alien ship is below 600 pixels on the screen.

```
if ((enemies[j].Alive) && (enemies[j].Position.Y > 600) &&
    (enemies[j].BoundingRect.Intersects(heroShip.BoundingRect)))
```

Part of game development is always looking for ways to do things smartly. For myself, it is one of the most enjoyable parts of the effort.

Conclusion

This chapter covered extensively the process of building out the game play leveraging existing samples like the GameScreen Game Management and the Sprite Sheet processor samples to build out 2D game. In the next chapter we focus on making enhancements to this game such as explosions for collisions as well as important housekeeping items such as adding support for saving and loading the game as well as the very important tombstoning support. The next chapter also provides an introduction to 3D game development.

CHAPTER 8

Advanced XNA Framework Development

In this chapter, we continue with our discussion of game development. In Chapter 1, we provided a basic overview of game development. In Chapter 7, we took the sample code from Chapter 1 and turned it into a structured 2D game, leveraging the AppHub Game Screen Management sample to provide a basic menu system and a base GameScreen class to help manage the various screens that users expect to have such as a main menu, options menu, and the game play screen. We covered 2D animation and encapsulated our game play using a GameObject class to represent the enemy alien ships, missiles, and the hero ship.

In this chapter we add a few key enhancements to the AlienShooter game. We take a copy of the code from the Chapter 7 solution and add support for saving and loading the game, as well as tombstoning support. We wrap up with a basic particle system to simulate explosions when the hero ship shoots down an alien enemy ship. We then shift gears with an introduction to 3D game development, covering key 3D concepts, a little bit of 3D math, and finally the 3D programming model provided by XNA Game Studio.

AlienShooter Enhancements

In this section we add support for functionality you would expect to see if this was a real Windows Phone 7 game. We first implement how to load and save game state. We modify the main menu game screen to have both new game and resume game menu items in the event that previous game state is present.

We next implement tombstoning support so that the user is restored to the main menu screen and has a chance to click resume to restart game play. The last section covers how to create a basic particle system that simulates expositions when a hero ship missile collides with an alien enemy spaceship.

Load and Save Game State

For our game, we automatically save game state when the user backs out of the GameplayScreen with a game in progress. The main menu screen is modified to include both New Game and Resume Game menu options that will resume an existing game if saved state is present. Automatic save keeps things simple and is a typical state management approach for many game developers.

We set about modifying the MainMenuScreen class, renaming the playGameMenuEntry object to newGameMenuEntry and adding another MenuEntry named resumeGameMenuEntry. Here is the modified constructor MainMenuScreen():

```
public MainMenuScreen()
  : base("Main Menu")
{
```

```
    // Create our menu entries.
    MenuEntry newGameMenuEntry = new MenuEntry("New Game");
    MenuEntry optionsMenuEntry = new MenuEntry("Game Options");

    // Hook up menu event handlers.
    newGameMenuEntry.Selected += newGameMenuEntrySelected;
    optionsMenuEntry.Selected += OptionsMenuEntrySelected;

    // Add entries to the menu.
    MenuEntries.Add(newGameMenuEntry);
    MenuEntries.Add(optionsMenuEntry);

    //robcamer - Only display resume game menu opion
    //if saved state is present.
    using (IsolatedStorageFile gameStorage = IsolatedStorageFile.GetUserStoreForApplication())
    {
      if (gameStorage.FileExists(AlienShooterStateFileName))
      {
        MenuEntry resumeGameMenuEntry = new MenuEntry("Resume Game");
        resumeGameMenuEntry.Selected += resumeGameMenuEntry_Selected;
        MenuEntries.Add(resumeGameMenuEntry);
      }
    }
}
```

We want to display the "Resume Game" menu option only when there is game state present, so in the MainMenu there is a FileExists check to determine if game state is present. We add a using System.IO.IsolatedStorage statement to the top of MainMenuScreen.cs as well as a constant declaration of the state filename to wire things up:

```
const string AlienShooterStateFileName = "AlienShooter.dat";
```

We modify the new game selected event handler named newGameMenuEntrySelected to delete any saved game state since a new game is desired:

```
void newGameMenuEntrySelected(object sender, PlayerIndexEventArgs e)
{
  //
  using (IsolatedStorageFile gameStorage = IsolatedStorageFile.GetUserStoreForApplication())
  {
    if (gameStorage.FileExists(AlienShooterStateFileName))
    {
      gameStorage.DeleteFile(AlienShooterStateFileName);
    }
  }

  LoadingScreen.Load(ScreenManager, true, e.PlayerIndex,
                     new GameplayScreen());
}
```

This sets things up for the GameplayScreen to load saved state or start a new game depending on what option is chosen in the MainMenuScreen UI. In the GameplayScreen object we create two new public methods to load and save state. For load state, we do the following:

- Check for saved state; if not present, initialize the variables as before.
- If saved state is present, restore saved state and begin game play.

To save state, we use a System.IO.StreamWriter object. We don't use object serialization because we need to instantiate the GameObject classes normally, just like when LoadContent is called. Instead, we simply save off the important state values to a text file in Isolated Storage such as the Position and Velocity vector values, the status board game score and remaining lives, and so on. The SaveAlienShooterState method always deletes the file first before saving. Also, the method does not save state if the game is over. Listing 8.1 shows the GameplayScreen. SaveAlienShooterState method.

Listing 8–1. GameplayScreen. SaveAlienShooterState

```
public void SaveAlienShooterState()
{
  //Only save game if not GameOver
  using (IsolatedStorageFile gameStorage =
    IsolatedStorageFile.GetUserStoreForApplication())
  {
    //Overwrite existing saved game state
    if (gameStorage.FileExists(AlienShooterStateFileName))
    {
      gameStorage.DeleteFile(AlienShooterStateFileName);
    }
    if (!statusBoard.GameOver)
    {
      using (IsolatedStorageFileStream fs =
        gameStorage.OpenFile(AlienShooterStateFileName,
                             System.IO.FileMode.Create))
      {
        using (StreamWriter streamWriter = new StreamWriter(fs))
        {
          //Only serialize interesting state
          //Other state MUST be initialized each time
          streamWriter.WriteLine(heroShip.Position.X);
          streamWriter.WriteLine(heroShip.Position.Y);
          streamWriter.WriteLine(heroShip.Velocity.X);
          streamWriter.WriteLine(heroShip.Velocity.Y);
          streamWriter.WriteLine(statusBoard.Score);
          streamWriter.WriteLine(statusBoard.Lives);
          for (int i = 0; i < maxEnemies; i++)
          {
            streamWriter.WriteLine(enemies[i].Alive);
            streamWriter.WriteLine(enemies[i].Position.X);
            streamWriter.WriteLine(enemies[i].Position.Y);
            streamWriter.WriteLine(enemies[i].Velocity.X);
            streamWriter.WriteLine(enemies[i].Velocity.Y);
          }
          streamWriter.Flush();
          streamWriter.Close();
        }
      }
    }
  }
}
```

The GameplayScreen.LoadAlienShooterState method instantiates the GameObjects and classes, i.e., heroShip. statusBoard GameStatus object, and the enemies alien ship collection. This code was cut from the GameplayScreen.LoadContent method and pasted into the GameplayScreen.LoadAlienShooterState method shown in Listing 8–2.

Listing 8–2. GameplayScreen.LoadAlienShooterState Method

```
public void LoadAlienShooterState()
{
  using (IsolatedStorageFile gameStorage = IsolatedStorageFile.GetUserStoreForApplication())
  {
    //Initialize all objects as before
    enemies = new List<AlienGameObject>();
    for (int i = 0; i < maxEnemies; i++)
    {
      enemies.Add(new AlienGameObject(alienShooterSpriteSheet, "spaceship", screenRect));
    }

    //Initialize Player Object
    heroShip = new UserGameObject(alienShooterSpriteSheet, "heroship", screenRect,
maxMissiles);
    heroShip.Position = new Vector2(screenRect.Width / 2, 720);
    heroShip.LoadContent(content);

    //Initialize Status Board
    statusBoard = new GameStatusBoard(gameFont);
    statusBoard.LoadContent(content);

    //Set saved state on objects
    if (gameStorage.FileExists(AlienShooterStateFileName))
    {
      using (IsolatedStorageFileStream fs =
      gameStorage.OpenFile(AlienShooterStateFileName, System.IO.FileMode.Open))
      {
        using (StreamReader streamReader = new StreamReader(fs))
        {
          heroShip.Position = new Vector2(
            (float)Convert.ToDouble(streamReader.ReadLine()),
            (float)Convert.ToDouble(streamReader.ReadLine()));
          heroShip.Velocity = new Vector2(
            (float)Convert.ToDouble(streamReader.ReadLine()),
            (float)Convert.ToDouble(streamReader.ReadLine()));
          statusBoard.Score = Convert.ToInt32(streamReader.ReadLine());
          statusBoard.Lives = Convert.ToInt32(streamReader.ReadLine());
          for (int i = 0; i < maxEnemies; i++)
          {
            enemies[i].Alive = Convert.ToBoolean(streamReader.ReadLine());
            enemies[i].Position = new Vector2(
              (float)Convert.ToDouble(streamReader.ReadLine()),
              (float)Convert.ToDouble(streamReader.ReadLine()));
            enemies[i].Velocity = new Vector2(
              (float)Convert.ToDouble(streamReader.ReadLine()),
              (float)Convert.ToDouble(streamReader.ReadLine()));
          }
          streamReader.Close();
        }
```

```
        }
      }
    }
}
```

The Save and Load code isn't the most elegant code you will ever see but it is simple and works fine. With this code in place, when you hit the Back hard button when playing the game, you get a Resume menu item. Figure 8–1 shows the updated MainMenuScreen class UI.

Figure 8–1. Updated main menu screen with Resume Game menu option

If you play the game until all of your lives are consumed and then hit the back button, the Resume Game menu option is not present, because there isn't any saved state.

One issue that remains is, if you are playing the game and then hit the Start button and then the Back button, the game resets to a new game on the GameplayScreen UI. What we want to happen is for state to be saved and the game resume back on the main menu screen, so that the user has a chance to get ready to play and then tap the Resume Game menu option. We cover how to implement tombstone support in the next section.

Tombstone Support

Adding tombstone support to your XNA Framework game is different from adding tombstone support in Silverlight. In Silverlight, the Deactivated and Activated events only fire when tombstoning and returning from tombstoning respectively. In Silverlight, these events do not fire when launching (Launching event) nor when closing (Closing event).

In the XNA Framework, the OnDeactivation (tombstoning) and OnActiviation (returning from tombstone) also fire when launching and closing the game, making it difficult to distinguish tombstoning events from regular launching/closing events.

To detect tombstoning events, you can use the PhoneApplicationService class available in the Microsoft.Phone.dll assembly. You must also add a reference to System.Windows.dll as well, or a compilation error will occur. Add a using Microsoft.Phone.Shell statement to the top of AlienShooterGame.cs (default name is game1.cs in a new project). In the AlienShooterGame() constructor (default name is Game1() in a new project), add this code at the end to hook the Activated and Deactivated events:

```
//Implement tombstoning support globally if managing
//multiple state objects across game gamescreens
PhoneApplicationService.Current.Activated += AlienGame_Activated;
PhoneApplicationService.Current.Deactivated += AlienGame_Deactivated;
```

You can then implement tombstoning for the application in the corresponding event handlers in AlienShooterGame.cs:

```
void AlienGame_Activated(object sender, ActivatedEventArgs e)
{
  //Globally handle return from tombstoning here
}

void AlienGame_Deactivated(object sender, DeactivatedEventArgs e)
{
  //Globally handle tombstoning here
}
```

As far as where to store game state, as with Silverlight, you can store transitional state in the PhoneApplicationService.Current.State Dictionary object, like this example:

```
PhoneApplicationService.Current.State[enemies] = enemies;
```

The other bit of information available to you is the PhoneApplicationService.Current.StartupMode property, which can have a value of StartupMode.Launch or StartupMode.Activate. This can be useful if you need to detect whether starting up a new application instance (StartupMode.Launch) or returning from tombstone (StartupMode.Activate) down within the game screens. Note that there isn't a corresponding way to check for deactivation. Only the PhoneApplicationService.Deactivated can help there.

For the AlienShooter game, we add code in the AlienGame_Deactivated to find the GameplayScreen and call the SaveAlienShooterState method. Here is the updated code:

```
void AlienGame_Deactivated(object sender, DeactivatedEventArgs e)
{
  //Globally handle  tombstoning here
  GameScreen[] screens = screenManager.GetScreens();
  foreach (GameScreen screen in screens)
    if (screen is GameplayScreen)
    {
      (screen as GameplayScreen).SaveAlienShooterState();
```

```
    }
}
```

We update the AlienGame_Activated method to load the MainMenuScreen upon restore from tombstoning, as shown here:

```
void AlienGame_Activated(object sender, ActivatedEventArgs e)
{
  //Globally handle return from tombstoning here
  if (!screenManager.DeserializeState())
  {
    // Activate the first screens.
    // Resume at Main Menu so that user isn't caught off guard
    screenManager.AddScreen(new BackgroundScreen(), null);
    screenManager.AddScreen(new MainMenuScreen(), null);
  }
}
```

There isn't anything else to show for game save/load or tombstoning. Run the code and play around with the functionality, including tombstoning the game. As you will see, the functionally works pretty well and has the feel of a "real" Windows Phone 7 game.

One thing that is missing from the game play is explosions when the missiles collide with the enemy alien space ships. A particle system can assist with implementing "random" looking stuff flying around like you would expect if something is blowing up or smoking from a missile strike.

Particle System

A particle system randomly generates points or small area sprites with a random velocity and rotation, as well as a lifetime, such that the points fly out and then disappear much like you see in Hollywood movie effects. Particle systems can be very simple or extremely sophisticated, capable of generating water effects, fire, smoke, and explosions. AppHub includes a simple particle system that generates smoke and fire for explosions or to show damage. Here is a link to the sample:

http://create.msdn.com/en-US/education/catalog/sample/particle

Modifying AlienShooter

In the AlienShooter project I add a folder named ParticleSystem and copy the following files from the AppHub Particle Sample into the new folder in the AlienShooter project, updating the namespace to AlienShooter.ParticleSystem:

- ParticleSystem.cs

- Particle.cs

- ExplosionSmokeParticleSystem.cs

- ExplosionParticleSystem.cs

- SmokePlumeParticleSystem.cs

The Particle System classes sample have some ties to the game project so the classes are refactored a bit to fit within the AlienShooter project. The ParticleSystem classes are dependent on the SpriteBatch being part of the Game class instance. In our case, the Game.Components collection in the

AlienShooterGame instance is accessed to grab the screenManager object, which then makes the ScreenManager.SpriteBatch accessible to the particle system classes:

```
((ScreenManager)game.Components[0]).SpriteBatch.Draw
```

Notice that the assumption is that the ScreenManager is the first Component added with the index of 0 in the Components collection, so it is something to be aware of.

Another modification required is to add the smoke.bmp and explosions.png content files to a new folder named ParticleSystem in the AlienShooter content project. The path values in the Particle System class files are updated by adding ParticleSystem/ path info in front of filenames so that the ContentManager can find them.

The random number-related helper functions were moved from the game class into the ParticleSystem classes directly, helping to encapsulate the functionality better within the classes themselves. Another option is to make the random number helper members a part of the ScreenManager object, which could be useful in other situations when a GameScreen instance may need a random number for game functionality. Either way, once all of the house keeping updates to the code are completed, we can now implement explosions and smoke for the AlienShooter game.

Adding Explosions and Smoke to AlienShooter

Once all of the modifications are completed to incorporate the AppHub Particle Sample code into the AlienShooter project, it is brain dead simple to add support for explosions and smoke plume in the game. In AlienShooterGame.cs, three additional fields are added:

```
ExplosionSmokeParticleSystem explosionSmokeParticleSystem;
ExplosionParticleSystem explosionParticleSystem;
SmokePlumeParticleSystem smokePlumeParticleSystem;
```

The first two are for the explosion, one for the smoke, the other for the fire. The third field added is for the smoke plume. In the AlienShooterGame class constructor, the particle system classes are instantiated and then added to the Game.Components collection:

```
explosionSmokeParticleSystem = new ExplosionSmokeParticleSystem(this, 2);
Components.Add(explosionSmokeParticleSystem);
explosionParticleSystem = new ExplosionParticleSystem(this, 1);
Components.Add(explosionParticleSystem);
smokePlumeParticleSystem = new SmokePlumeParticleSystem(this, 8);
Components.Add(smokePlumeParticleSystem);
```

The numbers represent the number of particles. Running on a device, you will see that if you set the number too high it will directly affect framerate and game performance can suffer.

Now that we have our particle system DrawableComponents configured, it is time to add explosions and smoke plume support to the GameplayScreen. We will add an explosion (both smoke and fire) each time an enemy alien ship is shot down. We will add a smoke plume to the hero ship when a life is lost due to a kamikaze enemy alien ship collision. Since this involves collision detection, you are right to guess that the code to draw the explosions and smoke is added there. Listing 8–3 has the updated CheckForCollisions method.

Listing 8–3. GameplayScreen.LoadAlienShooterState Method

```
private void CheckForCollisions()
{
  //Checking for two major collisions
  //1 - Has an in flight missile intersected an alien spaceship   score 5 pts
  for (int i = 0; i < heroShip.MaxNumberofMissiles; i++)
```

```
    if (heroShip.Missiles[i].Alive)
      for (int j = 0; j < maxEnemies; j++)
        if ((enemies[j].Alive) &&
            (enemies[j].BoundingRect.Intersects(heroShip.Missiles[i].BoundingRect)))
        {
          statusBoard.Score += 5;
          //Display Explosion

((ExplosionSmokeParticleSystem)ScreenManager.Game.Components[1]).AddParticles(enemies[j].Posit
ion);

((ExplosionParticleSystem)ScreenManager.Game.Components[2]).AddParticles(enemies[j].Position);
          enemies[j].ResetGameObject();
          heroShip.Missiles[i].ResetGameObject();
        }
  //2 - Has an alien spaceship intersected the hero ship - deduct a life
  for (int j = 0; j < maxEnemies; j++)
    if ((enemies[j].Alive) && (enemies[j].Position.Y > 600) &&
        (enemies[j].BoundingRect.Intersects(heroShip.BoundingRect)))
    {
      statusBoard.Lives -= 1;

((SmokePlumeParticleSystem)ScreenManager.Game.Components[3]).AddParticles(heroShip.Position);

      for (int i = 0; i < maxEnemies; i++)
        enemies[i].ResetGameObject();
      for (int i = 0; i < heroShip.MaxNumberofMissiles; i++)
        heroShip.Missiles[i].ResetGameObject();
    }
}
```

Essentially the desired particle system DrawableComponent instance is grabbed from the AlienShooterGame.Components collection and the correct position Vector2 is passed into the AddParticles method. Here is the call to draw a smoke plume at the hero ship's Position property:

```
((SmokePlumeParticleSystem)ScreenManager.Game.Components[3]).AddParticles(heroShip.Position);
      Note the use of the number index. If the value is incorrect you will get a invalid
cast exception at runtime. Figure 8-2 shows an explosion and smoke plume in action.
```

Figure 8–2. Explosion and smoke plume

I won't go into the actual particle system sample code; I'll leave that as an exercise for the reader, but you will see that it isn't terribly complicated code, which is pretty amazing given the robust effects that are provided. If anything, you may want to simplify the code in a real game to minimize performance impact. Try running the game on a device and you will see the frame rate drop occasionally if too many explosions occur at the same time.

This completes the coverage of the AlienShooter sample. What is great about this sample is that you can simply take it in whole, find and replace namespaces if desired to match your game, and essentially rewrite the GameplayScreen class and GameObject descendants to reflect your game logic. Otherwise, the Game Screen Manager, save and load, tombstoning, and particle system effects are available for use in your game immediately, though you will have to customize the actual code to save and load the correct state for your game.

In the next section we completely shift gears and provide an overview of the 3D game development capabilities available within the XNA Framework. The section won't make you a complete expert, but it will provide you with enough knowledge and understanding to dive into 3D game development if you find you cannot resist the allure of matrix mathematics and 3d model manipulation.

3D Game Development

The rest of this chapter covers 3D game development with XNA Game Studio. The goal is to provide you with the knowledge and understanding of how to develop 3D games, covering the fundamental principles, a little bit of 3D math, and the 3D programming model provided by the XNA Framework. In the next section, we cover the fundamentals of 3D development.

■ **Note** Many of the 2D concepts I have covered so far still apply in 3D game development as well, such as applying velocity, collision detection, and so on. This section focuses on drawing 3D models and some of the additional considerations related to 3D rendering.

3D Game Concepts

Hopefully by now, if you have read this book straight through – or at the very least have read the XNA Framework-related sections in Chapter 1, Chapter 3, and all of Chapter 7 – you have a solid understanding of 2D game development. Programming in 2D is similar in process to hand-drawing a cartoon on paper. You can draw a scene in 2D that makes objects appear near or in the background, providing perspective that models the 3D real world. 3D game development results in the same 2D projection on a flat 2D screen, however, the path to rendering is very different.

■ **Tip** It is not possible to cover 3D game development in a single chapter, so I recommend *Windows Phone 7 Game Development* (Apress, 2010) by Adam Dawes if you want to explore 3D game development in more detail.

In 3D game development, you create a 3D world using wireframe models with a skin over the wireframe that is a 2D texture. The view into the world is similar to viewing the real world behind a camera, where the front aspect of an object is visible and the back of an object is not; however, the back of an object still exists. As an example, Figure 8–3 shows a sample 3D rendering named Pac Man displayed in Caligri truSpace with views from different angles.

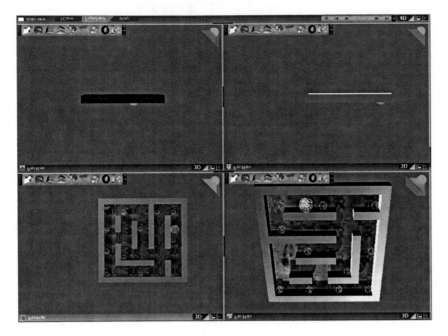

Figure 8–3. *3D model rendered in Caligri trueSpace*

You can spin, rotate, and zoom in on the model to get a different view of the environment. Just as in the real world, any view you pick is translated into a 2D rendering. However, with 3D game development, as hardware grows more powerful, the 3D model and rendering comes closer and closer to the real world. With the power of matrix mathematics, 3D vectors, and Algorithms, a game developer can fly around a 3D model of an imaginary world resulting in an immersive experience.

Modeling the Real World

For 3D game development, you mathematically create the camera view on the loaded model. As a user manipulates a game controller or tilts a phone in a mobile game experience, the Accelerometer readings can be measured and the movement is translated to affect the camera view in the model.

A 3D world can be quite expansive, so much so that trying to render an entire world model will bog down even the most powerful graphics cards. Just like viewing the real world through a camera, developers mathematically create a view that consists of a boxed 3D area that is rendered called the Frustum.

The Frustum consists of a near plane, a far plane, left and right plane that boxes an area of view, as shown in Figure 8–4.

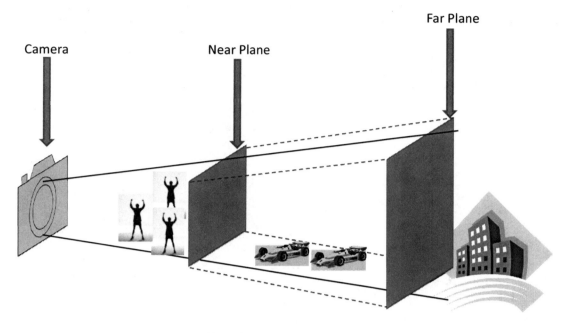

Figure 8–4. *Frustum area of a view*

Notice that some objects are shown outside of the Frustum; this means that if the scene is rendered those objects would not be shown. If the user moves the camera closer in, the people would come into view. Likewise, moving the camera towards the cars could begin to bring in the building in the background. Notice in Figure 8–4 that the developer could decide to make the Frustum longer, with the near plane in front of the crowd of people and behind the buildings. As mentioned before, this could overload the graphics card resulting in frame rate loss, especially in a high-speed racing game. This is the essence of 3D game development, building out a model and rendering it in such a way that user movement feels "natural" within the game.

3D Coordinate Systems

The XNA Framework is engineered to work with the modeling techniques in the previous section, modeling the real world via 3D coordinate systems and mathematics to project a view of a 3D experience to a game player. At the heart of 3D is the coordinate system.

Remember in 2D game development that the 2D origin (X,Y) is in the upper left-hand corner of the screen with positive X going left to right and positive Y going top to bottom. In 3D game development, the origin (0,0,0) can be at the center of a car model, or it could be at an arbitrary place in the overall 3D world. In reality, there are multiple 3D origins that are relatively positioned to each other. A model has a 3D origin that runs through the center of the model or could be centered at the bottom of the model, depending on what makes most sense for the game at that time. You can rotate around the model origin, and the model would spin like a top.

Likewise, the overall world will have an origin as well. You can also rotate a model about the 3D world origin like a plane orbiting the sun in our Solar System. These concepts will be explored as we proceed in this chapter but it is important to break your mind free from the comfort of the rigid 2D coordinate system.

One aspect of coordinate systems that needs to be consistent is how the three axis (X,Y,Z) are oriented. In 3D game development, this is called either a right-handed or left-handed coordinate system. Figure 8–5 shows the two coordinate systems taken from the DirectX documentation on MSDN.

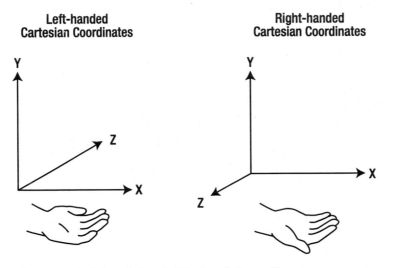

Figure 8–5. *Left-handed and right-handed coordinate systems*

So the idea is you can use your hand to remember the direction of the positive Z access. Point your fingers in the direction of the positive X axis and curl your fingers up toward the positive Y axis, and your thumb points in the direction of the positive Z axis.

The XNA Framework is a right-handed coordinate system, meaning that the Z axis is positive coming out of the screen. There are many programming models including DirectX that are left-handed systems so be cognizant of the coordinate convention when reviewing sample code and documentation.

Rendering 3D Primitives

Modern graphics hardware is optimized to render triangles. You can take it on to prove it to yourself by reviewing a 3D mathematics text but any 3D object can be modeled to have smooth edges with enough triangles. Zoom in close enough on a model and the edges can look jagged, but this does not stray too far from reality in this case either. As an example, a golf ball is round with bumps, but if you view it close enough you can see the imperfections, and take comfort in blaming your errant golf swing on the golf ball's imperfections and not your golf skills.

This is another aspect of 3D game development that is art as much as science in managing how many triangles you try to push through the graphics processor unit (GPU) versus rendering quality at different zoom levels. More triangles sounds better, but if the frame rate drops to far over a period of time a game can become unplayable.

We will work with 3D models in a bit, but let's start out by working with just a few triangles to dip our toe into the water of 3D game development. In the Chapter 8 solution, the XNA3DPrimitives project sample demonstrates programming with triangles, which we will walk through now.

Creating 3D Primitives

You don't generally create a 3D game using triangle primitives, but we go through the exercise to define key concepts of 3D development with the XNA Framework. In the end, when you render a 3D model created by a graphics artist, you are rendering bunches of triangles that have been predefined so the concepts covered in this section translate right over to working with models . To render a 3D scene in the XNA Framework, follow these steps:

- Load your content; in this case, a set of triangles defined as vertex collections where each vertex is one of the three points on a triangle.

- Load any textures that will render over the triangles; in this case, to provide a "skin" that is stretched over the triangle points.

- Pass the content to a vertex buffer containing the triangles that the GPU can render.

- Define the shader effect that will do the rendering.

- Modify the Update method as you did in 2D development to apply translation, rotation, and so on.

- Render the vertex buffer using the shader effect in the Draw method.

In the next section, we go through creating a 3D cube that is rendered to the screen.

From Triangles to Objects

We create a new project named XNA3DPrimitives in the Chapter 8 solution, where we go through the previously covered process in detail. We will draw a 3D cube and apply a color to the cube wireframe. We will then manipulate different aspects of drawing and movement to help you understand how 3D development works.

A cube has six square sides connected at 90 degree angles. Figure 8–6 shows how a cube consists of 12 triangles with two triangles per cube face.

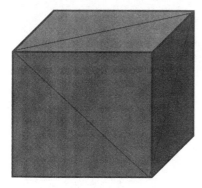

3D Cube

Each Cube Face

Figure 8–6. Building a cube with triangles

Each side has six indices (three per triangle) and four vertices per cube face representing each corner of the face. When thinking about positioning each cube face, remember that an object can have a coordinate system that goes through the geometric center. In the case of a cube, it is easily to visualize positioning each face on a 3D axis as shown in Figure 8–7.

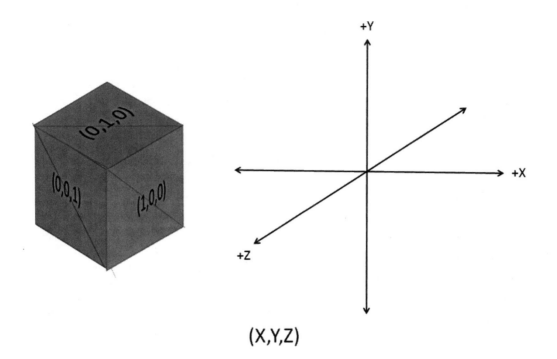

Figure 8–7. Positioning each cube face on a 3D axis

Notice the vector information in Figure 8–7 indicating which axis matches each cube face. Here is a full list of the "normal" vectors for each face, which is a Vector3 that shoots straight out of each cube face at a 90 degree angle, which is really shooting straight out of the two triangles that make up the cube face:

- (1,0,0): Positive X axis cube face
- (-1,0,0): Negative X axis cube face
- (0,1,0): Positive Y axis cube face
- (0,-1,0): Negative Y axis cube face
- (0,0,1): Positive Z axis cube face
- (0,0,-1): Negative Z axis cube face

3D game developers use normal vectors to figure out positioning between triangles, objects, etc. As an example, if you want to figure out how to move an object sideways, you figure out the normal to the front and top vectors to give you the "sideways pointing" vector. Mathematically, the cross product can find the normal vector between two vectors As an example, the Z axis is the normal vector to the Y axis and X axis. The Y axis is the normal to the X axis and Z axis and the X axis is the normal vector to the Y and Z vector.

Figure 8–7 makes it easy to visualize the normal vector between the X, Y, and Z axis. It is a little bit of math to calculate the normal vector between two vectors. Luckily, the Vector3.Cross method takes two vectors and finds the normal vector for the two vectors passed in to the method call. Now we can proceed with building the cube. We add a method call to CreateCubeObject in the Game.LoadContent() method. We will build up the cube object in the CreateCubeObject method.

To render the cube we use two buffers: one that contains the vertex information and the other that contains the index information. Index information allows you to reuse Vertex information. For example, when two triangles form a square such as a cube face, two points are shared between the triangles. While you could repeat the vertex information and have duplicates, for a large model this consumes precious memory and should be avoided. One way to avoid duplicates is to store only unique vertices in the vertex buffer and use an index buffer to represent the triangles that are drawn. Figure 8–8 shows how the vertex buffer relates to the index buffer.

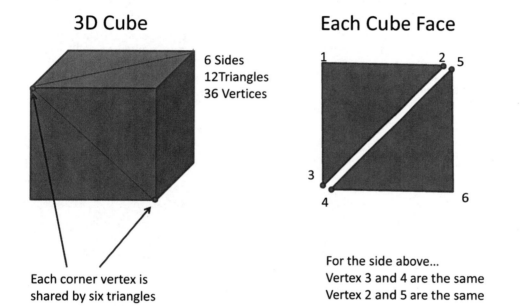

3D Cube

6 Sides
12 Triangles
36 Vertices

Each corner vertex is shared by six triangles

Each Cube Face

For the side above...
Vertex 3 and 4 are the same
Vertex 2 and 5 are the same

Figure 8–8. *Vertex buffer and index buffer relationship*

In looking at just the side on the right in Figure 8–8, the index buffer would have six slots to represent the two triangles, with three vertices each. However, the vertex buffer would only store four unique vertices. Here is what the vertex and index buffers would look like moving left to right around the side shown on the right in Figure 8–8:

- Vertex buffer - 1,2,3,6 (Vertices 4 and 5 are duplicates and removed)

- Index buffer 1,2,3,2,6,3 (Always six vertices for two triangles)

The actual drawing is done using the index buffer, because it fully represents each triangle with three vertices per triangle. When the GPU needs the three points to draw the triangle, it looks up the actual vertex in the vertex buffer based on the index buffer with some vertices used multiple times.

In our example, to draw the left / top triangle, the GPU uses vertices 1,2, and 3. To draw the right/bottom triangle, the GPU uses 2,6, and 3, reusing two vertices. Although in our example the memory savings may seem trivial, for a large complex model the savings can be significant.

Creating the Cube

Now that you have an understanding of how the vertex buffer relates to the index buffer, we return to the code to use this knowledge to create the cube object. Five new members are added to the Game1 class:

```
VertexBuffer vertexBuffer;
IndexBuffer indexBuffer;

//Lists and variables used to construct vertex and index buffer data
List<VertexPositionNormalTexture> vertices = new List<VertexPositionNormalTexture>();
List<ushort> indices = new List<ushort>();
float size = 3;
```

The vertices and indices List objects are used to construct the primitive cube model. Once the cube is constructed, the data is loaded into the vertexBuffer and indexBuffer members using the SetData method call. Once loaded, the vertexBuffer and indexBuffer objects are passed to the graphics device (the GPU) for rendering using the specified lighting effect. We cover lighting and drawing in a bit. First let's construct the cube model using the vertices and indices List objects in the CreateCubeObject method, which is called in the Game1.LoadContent method after the texture is loaded and shown in Listing 8–4.

Listing 8–4. The Game1.CreateCubeObject Method

```
private void CreateCubeObject()
{
  // A cube has six faces, each one pointing in a different direction.
  Vector3[] normals =
      {
          new Vector3(0, 0, 1),
          new Vector3(0, 0, -1),
          new Vector3(1, 0, 0),
          new Vector3(-1, 0, 0),
          new Vector3(0, 1, 0),
          new Vector3(0, -1, 0),
      };

  // Create each face in turn.
  foreach (Vector3 normal in normals)
  {
    // Get two vectors perpendicular to the cube face normal and
    //perpendicular to each other
    Vector3 triangleSide1 = new Vector3(normal.Y, normal.Z, normal.X);
    Vector3 triangleSide2 = Vector3.Cross(normal, triangleSide1);

    // Six indices (two triangles) per face
    indices.Add((ushort)(vertices.Count + 0));
```

```
    indices.Add((ushort)(vertices.Count + 1));
    indices.Add((ushort)(vertices.Count + 2));

    indices.Add((ushort)(vertices.Count + 0));
    indices.Add((ushort)(vertices.Count + 2));
    indices.Add((ushort)(vertices.Count + 3));

    // Four vertices per cube face
    vertices.Add(new VertexPositionNormalTexture(
      (normal - triangleSide1 - triangleSide2) * size / 2, normal,Vector2.One));
    vertices.Add(new VertexPositionNormalTexture(
      (normal - triangleSide1 + triangleSide2) * size / 2, normal,Vector2.One));
    vertices.Add(new VertexPositionNormalTexture(
      (normal + triangleSide1 + triangleSide2) * size / 2, normal,Vector2.One));
    vertices.Add(new VertexPositionNormalTexture(
      (normal + triangleSide1 - triangleSide2) * size / 2, normal,Vector2.One));
  }
}
```

The CreateCubeObject starts by creating the six vectors that represent each side of the cube. Each vector is normal to a cube face, positioned along a 3D axis as shown in Figure 8–7.

With each normal vector, two additional normal vectors are created that are perpendicular to the normal vector and to each other. These two new vectors named triangleSide1 and triangleSide2 are used to find the four vertices that represent the cube face corner vertices that are added to the vertices List. The indices List is updated to add vertex references in the correct order so that the object can be rendered properly.

Graphics Objects and the Effect Class

We next construct and initialize the graphics objects and buffers to render our cube primitive. We declare an effect object of type BasicEffect at the top of Game1.cs. With XNA 4.0, Microsoft defined several built-in effects classes that draw objects without having to resort to High Level Shader Language (HLSL) coding. Windows Phone 7 does not support HLSL so we do not dive into HLSL development but in short the language allows developers to directly program the GPU to crate dazzling visual effects.

It may seem like a major limitation to not be able to program in HLSL but the built in Effect class descendants provide several benefits:

- Cross-platform support is simplified by using the Effect class objects. This is known as the "reach" profile in XNA Game Studio 4.0.

- The Effect class objects are highly configurable, allowing a wide-range of visual effects programming in C#.

- Developers do not have to learn yet another language in HLSL.

Table 8–1 has a list of available effect classes in XNA Game Studio 4.0.

Table 8–1. Configurable Effect Classes in the XNA Framework

Effect	Description
AlphaTest	Contains a configurable effect that supports alpha testing.
BasicEffect	Contains a basic rendering effect.
DualTextureEffect	Contains a configurable effect that supports two-layer multitexturing.
Effect	Used to set and query effects, and to choose techniques that are applied when rendering.
EnvironmentMapEffect	Contains a configurable effect that supports environment mapping.
SkinnedEffect	Contains a configurable effect for rendering skinned character models.

Each Effect class in Table 8–1 has several configurable "knobs" that provide developers a wide range of control without having to delve into HLSL. This link has more information and samples on the various available Effect classes:

http://create.msdn.com/en-us/education/catalog/?contenttype=0&devarea=14&sort=2

The ConstructGraphicsObjectsForDrawingCube method initializes the graphics objects and the BasicEffect object:

```
private void ConstructGraphicsObjectsForDrawingCube()
{
    // Create a vertex buffer, and copy the cube vertex data into it
    vertexBuffer = new VertexBuffer(graphics.GraphicsDevice,
                            typeof(VertexPositionNormalTexture),
                            vertices.Count, BufferUsage.None);
    vertexBuffer.SetData(vertices.ToArray());

    // Create an index buffer, and copy the cube index data into it.
    indexBuffer = new IndexBuffer(graphics.GraphicsDevice, typeof(ushort),
                            indices.Count, BufferUsage.None);
    indexBuffer.SetData(indices.ToArray());

    // Create a BasicEffect, which will be used to render the primitive.
    basicEffect = new BasicEffect(graphics.GraphicsDevice);
    basicEffect.EnableDefaultLighting();
    basicEffect.PreferPerPixelLighting = true;
}
```

The vertex and index data calculated in the CreateCubeObject method are loaded into the vertexBuffer and indexBuffer objects, respectively. The BasicEffect is instantiated next. We discuss effects in more detail later, but essentially the BasicEffect object provides the environmental effects for the scene such as lighting and shading.

Drawing the Cube

To draw the cube we need several additional member variables that are added at the top of Game1.cs.

```
float yaw = .5f;
float pitch = .5f;
float roll = .5f;
Vector3 cameraPosition = new Vector3(0, 0, 10f);
```

The last method related to our cube is the Game1.DrawCubePrimitive method listed here:

```
private void DrawCubePrimitive (Matrix world, Matrix view, Matrix projection, Color color)
{
  // Set BasicEffect parameters.
  basicEffect.World = world;
  basicEffect.View = view;
  basicEffect.Projection = projection;
  basicEffect.DiffuseColor = color.ToVector3();
  basicEffect.Alpha = color.A / 255.0f;

  GraphicsDevice graphicsDevice = basicEffect.GraphicsDevice;
  // Set our vertex declaration, vertex buffer, and index buffer.
  graphicsDevice.SetVertexBuffer(vertexBuffer);
  graphicsDevice.Indices = indexBuffer;

  foreach (EffectPass effectPass in basicEffect.CurrentTechnique.Passes)
  {
    effectPass.Apply();
    int primitiveCount = indices.Count / 3;
    graphicsDevice.DrawIndexedPrimitives(
      PrimitiveType.TriangleList, 0, 0,vertices.Count, 0, primitiveCount);
  }
}
```

The DrawCubePrimitive method is called in the Game1.Draw method. This method instantiates the graphicsDevice object and passes in the calculated vertex and index information for rendering. Depending on the effect used, one or more passes are executed to create the scene, drawing the triangle primitives using the graphicsDevice.DrawIndexedPrimitives method.

The cube is ready for rendering within a 3D scene. We next move to incorporating the cube code into an XNA Framework game.

The Game Class

To draw a 3D scene a developer needs to set up a coordinate system and create a camera to view the rendered scene.

The Camera

We need to create a camera that will be a view into our 3D world of triangles that is rendered by the GPU. Right-click on the XNA3DPrimitives project and select Add ➤ New Item… ➤ click on XNA Game Studio 4.0 and select Game Component. Name the new game component Camera and click Add. Remember from our discussion above that the Camera object has a position within the model world, looks in a particular direction, and has a view defined by the Frustum. We modify the constructor to take three parameters: cameraUpVector, cameraPosition, and cameraDirection all of type Vector3..

The cameraPosition and cameraDirection parameters orient the Camera. As an example, if flying an airplane in the first person, you bank right to turn right, so it would make sense to have the Camera Up Vector oriented 45 degrees to the right through the turn. The camera direction defines the viewing Frustum and will be oriented to look towards our triangles when drawn to the screen.

The Camera GameComponent object will need two public properties: View and Projection of type Matrix. Don't worry about what it means to define these terms as a Matrix type – it isn't critical. It is more important to think of the concepts above as we define them programmatically.

▪ **Tip** If you desperately want to understand the math behind 3D game development, and eventually you will need to understand it if you pursue 3D game development, I recommend reading *3D Math Primer for Graphics and Game Development* (Jones & Bartlett Publishers, 2002) by Fletcher Dunn.

The Matrix class has a static method called CreatePerspectiveFieldOfView that defines the frustrum for the GPU. This method call takes four parameters:

- fieldOfView

- aspectRatio

- nearPlaneDistance

- farPlaneDistance

The fieldOfView parameter defines the angle width of the field of view for the Frustrum in radians, not degrees. Remember from geometry that 360 degrees equals 2pi Radians, 180 degrees equals pi Radians, and 90 degrees equals pi/2 radians. The MathHelper class defines these values for you so you can pass in MathHelper.PiOver4 to define a field of view of 45 degrees, which is a good starting point for most games.

The aspectRatio parameter is defined by the ratio of the screen width divided by screen height. The Game object has these values in this format: Game.Window.ClientBounds.Width /Game.Window.ClientBounds.Height.

The nearPlaneDistance parameter defines how far in front of the Camera object the near plane from Figure 8–4 is defined. A good starting point is one for our example, but in a real game you may not want the near plane to include every object in front of the Camera object. Lastly, the farPlaneDistance parameter defines the far plane, i.e., the how far into the distance the Camera can "see" past the Near Plane.

Now that we have defined the Frustrum box, we need to orient the frustrum box in a particular direction to look at our triangles that we are going to draw in just a bit. The handy Matrix class defines a static method named CreateLookAt that defines the direction that the Camera is facing. It takes three parameters:

- Camera Position

- Camera Direction

- Camera Up Vector

The CreateLookAt parameters match the three parameters that are passed into the Camera GameComponent object that we defined above so we pass them into the method call as shown in Listing 8–5.

Listing 8–5. *The Camera GameComponent Class*

```
using Microsoft.Xna.Framework;

namespace XNA3DPrimitives
{
  public class Camera : Microsoft.Xna.Framework.GameComponent
  {
    public Camera(Game game, Vector3 position, Vector3 direction, Vector3 upVector)
      : base(game)
    {
      // Initialize frustum matrix
      Projection = Matrix.CreatePerspectiveFieldOfView(
          MathHelper.PiOver4,
          this.Game.GraphicsDevice.Viewport.AspectRatio,
          1, 20);

      // Initialize "look at" matrix
      View = Matrix.CreateLookAt(position, direction, upVector);
    }

    public Matrix View { get; private set; }
    public Matrix Projection { get; private set; }

    public override void Initialize()
    {

      base.Initialize();
    }

    public override void Update(GameTime gameTime)
    {

      base.Update(gameTime);
    }
  }
}
```

We next update the Game1 class to include our new Camera object and use it to call the cube related methods to render the cube in a scene.

Rendering the Cube Scene

To leverage the Camera object we add it to Game1.cs in the Game1.Initialize method:

```
protected override void Initialize()
{ // Initialize camera
  camera = new Camera(this, cameraPosition,
      Vector3.Zero, Vector3.Up);
  Components.Add(camera);

  base.Initialize();
}
```

We update the DrawCubePrimitive method to leverage the Camera object. The method now just takes two parameters. Here is a snippet of the first part of the method where the changes are in effect:

```
private void DrawCubePrimitive (Matrix world,  Color color)
{
  // Set BasicEffect parameters.
  basicEffect.World = world;
  basicEffect.View = camera.View;
  basicEffect.Projection = camera.Projection;
  basicEffect.DiffuseColor = color.ToVector3();
  basicEffect.Alpha = color.A / 255.0f;
...
```

The basicEffect object now gets its View and Projection properties from the Camera object in the DrawCubePrimitive method. Here is the Game1.Draw method that renders the cube:

```
protected override void Draw(GameTime gameTime)
{
  GraphicsDevice.Clear(Color.CornflowerBlue);

  // TODO: Add your drawing code here
  Matrix world = Matrix.CreateFromYawPitchRoll(yaw, pitch, roll);
  DrawCubePrimitive (world, Color.Orange);
  // Reset the fill mode renderstate.
  GraphicsDevice.RasterizerState = RasterizerState.CullCounterClockwise;
  base.Draw(gameTime);
}
```

The World coordinate is obtained from configured, yaw, pitch, and role values at the top of Game1.cs resulting in the rendered cube shown in Figure 8–9.

```
float yaw = .5f;
float pitch = .5f;
float roll = .5f;
```

Figure 8–9. Rendered cube with configured color

The scene is static, which is a bit boring. Let's add some movement to the scene in the next section via yaw, pitch, and roll.

Adding Movement

In the previous section, the cube object is positioned using world Matrix object, which is created using the Matrix.CreateFromYawPitchRoll(yaw, pitch, roll) static method call. The world Matrix object is passed to DrawCubePrimitive method and assigned to the basicEffect.World property to render the object with the configured yaw, pitch, and roll applied to its coordinates. Figure 8–10 describes these parameters visually.

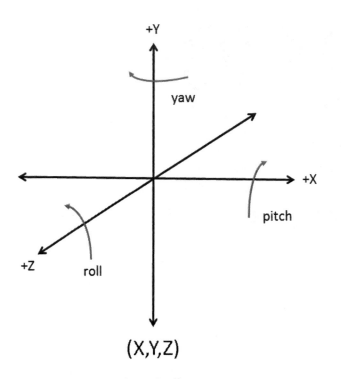

Figure 8–10. *Yaw, pitch, and roll*

We apply a simple way to manipulate the object by updating the yaw, pitch, and roll members in the Update method shown here:

```
protected override void Update(GameTime gameTime)
{
  // Allows the game to exit
  if (GamePad.GetState(PlayerIndex.One).Buttons.Back == ButtonState.Pressed)
    this.Exit();

  float time = (float)gameTime.TotalGameTime.TotalSeconds;

  yaw = time * 0.5f;
  pitch = time * 0.5f;
  roll = time * 0.5f;

  base.Update(gameTime);
}
```

The gameTime.TotalGameTime.TotalSeconds value is fairly small as it is the elapsed time between frames. Applying the modification on each call to Update results in smooth animation. A screenshot doesn't do it justice, so run the sample code to observe the lighting provided by the BasicEffect instance when rendering the object as it rotates.

Now that we covered 3D programming basics and rendering 3D objects generated from triangle primitives in code, we can move on to rendering rich 3D models, building on the 3D game development concepts presented so far.

Rendering 3D Models

A 3D model consists of triangle primitives, but are generally created in a third-party tool, such as Softimage Mod Tool, Daz Studio 3D, blender, or Caligari trueSpace, to name a few of the freely available modeling tools. Paint.NET is a free tool to create 2D textures. Professional modeling tools for purchase are Autodesk's 3ds Max, Autodesk's Maya, and Adobe's Creative Suite for texture creation. XNA Game Studio 4.0 supports importing 3D models in both Autodesk .fbx and DirectX .x formats generated from any of these tools.

Creating 3D models is beyond scope of this book. Instead we leverage models available under the MS-PL license up at AppHub located at http://create.msdn.com. I grab the spaceship.fbx file from the samples located at AppHub and I grabbed the background texture from the AlienShooter project, adding them to the content project for a new project named XNA3DModels in the Chapter 8 code solution.

Movable Camera

For the new project named XNA3DModels we need a Camera object to view the 3D scene and model. In the previous sample the Camera was fixed in location. In this sample we create a Camera that can create the appearance of movement based on user input.

■ **Tip** The Camera Projection or field of view does not change; think of that aspect of the Camera as fixed, like looking through a pair of binoculars. The Camera.View property is the direction that the binoculars are pointed and can change based on user input.

For this sample, we demonstrate shifting the View property of the Camera based on Accelerometer input. For more information on the Accelerometer sensor, refer to Chapter 3.

We start with a copy of the Camera class from the XNA3DPrimitives project. Properties for View, Position, Up are added to the Camera class. We also add a private variable named direction of type Vector3 that is calculated by taking the target Vector3 (the spaceship model) and subtracting the Position Vector3. The Projection property is calculated as before.

The Up Vector3 value is set to Vector3.Up as before and the View property is recalculated each time it is accessed via this read-only property declaration:

```
public Matrix View
{
  get { return Matrix.CreateLookAt(Position, Position+direction, Up); }
}
```

The recalculation is necessary since the Camera Position and direction values will change based on user input in the Camera.Update method. Listing 8–6 has the Camera source code.

Listing 8–6. Updated Camera Class with Support for User Input

```
using System;
using Microsoft.Devices.Sensors;
using Microsoft.Xna.Framework;

namespace XNA3DModels
{
  public class Camera : Microsoft.Xna.Framework.GameComponent
  {
    #region private members
    //Camera properties
    Vector3 direction;
    Vector3 Up;

    //Accelerometer input
    Accelerometer accelerometer;
    AccelerometerReading currentReading;

    //Movement parameters
    float speed = 100f;
    //Yaw movement
    float maxLeftRight = MathHelper.PiOver4 / 10;
    float stepLeftRight = MathHelper.PiOver4 / 10000;
    float currentLeftRight = 0;
    #endregion

    public Camera(Game game, Vector3 position, Vector3 target, Vector3 upVector)
      : base(game)
    {
      Position = position;
      direction = target - position;
      direction.Normalize();
      Up = upVector;

      // Initialize frustum matrix, which doesn't change
      Projection = Matrix.CreatePerspectiveFieldOfView(
          MathHelper.PiOver4,
          this.Game.GraphicsDevice.Viewport.AspectRatio,
          1, 20000);

      currentReading = new AccelerometerReading();
    }

    public Matrix View
    {
      get { return Matrix.CreateLookAt(Position, Position + direction, Up); }
    }
    public Matrix Projection { get; private set; }
    public Vector3 Position { get; private set; }

    public void ResetPosition()
    {
```

```
      Position = new Vector3(0, 1000, 15000);
      direction = Vector3.Zero - Position;
      direction.Normalize();
      Up = Vector3.Up;
}

public override void Initialize()
{
    accelerometer = new Accelerometer();
    accelerometer.ReadingChanged += accelerometer_ReadingChanged;
    accelerometer.Start();

    base.Initialize();
}

public override void Update(GameTime gameTime)
{
    ApplyThrust();

    ApplySteering();

    base.Update(gameTime);
}

private void ApplySteering()
{
    if ((Math.Abs(currentLeftRight) < maxLeftRight) &&
(Math.Abs(currentReading.Y) > .4))
    {
        direction = Vector3.Transform(direction,
                    Matrix.CreateFromAxisAngle(Up, currentLeftRight));
        if (currentReading.Y > .2)
        {
            currentLeftRight += stepLeftRight;
            if (currentLeftRight < 0)
                currentLeftRight = currentLeftRight * -1;
        }
        if (currentReading.Y < -.2)
        {
            currentLeftRight -= stepLeftRight;
            if (currentLeftRight > 0)
                currentLeftRight = currentLeftRight * -1;
        }
    }
}

private void ApplyThrust()
{
    //Travel forward or backwards based on tilting
    //device forwards or backwards (Z axis for Accelerometer)
    if (currentReading.Z < -.65)
        Position += direction * speed;
    if (currentReading.Z > -.5)
        Position -= direction * speed;
```

```
      }

      protected override void OnEnabledChanged(object sender, System.EventArgs args)
      {
        if (this.Enabled)
          accelerometer.Start();
        else
          accelerometer.Stop();

        base.OnEnabledChanged(sender, args);
      }

      private void accelerometer_ReadingChanged(
        object sender, AccelerometerReadingEventArgs e)
      {
        currentReading.X = e.X;
        currentReading.Y = e.Y;
        currentReading.Z = e.Z;
        currentReading.Timestamp = e.Timestamp;
#if DEBUG
        System.Diagnostics.Debug.WriteLine("X: " + e.X);
        System.Diagnostics.Debug.WriteLine("Y: " + e.Y);
        System.Diagnostics.Debug.WriteLine("Z: " + e.Z);
#endif

      }
    }

    class AccelerometerReading
    {
      public double X { get; set; }
      public double Y { get; set; }
      public double Z { get; set; }
      public DateTimeOffset Timestamp { get; set; }
    }
}
```

User input is based on Accelerometer sensor input. Z axis accelerometer value changes, i.e., tilting the phone forward and backward in landscape orientation will move the Camera object closer or further in the direction it is pointed, think of it as thrust. Tilting the phone left or right, i.e., Y axis accelerometer changes, steers the Camera left or right. The hard-coded values used to manage user input were derived empirically based on the size of the spaceship model size, Projection size, etc. Finding the right balance based on all the factors in a game are part of the art of providing good game play.

In Listing 8–6 you can find the code to wire up the accelerometer, also covered in Chapter 3. The OnEnabledChanged event shown here is overridden to allow Starting and Stopping the Accelerometer object readings based on whether the GameComponent is enabled:

```
protected override void OnEnabledChanged(object sender, System.EventArgs args)
{
  if (this.Enabled)
    accelerometer.Start();
  else
    accelerometer.Stop();
```

```
    base.OnEnabledChanged(sender, args);
}
```

This is a good programming practice to do, so that collecting Accelerometer input does not needlessly run the battery down. The Camera class also contains a ResetPosition method for testing purposes in the event that you fly off into 3D space and want to get back to a known good position for the movable Camera object.

The Update method in Listing 8–6 calls to private methods, ApplyThrust and ApplySteering. ApplyThrust is pretty straight forward. It adjusts the Position of the Camera along the direction the Camera object is pointing, moving the Camera backwards and forwards.

The ApplySteering method detects changes in the left/right tilt of the phone and applies the change to the currentLeftRight float value. This is used to calculate a new value for direction with this line of code:

```
direction = Vector3.Transform(direction,
          Matrix.CreateFromAxisAngle(Up, currentLeftRight));
```

This handy piece of code applies a transform to the direction Vector3 object. The transform matrix is calculated by taking the Up Vector3 value and an angle in radians that is based on the tilt of the phone. Now that the Camera class is updated, we move on to creating a new class for 3D game objects and a 3D game object coordinator class.

3D Game Object Management

In the AlienShooter 2D game, we created a class named GameObject to represent the sprite objects in the game. In the XNA3DModels project we create a class named GameObject3D to represent 3D model objects. We also create a SceneManager class that can manage multiple GameObject3D instances as part of a 3D game.

GameObject3D Class

The GameObject3D class is pretty simple. Just like GameObject took a 2D sprite Texture2D object, GameObject3D takes a Model instance loaded from the content project. In our case, the spacehip.fbx sample spaceship object located in the XNA3DModelsContent project Models folder. We haven't delved too deeply yet into what a Model is, except that it is a computer generated object created by a graphics designer using a tool similar to the tools listed at the beginning of the section titled "3D Game Development" earlier in this chapter. The XNA Game Studio 4.0 documentation covers this in detail at this link:

```
http://msdn.microsoft.com/en-us/library/dd904249.aspx
```

Figure 8–11 is taken from the above page and describes the relationships between the Model, Mesh and bones objects.

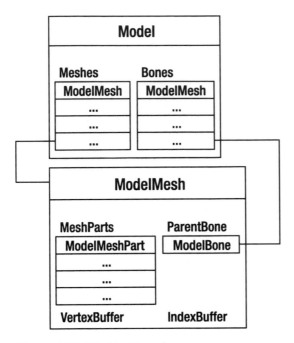

Figure 8–11. Model internals

A Model object is made up of many vertices and materials organized into a set of meshes. In the XNA Framework, a model is represented by the Model class. A model contains one or more meshes, each of which is represented by a ModelMesh class. Each mesh is associated with one bone represented by the ModelBone class. Notice the familiar VertextBuffer and IndexBuffer that makes up the ModelMesh, which is essentially a collection of triangles under the covers.

The bone structure is set up to be hierarchical to make controlling each mesh (and therefore the entire model) easier. At the top of the hierarchy, the model has a Root bone to specify the overall position and orientation of the model. Each ModelMesh object contains a ParentBone and one or more ModelBone. You can transform the entire model using the parent bone as well as transform each individual mesh with its bone.

To animate one or more bones, update the bone transforms during the render loop by calling Model.CopyAbsoluteBoneTransformsTo Method, which iterates the individual bone transforms to make them relative to the parent bone. To draw an entire model, loop through a mesh drawing each sub mesh. It is through transforming bones over time that a Model can appear to walk, rotate, fly, etc. in a 3D game. With the above background out of the way, Listing 8–7 describes how to work with a Model in code when rendering.

Listing 8–7. The GameObject3D class

```
using Microsoft.Xna.Framework.Graphics;
using Microsoft.Xna.Framework;

namespace XNA3DModels.Models
{
  class GameObject3D
  {
```

```
    Matrix[] boneTransforms;

    public GameObject3D(Model m)
    {
      SpaceshipModel = m;
      boneTransforms = new Matrix[SpaceshipModel.Bones.Count];
    }

    public Matrix World
    {
      get { return Matrix.Identity; }
    }
    public Model SpaceshipModel { get; protected set; }

    public void Update()
    {

    }

    public void Draw(Camera camera)
    {
      SpaceshipModel.CopyAbsoluteBoneTransformsTo(boneTransforms);

      foreach (ModelMesh mesh in SpaceshipModel.Meshes)
      {
        foreach (BasicEffect be in mesh.Effects)
        {
          be.World = World * mesh.ParentBone.Transform;
          be.Projection = camera.Projection;
          be.View = camera.View;
          be.TextureEnabled = true;
          be.EnableDefaultLighting();
          be.PreferPerPixelLighting = true;
        }
        mesh.Draw();
      }
    }
  }
}
```

Notice that we pass the Camera object into the Draw method to ensure that the Model is rendered within the coordinates of the Camera. Just like when we rendered primitives in the XNA3DPrimitives project, an Effect class is used to apply textures and provide lighting. In the next section we cover the SceneManager class that manages GameObject3D objects.

SceneManager Class

The SceneManager class inherits from the DrawableGameComponent class. It maintains a collection of GameObject3D objects in a Generic List collection. As a minimum it loops through each object and calls the Update and Draw methods for all managed objects as shown in Listing 8–8.

Listing 8–8. *The SceneManager class*

```
using System.Collections.Generic;
using Microsoft.Xna.Framework;
using Microsoft.Xna.Framework.Graphics;

namespace XNA3DModels.Models
{
  public class SceneManager : DrawableGameComponent
  {
    List<GameObject3D> gameObjects3D = new List<GameObject3D>();

    public SceneManager(Game game)
      : base(game)
    {
    }

    public override void Initialize()
    {
      base.Initialize();
    }

    protected override void LoadContent()
    {
      gameObjects3D.Add(new GameObject3D(Game.Content.Load<Model>("Models/spaceship")));
      base.LoadContent();
    }

    public override void Update(GameTime gameTime)
    {
      for (int i = 0; i < gameObjects3D.Count; ++i)
      {
        gameObjects3D[i].Update();
      }

      base.Update(gameTime);
    }

    public override void Draw(GameTime gameTime)
    {
      for (int i = 0; i < gameObjects3D.Count; i++)
      {
        gameObjects3D[i].Draw(((Game1)Game).Camera);
      }
      base.Draw(gameTime);
    }
  }
}
```

The SceneManager class provides support for managing numerous GameObject3D classes and can be the basis for creating a more complex application in combination with the GameObject3D and Camera class we have covered so far. We now pull all of the previous pieces together to compete the XNA3DModels project sample in the next section.

XNA3DModels Game Class

The Game class Game1.cs is updated to have three additional private members at the top:

```
SceneManager sceneManager ;
Texture2D backgroundTexture;
GestureSample gestureSample ;
```

A SceneManager instance is added as well as a Texture2D to display a background image. The GestureSample field is used to obtain a touch screen gesture by the user. If a Tap gesture is detected, the Camera.ResetPosition method is called to reposition the Camera in front of the rendered 3D model.

The Camera object is declared as a public property to the Game1 class so that it can be passed into the Draw method of GameObject3D instances. Here is the Camera and SceneManager initialization code in the Game1 class:

```
protected override void Initialize()
{
  // Initialize Camera
  Camera = new Camera(this, new Vector3(0, 1000, 15000),
      Vector3.Zero, Vector3.Up);
  Components.Add(Camera);

  //Initialize SceneManager
  sceneManager = new SceneManager(this);
  Components.Add(sceneManager);

  TouchPanel.EnabledGestures = GestureType.Tap;

  base.Initialize();
}
```

The code also enables the Tap Gesture so that the user can reset the Camera position. The Update method is modified to call the HandleInput method shown here:

```
private void HandleInput()
{
  if (TouchPanel.IsGestureAvailable)
  {
    gestureSample = TouchPanel.ReadGesture();
    if (gestureSample.GestureType == GestureType.Tap)
      Camera.ResetPosition();
  }
}
```

The only other code modified in the Game1 class is to load the backgroundTexture and draw the backgroundTexture using a SpriteBatch object as before. Note that you can inter-mingle 2D code to render textures and screen text with 3D code. Figure 8–12 shows the rendered spaceship model against a space background.

Figure 8–12. 3D Rendered spaceship model

You should run the sample on a phone to test out the Accelerometer input. While the sample isn't super exciting, it demonstrates how to render basic 3D models in the XNA Framework including a few classes to help you get started with 3D game development.

Conclusion

In this chapter, we started off by adding the finishing touches to the 2D AlienShooter project, including support for loading and saving the game as well as support for tombstoning. We also added a basic particle system to the 2D AlienShooter project to have nice explosions when missiles strike enemy alien space ships.

We switched gears and provided an introduction to 3D game development with extensive coverage of 3D game development concepts. We next moved on to two 3D game sample projects. The first sample demonstrated basic 3D concepts by rendering triangles to form a cube. The second sample rendered a 3D Model that also had a movable Camera controlled by the user via the Accelerometer sensor.

Index

■ ■ ■

CPSIA information can be obtained at www.ICGtesting.com
228012LV00006B/2/P

9 781430 232193